CONTESTED GOVERNANCE

Culture, power and institutions in Indigenous Australia

Janet Hunt, Diane Smith, Stephanie Garling
and Will Sanders (Editors)

ANU
THE AUSTRALIAN NATIONAL UNIVERSITY

E PRESS

Centre for Aboriginal Economic Policy Research
College of Arts and Social Sciences
The Australian National University, Canberra

Research Monograph No. 29
2008

ANU

E PRESS

Published by ANU E Press
The Australian National University
Canberra ACT 0200, Australia
Email: anuepress@anu.edu.au
This title is also available online at: http://epress.anu.edu.au/c29_citation.html

---

National Library of Australia
Cataloguing-in-Publication entry

Title: Contested governance : culture, power and institutions in indigenous
                  Australia / editors: Janet Hunt ... [et al.].

ISBN: 9781921536045 (pbk.)
                  9781921536052 (pdf)

Series: Research monograph (Australian National University. Centre for
                  Aboriginal Economic Policy Research) ; no. 29.

Subjects: Aboriginal Australians--Politics and government.
                  Aboriginal Australians--Economic conditions.
                  Aboriginal Australians--Social conditions.
                  Community development--Australia.

Other Authors/Contributors:
                  Hunt, Janet.
                  Australian National University. Centre for Aboriginal Economic
                  Policy Research.

Dewey Number: 320.0899915

Cover design by ANU E Press.

Contents

Part 1. The governance environment

Part 2. Culture, power and the intercultural

Part 3. Institutions of Indigenous governance

List of Figures

List of Tables

Notes on contributors

Jon Altman

Jon Altman is Director of the Centre for Aboriginal Economic Policy Research at The Australian National University, Canberra. He has a disciplinary background in economics and anthropology. Professor Altman has undertaken research in the Maningrida region and with the Bawinanga Aboriginal Corporation since 1979 on a diversity of issues, including the customary economy, resource management, land rights and the outstations movement, the arts industry, and the Community Development Employment Projects scheme. His current research focuses on the Indigenous hybrid economy in the tropical savanna, and the potential of equitable payment for environmental services delivered to provide viable livelihood options for Indigenous people.

Manuhuia Barcham

Manuhuia Barcham is the former Director of the Centre for Indigenous Governance and Development at Massey University, New Zealand, and is now a Director of Synexe, a private sector research and consulting firm. He has field experience in eastern Indonesia, Melanesia, Australasia, eastern Polynesia and North America. A key practical goal of his work is to explore how indigenous and introduced governance structures and processes can come together constructively so as to maximise their developmental utility for local communities.

Sarah Holcombe

Sarah Holcombe is a social anthropologist and Research Fellow at the National Centre for Indigenous Studies at The Australian National University. Prior to this she was a Postdoctoral Fellow and Research Fellow at the Centre for Aboriginal Economic Policy Research (CAEPR) on two Australian Research Council projects: 'Indigenous community organisations and miners: partnering sustainable regional development?' and the 'Indigenous Community Governance Project'. The research in the latter project was also supported by the Desert Knowledge Cooperative Research Centre (CRC) as part of the 'Sustainable Settlements' research program. In her later period at CAEPR Dr Holcombe also held the position of Social Science Coordinator for the Desert Knowledge CRC. She has a balance of applied and academic anthropology, having worked earlier for the Central and Northern Land Councils as a regional staff anthropologist.

Janet Hunt

Janet Hunt is a Fellow at the Centre for Aboriginal Economic Policy Research at The Australian National University where she manages the Indigenous

Community Governance Project. She has worked for many years in international development with a particular focus on non-government organisations (NGOs), gender and development, and the Pacific and South East Asia regions. She was Executive Director of the Australian Council for Overseas Aid, the peak body of international development NGOs, from 1995–2000. Since 1999 she has worked with a range of local and international NGOs in East Timor. She has published about education, aid and development, East Timor, and Indigenous governance; and has lectured in international and community development at RMIT and Deakin universities. Her most recent book, co-authored with four others, is *International Development: Issues and Challenges*, published by Palgrave in 2008.

Bill Ivory

Bill Ivory is a PhD scholar with Charles Darwin University/Menzies School of Health Research in Darwin, Northern Territory (NT). He has a background in anthropology and community development. Bill has worked in Indigenous affairs since 1972 with the NT and Commonwealth Governments. He graduated from the Australian School of Pacific Administration in 1972, and since then has been involved primarily as a field operative with projects in remote community contexts. Bill has a special interest in the sphere of Indigenous economic development. During the late 1990s he was a ministerial adviser to the NT Minister for Aboriginal Affairs. Since 2002, he has worked intensively in the Port Keats region in the northwest of the NT, with a specific focus on Indigenous leadership development.

Christina Lange

Christina Lange has worked with Aboriginal organisations and government agencies for over 20 years, predominantly in the areas of native title, social justice and capacity development. Christina is an accredited trainer and assessor, and uses this qualification in her work with organisations to develop their capacity in governance and strategic planning. Christina has an honours (first class) degree in anthropology from The University of Western Australia (UWA), and is currently undertaking PhD research on a postgraduate award from UWA. Her research on governance and service delivery in remote Western Australia is supported by the Indigenous Community Governance Project, on which she is a research collaborator.

Frances Morphy

Frances Morphy is a Fellow at the Centre for Aboriginal Economic Policy Research (CAEPR) at The Australian National University. An anthropologist and linguist, she has worked with Yolngu people of northeast Arnhem Land over a period of nearly 35 years. She is editor of *Agency, Contingency and Census Process: Observations of the 2006 Enumeration Strategy in Remote Australia* (CAEPR

Monograph No. 28, ANU E Press, 2007), which reports on her research with other CAEPR colleagues on the 2006 Census, and co-editor of *The Social Effects of Native Title: Recognition, Translation, Coexistence* (CAEPR Monograph No. 27, ANU E Press 2007), which includes a chapter in which she reflects on the response of the Yolngu applicants to their involvement in the Blue Mud Bay native title claim.

Will Sanders

Will Sanders joined the staff of the Centre for Aboriginal Economic Policy Research at The Australian National University (ANU) in 1993, having previously undertaken research and taught in three other departments of the ANU. Will's disciplinary training is in politics and public administration. He has, over the last 25 years, worked on many aspects of Australian Indigenous affairs policy, from housing, employment and inclusion in the social security system, to local government, inter-governmental relations and elections.

Benjamin Smith

Benjamin Richard Smith is currently Honorary Visiting Fellow at the University of Manchester and Visiting Fellow at the Centre for Aboriginal Economic Policy Research (CAEPR). His research interests include the social effects of customary land claims, the relationship between Indigenous Australians and the state, and the intercultural character of contemporary Indigenous life-worlds. He has carried out both academic and applied research with Aboriginal people in Cape York Peninsula and other locations across northern Queensland. His recent publications include *The Social Effects of Native Title: Recognition, Translation, Coexistence* (CAEPR Research Monograph No. 27), co-edited with Frances Morphy. He is currently working on a book, *Between People, Between Places: The Grounds of Sociality in Central Cape York Peninsula*.

Diane Smith

Diane Smith is an anthropologist with over 35 years field and research experience with Indigenous Australian communities and organisations in remote, rural and urban locations across Australia. Along with Mick Dodson, Jon Altman and Will Sanders she is a chief investigator on the Indigenous Community Governance Project and has undertaken related field-based case studies in West Arnhem Land and Newcastle, and research analysis of Western Australian, Northern Territory and Australian government policy and funding frameworks. She has carried out applied research and published widely on issues including Indigenous poverty, the socioeconomic status of families and households, the Community Development Employment Projects scheme, family welfare and community participation agreements, Indigenous land tenure systems, land rights and native title, resource development agreements and royalty associations, representative

Indigenous organisations, regional and community governance, and evaluation of changing government policy and funding arrangements in Indigenous affairs. Diane has been a member of the National Native Title Tribunal; is a member of the New South Wales Indigenous Dispute Resolution Reference Group; and has sat on numerous Indigenous organisational reviews and inquiries over the last three decades. She is currently a Visiting Fellow at the Centre for Aboriginal Economic Policy Research, and a principal consultant with Westbury Smith and Associates.

Kathryn Thorburn

Kathryn Thorburn is a PhD scholar on the Indigenous Community Governance Project at the Centre for Aboriginal Economic Policy Research, The Australian National University. Her disciplinary background is in geography and politics. Her PhD will examine the governance practice of two Indigenous organisations: one in Fitzroy Crossing, the other based at Kupartiya around 120 kilometres to the east of Fitzroy Crossing. Both are situated in the West Kimberley. As part of the doctoral process she spent 2005–2006 living in and around Fitzroy Crossing, and working with communities associated with each organisation.

Abbreviations and acronyms

ABC	Australian Broadcasting Corporation
ACAA	*Aboriginal Councils and Associations Act 1976* (Cth) (now CATSIA)
ACGC	Anmatjere Community Government Council
AGM	Annual General Meeting
AGPS	Australian Government Publishing Service
AIATSIS	Australian Institute of Aboriginal and Torres Strait Islander Studies
ALGA	Australian Local Government Association
ALRA	*Aboriginal Land Rights (Northern Territory) Act 1976* (Cth)
ALSWA	Aboriginal Legal Service of Western Australia (Inc)
ANU	The Australian National University
ARC	Australian Research Council
ATSI	Aboriginal and Torres Strait Islander
ATSIC	Aboriginal and Torres Strait Islander Commission
ATSISJC	Aboriginal and Torres Strait Islander Social Justice Commissioner
BAC	Bawinanga Aboriginal Corporation
BOM	Bureau of Meteorology
BSRSF	*Building Stronger Regions, Stronger Futures* policy (NT)
CAA	Council for Aboriginal Affairs
CAC	Chuulangun Aboriginal Corporation
CAEPR	Centre for Aboriginal Economic Policy Research
CATSIA	*Corporations (Aboriginal and Torres Strait Islander) Act 2006* (Cth)
CDEP	Community Development Employment Projects (Cth)
CDO	Community Development Officer
CDU	Charles Darwin University
CEO	Chief Executive Officer
CHIP	Community Housing and Infrastructure Program (Cth)
COAG	Council of Australian Governments
CAONT	Combined Aboriginal Organisations of the Northern Territory
CLC	Central Land Council
CLP	Country Liberal Party (NT)
CRAC	Coen Regional Aboriginal Corporation
CRC	Cooperative Research Centre
CYI	Cape York Institute
DAFWA	Department of Agriculture and Food (WA)
DCDSCA	Department of Community Development, Sport and Cultural Affairs (NT) (now DLGHS)

DEC	Department of Environment and Conservation (WA)
DEWR	Department of Employment and Workplace Relations (Cth)
DIA	Department of Indigenous Affairs (WA)
DKCRC	Desert Knowledge Cooperative Research Centre
DLGHS	Department of Local Government, Housing and Sport (NT)
DOGIT	Deed of Grant in Trust
DPI	Department of Planning and Infrastructure (NT)
EHSC	Education and Health Standing Committee (WA)
FaCSIA	Department of Families, Community Services and Indigenous Affairs (Cth, former Coalition Government)
FaHCSIA	Department of Families, Housing, Community Services and Indigenous Affairs (Cth, Labor Government)
HREOC	Human Rights and Equal Opportunity Commission
HRSCAA	House of Representatives Standing Committee on Aboriginal Affairs (Cth)
ICC	Indigenous Coordination Centre
ILC	Indigenous Land Corporation
IPA	Indigenous Protected Area
km	kilometre(s)
km^2	square kilometres
LAA	*Lands Administration Act 1997* (WA)
LANT	Legislative Assembly of the Northern Territory
Laynha	Laynhapuy Homelands Association Incorporated
LGANT	Local Government Association of the Northern Territory
MAC	Maningrida Arts and Culture
MSP	Municipal Services Program
NGO	non-government organisation
NIC	National Indigenous Council
NLC	Northern Land Council
NSW	New South Wales
NT	Northern Territory
NTRB	Native Title Representative Body
OIPC	Office of Indigenous Policy Coordination (Cth)
ORA	Outstation Resource Agency
ORAC	Office of the Registrar of Aboriginal Corporations (Cth) (now Office of the Registrar of Indigenous Corporations, ORIC)
PLB	Pastoral Lands Board (WA)
RA	Reconciliation Australia
RADA	Reform and Development Agenda

RCIADIC	Royal Commission into Aboriginal Deaths in Custody
RPA	Regional Partnership Agreement
RSPCA	Royal Society for the Prevention of Cruelty to Animals Incorporated
SGIA	Secretaries Group on Indigenous Affairs
SCRGSP	Steering Committee for the Review of Government Service Provision
SNC	Single Noongar Claim
SRA	Shared Responsibility Agreement
STEP	Structured Training and Employment Projects
SWALSC	South West Aboriginal Land and Sea Council
TET	Top End Triangle
TRC	Thamarrurr Regional Council
UWA	University of Western Australia
WA	Western Australia
WAC	Windidda Aboriginal Corporation
WASTC	West Arnhem Shire Transitional Committee
YATSIC	Yarnteen Aboriginal and Torres Strait Islanders Corporation
WCARA	West Central Arnhem Regional Authority (Interim Council)

Foreword

Governance has become a concern for Indigenous peoples worldwide, so it is significant that the research that informed this book grew out of early linkages between Australian researchers and Indigenous leaders with their Canadian and US counterparts. These early relationships, with people associated with the landmark *Delgamuukw v British Columbia* case, the Harvard Project on American Indian Economic Development and the Native Nations Institute at the Udall Centre at the University of Arizona, developed into a series of exchanges across the Pacific Ocean that have been ongoing since the late 1990s.

In April 2002, the first national *Indigenous Governance Conference* was held in Canberra, under the auspices of Reconciliation Australia. It drew on international and Australian speakers and its outcomes raised key points, which were articulated on behalf of the organisers in a closing speech by Fred Chaney:

> First we'd say that it's been pretty clearly indicated that good governance requires communities having genuine decision-making powers, and that's overwhelmingly confirmed by the evidence presented at this conference.

> Second, the compelling evidence presented to us from local experience, as well as our friends from overseas, shows that sustained and measurable improvements in the social and economic wellbeing of Indigenous people only occurs when the real decision-making power is vested in their communities, when they build effective governing institutions, and when the decision-making processes of those institutions reflect the cultural values and beliefs of the people.

A second conference was convened 18 months later at Jabiru in the Northern Territory (NT). It focused on presenting Indigenous Territorians' stories of their initiatives to develop practical, capable and legitimate governance in that jurisdiction. The timing coincided with a new NT policy for the development of Regional Authorities, which were to have the jurisdictional powers of local governments and reflect 'Indigenous cultural relationships and communities of traditional interest'.[1] This promised a significant reshaping of Indigenous governance arrangements. The timing also coincided with the Australian Government's abolition of the peak Indigenous representative body for the country, the Aboriginal and Torres Strait Islander Commission (ATSIC) and its 35 Regional Councils, and the commencement of a Council of Australian Governments (COAG) trial of 'whole-of-government' coordination in several Indigenous communities across Australia.

---

[1] See D. Smith, 2004, 'From Gove to governance: reshaping Indigenous governance in the Northern Territory,' *CAEPR Discussion Paper No. 265*, CAEPR, ANU, Canberra, p. 9.

The national and international research presented at both conferences, reinforced by local speakers' own experiences, was that a number of preconditions were essential to successful Indigenous governance. Dr Neil Sterritt, a Gitxsan leader and First Nations governance expert from Canada, noted at the 2002 conference that strong Indigenous governance could be characterised as having four main attributes or dimensions: legitimacy, power, resources and accountability. These preconditions resonated with many of the conference participants, who noted their absence from the Australian context.

The Harvard Project on American Indian Economic Development derived a similar set of prerequisites from their long-term research among over 60 Native American tribal governments in the United States. This international research emphasised four fundamental preconditions to strong and effective Indigenous governance:

- power ('de facto sovereignty' or genuine decision-making authority for 'self-rule');
- ownership and access to resources (natural, human, capital etc.);
- effective governing institutions and accountability; and
- legitimacy and 'cultural match'.

But we needed to know whether these preconditions were necessary, similar or even sufficient in the intercultural and political context of Indigenous Australia.

It was against this backdrop that researchers at the Centre for Aboriginal Economic Policy Research at The Australian National University, in partnership with Reconciliation Australia, initiated the Indigenous Community Governance Project (ICGP), an Australian Research Council project, as a longitudinal, comparative study. National in coverage, and community and regional in focus, it pulled together a multidisciplinary team to work with partner communities and organisations to investigate Indigenous governance arrangements—the processes, structures, scales, institutions, leadership, powers, capacities, and cultural foundations—across rural, remote and urban settings.

The ICGP has been ambitious. It aimed to elucidate the diverse conditions and models of contemporary Indigenous governance in different community and regional settings, with a focus on governing bodies and leaders, and the underlying cultural systems within which their governance is embedded. Recognising the dominant powers and institutions of Australian governments in Indigenous affairs, the project also sought to explicate the nature of the broader governance environment (at regional, state and national levels), its differing governance values and rationales, and its impacts on Indigenous community governance.

ICGP researchers have explored the diverse forms of governance in Indigenous communities and the ramifications of these for community and regional self-determination, and for sustainable socioeconomic development. In doing so, the project aimed to identify broadly relevant insights and enduring Indigenous 'design principles' that might assist other initiatives to strengthen community governance, including options that address intercultural matters of power, autonomy, scale, representation, legitimacy and accountability.

As part of this process, the researchers also analysed the nominations from the 2005 and 2006 *Indigenous Governance Awards*, a related initiative of Reconciliation Australia, to recognise and reward standards of excellence in Indigenous governance. Both the research and the awards processes have revealed highly competent organisations that have found ways to balance their cultural imperatives and practice with the demands of legal incorporation and government funding regimes. In doing so, they demonstrate how to build practical capacity and secure community legitimacy, and the importance of developing strong Indigenous leadership across the generations.

My thinking has been profoundly altered by my involvement in both the research project and the governance awards. Both have demonstrated to me the value of the research and the fact of Indigenous success: built on innovation, ingenuity, determination and community initiative. We have a duty to ensure that this success is replicated across the country.

In confronting the challenges posed in getting governance right we should not lose sight of the successful models of governance that Indigenous peoples and their organisations and communities are already employing.

This book is one of many publications from the ICGP, and it complements other materials directed specifically to governments and Indigenous communities. In this way, I trust that the research counts in terms of the evidence and practical guidance it can provide to governments and Indigenous leaders about community governance in Indigenous Australia, and contributes to enhancing the success I have mentioned. In the chapters that follow, the researchers document many of the challenges, opportunities and issues facing those engaged in trying to achieve legitimate and effective governance on the ground. I trust that the insights this book offers will, in their own way, help in that very practical and important endeavour.

Finally, I would like to acknowledge the valued collaboration of the many Indigenous communities and organisations participating in the research, the detailed intellectual and practical governance work of the research team, the support of the funding partners, and the valuable contribution of the International Advisory Committee for the project. In particular, I wish to thank Professor Stephen Cornell, Dr Manley Begay and Dr Neil Sterritt for planning and hosting an Australian Indigenous delegation on a visit to North America to examine governance issues confronting Native Americans and Aboriginal Canadians. All have contributed enormously to this ground-breaking book, which sheds new light on the significant underlying problems that have to be resolved if Indigenous social and economic development is to be achieved and sustained.

Professor Mick Dodson
Chair, International Advisory Committee for the ICGP
Director, National Centre for Indigenous Studies, The Australian National University
Co-Chair, Reconciliation Australia.

Acknowledgements

This research was conducted with financial support from the Australian Research Council (ARC Linkage Project No. 0348744), and with Reconciliation Australia as an industry partner.

In a project as large as this, carried out over several years with Indigenous groups and leaders from many different parts of Australia, with government agencies and officers across jurisdictions, and with national and international research institutions, there are many people to thank.

Firstly, we would especially like to acknowledge and thank all the Indigenous communities, organisations and leaders who have welcomed us to work with them. These research partnerships have been crucial to the project and have involved considerable time, patience, good humour and intellectual engagement on their part. We particularly appreciate the contribution of the following organisations and people to the development of chapters for this book:

Anmatjere Community Government Council

West Arnhem Shire Transitional Committee and community organisations

Laynhapuy Homelands Association Incorporated

Aboriginal people of the Kaanju homelands

Bawinanga Aboriginal Corporation

Yarnteen Aboriginal and Torres Strait Islanders Corporation

Thamarrurr Regional Council

South West Aboriginal Land and Sea Council

Windidda Aboriginal Corporation

Kurungal Incorporated

The Indigenous Community Governance Project (ICGP) has brought together a multi-disciplinary team of researchers largely from the Centre for Aboriginal Economic Policy Research (CAEPR), as well as from the National Centre for Indigenous Studies (NCIS), at The Australian National University (ANU), and from the following institutions: Charles Darwin University, the Centre for Anthropological Research at The University of Western Australia, the Australian Institute of Aboriginal and Torres Strait Islander Studies, and the Centre for Indigenous Governance and Development at Massey University, New Zealand. We appreciate the collegial spirit in which they have all undertaken very practical research and fieldwork collaboration. Collectively, they have made an inspiring intellectual contribution to both the Australian debate and practical consideration of the critical issue of Indigenous governance.

The research was made possible by the partial grant support of the ARC and the valuable collaboration of our ARC Linkage Partner, Reconciliation Australia (RA), particularly their board; the Chair of their Governance theme, Professor Mick Dodson; our RA Partner Investigator, Jason Glanville; and the RA Governance Program team (Kate Brodie, Rowena Withers and Marianne Pinnington). The partnership has had its own governance issues to periodically resolve, but the project would not have been possible without the tireless support and commitment of RA, and Jason Glanville in particular.

Through RA, we would also like to express our appreciation for the financial support and engagement of the Northern Territory, Western Australian and Australian governments and their senior officers, several of whom have put considerable effort into raising governance policy and program issues within their respective departments and ministries. Part of the ICGP's research in Central Australia was financially supported by the Desert Knowledge Cooperative Research Centre, and this has enabled the case study research to feed into other forums and practical applications.

The project's research has been overseen by an International Advisory Committee. Over several meetings, the Chair and members of the committee provided thoughtful input to the research approach and focus, and to discussion of practical and policy issues currently affecting Indigenous governance in Australia and elsewhere.

Our final thanks go to the project management and research team at CAEPR, including John Hughes for assistance with maps and Hilary Bek and Kitty Eggerking for proofreading this volume. The project has required and received intensive research coordination, administrative support, fieldwork facilitation, communication expertise, and intellectual leadership. The project team has unfailingly delivered on these.

Janet Hunt
Diane Smith
Stephanie Garling
Will Sanders
CAEPR, June 2008

1. Understanding Indigenous Australian governance—research, theory and representations

Diane Smith and Janet Hunt

An intercultural allegory

Scene 1: the opening of Parliament House, Canberra, May 1927

Crowds gather on a flat, dusty, ceremonial ground—witnesses to the first steps in the invention of a capital city. The Duke and Duchess of Kent have travelled from the mother country to preside over proceedings. The sovereign Crown come down under.

In the midst of the huddle one figure stands out. He is an Aboriginal man dressed in an old suit, dogs at his side ... A report from the *Canberra Times* referred to him as 'a lone representative of a fast vanishing race' who had come only to salute 'visiting Royalty'. His name was Jimmy Clements. Whitefellas, as was their way, referred to him as 'King Billy'. On seeing Clements, a policeman immediately asked him to leave. He was apparently dressed inappropriately for the occasion—a King not fit to be in the presence of English royalty. But Clements did not want to be moved on; this country was his after all.

... the crowd on the stands rallied to his side. There were choruses of advice and encouragement for him to do as he pleased. A well known clergyman stood up and called out that the Aborigine had a better right than any man present to a place on the steps of the House of Parliament and in the Senate during the ceremony. The old man's persistence won him an excellent position, and also a shower of small change ...

The following day, May 10, prominent citizens were paraded before the Duke and Duchess as they stood atop the steps of Parliament House. Clements was among those who passed before them ... *The Argus* reported, 'an ancient aborigine, who calls himself King Billy and who claims sovereign rights to the Federal Territory, walked slowly forward alone, and saluted the Duke and Duchess. They cheerily acknowledged his greeting.'

... the Aboriginal man who 'claims sovereign rights' at the very moment the sovereignty of the Crown and the Australian parliament is asserted.

(McKenna 2004)

Scene 2: the opening of Parliament, Canberra, February 2008

Politicians and dignitaries have gathered in the centre of Parliament House for the first-ever indigenous welcome. With rain gently falling across Canberra ... Ngambri elder Matilda House-Williams ... accompanied by a didgeridoo player and her two grandchildren, greeted Prime Minister Kevin Rudd and presented him a message stick.

She said her welcome, on this occasion, was far different from that accorded Jimmy Clements in 1927 ... Ms House-Williams described the day as significant because it was the first time parliament had opened with an Indigenous welcome to country ceremony ... 'A welcome to country acknowledges our people and pays respect to our ancestors' spirits who've created the lands,' she said. 'In doing this the prime minister shows what we call proper respect, to us, to his fellow parliamentarians and to all Australians.' ... The welcome symbolised a united Australia, Ms House-Williams said. 'The hope of a united nation through reconciliation, we can join together the people of the oldest-living culture in the world and with others who have come from all over the globe and who continue to come.'

A smiling Mr Rudd said he would respond, first by honouring the traditional owners of the land, now occupied by Parliament House, as well as the traditional owners of all lands across Australia ... He said exactly 100 years ago Canberra was chosen as the site of the nation's capital, 80 years ago the first parliament house was built and 20 years ago new parliament house opened. 'Yet the human history of this land stretches back thousands of years to the Dreamtime,' he said.

'Despite this antiquity among us, despite the fact that parliaments have been meeting here for the better part of a century, today is the first time in our history that as we open the parliament of the nation, that we are officially welcomed to country by the first Australians of this nation,' ... 'Today we begin with one small step, to set right the wrongs of the past, and in this ceremonial way it is a significant and symbolic step.' Mr Rudd said the ceremony should become a permanent practice for future governments. 'Let this become a permanent part of our ceremonial celebration of the Australian democracy.'

(AAP 2008)

The debate about Indigenous governance in Australia teeters on the brink of becoming inane and unilateral. As McKenna (2004) details above, in 1927, Jimmy Clements, or King Billy as he was known to the citizens of Canberra, was seen as 'a lone representative of a fast vanishing race'. At the same time as his 'race' was supposedly vanishing, he 'claim[ed] sovereign rights' at the very moment 'the sovereignty of the Crown' was being asserted in the opening of the first Australian Parliament. Eighty years later, Indigenous Australians have not disappeared. They are still asserting their sovereign rights and interests as the First Australians, and still doing so within a highly charged and contested environment in which the Australian state holds pre-eminent power. In many ways, government discourse and public understanding of the nature of Indigenous Australians' own systems of governance, and how these function within contemporary Australian society, have not progressed far since 1927. Their views continue to be pervaded by misunderstanding, half truths and convenient assumptions.

The two news events related above, linked across almost 80 years, stand as a rich allegory for the struggle, vulnerability and sustaining practices of Indigenous governance in Australia. They pose Indigenous systems of governance squarely within an intercultural post-colonial frame, in which the Australian state has overarching sovereign power and jurisdiction. Today, Indigenous Australians have secured only limited jurisdictional authority through the erratic enactment of land rights, native title and local government legislation in the states and territories. In the absence of treaties or constitutional recognition, they are having to find their pathways to self-governance within the wider 'governance environment' that encompasses them. This continues to bring them face to face with the governance systems, structures, concepts and values of non-Indigenous Australia—many of which are incompatible with their own.

A broad theme running through *Contested Governance: Culture, Power and Institutions in Indigenous Australia* is that the engagement between Indigenous people, their organisations and the Australian state is essentially intercultural in nature (cf. Hinkson and Smith 2005; Merlan 1998). That is, what we are trying to understand is a heterogeneous and relational field of governance (see B. Smith this volume, Chapter 6). The case studies presented here illustrate this point vividly. It is simply impossible to understand the governance of Australian Indigenous communities and organisations as separate from the encapsulating governance environment of the Australian state.

This is not an assertion of categorical control or domination by the Australian state. Rather, it identifies the importance of the interplay of relationships, practices and agency taking place in the intercultural governance field. The inter-penetration evolves and is neither uniform nor unidirectional. The focus of the book is squarely on that field, for it is where our research has found contemporary Indigenous governance practices are being shaped and often actively asserted, and where differences between the cultures of governance are being contested and negotiated. In other words, there is significant 'inter-influence' (Merlan 1998, 2005).

The case study research presented here indicates that Indigenous and non-Indigenous governance systems are far from separate in respect to issues of power, authority, institutions and relationships. And there are intended and unintended consequences—beneficial and negative—for both Indigenous and non-Indigenous Australians arising from what Hinkson and Smith (2005: 160) refer to as 'the complexities of lived interculturalism'. In particular, the contemporary governance systems of Indigenous communities, their organisations and leaders have been influenced by their interactions with the Australian state over many decades. To a lesser extent, the state has in turn been influenced by its interactions with Indigenous Australian governance systems, an influence that is most apparent at the level of its institutional engagement and policy implementation.

Contesting governance

Because one cannot simply demarcate the colonial past from struggles in the present, the contemporary exercise of Indigenous governance is a process that must constantly attempt to renegotiate the balance of domination, subordination and contestation in its interactions with the Australian state (Pels 1997: 163). Furthermore, 'the state' does not sit in splendid isolation in the nation's capital. Nor is it homogeneous. In its governmental, departmental and bureaucratic guises, the state daily manifests itself in Indigenous communities and organisations. The governmentality of the state can be understood as a pattern of power and set of supporting institutions that are dispersed—and not uniformly so—through the Indigenous social body. Contestation also highlights relationships between sets of individuals, as well as systems. These relationships may vary from local, familiar and seemingly benign, to distant, alien and antagonistic.

A broad perspective running through this book is that we must therefore study Indigenous governance as relationships between and among Australian governments and Indigenous groups, and as contestation and negotiation over the appropriateness and application of policy, institutional and funding frameworks within Indigenous affairs. The self-determination policy initiated various government experiments with community management, service delivery and institutional mechanisms for Indigenous-specific funding. More recently, a dominant mode of the state has been increased unilateral intervention into the political, social, family and economic lives of Indigenous communities. This has been particularly evident with the exercise of Commonwealth powers in the Northern Territory (NT).

There is little doubt that the difficulties of Indigenous governance in the context of extremely limited self-determination have long been apparent to those who study the aftermath of Indigenous struggles in the post-colonial world. In Australia it is evident, for example, in lost economic and resource rights, ruptured social fabrics, diminished law, language and ceremony, ill health, broken families and extreme welfare dependency. It is not surprising then that some commentators, including influential Indigenous spokespersons, argue that direct intervention by the state is long overdue and is justified to end dysfunction. But in these unilateral interventions, government support for Indigenous self-governance and related capacity-building is noticeably absent.

Indigenous self-determination in Australia is now widely disparaged. It has failed to deliver expected improvements in socioeconomic outcomes and has been poorly implemented by governments (Hunt this volume, Chapter 2). While there are some examples of outstanding Indigenous governance success (Reconciliation Australia 2006, 2008), there are also examples that have tragically failed to provide for the most basic rights of the people they are meant to represent. A preoccupation with Indigenous governance failure and dysfunction, however, has taken hold among policy makers and commentators alike, to the point that Indigenous institutions and capacity are now commonly seen through the lens of a deficit model of, and a problem for, 'good governance'.

Within this environment, Indigenous peoples in Australia have also been determined to increase their authority and capacity over their own affairs, resources and futures. They also point to the dysfunction and lack of governance capacity within governments as being equally relevant causal factors contributing to their poor community governance and socioeconomic disadvantage.

Partly as a result of these outcomes and public debates, the issue of governance and more particularly 'good governance' has come into greater prominence in Australian Indigenous affairs. As the concept of 'good governance' has rapidly transferred from the arena of international development and corporate management into policy making and bureaucratic language, some State and Territory governments have shown an interest in paying attention to Indigenous governance, but have found implementation difficult; their own capacities have been challenged by the task. The issue of governance also preoccupies Indigenous communities, organisations and leaders who have been bitterly disappointed with the political rhetoric and institutional failures of the Australian state over many decades. Indigenous groups are increasingly considering whether governance offers them an avenue to greater self-determination, when the official policy by that name did not, and while many remain so dependent on the state.

Getting governance right is gradually being recognised by both Indigenous and non-Indigenous Australians as fundamental to improving Indigenous well-being and generating sustained socioeconomic development. But its introduction into

Australia has been loaded with unrealistic expectations and contradictory assumptions. There is little critical understanding or consensus about its meaning, or how effective governance in Indigenous communities and regions might be developed, so that people talking about governance are often 'talking past each other', as Thorburn's chapter (Chapter 13) in this volume illustrates.

The purpose of the book

Contested Governance looks to this intercultural arena to put forward ethnographic accounts of the 'cultures of governance' of both Indigenous peoples and the Australian state, and explores their institutional inter-relationship. The book seeks to unite empirical, theoretical and action research by using these accounts to critique the concept and meanings of governance, and to pose questions about the nature and future of Indigenous governance in 'post-colonial' Australia.

From a scholarly perspective, the contributors seek to understand and problematise how Indigenous governance operates—in all its diversity—at the local level: its cultural foundations, values and principles, what is working, what is not, and why. The chapters collectively aim to better elucidate the relationship between the effectiveness of governing arrangements in diverse contexts, and factors of institutional form, scale, power, autonomy, legitimacy, representation and accountability. A key aim is to instil comparative data, greater analytical rigour and theoretical content into debates on these issues.

From policy and practical perspectives we believe that high quality research can have significant value to both Indigenous groups and governments concerned with enabling community 'governance building'. For the communities involved, the field research has been applied and collaborative—it has aimed to make research 'count' on the ground (see Holcombe this volume, Chapter 3). All the authors have worked on practical initiatives with Indigenous communities, organisations and leaders to identify the shortfalls and assets in governance power, institutions and capabilities, and to highlight successful governance strategies and solutions for wider dissemination. To that extent, the authors seek to make an empirical, conceptual and practical contribution to the governance field in Indigenous affairs in Australia and more widely.

Authors of the various chapters explore fundamental questions about the histories, nature and exercise of Indigenous governance, and its place in Indigenous communities and the wider Australian state. These issues have taken on an added urgency since the unilateral intervention by the previous Australian Government into NT communities (see Altman, Hunt, Smith, Ivory, this volume), and the current Federal Labor Government's formal apology to the Stolen Generations following the opening of the Australian Parliament in early 2008, referred to at the beginning of this introduction.[1] These two events, though diametrically different in character and intention, have focused attention squarely back onto issues of Indigenous legal rights, socioeconomic status and self-determination and, by implication, onto Indigenous self-governance.

Researching governance

The research on which this volume draws has arisen from a comparative research project—the 'Indigenous Community Governance Project' (ICGP)—which has been carried out over the five years 2004–08. The project involves a partnership between researchers from the Centre for Aboriginal Economic Policy Research at The Australian National University and Reconciliation Australia, as well as individual researchers from several other tertiary institutions. While national in coverage, the project is community and regional in focus, bringing together a multidisciplinary team[2] to investigate Indigenous governance arrangements and processes across different rural, remote and urban settings.

Researching governance is challenging given the multidimensional complexities of politics, ideology and institutions that are encompassed, and all the more so given its different cross-cultural meanings and expressions and the multiple agents involved (see Holcombe and Hunt this volume, Chapters 3 and 2 respectively). With these conditions in mind, and in order to support the objectives of the research project, the team leaders developed an overarching comparative methodological framework with several core components (see Smith 2005).

At the heart of the project are a number of ethnographic case studies undertaken with participating Indigenous communities and organisations. These include a sample of different 'types' of Indigenous 'communities' in diverse geographical locations (see Fig. 1.1). Researchers were engaged with the same communities and organisations over three to five years so that the dynamic aspects of local governance could be documented over time. A community collaboration strategy was developed that aimed to engage Indigenous organisations, leaders and community residents as active researchers in these case studies.

---

[1] See Altman and Hinkson (2007) for several authors' descriptions and analyses of the Australian Liberal Government's intervention strategy in 2007. See also the text of the Prime Minister's apology speech to Australia's Indigenous peoples (Rudd 2008).

[2] The ICGP brought together researchers with professional expertise in political science, anthropology, demography, geography, development studies and economics. The researchers worked alongside community research collaborators with expertise in local culture, business development, social organisation, language, history and local politics.

Fig. 1.1 The ICGP case study sites included in this volume

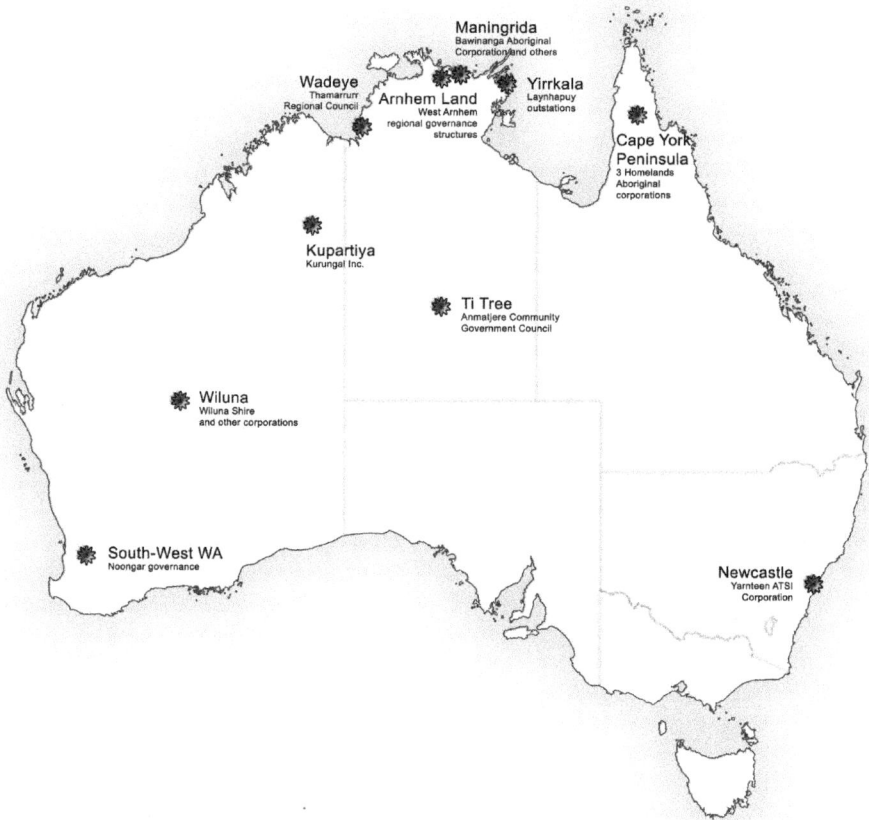

Maningrida
Bawinanga Aboriginal
Corporation and others

Wadeye
Thamarrurr
Regional Council

Arnhem Land
West Arnhem
regional governance
structures

Yirrkala
Laynhapuy
outstations

Cape York
Peninsula
3 Homelands
Aboriginal
corporations

Kupartiya
Kurungal Inc.

Ti Tree
Anmatjere Community
Government Council

Wiluna
Wiluna Shire
and other corporations

South-West WA
Noongar governance

Newcastle
Yarnteen ATSI
Corporation

ICGP researchers also undertook case studies of the 'governance environment', which was conceptualised separately for analytical purposes. These studies focused on the changing policy, service delivery and funding frameworks being implemented by different levels of government. The goals and rationale of government strategies were analysed and their impacts on the ground investigated. Language is a key feature of political and policy processes. Indigenous and government discourse about governance was thus a key component of the analysis. Within their host communities, project researchers mapped the wider field of players, and external conditions and relationships that impinge directly on the legitimacy, effectiveness and outcomes of Indigenous governance.

Researchers employed a variety of methodologies, including: demographic analysis; investigation of the governance histories of communities and organisations; participant observation; language and discourse analysis; mapping the community and governance environment; conducting organisational evaluations; documentation of decision-making processes and meetings; analyses of policy and legal frameworks; recording the life histories of individual leaders; and a range of interview, survey and questionnaire techniques. This approach was designed to elicit valid and meaningful information about the diverse conditions and attributes of Australian Indigenous community governance, and to help elucidate both the Indigenous and government 'cultures of governance'.

A comparative analysis of the case study evidence was undertaken (see Hunt and Smith 2006, 2007; Smith 2005). To enable comparative data to be collected at each field site the research leaders developed a set of questions and issues in a field manual, which each researcher investigated and subsequently reported upon. This enabled the project leaders to test hypotheses and location-specific evidence, in order to generate more broadly relevant insights into principles about Indigenous governance. These findings were then scrutinised at research workshops and the project's advisory committee meetings. Across the research sites, fundamental concepts such as 'governance', 'community', 'leadership', 'institutions', 'capacity', 'accountability' and 'legitimacy' were unpacked. The research team was endeavouring to identify underlying values, meanings and norms, and to test what might constitute valid criteria and principles for designing and evaluating Indigenous governance (Hunt and Smith 2006, 2007).

Conceptualising governance

The concept of governance has multiple origins and meanings. The academic literature is eclectic and rather disjointed and the term can sometimes serve to obscure rather than clarify issues. For the purposes of the ICGP, we define 'governance' as: the evolving processes, relationships, institutions and structures by which a group of people, community or society organise themselves collectively to achieve the things that matter to them. To do this they need to make decisions about:

- their group membership and identity (who is the 'self' in their governance);
- who has authority within the group, and over what;
- their agreed rules to ensure authority is exercised properly and decision-makers are held accountable;
- how decisions are enforced;
- how they negotiate their rights and interests with others; and
- what arrangements will best enable them to achieve their goals (see Hunt and Smith 2006).

In other words, governance is as much about people, power, and relationships as it is about formal structures, management and corporate technicalities. Indeed, the relational aspects of governance are often critical factors in effective performance (Hunt and Smith 2006).

Governance is not culture-neutral. Assessments of what is 'good' about governance cannot be separated from culturally-based values and normative codes about what is 'the right way' to get things done. In an intercultural milieu, determining whose way is the 'right way' is frequently a contested issue. A related undercurrent running through recent Australian debates about Indigenous governance is the role of 'culture'. To put it most starkly, some commentators question whether Indigenous people are culturally capable of 'good' governance in western terms. Blame for the failings of community and organisational governance are variously laid at the door of a perceived unchanging culture, whose values are supposedly antithetical to good governance; of leaders who are abnormally corrupt; or a culture now so dysfunctional that it is unable to deliver good governance (Hughes 2007; Vanstone 2005).

In a highly charged debate, what constitutes 'Indigenous' governance, 'leadership' and 'community' is also contested, and so has been problematised and closely examined by several authors in this volume.

The ICGP defines a 'community' as 'a network of people and organisations linked together by a web of personal relationships, cultural and political connections and identities, networks of support, traditions and institutions, shared socioeconomic conditions, or common understandings and interests' (Hunt and Smith 2006: 5). The concept can therefore encompass different types of 'community' including: a discrete geographic location; a 'community of identity' comprising a network of Indigenous people or organisations whose membership is based on cultural and historical affiliations, rather than geographic co-residence; a 'community of interest' comprising people who may not necessarily share the same world view or customs, but who share a set of common goals; and a political or policy community, such as a bureaucratic network of individuals (ibid.).

Such distinctions are useful for analytic purposes, but as the authors document here, several of these different types of community can be found in a single location. Communities are more than just residential locations or interpersonal networks. They can take on enduring social patterns, institutional voices, roles, functions, collective identities and structures.

The 'communities' that feature in this volume reflect much of the complexity and diversity elaborated above. In the context of governance, the concept of community immediately raises issues of scale, cultural geographies and boundaries, and contestation over those. The ICGP research therefore focused beyond the geographic boundaries of discrete communities to include the more permeable and mobile collectivities to be found dispersed across wider regions, and which are often seen by Indigenous people as constituting the more legitimate bases for the 'self' in their community self-governance.

Theorising governance

The chapters in this volume speak collectively to a pluralistic understanding of governance. The relatively under-theorised nature of the concept of governance encourages the broad methodological approach researchers have adopted. Accordingly, amongst the following papers, the authors critically test the relevance of theories of transformation and transition; political economy; network theories of governance; leadership theory; intercultural theory; and interpretative policy analysis.

At the same time, an underlying concern common to all the authors is to examine Indigenous governance as a site for the unfinished business of post-colonial struggle, which constantly contests and renegotiates the balance of power and relationships between Indigenous Australians and the Australian state. Collectively, the chapters call attention to the hyper-fluidity of the current government policy and institutional conditions under which Indigenous Australians are seeking to develop their community, regional and national governance arrangements.

Another broad finding evident in this volume is the relevance of 'culture', both as an object of governance and as an explanatory variable for differences in the workings and effectiveness of governance regimes within Indigenous societies, and in its contested mode within the Australian state. In each chapter, different authors investigate particular dilemmas and issues that come to the fore in the everyday experience of Indigenous community and organisational governance.

We believe that the multi-disciplinary and methodologically varied research framework, when combined with a comparative exploration of common research issues, has provided a rich source of data and critical analysis from different perspectives about the same fundamental issues. As a consequence, it is possible to look at the papers overall and extrapolate a set of broader theoretical propositions about 'governance' (see also Kooiman 2003; Pels 1997; Stoker 1998), and 'Indigenous governance' in particular.

The first proposition about the governance of Indigenous communities that emerges from the collected papers is that the concept refers to a field characterised by a plurality of actors, institutions and systems, and a multiplicity of forms of action. Today these are drawn from both the public and private sector, and Indigenous societies. As several authors note, the field of governance in Australia has been significantly widened in the last 40 years through the burgeoning of Indigenous community service organisations. That sector has taken over some of the usual tasks of government in Indigenous affairs. Conversely, the increased involvement of the private and voluntary sectors, and unilateral intervention by the public sector into Indigenous organisations and community life, highlights the potentially greater role of all these external players in either facilitating or undermining local governance arrangements.

The second proposition that emerges is that culture matters for governance. By culture we mean the shared values, meanings, ways of understanding the world, and beliefs of a group that inform their everyday practice. It underpins the way Indigenous people work together in their communities and organisations, and it flows through their governance arrangements in persistent and innovative ways. It is clearly relevant both as a dimension and object of governance, and as an explanatory variable for differences in the operation and the effectiveness of governance. It is also a critical factor in the outcome of encounters between Indigenous Australians and the state.

Acknowledging the first proposition also means recognising that there are several different 'cultures' of governance operating within the broad field of governance in Australia. The book examines this complex diversity and the contestation that occurs over the role of 'culture' in governance. The research findings of several authors testify to the fact that culture cannot simply be quarantined outside of the workings of governance. Indeed, they demonstrate how it can constitute an important component of governance legitimacy and effectiveness. Overall, the papers suggest that what is required is a far more sophisticated understanding of how Indigenous peoples are inserting their culturally-based world views, values and institutions into their contemporary governance arrangements, and the ways these interact with the cultural values and institutions underlying the western systems of governance in Australia.

A crucial issue that is highlighted by the collection of papers is that the expectations and values imposed by the state for 'good governance' are often counterproductive to the establishment of workable forms of Indigenous governance. On the other hand, several chapters address the argument that governance should not be reduced simply to cultural relativism; there may be principles for effective governing that apply or resonate across many cultures, and several authors address these.

The third proposition about governance that emerges from the collected papers is the blurring of boundaries and responsibilities that occurs in tackling social, economic, law and order, and political issues. Given the entrenched levels of Indigenous socioeconomic disadvantage, this proposition identifies that there may be a concomitant blurring of departmental accountability for allocation of resources and for key outcomes, where governments can shift blame onto Indigenous organisations and people for their failures.

Within Indigenous communities, this proposition partly explains the institutionalised forms of competition between organisations for scarce government resources, and the pressure organisations endure due to the administrative overload of multiple program grants that are necessary for them to meet immediate community needs. These pressures are counterproductive to organisations taking on more strategic governance roles.

The fourth proposition about governance identifies the power dependence and inequalities involved in the relationship between the institutions of the state on the one hand, and those of Indigenous Australia on the other. This proposition acknowledges that governance is inseparable from the contestation, negotiation and construction of political identity and the exercise of institutional power; that is, who gets to decide the rules and make the decisions about important matters. In an intercultural milieu, it highlights the fact that governance is also about the politics of cultural identities.

This proposition also identifies a major challenge currently confronting Indigenous Australians: can their culturally-based predeliction for small-scale, local autonomy be sustained in the context of living in contemporary Australia, where not only governments but also some Indigenous leaders and organisations are contemplating other scales of cultural geography for Indigenous governance?

The fifth proposition highlighted by the papers is about the inter-connectedness and autonomy of self-governing networks of actors, and communities of identity and interest. Here, governance describes the interaction of self-organising networks. This proposition suggests that the institutions of governmentality are now dispersed beyond governments to the private, voluntary and Indigenous sectors, which have their own forms of authority and rules. These sectors form networks with more and less enduring features and alignments of cultural values.

This proposition suggests that governance is always an interactive process—it is about relationships; a point noted by all the papers in this volume. Indigenous and non-Indigenous governance networks are inter-linked. Several authors in the volume investigate how Indigenous actors come to form networks, what holds them together, how they maintain identity, how they mobilise resources, what determines their choices, and how they influence their joint governing decisions. They document the anticipated problems of scale and autonomy emerging, as Indigenous networks and communities struggle to develop and maintain effective governing capacity and deliver outcomes. They also examine the nature and extent of the interaction between Indigenous and non-Indigenous governance networks, and the degree of their mutual commensurability.

The final theoretical proposition emerging from the collected papers is that governance recognises that the legitimacy and capacity to get things done does not rest alone on the power of government to command or use its authority. This proposition suggests that Indigenous governance poses a challenge to the authority of the state, and to its capacity to facilitate (rather than unilaterally impose) governance institutions and effectiveness.

A dilemma documented by the papers is the issue of the inertia or self-interest of policy makers (and departments) who seek to maintain policy and implementation choices that prove counterproductive to the achievement of effective, legitimate Indigenous governance. But a related dilemma is where

Indigenous leaders and organisations also resist internal governance reform because it erodes their power base. This proposition implies that governance capacity and legitimacy are, first and foremost, internal matters for the members of the Indigenous group or community concerned, and can only be enduringly transformed by them.

These theoretical propositions arising from the collective analyses presented in the following chapters are inter-related. They demonstrate that 'governance' is at times an analytical, at times a normative, concept; at other times it defines a specific policy, system, process, structure or political environment. All these meanings of governance are the product of cultural values, norms, institutions, behaviours and motivations.

The chapters in this volume are clustered according to these common themes and issues, which have determined the five sections of the book.

Part One sets the scene, both in terms of the policy environment and the research challenge. Janet Hunt outlines the recent history of the Australian Government's policy frameworks for Indigenous affairs. The period during which the ICGP was being undertaken witnessed a large shift away from self-determination and acceptance of the rights of Indigenous people in Australia—a process experienced by all of the communities in which the authors worked. Some representative Indigenous organisations were dismantled by the Australian state; other organisations collapsed or struggled in the face of the overload attached to the dramatic policy changes of the past decade. She argues that resilient Indigenous governance structures and reinvigorated networks of mutual support might provide the basis for Indigenous people to regain some momentum for self-determination.

At the same time, Hunt highlights the need for governments to reform their own internal institutional arrangements. She exposes several key areas of policy and funding where this might be undertaken, and which would significantly improve both the quality of services due to all Indigenous people as citizens, and the scope for their legitimate exercise of self-determination.

Sarah Holcombe illustrates some of the dilemmas and challenges of undertaking research in the intercultural arena of Indigenous community governance. She examines what happened to the knowledge produced by the researchers in one location, Ti Tree in the NT, and demonstrates how, through the course of the research, power relationships between Indigenous people and the state—as well as relationships within their own council—were slowly revealed and activated.

Holcombe's chapter also sheds light on what 'policy' is, and how it is promulgated and rationalised. She challenges the concept of 'equity' in service provision, and raises questions about ideas of Aboriginal choice and demand-driven development. The impact of a multitude of different players with an interest in the situation of some 100 Aboriginal people camping on unserviced land close to the Ti Tree township is highlighted. Holcombe thus shows the governance complexities and the blurring of responsibilities that are inherent in resolving many of the entrenched socioeconomic problems experienced by Indigenous Australia.

In **Part Two** of the book, Diane Smith, Frances Morphy and Ben Smith directly examine issues of culture and power inequalities in the operation of Indigenous governance. The papers foreground the issues of different cultural assumptions and ways of doing things, and how the complex 'field of governance' in which Indigenous communities and organisations operate influences their governance decision making, systems of representation, legitimacy and effectiveness.

Diane Smith's study (Chapter 4) of the processes of regionalising governance in West Arnhem Land in the NT highlights the continuing assertion of state power through both the minutiae of policy implementation processes and bureaucratic institutions. She describes Indigenous efforts to negotiate space within these processes, in order to reassert their own governance values and institutions. She introduces the concepts of 'cultures of governance' and the 'governance of culture' to elucidate the nature of the interaction and contestation between Indigenous community leaders and organisations, and the state.

Over several years, the Bininj people have tried to assert and insert their decision-making processes, cultural geographies and institutions into a government-initiated regionalisation of local government. In doing so, they have been confronted by non-Indigenous notions of what is 'right', legitimate and 'fair'. As Smith observes: 'the Australian state exercises overwhelming legal, policy and financial powers to govern Indigenous culture, and through that power seeks to make Indigenous governance and people "good" in western terms'. However, as Smith demonstrates, Indigenous peoples' capacity to transform and recreate their own institutions can also operate as a powerful tool, not only to positively build governance institutions that suit new conditions, but also to modify the state's efforts to govern Indigenous culture.

Frances Morphy's study describes an outstation resource agency, Laynhapuy Homelands Association Incorporated (Laynha), located in northeast Arnhem Land, which finds itself at the centre of an intercultural process: attempting to mediate between a highly structured, yet flexible Yolngu system and the world of the encapsulating settler state. Over the period of her case study research, the impact of government policies on the organisation has created major tensions. Yolngu conceptualisations of their own organisation and those of its government funders have come into direct conflict, and the very survival of the organisation has been at stake.

Just as in the West Arnhem case described by Smith, underlying the struggles that Laynha is experiencing are different culturally based conceptions and values of what 'good' governance looks like. Morphy recognises that the state and Yolngu have to recognise that *both* systems of value are at play and are complex, and both have to get beyond a simple deficit view of each other. Above all, resolving the tensions will require the state, as the more powerful party, to accept cultural difference and diversity into its policy and institutional thinking, rather than viewing it as a problem. This implies the need for governments to negotiate strategies that will work across the systems of Indigenous and non-Indigenous governance, to achieve mutually agreed outcomes.

Ben Smith provides a detailed account of the efforts of Kaanju people of the upper Wenlock and Pascoe River regions in Cape York to establish outstations on their traditional country, a process which again testifies to the complex field of governance in which Indigenous and non-Indigenous aspects of governance are irrevocably intertwined. Contemporary Kaanju identities and interests are now intercultural.

The interaction between local Indigenous interests and those outside the region produces, he argues, three key tensions: between the homelands-based, and other sub-regional and regional Aboriginal organisations; between contemporary Indigenous law and custom and 'mainstream' governance systems; and between different articulations of Indigenous identity at various scales. But for Smith the distinction between the Indigenous domain and the Australian 'mainstream' fails to provide a full account of the contemporary dynamics of the governance field. Thus, conflicts over appropriate governance are conflicts about interconnected institutions at a variety of scales and with diverse mandates. 'Cultural match', the idea of matching an institution to an underlying social order, is similarly problematised. Smith envisages it as a complex, contested institutional field in which Indigenous organisations extend the realm of Indigenous politics and assert differing Indigenous identities.

In Part Three, Jon Altman and Diane Smith focus on the Indigenous design, form and role of institutions of governance, and the challenges these pose for both indigenous leaders, communities and their organisations, and for governments. Bill Ivory explores similar themes through an investigation of the concept of Indigenous leadership; an often poorly understood institution of Indigenous governance systems.

Jon Altman examines how the Bawinanga Aboriginal Corporation (BAC), in the township of Maningrida in the NT, has managed similar governance tensions as those described by Diane Smith and Frances Morphy, and how over the almost 30 years of its existence it has grown considerably and transformed its roles. The BAC now services the social and economic interests of an extremely diverse population, including widely dispersed outstation communities.

Altman emphasises the intercultural checks and balances that lie at the heart of BAC's ability to straddle both the Indigenous and western worlds. He identifies factors that have been instrumental to the organisation's resilience over periods of external and internal change, including the carefully negotiated balance of power amongst the local Indigenous leadership; the role of long standing non-Indigenous senior staff in attempting to balance the organisation's customary and community obligations with legal compliance and business goals; and efforts to build informal institutions that foster openness and transparency. Despite recent threats to its major programs, Altman concludes that BAC's continuing success can be attributed to its ability to evolve into an intercultural organisation which supports hybrid local economies and enables residential mobility between the outstations and township.

Diane Smith's study of a dramatically different context in urban Newcastle, Yarnteen Aboriginal and Torres Strait Islanders Corporation, provides another governance and economic success story. In this chapter, Smith poses the concepts of 'community' and 'family' as issues for Indigenous governance, especially in the context of economic development initiatives. She explores the current myths and negative assumptions held about these two concepts, and the ways in which they are variously cast as either antithetical or fundamental to 'good' Indigenous governance and economic success. Smith describes how Yarnteen's leaders have attempted to address these expectations and assumptions in order to develop a robust, evolving governance model that supports both its enterprise and community development goals.

Smith argues that integral to the organisation's acknowledged success in business is the critical role of its formal and informal institutions of governance, and the ways these have been deliberately embedded in Yarnteen's modus operandi. The organisation's governance institutions create a system of incentives, constraints, limits and processes that direct the board, senior management and individual staff members to behave and perform in particular ways. For Yarnteen, these institutions are a form of capital—governance capital—to which there is a distinctly Indigenous character.

In the final chapter of this section, Bill Ivory (Chapter 9) explores the particular institution of men's leadership in the Port Keats region of the NT. He analyses the governance and leadership histories of the Indigenous clans over their contact history, up to their recent establishment of a new regional governance structure based on a revitalisation of their traditional concept of *thamarrurr*. At different points in their governance history, clan leaders have attempted to create a 'responsive engagement' with the sequence of outsiders who have generated massive changes in their society.

Ivory traces the leadership development of different generations through personal and group case studies, and concludes that leadership operates in a 'flexible field of authority' centred on relatively fluid networks in which leaders operate as core nodes. These nodal leadership networks serve to satisfy the duality of a simultaneously egalitarian and hierarchical society. However, the networked leadership model has been barely perceived or understood by those outside it, much less engaged with. Ivory echoes Morphy's plea for a mutual appreciation of the systemic differences as a basis for moving forward. He emphasises the contemporary significance of the clan unit and the concept of *thamarrurr*, the enduring way that clans cooperate together, and the positive ongoing role of the local world view within their governance system.

In Part Four, papers by Will Sanders and Manuhuia Barcham focus on the cultural geographies of Indigenous governance—its changing scales, sociology and boundaries—and the contestation and negotiation that occurs within and between Indigenous communities and governments around definitions of the collective 'self' in governance arrangements. The challenge of developing larger, regional aggregations that have legitimacy and respect local autonomy, but which also generate greater capacity to achieve Indigenous goals, is the issue these chapters address. Traditionally, Indigenous governance has been highly localised and small scale, but with groups linked into ever-widening relationships and shared decision making. These pose the potential for larger scale, bottom-up alliances and confederations.

In Chapter 10, Manuhuia Barcham traces the story behind the development of the successful Noongar native title claim over the Perth Metropolitan area; the first of six claims over southwest Western Australia (WA). After several false starts and seemingly interminable and debilitating problems of governance, Noongar people eventually developed a process and structure to articulate and progress their aspirations in the southwest.

Finding the right organisational and decision-making structure to represent their diverse interests was critical. The South West Aboriginal Land and Sea Council (SWALSC) achieved it. A process of detailed and lengthy genealogical work using participatory family research provided the basis for a family based representative structure for native title working parties and claimant groups. This was widely perceived to be legitimate and effective. SWALSC's experience indicates that aggregation of Indigenous interests beyond the local is possible if approached in a culturally legitimate and inclusive way.

Will Sanders explores how the Anmatjere Community Government Council (ACGC) has managed the tensions between regionalism and local autonomy in Central Australia over the past 15 years. The ACGC operated with a form of 'regional federalism', which had demanding quorum rules that became unworkable and were eventually reformed. But its success in supporting what Sanders describes as 'dispersed single settlement localism', while still managing its regional mandate, provides another illustration of how regionalism and localism can coexist successfully as a governance model; a conclusion that mirrors Diane Smith's analysis from West Arnhem Land.

In Part Five, papers by Christina Lange and Kathryn Thorburn examine two very different contexts in WA, where Indigenous groups are attempting to rebuild their governance arrangements and develop locally relevant governance capacities. These papers focus on how organisations and those who support them work to strengthen their governance in contexts where problems have been identified by external government agents who then take various kinds of action.

Christina Lange describes how the governance of Windidda Station, a pastoral lease owned by the Windidda Aboriginal Corporation (WAC) in the Shire of Wiluna, came to public attention through a complaint alleging neglect of cattle during the 2005 drought. At risk was the organisation's major asset, its pastoral lease. Contemporaneously, an investigation by the Registrar of Aboriginal Corporations demanded compliance with numerous conditions if WAC was to retain its registration. As Lange notes: 'Over an 18 month period the organisation had to deal with a barrage of bureaucratic and legislative challenges.' Power inequalities and misunderstanding of governance roles and responsibilities came to the fore.

However, the community had networks of support that it was able to call upon. These assisted it to confront and overcome its governance and management problems. Capacity building support of various kinds, including support from Lange herself, enabled the organisation to regain control of its pastoral lease, develop a plan for the pastoral business, and build the governance skills of its members. Importantly, in this process, governance came to be seen as a tool to enable the community to achieve its aspirations, rather than simply a compliance matter—an important lesson for strengthening self-governance.

Kathryn Thorburn analyses a different type of intervention; namely, a governance review exercise undertaken by a remote Aboriginal organisation in the West Kimberley region, which was experiencing some governance problems and thereby drawing unfavourable government scrutiny. Her study exposes the very different perceptions of the organisation: those held by the key government funding agency; the internal differences of views about what 'governance' might mean among the members of the organisation; and the views of its coordinator. The external consultant engaged to lead the review identified major cross cultural misunderstandings as factors contributing to the stresses being experienced by the organisation.

As with Ivory's chapter, Thorburn demonstrates that the history of the organisation and its community members are powerful factors shaping the extent of its Indigenous legitimacy and the ongoing tensions within it. Furthermore, the coordinator was clearly caught between two increasingly incompatible forms of bureaucratic demands and Indigenous expectations. The review itself, as a one-off exercise, was able to identify many of the underlying problems. But whilst 'governance' language opened up space for problems to be better understood, the time allocated to the review and the lack of follow-up, meant that the specifics revealed went largely unresolved. The timeframes for capacity building interventions clearly need to be longer.

Conclusion

The two stories that opened this chapter stand as a testimony to the Indigenous struggle for the recognition and rights of their governance in Australia. The following chapters highlight the dilemmas and challenges involved in this, the nature of the contestation and negotiation between Australian governments, their agents and Indigenous groups over the appropriateness of different governance processes, values and practices, and over the application of related policy, institutional and funding frameworks within Indigenous affairs.

Collectively, the papers in this volume demonstrate that the facilitation of effective, legitimate governance should be a policy, funding and institutional imperative for all Australian governments—yet by and large it is not. There are examples of Indigenous groups successfully designing innovative governance arrangements, transforming their institutions, building new capacities and revitalising trusted processes. However, the contributions to this volume overwhelmingly point to the continuing challenges that Indigenous people face in their efforts to secure and exercise genuine decision-making authority and capacity over issues that matter to them, and therefore, to the related challenges facing the Australian state and its agents.

Today Indigenous systems of governance remain squarely located within an intercultural, post-colonial frame in which the Australian state has overarching sovereign power and jurisdiction, as they were 80 years ago when Jimmy Clements attempted to assert his sovereign rights at the opening of Australia's first parliament. Research for this book occurred during a period which has seen major interventions by governments in Indigenous affairs at national, State and Territory levels. In combination, the chapters also document the significant and ongoing negative impacts that the poor 'governance of governments' is having on the operation of Indigenous governance, and on people's daily experience of living and working in their communities and organisations.

Importantly, the chapters point to the need to rectify the common assumption that Indigenous cultures across the country are so completely different that general principles of Indigenous governance cannot be discerned. Whilst there is enormous variety of circumstance, the ICGP and the detailed accounts presented here do identify some common Indigenous 'design principles', which underpin governance across the diverse settings (Hunt and Smith 2007). Greater attention to these principles may be a fundamental factor in strengthening Indigenous governance.

Common Indigenous principles of governance include the relevance and legitimacy of:

- networked governance models;
- nodal networks and gendered realms of leadership;
- governance systems arising out of locally dispersed regionalism and 'bottom-up' federalism;
- subsidiarity and mutual responsibility as the bases for clarification and distribution of roles, powers and decision making across social groups and networks;
- cultural geographies of governance; and
- an emphasis on internal relationships and shared connections as the foundation for determining the 'self' in self-governance, group membership and representation.

In activating these principles, the institutional and organisational dimensions of Indigenous governance are both important. Institutions are often longer-lasting and more influential on people's behaviour than organisations. They are especially influential in determining the extent to which governance arrangements are judged to be proper and legitimate. To that extent, the chapters collectively remind us that institutional strength is not only fundamental to achieving effective Indigenous governance, but that it must be created from the considered and informed choice of Indigenous people themselves, not through external imposition.

To outsiders, Indigenous organisations and their leaders are often the most visible expression of governance in communities. But 'community governance' for Indigenous people is in fact a form of multi-networked, nodal governance that includes not only organisations, but also wider networks of leaders, families and communities. These nodal networks are embedded within the more formal wider governance environment that includes governments, bureaucratic and policy networks, private sector companies, voluntary organisations, and their individual officers.

The case study research presented here demonstrates that Indigenous and non-Indigenous governance systems are intercultural in respect to issues of power, authority, institutions and relationships. It also documents the intended and unintended consequences—beneficial and negative—arising for both Indigenous and non-Indigenous Australians from the realities of contested governance. In particular, the contemporary governance arrangements of Indigenous communities, their organisations and leaders have been significantly affected by their interactions with the Australian state over many decades. To a lesser extent, and at specific points, the state has in turn been influenced by its interactions with Indigenous Australians' systems of governance. That influence is most apparent at the level of the state's institutional engagement and policy implementation in Indigenous affairs. It is likely, therefore, that the legitimacy and effectiveness of both Indigenous governance and the 'governance of governments' in Australia will continue to be inextricably linked, not only to the priorities, normative codes and institutional predilections of each, but to the extent of their mutual understanding and engagement.

References

AAP 2008. 'Politicians welcomed to Canberra with indigenous ceremony', *Herald-Sun*, 12 February, available at <http://www.news.com.au/heraldsun/story/0,21985,23200274-662,00.html> [accessed 5 May 2008].

Altman, J. and Hinkson, M. 2007. *Coercive Reconciliation: Stabilise, Normalise, Exit Aboriginal Australia*, Arena Publications, Melbourne.

Hinkson, M. and Smith, B. 2005. 'Introduction: conceptual moves towards an intercultural analysis', in M. Hinkson and B. Smith (eds), *Figuring the Intercultural in Aboriginal Australia*, Special issue of *Oceania*, 75 (3): 157–66, Sydney University Press, Sydney.

Hughes, H. 2007. *Lands of Shame: Aboriginal and Torres Strait Islander 'Homelands' in Transition*, Centre for Independent Studies, St Leonards, NSW.

Hunt, J. and Smith, D. E. 2006. 'Building Indigenous community governance in Australia: preliminary research findings', *CAEPR Working Paper No. 31*, CAEPR, ANU, Canberra.

—— and ——2007. 'Indigenous Community Governance Project: year two research findings', *CAEPR Working Paper No. 36*, CAEPR, ANU, Canberra.

Kooiman, J. 2003. *Governing as Governance*, Thousand Oaks Press, London.

McKenna, M. 2004. 'The need for a reconciled republic', Manning Clark House Inc, Canberra, available at <http://www.manningclark.org.au/papers/reconciled_republic.htm>.

Merlan, F. 1998. *Caging the Rainbow: Places, Politics and Aborigines in a North Australian Town*, University of Hawaii Press, Honolulu.

——2005. 'Explorations towards intercultural accounts of socio-cultural reproduction and change', in M. Hinkson and B. Smith (eds), *Figuring the Intercultural in Aboriginal Australia*, Special issue of *Oceania*, 75 (3): 167–82, Sydney University Press, Sydney.

Pels, P. 1997. 'The anthropology of colonialism: culture, history, and the emergence of western governmentality', *Annual Review of Anthropology*, 26: 163–83.

Reconciliation Australia (R. Withers and R. Beattie [eds]) 2006. *Celebrating Indigenous Governance: Success Stories of the Indigenous Governance Awards*, 2005 IGA, Reconciliation Australia, Canberra.

——(R. Withers and J. Jeeves [eds]) 2008. *Celebrating Indigenous Governance: Success Stories of the Indigenous Governance Awards*, 2006 IGA, Reconciliation Australia, Canberra.

Rudd, K. The Hon. 2008. 'Apology to Australia's Indigenous peoples, House of Representatives, Parliament House, Canberra', Speech as Prime Minister of Australia, 13 February, available at <http://www.pm.gov.au/media/Speech/2008/speech_0073.cfm> [accessed 29 May 2008].

Smith, D. E. 2005. 'Researching Australian Indigenous governance: a methodological and conceptual framework', *CAEPR Working Paper No. 29*, CAEPR, ANU, Canberra.

Stoker, G. 1998. 'Governance as theory: five propositions', *International Social Science Journal*, 155: 17–28.

Vanstone, A. The Hon. 2005. 'Beyond conspicuous compassion: Indigenous Australians deserve more than good intentions', Speech as Minister for Immigration and Multicultural and Indigenous Affairs to the Australia and New Zealand School of Government, 7 December, ANU, Canberra, available at <http://epress.anu.edu.au/anzsog/policy/mobile_devices/ch03.html>.

Part 1: The governance environment

2. Between a rock and a hard place: self-determination, mainstreaming and Indigenous community governance

Janet Hunt

The first few years of the new century saw major change in the Australian Government's approach to Indigenous affairs. These developments combined with simultaneous policy shifts in State and Territory jurisdictions to create a period of enormous flux and uncertainty in Indigenous communities and organisations. This chapter aims to help readers understand these changes and the resulting challenges facing the Indigenous community governance bodies involved in our research. Subsequent chapters will indicate that Indigenous people and their organisations actively engaged through this period, trying to manoeuvre their way through these new arrangements towards their own goals. The changes presented opportunities as well as constraints, but this chapter will argue that there is an underlying contradiction that the organisations confront. They are, in a sense, between a rock and a hard place: the assumptions and principles of self-determination underlying the policy environment in which many of them were created have changed. Some new ideas like 'mainstreaming' have been introduced and organisations are finding themselves caught at an uncomfortable intersection between communities operating with one set of assumptions, and governments another. They are also squeezed in the shifting policy space between jurisdictions as different interests exert their influence around them. These organisations are the intercultural space where different 'framings' of the governance challenge (cf. Leach et al. 2007) meet or, at times, collide. At the end of 2007, as this research concluded, a change of government at the national level signalled the potential for a more productive engagement with Indigenous people to address the challenges this paper outlines.

Background

Between the early 1970s and the mid 1990s, under both Labor and Coalition Governments, many of the organisational arrangements for Indigenous community governance developed under policies favourable to the principle of Indigenous self-determination. Although this principle was enormously circumscribed in practice, and self-management might better describe what actually occurred (Moreton-Robinson 2007), the period saw the creation of an 'Indigenous sector' across the country and diverse land rights regimes in a number of jurisdictions. The sector comprised statutory bodies such as land councils, native title bodies, Aboriginal and Torres Strait Islander Commission

(ATSIC) Regional Councils, community government councils acting as local governments, and several thousand Indigenous associations and corporations providing legal, employment, health, housing, education and many other services, which burgeoned across the country (Rowse 2005). This diverse expression of Indigenous agency and collective effort to take greater control over Indigenous lives was encouraged by key pieces of legislation[1] and by governments' program arrangements. The idea that Indigenous peoples' organisations may be best placed to address Indigenous problems was well-supported through special Indigenous programs, which funded Indigenous-controlled services. The mosaic of organisations also reflected the desire of Aboriginal people for a very local level of organisation and representation. Nevertheless, the establishment of ATSIC in 1990 provided an important form of Indigenous representation at the national level, albeit government-designed and under Ministerial control (Morrisey 2006). Though severely constrained by the complex federal legislative and policy context, the lack of Indigenous economic independence, the poor educational levels of many Indigenous people, and the limited national efforts towards Indigenous capacity building, self-determination as a principle was well accepted, if implemented without adequate support and in quite different ways from the Torres Strait to remote communities and urban settings (House of Representatives Standing Committee on Aboriginal Affairs (HRSCAA) 1990). As a result, it did not deliver quickly enough on the aspirations of those who championed and supported it. The statistics on Indigenous disadvantage seemed hard to budge, and the rapid growth of a youthful population with poor education and health, few employment prospects, and many associated social problems seemed, to many, to demand a new response.

Changing the arrangements

Change began with the election in 1996 of the Howard Coalition Government (P. Dodson 1996; Dodson and Pritchard 1998). This occurred just over half-way through the 10-year national reconciliation process led by the Council for Aboriginal Reconciliation (CAR), which was expected to lead to a negotiated agreement between Indigenous and other Australians. CAR was due to report to the national parliament in 2000. By then, for a variety of reasons, Australian Government relations with Indigenous Australia were deteriorating (Sanders 2006). From the outset, the Howard Government had been promoting what became known as 'practical reconciliation'—essentially focusing on Indigenous socioeconomic disadvantage (Aboriginal and Torres Strait Islander Social Justice Commissioner (ATSISJC) 2000, 2001). The Government's approach was to emphasise that, after many years of self-determination policies and focus on 'rights' (including land rights), Indigenous social and economic outcomes

---

[1] For example: *Aboriginal Land Rights (Northern Territory) Act 1976* (Cth); *Aboriginal Land Rights Act 1983* (NSW); *Aboriginal Councils and Associations Act 1976* (Cth); *Native Title Act 1993* (Cth).

remained woefully below the levels of other Australians, and these earlier ideas were now off the agenda[2] —despite evidence of at least some gains having been made (Altman 2004). The Government was tackling Indigenous disadvantage as its contribution to the reconciliation decade and would continue this focus in response (Commonwealth of Australia 2002). It was thus highly selective in its response to the Council's recommendations on sustaining the reconciliation process, promoting recognition of Indigenous rights, overcoming disadvantage, and fostering economic independence (CAR 2000). Aboriginal critics directly and implicitly highlighted the false dichotomy implied in the distinction between 'practical reconciliation' and rights-based approaches (Behrendt 2001, 2002; P. Dodson 1996; Dodson and Strelein 2001), but their voices were ignored. Nor was the Government concerned about undermining the very foundation of the concept of reconciliation—the expression of collective responsibility for past wrongs (Gaita 2007).

Thus, in the year 2000 the Council of Australian Governments (COAG) initiated a process to collaborate in addressing Indigenous disadvantage. It established nationally agreed priority outcomes and pledged periodic assessment of progress through Overcoming Indigenous Disadvantage reports (Steering Committee for the Review of Government Service Provision (SCRGSP) 2003, 2007). However, it offered no agreed national plan. Instead, COAG established eight 'whole-of-government' community trials to test new ways of working. Although progress in these was reportedly slow, in mid 2004 the Australian Government announced a set of 'new arrangements' in Indigenous affairs, which appeared to draw from this approach and were to apply nationally (Office of Indigenous Policy Coordination (OIPC) 2005).

The new arrangements involved the abolition of ATSIC, including its network of 35 elected regional councils (ATSISJC 2005b; OIPC 2005; Sanders 2004). Government would no longer work through these representative bodies, but instead would operate in direct partnership with Indigenous communities in a coordinated whole-of-government approach, emphasising Indigenous self-responsibility and mutual obligation (Shergold 2005). Proposed new regional Indigenous consultation arrangements (OIPC 2007) failed to materialise nationally, but the whole-of-government concept was implemented through various new processes or mechanisms, notably the leadership of the Secretaries Group on Indigenous Affairs (Gray and Sanders 2006), a single Indigenous budget, the establishment of Indigenous Coordination Centres (ICCs) in 30 locations around Australia, Shared Responsibility Agreements (SRAs) and Regional Partnership Agreements (RPAs). The idea was to 'harness the mainstream' to address Indigenous disadvantage, an idea reminiscent of one that had been tried—and

---

[2] Some years later, the Minister for Indigenous Affairs, the Hon. Amanda Vanstone, put the government's view this way: 'being land-rich but dirt poor is not good enough' (Vanstone 2005).

failed—much earlier (Arabena 2005). Altman (2004) described this 'new' approach as simply moving Indigenous-specific programs to mainstream departments, which themselves had demonstrated little capacity to meet Indigenous needs.

The key new players established in terms of partnerships with Indigenous communities are the ICCs. Their role is to coordinate 'Indigenous-specific programs' and 'negotiate regional and local agreements' (OIPC 2005: 15). These centres are meant to be 'one-stop-shops' for Indigenous interaction with the Australian Government and, ideally, for other jurisdictions as well. But they have struggled to satisfy Indigenous communities in this regard, with some communities concerned about a lack of ICC activity or access, and others experiencing a proliferation of new departmental relationships, funding applications and reporting processes (ATSISJC 2007a; Gilligan 2006; Gray and Sanders 2006; Hunt and Smith 2006; Jeffries 2006; McCarthy 2006). Obviously, the 'silo' behaviour of different departments, which whole-of-government approaches were meant to overcome, was proving difficult to change.

Self-determination gave way to 'sharing responsibility'. SRAs became the 'front line' of the partnership between government and Indigenous communities (Secretaries Group on Indigenous Affairs (SGIA) 2005). These local agreements sit within a broader context of 'mutual obligation' policy, as the key policy tools for a new *direct* conversation with Indigenous communities (Vanstone 2005). There have been many criticisms of SRAs, notably that government is by-passing competent Aboriginal organisations with existing capacity in order to negotiate directly with families and individual communities (ATSISJC 2005a, 2005b; McCausland 2005a, 2005b). With less than 250 negotiated in four years, and many of the easiest to finalise agreed first, SRAs appeared from the outset to be a very cost-inefficient and patchy means of delivering services to Indigenous Australians across the nation, even if some communities were relatively satisfied with them (ATSISJC 2007a).[3] SRAs obviously contribute to the existing burden of 'red tape' (Morgan, Disney and Associates 2006a). More significantly, SRAs suggest that Aboriginal people can have a voice in a limited range of local matters, but remain voiceless and unrepresented on the far more significant backlogs of housing, health, education and other essential services due to them as citizens. The development of RPAs, which appeared by 2007 to be replacing the focus on SRAs, has been much slower, however, with less than a handful negotiated by early 2008 (Australian Government 2008); their responsiveness to Indigenous priorities is already being questioned (ATSISJC 2007b; Shire of Naaanyatjarruku and Ngaanyatjarra Council 2007).

---

[3] There are over 1200 discrete Indigenous communities, without consideration of the regional and urban populations living in mixed settlements (ABS 2001).

Development discourses and the alleged 'failure' of self-determination

While these changes were proceeding, the discourse of 'failure' about past policies strengthened. Concern about social problems in Aboriginal communities is neither new nor confined to people or groups of any particular political persuasion (Hinkson 2007). However, by 2005, public debate about the 'failure' of self-determination, and suggestions that this had led to a form of separatism, were being escalated by those associated with right-wing think tanks and associations such as the Centre for Independent Studies and the Bennelong Society (Dillon 2005; Johns 2006), as well as by the Australian Government itself (Vanstone 2005).

When Minister Brough announced his 'Blueprint for Action in Indigenous Affairs' (Brough 2006a), his key messages were about giving Indigenous Australians equitable access to services on the same basis as other Australians, and removing barriers to economic opportunity. Asserting that culture should not 'stand in the way of progress', the Minister emphasised that individual, not community, decision making was critical, and suggested that the term 'partnership' would:

> signal the beginning of a redefinition of relationships ... to a point where responsibilities between governments, Indigenous people and other Australians are better aligned to normal Australian life ... We need to move beyond the fact that because a community is largely Indigenous that state and local governments relinquish their responsibilities for providing municipal and other basic services (Brough 2006a: 3–4).

Whilst such debates about treating Aboriginal people like all other Australian citizens, or treating them differently based on their group identity, have featured over decades of Indigenous policy (Attwood 2003), at this time the Commonwealth was clearly signalling that it planned to shift some financial responsibilities for remote Indigenous communities, which it had historically supported, to other jurisdictions. The broader strategy was three-pronged. In urban areas mainstream services would be improved to cater better for Indigenous people and improve their access to jobs. In remote areas the Government would be 'working with other governments to improve standards of service and to open these communities to the broader Australian community and the market economy' (Brough 2006a: 9). Some 'priority communities' would be the subject of 'intensive intervention' (ibid.), land tenure changes would be introduced, and 'normal' economic activity and home ownership would be encouraged. Thus, collective self-determination was being rejected and replaced by emphasis on an *individual's* ability to choose a particular way of life (Brough 2006a; Dillon

2005), notably one which embraced the 'mainstream'.[4] The 'mainstream' implied full engagement in a market economy. While for many Indigenous people who have experienced considerable exclusion from such economic opportunities this may be welcome, the features of Aboriginal life which marked out 'difference', such as communal land ownership and living on remote 'homelands', came under threat.

The Howard Government argued that communal land ownership was a key brake on economic development, that individual property rights were essential, and that reform of land tenure in Aboriginal townships under the *Aboriginal Land Rights (Northern Territory) Act 1976* (Cth) (ALRA) to allow 'head leases' was necessary. In fact, changes to this Act had already been passed to 'provide more choice and opportunity for Aboriginal people in the Northern Territory … and enable Aboriginal communities to operate like normal Australian towns' (Brough 2006b). Some 'intensive interventions' were also already underway, generating controversy about land tenure arrangements (Scrymgour 2007). Commonwealth funding for Indigenous home ownership to all jurisdictions in Australia was also to require 99-year head leases on Aboriginal land (ATSISJC 2007b). As Dodson and McCarthy (2006: 26) concluded, the changes to the ALRA were 'squarely aimed at drawing residents in remote communities away from real communal ownership of land and into individuated relationships with the wider economy'. The permit system, which enabled Aboriginal people to control access to their freehold land, was also to be changed, as it apparently 'hindered effective engagement between Aboriginal people and the Australian economy' (FaCSIA 2006: 4), an argument strongly disputed by David Ross, director of the Central Land Council, a major body that issued permits (Ross 2007).

If the first set of changes were designed to foster economic development on Indigenous land, the second tranche was to force greater Indigenous mobility to existing job markets. According to critics, Indigenous Australians were insular, indulgent, and needed to move into modern Australian society:

> If people want goods and services that a modern economy can provide, they will have to generate an income in order to purchase them. In order to generate an income they will have to work. If work is not available where they live, they will have to move to find it (Johns 2006: 1).

Changes to labour market and income support programs that would affect individual behaviour were seen as the solution. In other words, Indigenous Australians needed to accept the tenets of liberal democracy and individual property rights, and fully embrace the market and modernisation. They were to be pressured to assimilate. The fact that many Indigenous people already

---

[4] Of course, self-determination for a people was never in conflict with an individual's right to choose a way of life—indeed it was intended to strengthen the choices available to individuals within defined groups, whose rights have often been curtailed.

living in close proximity to employment opportunities in urban centres remain poor and experience high rates of unemployment, seemed to be overlooked (Taylor 2006).

Indigenous discourses

These changes were not driven by the Government alone. The Indigenous leadership network, which had worked together closely in the early 1990s, was no longer of one voice. Some key Indigenous individuals were actively promoting many of these policy changes, to both the Coalition Government and the Labor Party, then in Opposition. The most prominent was Noel Pearson. He vigorously promoted a change to perverse economic incentives, arguing passionately that welfare was killing his people in Cape York. He argued that social norms had broken down, and that nothing less than radical welfare reform was required to ensure that Aboriginal people regained their dignity, took responsibility for their lives and those of the next generation, and indeed survived as a people (Pearson 2000, 2005b). Drawing on ideas from development economist Amartya Sen (1999), Pearson was concerned about people's *capability to be self-determining and to make choices* through liberation from alcohol dependence, better education, exposure to the 'mainstream', and through economic development of their lands (Pearson 2000, 2005b).[5] Pearson argued for Indigenous mobility and the education necessary to enable young people to move for work. He also urged reform of the Community Development Employment Projects (CDEP) program which, combined with other family payments, he saw as providing a disincentive to people entering the so-called 'real economy', accessing the formal job market or generating businesses (Pearson 2005a, 2006).

Pearson nevertheless remained a supporter of Aboriginal native title, of collective ownership of land and the rights of Indigenous people, although he downplayed these issues. He also argued for engagement with Aboriginal organisations and leaders. His argument was essentially about re-balancing collective rights with individual responsibilities, and he asserted that social dysfunction was a higher priority to address than land rights issues (Cape York Institute (CYI) 2007; Pearson 2007a, 2007b). Pearson's views about Indigenous rights as first peoples, the value of Indigenous cultural identity and the role of Indigenous organisations, clearly differed from Government's, but his other ideas were sufficiently close to theirs for him to gain considerable Government support for his initiatives. He was appointed an Adviser on Welfare Reform to the Prime Minister, and the 'Cape York Agenda' began to dominate national policy discourse. His approach

---

[5] Sen's (1999) work, though valuable in broadening the concept of development beyond narrow economics, seems to neglect the interaction between individuals and social structures, and he views individual 'freedom' as a value overriding all others. Sen's theory may seriously underestimate the discord between these assumptions and the relationships and obligations that underpin contemporary Indigenous societies and worldviews, and may thus fail to provide a strong basis for successful Indigenous development (Adams 2007).

was not without its critics (Behrendt 2007; Calma 2007; Hart, Herbert and Tripcony 2004; Education and Health Standing Committee (EHSC) 2007a), and Government adopted it selectively, ignoring the Indigenous rights, cultural identity and Indigenous organisational leadership aspects.

Other Indigenous individuals, including Warren Mundine, a senior figure in the Australian Labor Party, accepted the Coalition Government's invitation to join a new National Indigenous Council (NIC) to advise the Government after ATSIC's abolition in 2004.[6] Chaired by Western Australian magistrate Sue Gordon, this advisory council supported and gave some legitimacy to the Government's new approach (NIC 2006). Thus, the Government drew on the support of selected Indigenous people who shared its view of the problem. Other Indigenous leaders were marginalised from the national debate, their focus on rights-based approaches characterised as inappropriate in light of the growing sense of past policy failure and current crisis.

A number of specific policy changes highlight some of the key issues under contention. These included the debate about outstations (or 'homelands' communities), as well as the abolition or reform of CDEP and the Community Housing and Infrastructure Program (CHIP).

The Homelands debate

The debate about collective ownership of land was linked to the issue of the viability of small, remote outstation communities. On a number of occasions, Ministers (see Brough 2006a; Vanstone 2005) and the Prime Minister took the opportunity to emphasise that they perceived Aboriginal people living in remote settlements as enduring a second-rate existence in undesirable segregation from mainstream society:

> The right of an Australian to live on remote communal land and to speak an Indigenous language is no right at all if it is accompanied by grinding poverty, overcrowding, poor health, community violence and alienation from mainstream Australian society. Reconciliation has little meaning in a narrative of separateness from that society (Howard 2007a: 2).

Support for these views came from the book *Lands of Shame* (Hughes 2007), a Centre for Independent Studies publication, which argued that 'exceptionalist' policies that enabled Indigenous people to subsist in 'living museums' had left Indigenous people illiterate, without economic sustenance, welfare dependent and without access to the protections and standards of living expected by other Australians. But while conditions may be inadequate, evidence about homeland outstations suggests that relative to larger Indigenous communities, housing is less crowded, median income is similar, employment and health is better, and

---

[6] He later resigned under pressure from within the Labor Party over conflicts of interest and policy.

most have good access to essential infrastructure services, such as clean water and electricity (Altman 2006). Customary wildlife harvesting is also likely to be greater, thus livelihoods may be better than income data would reveal, while natural and cultural resource management activities associated with homelands contribute significantly to positive health outcomes (Burgess and Johnstone 2007).

Furthermore, it became clear that if Aboriginal people choose to remain on the lands to which they returned so determinedly two or three decades before, the Australian Government was no longer going to support them (Howard 2007a). Nor were State/Territory Governments clear about how they would move forward from a legacy of several levels of government conflict about, and abdication of, their responsibilities to Aboriginal citizens, particularly in remote regions (EHSC 2007b). The Law Reform Commission of Western Australia (2006: 352) was one of the most recent organisations to recognise this:

> The rhetoric of self determination has, in the past, allowed governments to abdicate their responsibilities to provide services that are an entitlement of citizenship and which non-Aboriginal Australians take for granted.

Community governance in such remote locations was clearly going to be squeezed, with poorly-funded organisations attempting to provide continuity of services in such a shifting policy and funding environment.

Mainstreaming CDEP and CHIP

ATSIC's two largest programs, which were 'mainstreamed' in mid 2004, were CDEP and CHIP. Both programs functioned through a wide network of Aboriginal-controlled organisations, and CDEP had around 35 000 participants. The CDEP transfer in particular was to have dramatic impacts.

The handover of CDEP to the Department of Employment and Workplace Relations (DEWR) brought it into close contact with other mainstream labour market programs. The 'old' CDEP model, which offered close to guaranteed, relatively flexible, annual funding for community organisations, and provided continuing support for a broad range of community-defined work for participants (albeit with none of the usual benefits and conditions of regular employment or superannuation entitlements), was gradually replaced with a model in which contracts specified clear job targets, defined what work was more narrowly (e.g. excluding some cultural work), and did not provide continuing job subsidy support[7] (Sanders 2007a, 2007b). DEWR was transforming CDEP into a narrower skill development and employment program, more reflective of that department's

---

[7] 'Changes to CDEP', Department of Employment and Workplace Relations (DEWR) website, available at <http://www.workplace.gov.au/workplace/Category/SchemesInitiatives/IndigenousProgs/ChangestoCDEP.htm> [accessed 17/06/07].

wider employment philosophy.[8] Around 60 urban and regional CDEPs across Australia were closed in mid 2007,[9] and another 50 in the Northern Territory (NT) were expected to close by mid 2008, until some of these were given a reprieve with the late 2007 change of Australian Government (Brough and Hockey 2007; Koori Mail 2007; Murdoch 2007). CDEP activity underpinned a number of other government programs and economic development initiatives with Indigenous people, among them the Indigenous Protected Areas Scheme (Gilligan 2006), art programs, municipal services, and the activities of outstation resource agencies, yet the implications of DEWR's changed approach for these activities seemed not to have been fully considered. However, some 800 former CDEP jobs in government programs were fully funded by the Australian Government (ABC News 2007a, 2007b; Altman 2007a; Brough 2007; Hunt and Smith 2007). Clearly, the Australian Government expected State and Territory Governments to take up more of the employment challenge. In December 2007, the Labor Government transferred responsibility for CDEP to the new Department of Families, Housing, Community Services and Indigenous Affairs (FaHCSIA), indicating some rethinking about the program for the future.

In May 2007, the Australian Government also announced the abolition of the major Aboriginal housing scheme, CHIP, which had been managed by the Department of Families and Community Services and Indigenous Affairs (FaCSIA) since July 2004, and delivered by State and Territory Governments, local government and around 600 Aboriginal community housing organisations. An independent review had found extensive problems with the program (PricewaterhouseCoopers 2007). It is being replaced by new arrangements that involve mainstreaming Indigenous housing into public housing programs, policies to encourage Indigenous people to move to new public housing in locations where education, health and other services are available (i.e. no more new housing at outstations or homelands), and encouraging home ownership (Brough 2007). Whilst Dillon and Westbury (2007) argue strongly that parallel housing schemes for Indigenous and other Australians have seriously disadvantaged Indigenous people,[10] the impact of the policy announcement is nevertheless the redundancy of many Indigenous community housing sector organisations.

This transformation of the CDEP and community housing programs has clearly impacted on the Indigenous organisational landscape in some regions, as smaller

---

[8] 'Community Development Employment Projects (CDEP) Programme', workplace.gov.au website, Australian Government, available at <http://www.workplace.gov.au/workplace/Programmes/ IndigenousProgs/Community+Development+Employment+Projects+%28CDEP%29+Programme/> [accessed 17 June 2007].

[9] Other CDEPs not wishing to, or unable to, meet new program requirements lost funding. It is unclear how many successfully tendered for the Structured Training and Employment Program (STEP) (Cth), designed to prepare people for jobs.

[10] Dillon and Westbury (2007), however, disagreed about stopping new housing and infrastructure in outstations.

organisations close down, coalesce or become dormant, and larger ones juggle new responsibilities. As this organisational adjustment process has been occurring (which at best may lead over time to fewer organisations with greater capacity, or at worst may leave communities without programs and services), other programs have inevitably, if unintentionally, been affected (Altman 2007a).

The outcomes of the COAG trials

In April 2007, evaluations of the COAG trials were quietly released. Despite some diplomatic language, the reports revealed many problems; although there had been more progress at some sites than others, achievements were relatively limited in light of the significant resources dedicated to the trials. The evaluations identified the importance of building relationships and developing trust for successful partnerships, yet indicated that a number of factors militated against this. The trials had not emphasised enough how governments would need to work differently from how they had worked in the past to address community priorities; clearly insufficient attention had been given to new governance arrangements (Morgan, Disney and Associates 2006b).

The trials showed that an urgent priority is to address the capacity constraints within and between governments engaging with Indigenous communities. There is a need for clear, agreed policy frameworks and a simplification of program and funding arrangements, cultural change and staff development for whole-of-government work in Indigenous communities, as well as realistic expectations. They demonstrated that a successful framework needs to enable Indigenous people to have sustained, properly resourced opportunities to build their governance and participate in planning and decision-making. Building community governance and capacity at local and regional level through community development approaches is seen as a high priority for partnership working—to provide the foundation stone on which effective partnerships and programs can be built.

The COAG experience indicates that the factors that frustrated earlier self-determination policies were equally capable of frustrating positive outcomes from the 'new arrangements'. In 1991, the Royal Commission into Aboriginal Deaths in Custody (RCIADIC) had recognised that the years of self-determination policy were 'a cruel hoax' for Aboriginal people:

> They were not really being offered self-determination, just the tantalising hint of it. Instead they were being bequeathed the administrative mess which non-Aboriginal people had left, and were being told to fix it up. It was their mess now (RCIADIC 1991 Vol 4: 27.6.1).

That mess was the multitude of different funding arrangements, the inter-departmental competition, or what amounted to a 'ludicrously complicated funding super-structure' (RCIADIC 1991 Vol 4: 27.3.13), which remained the source of many problems; 15 years after the Royal Commission it was still a non-Indigenous responsibility to fix it. Yet governments seemed unable to. Inter-governmental rivalries, arguments about funding levels and responsibilities, and political posturing frequently combined to frustrate improvements. As Dillon and Westbury (2007: 208) argue, '[t]here has been a fundamental failure in the governance of governments in relation to Australian Indigenous affairs'.

However, while the mainstreaming approach to service delivery applied across the nation, with the consequent tendency to circumvent, undermine and de-fund Indigenous organisations,[11] there was even greater change to come in the NT, which accounts for some 10 per cent of the national Indigenous population.

The 2007 intervention in the NT

By June 2007, these policy changes in Indigenous Australia were well underway, yet barely noticed in 'mainstream Australia', when a dramatic announcement by the Prime Minister hit the headlines.[12] Within days of the *Little Children are Sacred Report* (Anderson and Wild 2007) being publicly released in the NT, the Commonwealth Government moved with an intervention in the Territory, which it called a national emergency and likened to Hurricane Katrina (Howard 2007b). Others referred to it as 'martial law' (P. Dodson 2007; Smith 2007b). The intervention had a number of elements, with law and order 'a central focus', and the army called in to provide logistic and other support. These elements included an immediate increase in policing levels, widespread alcohol restrictions on Aboriginal land (much of which was already 'dry'), medical examinations of Indigenous children, quarantining of 50 per cent of income support for food and other essentials, enforced school attendance, abolition of the permit system for common areas and road corridors on Aboriginal lands, and government-controlled leases over Aboriginal townships for five years, with administrators appointed to each township (Howard 2007b). Initially, 60 Indigenous communities were indicated but the number increased to 73.

Responses to this announcement ranged from welcoming the fact that the national Government had finally recognised the crisis facing Aboriginal communities

---

[11] The only Indigenous community-controlled sector that remained relatively unscathed was the health sector, although it was challenged to meet the accountability standards and processes associated with new public management approaches, while also meeting the expectations of its Indigenous clients for a more holistic health approach.

[12] In 2006, the outspokenness of an Alice Springs Crown Prosecutor, a media exposé of violence, and the Minister's allegations of paedophilia in a central Australian community had been the trigger for a flurry of media and political activity on these issues, culminating in a Ministerial Summit on Family Violence held in Canberra in June. The almost total absence of Indigenous participants in that summit sent a message that the Government was not prepared to work in partnership with Indigenous people with expertise in these issues. In June 2007, the Government argued that a delay by the NT Government in response to a major report into child sexual abuse in the NT forced it to act. The Commonwealth suggested that it was only the persistence of the Aboriginal Affairs Minister in 2006 that had led the NT Government to undertake this enquiry in the first place.

and responded, to sharp criticism at the racial basis and centralist response (Altman and Hinkson 2007; Atkinson 2007; CLC 2007; Grattan 2007). Many who welcomed the fact that a response was being made were nevertheless sceptical about the motives, the effectiveness and sustainability of the approach, particularly the very top-down and militaristic style (Anderson 2007). This was ironic, since the very first recommendation of the report that the Government was using to justify its actions said: 'It is critical that both governments commit to genuine consultation with Aboriginal people in designing initiatives for Aboriginal communities' (Anderson and Wild 2007: 22).

Across the NT there was generally a high level of confusion and some fear about the implications of the announcement. While improved police and medical services had long been called for and were generally welcomed in the short-term, there was fierce Indigenous opposition to some of the measures, particularly in relation to land and the permit system, which most argued were unrelated to the issue of child protection. As Patrick Dodson observed, the ALRA:

> was the first expression of the constitutional powers mandated by the 1967 referendum for the Australian Parliament to make laws for Aboriginal people … The Act liberated Aboriginal people in the Northern Territory from their subordinate and colonial status and became an inspiration for a raft of Aboriginal land legislation that has been passed in every Australian jurisdiction with the exception of Western Australia (P. Dodson 2007: 9).[13]

The attack on the ALRA was seen as a racist attack on self-determination and on Indigenous people's right to a distinctive and different way of life. A coalition of NT Aboriginal organisations prepared a detailed response to the intervention, critiquing the Government's actions and putting forward their own proposals to tackle the deep-seated problems based on a community-driven, evidence-based approach, in partnership with governments (Combined Aboriginal Organisations of the Northern Territory (CAONT) 2007). The proposed abolition of the CDEP added to the radical transformation being suggested. The Government justified it both in terms of the need to create 'real jobs' and in terms of the need to be able to quarantine welfare payments (Brough and Hockey 2007). The 'real jobs' to be created by governments (estimated at 1600), while very welcome, would not replace 7500 CDEP positions to be abolished. Those people not transferred to jobs would find their income drop as 'Work for the Dole' participants.

From a governance point of view, the Australian Government's June 2007 announcement was a dramatic development that strongly reflected a triumph

---

[13] Technically this is not quite correct as the ALRA could be justified under the Commonwealth 'Territories' Power. However, the fact that Patrick Dodson sees and reports it this way is a powerful reminder of the symbolic importance of the 1967 constitutional change.

for the conservative think tanks and their assimilationist approach. As Patrick Dodson recognised:

> They have asserted that communal land ownership and governance structures that reflect Indigenous traditional decision-making, imprisons Indigenous people in welfare ghettos and locks them out of the benefits of modernity (P. Dodson 2007: 9).

Furthermore, in contrast to earlier collaborative 'partnership' approaches with both the NT Government and Indigenous leaders, it was a return to command-and-control-style hierarchical governance (Davis and Rhodes 2000; Rhodes 2005), as well as a complete reversal of any remnants of self-determination for Indigenous Australians. Indigenous governance was to be shunted aside while public service administrators with extraordinary powers took over again (Siewart 2007). While the intervention and subsequent announcements clearly deployed considerable additional resources for NT Indigenous communities, the cost-effectiveness and sustainable impact of the strategies employed are open to question.

The intervention also coincided with a period of local government reform in the NT, which had begun in 2003 (Smith 2004) and already undergone policy change in October 2006. A shift from a relatively bottom-up process of regional authority development based on culturally-defined and negotiated boundaries was shelved in favour of nine proposed shires, almost all of which were considerably larger than existing proposals, and incorporated non-Indigenous landholders and small urban areas (Smith 2007a, 2007b). The future of many community government councils was limited or unclear, as their roles were to be largely taken over by the new regional shires. The combined raft of Federal and NT Government changes added up to a context of extraordinary flux and uncertainty for many Indigenous organisations.

Governance complexity and contestation

The picture that emerges is one of continued complexity and policy contestation in Indigenous governance. The period during which the case study research was undertaken is one more iteration of the continuing tensions that arise from the false dichotomy of treating Indigenous people as equal citizens or treating them as holders of special Indigenous rights. The pendulum has swung heavily towards treating them as individual citizens to be 'brought into the mainstream' and 'normalised' to the dominant way of life. In doing so, it is jeopardising deeply-valued Indigenous rights, especially the right of self-determination. As Kerry Arabena recognised:

> The government is ill-equipped to deal with the contemporary political consequences of Indigenous identity (including separate representative structures and inclusive cultural aspirations) and this incapacity

significantly influences how government treats those who are different. This is the core matter for me. In the new arrangements, Aboriginal and Torres Strait Islander peoples are beholden to government, who determines whether we can control our own affairs (Arabena 2005: 28).

The Indigenous Community Governance Project's research has confirmed that on the ground it is self-determination that Indigenous people are still seeking. They may call it 'self-control' or 'independence from government', but fundamentally they are striving to gain greater control over their lives and to promote the kind of development that they value (Hunt and Smith 2007). In 2003, Dodson and Smith argued that Indigenous people should focus on areas of development over which they had control, and they particularly highlighted governing structures, processes, and institutions and local development strategies (Dodson and Smith 2003). Since that was written, some of those governance structures have been dismantled, have collapsed or are struggling in the face of the dramatic changes of the past four years. This has left a significant vacuum of national Indigenous networking and organisational infrastructure to assert Indigenous rights (ATSISJC 2007a).

In the meantime, local and regional organisations within the Indigenous sector have been experiencing considerable tensions as they try to reflect Indigenous aspirations and expectations to be self-determining, while being dependent for funding on mainstream government departments that are applying increasingly incompatible mainstream principles to their Indigenous 'clients'. Indigenous community organisations have become the front line in these inevitable tensions, and this generates conflict and pressures on them, which only the most resilient can manage successfully. RCIADIC warned as early as 1991 that when the government funded services through Indigenous organisations they were subjected to 'minute and suspicious scrutiny' and that the 'whole process of delivery of such services was one of further control of their lives, and not one which offers autonomy' (RCIADIC Vol 4: 20.4.7). If that was true in the previous era, it was more so now. In fact, mainstreaming, as Finlayson (2005) observed, has been accelerating the effects of corporate management policies and competition policy across the board in Indigenous affairs, and this has been most evident in employment programs. Yet Indigenous success stories reflect a different approach, one that has involved government support for Indigenous-driven programs, based on Indigenous values, towards Indigenous-driven goals (Finlayson 2004; Gilligan 2006; Reconciliation Australia 2006).

Furthermore, the experience of the COAG trials demonstrates that for 'mainstreaming' and whole-of-government approaches to work, it has to be in partnership with Indigenous communities and their organisations. It requires effective and legitimate governance in Indigenous communities as well as improved governance by governments themselves. If weak or 'dysfunctional' Indigenous governance undermined outcomes in the self-determination era, the same problems are likely to frustrate success in whole-of-government mainstreaming as well, particularly as governments are struggling within themselves to make these new approaches work.

The difficulties facing Indigenous community government are further compounded by tensions between the three levels of government, and particularly State and Federal levels, about their respective responsibilities for service provision in remote areas. An African proverb—'When the elephants fight the grass gets trampled'—sums up the problem. While governments resist each others' attempts to cost-shift, the gaps have to be picked up by seriously under-resourced Indigenous community bodies. The need for a properly planned and negotiated process to address the historical anomalies and shortfalls is urgent. It is something the COAG, with all the governments at the table, could usefully lead as part of its Overcoming Disadvantage strategy. It is to be hoped that the new Australian Government's emphasis on COAG addressing duplication and overlap in jurisdictional responsibilities in Indigenous affairs, and working cooperatively to resolve these, may over time improve the situation (COAG 2007).

Across much of remote Australia, the policy of self-determination faltered when State Governments walked away from their responsibilities, local governments were not engaged, and Indigenous policy was left to the Australian Government, which exercised its role largely through the limited powers and resources of ATSIC. Gradually, as public services and the private sector withdrew from remote regions and ATSIC was axed, a vacuum of governance was left. The long-term strategic development of regional Australia is being ignored (Sanderson 2007). Many levels of government failure have been identified, among them, Commonwealth Grants Commission formulae, which fail to address infrastructure backlogs, the fact that funds allocated to States and Territories on the basis of Indigenous disadvantage are not tied to such expenditure, and the dysfunctional funding arrangements for Indigenous communities (Dillon and Westbury 2007; Morgan, Disney and Associates 2006a; Smith 2007a). Some have argued that the situation has reached crisis proportions and that remote Australia is a 'failed state' (Westbury and Dillon 2006). But this is not a classic failed state in the sense used in international development. The state certainly has failed to provide services, but it creates enormous complexity at the same time, due to the difficult legal, regulatory and policy environment that it has constructed. The state is both absent and ever-present; and the context it creates is not conducive to Indigenous capacity to resolve the challenges Indigenous communities face. Meanwhile, in the urban areas it is clear that mainstream services remain insufficiently responsive to Indigenous needs, while Indigenous-specific services are being dismantled in some sectors or continue to struggle with inadequate, short-term and unreliable funding in others.

Finally, it seems that 'welfare' has to a large degree substituted for development in Indigenous Australia and this has had very negative effects on people's capacities to be self-determining. Australian governments have used 'welfare' while ignoring the need for remote communities to engage in community and economic development, to create the economic base so essential to genuine self-determination. The drip-feed of welfare has maintained them, but not enabled them to develop in ways they may have wished. Indigenous peoples' idea of CDEP was to try to move in that direction (Whitby 2001), but it was inadequately resourced for the kind of community or economic development necessary. However, Indigenous organisations in the NT pushed again in late 2007 for a greater CDEP focus on community and business development (CDEP Reform 2007). With a welfare economy entrenched, and with very limited support by governments to help communities develop their livelihoods and economic base to date, it is now much harder than it might have been 30 years ago. Nevertheless, it is clear that Indigenous communities are turning their attention to economic development, but using a variety of models and strategies that embrace capitalist entrepreneurialism (Elu 2007; Smith 2006) and hybrid approaches (Altman 2001, 2007b). Those able to operate from self-generated resources, without government funding, are in a stronger position to demonstrate what their ideas of self-determination look like, even in an era of 'mainstreaming' (Smith 2006).

Conclusion

There are no guarantees that the approaches introduced since 2004 will be any more successful than the old ones if the wider governance issues facing both Indigenous communities and governments are not addressed. The COAG change agenda requires that governments give their own governance capacities and the 'funding mess' urgent attention if they are to provide the quality of services due to all Indigenous people as citizens. Sustained, facilitative support from governments to strengthen the capacity of Indigenous community governance is also necessary if they are to develop effective partnerships with Indigenous communities to achieve that. There are only limited signs of either happening at present, but a reinvigorated COAG, through its Indigenous Working Group (COAG 2007), could provide the political drive needed.

The conservative national ideology that prevailed through this period left little room for the essential reforms and capacity strengthening support that was needed. By trying to enforce a single definition of the problem (the need to bring Indigenous people into the mainstream) within a complex systems context, power holders in Australia in the last decade have countenanced only a singular solution. Whilst that may meet some Indigenous aspirations, recent literature about governance suggests that an analysis and synthesis of *multiple* dimensions and knowledge-frameworks about complex social issues is required. The 'framings' of the governance challenges that Indigenous people bring to the fore vary, as do the framings of the non-Indigenous players who surround them. Top-down approaches to problems framed by the powerful is the approach that has been exercised increasingly forcefully in Australia throughout the period of this research, at least until late 2007. An alternative is to adopt a more reflexive and adaptive approach to governance, which appreciates the significance of political history, pays attention to power, knowledge and different 'framings' of problems, and leaves open a range of pathways for Indigenous people (Leach et al. 2007). What self-determination means now, and how governance processes can enable it, remains a matter for dialogue. A serious, respectful and engaged conversation is needed between governments and Indigenous people about how to meet diverse Indigenous goals and expectations through a negotiated process at many levels, from the local to the national. A governance of diverse possibilities is required. Whether the new Australian Labor Government can lead such a process remains to be seen.

Acknowledgements

I am most grateful for insightful comments from Jon Altman, Bill Ivory, Diane Smith and Will Sanders, other colleagues participating in the ICGP researchers' workshop in August 2007, as well as two anonymous referees on earlier versions of this chapter.

References

ABC News 2007a. 'Scrapping CDEP puts services at risk: NT Govt', *ABC Online*, 24 July, available at <http://www.abc.net.au/news/stories/2007/07/24/ 1987085.htm> [accessed 24 July 2007]

———2007b. 'Scrapping work-for-the dole a disaster: NT Minister', *ABC Online*, 24 July, available at <http://www.abc.net.au/news/stories/2007/07/24/ 1986458.htm> [accessed 24 July 2007].

Aboriginal and Torres Strait Islander Social Justice Commissioner (ATSISJC) 2000. *Social Justice Report 2000*, Human Rights and Equal Opportunity Commission (HREOC), Sydney.

———2001. *Social Justice Report 2001*, HREOC, Sydney.

———2005a. *Social Justice Report 2004*, Report No. 1/2005, HREOC, Sydney.

———2005b. *Social Justice Report 2005*, Report No. 3/2005, HREOC, Sydney.

———2007a. *Social Justice Report 2006*, Report No. 1/2007, HREOC, Sydney.

———2007b. *Native Title Report 2006*, Report No. 2/2007, HREOC, Sydney.

Adams, A. 2007. The Individual and Social Transformation: A Critique of the Capability Approach, MA Thesis, ANU, Canberra.

Altman, J. C. 2001. 'Sustainable development options on Aboriginal land: the hybrid economy in the twenty-first century', *CAEPR Discussion Paper No. 226*, CAEPR, ANU, Canberra.

——2004. 'Practical reconciliation and the new mainstreaming: will it make a difference to Indigenous Australians?', *Dialogue*, 2: 35–45, Academy of the Social Sciences, Canberra.

——2006. 'In search of an outstations policy for Indigenous Australians', *CAEPR Working Paper No. 34*, CAEPR, ANU, Canberra.

——2007a. 'Neo-paternalism and the destruction of CDEP', *Arena*, August-September, 90: 33–35.

——2007b. 'Alleviating poverty in remote Indigenous Australia: the role of the hybrid economy', *Development Bulletin*, 72: 47–51.

—— and Hinkson, M. (eds) 2007. *Coercive Reconciliation: Stabilise, Normalise, Exit Aboriginal Australia*, Arena Publications Association, Melbourne.

Anderson I. 2007. 'Remote communities: unexplained differences', *Australian Policy Online*, 29 June, available at <http://www.apo.org.au> [accessed 2 July 2007].

Anderson, P. and Wild, R. 2007. *Ampe Akelyernemane Meke Mekarle—Little Children Are Sacred, Report of the Northern Territory Board of Inquiry into the Protection of Aboriginal Children from Sexual Abuse*, Report to the Northern Territory Government, Darwin, available at <http://www.nt.gov.au/dcm/inquirysaac/>

Arabena, K. 2005. 'Not fit for modern Australian society? Aboriginal and Torres Strait Island people and the new arrangements for the administration of Indigenous Affairs', *Research Discussion Paper No. 16*, AIATSIS, Canberra.

Atkinson, J. 2007. 'What I would do', *Australian Policy Online*, 25 June, available at <http://www.apo.org.au/webboard/print-version.chtml?filename_num =154957> [accessed 26 June 2007].

Attwood, B. 2003. *Rights for Aborigines*, Allen & Unwin, Crows Nest, NSW.

Australian Bureau of Statistics (ABS) 2001. *Housing and Infrastructure in Aboriginal and Torres Strait Islander Communities*, ABS, Australian Government, Canberra.

Australian Government. 2008. 'Regional Partnership Agreements', SRAs and RPAs Website, available at <http://www.indigenous.gov.au/sra.html #rpa> [accessed 8 February 2008].

Behrendt, L. 2001. 'What path forward for reconciliation? The challenges of a new relationship with Indigenous people', *Public Law Review*, 12 (2): 79–83.

——2002. 'Unfinished journey—Indigenous self-determination', *Arena Magazine*, April-May, 58: 24–7.

——2007. 'Shaping a nation: visionary leadership in a time of fear and uncertainty', Ninth John Curtin Prime Ministerial Library Anniversary Lecture, Curtin University, Perth.

Brough, M. The Hon. 2006a. 'Blueprint for action in Indigenous affairs', Speech as Minister for Families, Community Services and Indigenous Affairs, *Indigenous Affairs Governance Series*, 5 December, National Institute of Governance, University of Canberra, Canberra, available at <http://www.facsia.gov.au/internet/Minister3.nsf/content/051206.htm>.

——2006b. 'Northern Territory Indigenous now free to choose', Media Release, Minister for Families, Community Services and Indigenous Affairs, 17 August, Australian Government, Canberra,.

——2007. 'Government tackles overcrowding in remote Indigenous communities', Media Release, Minister for Families, Community Services and Indigenous Affairs, 8 May, Australian Government, Canberra.

—— and Hockey, J. The Hon. 2007. 'Jobs and training for Indigenous people in the NT', Joint Media Release, Minister for Families, Community Services and Indigenous Affairs and Minister for Employment and Workplace Relations, 23 July, Australian Government, Canberra.

Burgess, C. P. and Johnstone, F. H. 2007. Indigenous Natural and Cultural Resource Management and Health, Stakeholder debriefing paper, 8 May, Menzies School of Health Research, Charles Darwin University, Darwin.

Calma, T. 2007. 'Article muddied the waters', *National Indigenous Times*, Issue 124, 8 March, available at <http://www.nit.com.au/Opinion/story.aspx?id= 9849> [accessed 12 March 2007].

Cape York Institute for Policy and Leadership (CYI). 2007. *From Hand Out to Hand Up: Cape York Welfare Reform Project Design Recommendations*, CYI, Cairns.

Central Land Council (CLC). 2007. 'Commonwealth indigenous policy changes', Media Release, 22 June, Alice Springs, available at <http://www.clc.org.au/media/releases/2007/cwealth_changes.asp> [accessed 23 June 2007].

Combined Aboriginal Organisations of the Northern Territory (CAONT) 2007. 'A proposed *Emergency Response* and *Development Plan* to protect Aboriginal children in the Northern Territory: a preliminary response to the Australian Government's proposals', 18 July, available at <http://www.racgp.org.au/news/23018> [accessed 19 July 2007].

Commonwealth of Australia 2002. Commonwealth Government Response to the Council for Aboriginal Reconciliation Final Report—*Reconciliation: Australia's Challenge*, AGPS, Canberra.

Council for Aboriginal Reconciliation (CAR) 2000. *Roadmap for Reconciliation*, CAR, Kingston, ACT.

Council of Australian Governments (COAG) 2007. 'Communique', Meeting 20 December, Melbourne.

CDEP Reform. 2007. '14 Point Action Plan for CDEP reform, 15.12.07', Unpublished paper prepared by Top End CDEP organisations following meeting of CDEP organisations with Warren Snowdon MP and Trish Crossin MP, 10 December 2007, Yirrkala.

Davis, G. and Rhodes, R. A. W. 2000. 'From hierarchy to contracts and back again: reforming the Australian public service', in M. Keating, J. Wann and P. Weller (eds), *Institutions on the Edge? Capacity for Governance*, Allen & Unwin, Crows Nest, NSW.

Department of Families, Community Services and Indigenous Affairs (FaCSIA). 2006. 'Access to Aboriginal land under the Northern Territory Aboriginal Land Rights Act—time for a change?' *Discussion Paper*, October, Canberra.

Dillon, A. 2005. 'Separatism', *Occasional Paper*, November, The Bennelong Society, Melbourne.

—— and Westbury, N. 2007. *Beyond Humbug: Transforming Government Engagement with Indigenous Australia*, Seaview Press, West Lakes, SA.

Dodson, M. 1996. 'Assimilation versus self-determination: no contest', *Northern Australia Research Unit (NARU) Discussion Paper No. 1*, NARU, ANU, Darwin.

—— and Pritchard, S. 1998. 'Recent developments in Indigenous policy: the abandonment of self-determination?' *Indigenous Law Bulletin*, 4 (15): 4–6.

—— and Smith, D. 2003. 'Governance for sustainable development: strategic issues and principles for Indigenous Australian communities', *CAEPR Discussion Paper No. 250*, CAEPR, ANU, Canberra.

—— and Strelein, L. 2001. 'Australia's nation-building: renegotiating the relationship between Indigenous peoples and the state', *University of NSW Law Journal*, 24 (3), available at <http://www.austlii.edu.au/au/journals/UNSWLJ/2001/68.html> [accessed 2 July 2007].

—— and McCarthy, D. 2006. 'Communal land and the amendments to the Aboriginal Land Rights Act (NT)', *Research Discussion Paper No. 19*, Native Title Research Unit, AIATSIS, Canberra.

Dodson, P. 1996. 'Reconciliation at the crossroads', Address to the National Press Club of Australia, April, Canberra, available at <http://www.austlii.edu.au/au/special/rsjproject/rsjlibrary/car/dodson.html> [accessed 2 July 2007].

——2007. 'An entire culture is at stake', *The Age*, 14 July, p. 9.

Education and Health Standing Committee (EHSC) 2007a. 'Initiatives in the remote Indigenous communities of Cape York', Report No. 7 in the 37th Parliament, Legislative Assembly, Parliament of Western Australia, Perth.

EHSC 2007b. 'Where from? Where to? A discussion paper on remote Aboriginal communities', Report No. 6 in the 37th Parliament, Legislative Assembly, Parliament of Western Australia, Perth.

Elu, J. 2007. 'Embracing economic development to achieve economic independence', Paper presented to *Tides of Native Title* conference, 6–8 June, Cairns.

Finlayson, J. 2004. *Success in Aboriginal Communities: A Pilot Study*, AIATSIS, Canberra.

——2005. 'Guest Editorial', *Australian Aboriginal Studies*, 2: 1–3.

Gaita, R. 2007. 'Comment', *The Monthly*, August: 10–14.

Gilligan, B. 2006. *The Indigenous Protected Areas Programme: 2006 Evaluation*, Department of the Environment and Heritage, Commonwealth of Australia, Canberra, available at <http://www.deh.gov.au/indigenous/publications/ipa-evaluation.html> [accessed 3 July 2007].

Grattan, M. 2007. 'Aboriginal group lashes PM's plan', *The Age online*, 11 July, available at <http://www.theage.com.au/news/national/aboriginal-group-lashes-pms-plan/2007/07/10/1183833519338.html?page=fullpage> [accessed 11 July 2008].

Gray, B. and Sanders, W. 2006. 'Views from the top of the "quiet revolution": secretarial perspectives on the new arrangements in Indigenous affairs', *CAEPR Discussion Paper No. 282*, CAEPR, ANU, Canberra.

Hart, V., Herbert, J. and Tripcomy, P. 2004. 'Accountability the key to change through education', *National Indigenous Times*, 24 November, p. 69, available at <http://www.nit.com.au/Opinion/story.aspx?id=4067> [accessed 2 July 2007].

Hinkson, M. 2007. 'Introduction: in the name of the child', in J. Altman and M. Hinkson (eds), *Coercive Reconciliation: Stabilise, Normalise, Exit Aboriginal Australia*, Arena Publications Association, Carlton.

House of Representatives Standing Committee on Aboriginal Affairs (HRSCAA) 1990. *Our Future Our Selves: Aboriginal and Torres Strait Islander Community Control, Management and Resources*, Commonwealth of Australia, AGPS, Canberra.

Howard, J. W. The Hon. 2007a. Address to 'Their Spirit Still Shines', Commemorating the 40th Anniversary of the 1967 Referendum Parliament House, 27 May, Canberra.

———2007b. Address to the Sydney Institute, 25 June, Four Seasons Hotel, Sydney.

Hunt, J. and Smith, D. 2006. 'Building Indigenous community governance in Australia: preliminary research findings', *CAEPR Working Paper No. 31*, CAEPR, ANU, Canberra.

——— and ———2007. 'Indigenous Community Governance Project: year two research findings', *CAEPR Working Paper No. 36*, CAEPR, CASS, ANU, Canberra.

Hughes, H. 2007. *Lands of Shame: Aboriginal and Torres Strait Islander 'Homelands' in Transition*, The Centre for Independent Studies Ltd, St Leonards, NSW.

Jeffries, S. 2006. 'Shared responsibility: mutual obligation', *Background Briefing*, ABC Radio National, 12 March.

Johns, G. 2006. 'Social stability and structural adjustment', Paper presented to *Leaving Remote Communities*, Bennelong Society Sixth Annual Conference, 1–2 September, Sydney.

Koori Mail. 2007. 'Axe falls on CDEPs', 4 July, p. 12.

Law Reform Commission of Western Australia 2006. *Aboriginal Customary Laws: The Interaction of Western Australian Law with Aboriginal Law and Culture, Final Report*, Project 94, Government of Western Australia, Perth.

Leach, M. Bloom, G. Ely, A. Nightingale, P. Scoones, I. Shah, E. and Smith, A. 2007. 'Understanding governance: pathways to sustainability', *STEPS Working Paper 2*, STEPS Centre, Brighton.

McCarthy, M. MLA. 2006. 'Adjournment debate', *Parliamentary Record No. 6*, Legislative Assembly of the Northern Territory, Tenth Assembly, First Session, 29 March, Darwin.

McCausland, R. 2005a. 'The "new mainstreaming" of Indigenous affairs', *Briefing Paper No. 3*, Ngiya Institute for Indigenous Law, Policy and Practice, Jumbunna Indigenous House of Learning, University of Technology, Sydney.

——2005b. 'Shared Responsibility Agreements', *Briefing Paper No. 1*, Ngiya Institute for Indigenous Law, Policy and Practice, Jumbunna Indigenous House of Learning, University of Technology, Sydney.

Morgan, Disney and Associates Pty Ltd. 2006a. *A Red Tape Evaluation in Selected Indigenous Communities*, Final Report for OIPC, Canberra.

—— with Tracey Whetnall Consulting and Wis-Wei Consulting Pty Ltd. 2006b. *Synopsis Review of the COAG Trial Evaluations*, Report to OIPC, Canberra.

Morrisey, M. 2006. 'The Australian state and Indigenous people 1990–2006', *Journal of Sociology*, 42 (4): 347–54.

Moreton-Robinson, A. 2007. 'Introduction', *Sovereign Subjects: Indigenous Sovereignty Matters*, Allen & Unwin, Crows Nest.

Murdoch, L. 2007. 'Macklin quarantines welfare, calls summit on intervention', *The Age*, 11 December, available at <http://www.theage.com.au/news/national/macklin-quarantines-welfare-calls-summit-on-intervention/2007/12/10/1197135374439.html> [accessed 11 December 2007].

National Indigenous Council (NIC). 2006. *Report to Government January-December 2006*, available at <http://www.atsia.gov.au/NIC/reports.aspx> [accessed 15 June 2007].

Office of Indigenous Policy Coordination (OIPC) 2005. *New Arrangements in Indigenous Affairs*, DIMIA, Australian Government, Canberra.

——2007. 'Regional Indigenous engagement arrangements', OIPC, available at <http://www.oipc.gov.au/documents/RegionalIndigenousEngagement Arrangements_Parameters.pdf> [accessed 18 December 2007].

Pearson, N. 2000. *Our Right to Take Responsibility*, Noel Pearson and Associates, Cairns, QLD.

——2005a. 'Can Cape York communities be economically viable?' *Viewpoint*, November, CYI , Cairns, QLD.

——2005b. 'The Cape York Agenda', Speech to the National Press Club of Australia, 30 November, Canberra.

——2006. 'Address to the Treasury on the Cape York Peninsula reform agenda', Commonwealth Department of Treasury, 25 September, Canberra.

——2007a. 'Give us help to help ourselves', *The Weekend Australian*, 17–18 March, p. 28.

———2007b. 'Action only way forward', *The Weekend Australian*, 7–8 July, p. 23.

PricewaterhouseCoopers 2007. *Living in the Sunburnt Country—Indigenous Housing: Findings of the Review of the Community Housing and Infrastructure Programme*, Final report to FaCSIA, February, Canberra.

Reconciliation Australia (R. Withers and R. Beattie [eds]). 2006. *Celebrating Indigenous Governance: Success Stories of the Indigenous Governance Awards*, RA, Canberra.

Rhodes, R. 2005. 'The unholy trinity of governance', The Blake Dawson Waldron Lecture, 23 August, National Museum of Australia, Canberra.

Ross, D. 2007. 'Permits protect,' in J. Altman and M. Hinkson (eds), *Coercive Reconciliation: Stabilise, Normalise, Exit Aboriginal Australia*, Arena Publications Association, Carlton, VIC.

Rowse, T. 2005. 'The Indigenous sector', in D. Austin-Broos and G. Macdonald (eds), *Culture, Economy and Governance in Aboriginal Australia: Proceedings of a Workshop of the Academy of the Social Sciences in Australia held at the University of Sydney 30 November–1 December 2004*, University of Sydney Press, Sydney.

Royal Commission into Aboriginal Deaths in Custody (RCIADIC) 1991. *National Report*, Volume 4, available at <http://www.austlii.edu.au/au/other/IndigLRes/rciadic/national/vol4/5.html> [accessed 3 July 2007].

Sanders, W. 2004. 'ATSIC's achievements and strengths: implications for institutional reform', *Journal of Australian Indigenous Issues*, 7 (3): 14–21.

———2006. 'Indigenous affairs after the Howard decade: an administrative revolution while defying decolonization', Paper presented to the *John Howard's Decade* conference, 3–4 March, ANU, Canberra.

———2007a. 'Changes to CDEP under DEWR: policy substance and the new contractualism', *Topical Issue No. 6*, CAEPR, ANU, Canberra.

———2007b. 'The contraction of the CDEP scheme under new management after thirty good years: growing old or returning to remote area origins in times of low unemployment?' Paper presented in *CAEPR Seminar Series I*, 23 May, CAEPR, ANU, Canberra.

Sanderson, Lt Gen J. 2007. 'Federal renewal and unity in reconciliation: a return to government by the people', Annual Oration 2007, Order of Australia Association, available at <http://www.theorderofaustralia.asn.au/news/initiatives_and_activities.php>.

Scrymgour, M. MLA. 2007. 'Comments On Mantiyupwi Negotiating Team Document' Dated 20/5/07, Member For Arafura, 21 May, Northern Territory Government, Darwin.

Secretaries Group on Indigenous Affairs (SGIA) 2005. *Secretaries Bulletin*, 1, available at <http://www.apsc.gov.au/indigenousemployment/bulletin0105.htm> [accessed 8 September 2006].

Sen, A. 1999. *Development as Freedom*, Oxford University Press, New York.

Shergold, P. 2005. 'Delivering services to Indigenous Australians—a whole-of-government approach', Presentation to the *Australian Government Indigenous Affairs Forum for the Northern Territory*, 17 February, Darwin.

Shire of Naaanyatjarruku and Ngaanyatjarra Council 2007. *Response to Western Australia Legislative Assembly Education and Health Standing Committee: Discussion Paper on Remote Communities*.

Siewart, R. The Hon. 2007. 'Ministerial powers to seize assets of service providers in prescribed areas within the Northern Territory', Background Briefing, Parliament House, Canberra, available at <http://www.rachelsiewert.org.au/files/campaigns/extras/Briefing_on_NT_seizure_powers.pdf>.

Smith, D. 2004. 'From Gove to governance: reshaping Indigenous governance in the Northern Territory', *CAEPR Discussion Paper No. 265*, CAEPR, ANU, Canberra.

——2006. 'Evaluating governance effectiveness: a facilitated process with the Board of Yarnteen Aboriginal and Torres Strait Islanders Corporation', *ICGP Case Study Report No. 2*, ICGP, CAEPR, ANU, Canberra.

——2007a. 'Networked governance: issues of policy, power and process in a West Arnhem Land regional initiative', *Ngiya: Talk the Law*, 1: 24–52.

——2007b. 'From COAG to coercion: a story of governance failure, success and opportunity in Australian Indigenous affairs', Paper presented to the *Governing Through Collaboration: Managing Better Through Others* conference, Australia and New Zealand School of Government (ANZOG), 28–9 June, Canberra,.

Steering Committee for the Review of Government Service Provision (SCRGSP) 2003. *Overcoming Indigenous Disadvantage: Key Indicators 2003 Report*, Commonwealth of Australia, Canberra.

——2007. *Overcoming Indigenous Disadvantage: Key Indicators 2007 Report*, Commonwealth of Australia, Canberra.

Taylor, J. 2006. 'Population and diversity: policy implications of emerging Indigenous demographic trends', *CAEPR Discussion Paper No. 283*, CAEPR, ANU, Canberra.

Vanstone, A. (The Hon.) 2005. 'Beyond conspicuous compassion: Indigenous Australians deserve more than good intentions', Address as Minister for Immigration and Multicultural and Indigenous Affairs to the Australia and New Zealand School of Government, 7 December, ANU, Canberra.

Westbury, N. and Dillon, M. 2006. 'Australia's institutionalised second class', *The Australian Financial Review*, 8 December.

Whitby, T. 2001. 'Reforming the CDEP Scheme', in F. Morphy and W. Sanders (eds), *The Indigenous Welfare Economy and the CDEP Scheme*, CAEPR Research Monograph No. 20, CAEPR, ANU, Canberra.

3. Constraints on researchers acting as change agents

Sarah Holcombe

This chapter reflects on the role of research and the constraints on researchers acting as change agents in the context of a project on an Aboriginal governance issue. By examining what has happened to the knowledge produced in the context of this project, with the Anmatjere Community Government Council (ACGC) about a fringe camp within the Ti Tree township in the Northern Territory (NT), the tensions between advocacy and impartiality are explored. This fringe camp is without any basic servicing, although there has been a permanent Aboriginal population there since settlement of the town from the late 1880s. The conundrum raised by this research project was that although we found pathways to change, our suggestions were not pursued either by the ACGC or the NT Government. Considering why this was the case leads to an examination of power relationships between Aboriginal people and the state, as mediated through the council, and an exploration of the impacts of policy in this context. Thus, the challenges of operating as a researcher within this environment suggest that the impact of research is constrained by the limits to collaboration, both by the means through which policy becomes a rationalising tool of the NT Government and the deeper local history of colonialism.

Background

The Ti Tree fringe camp came to the attention of the then Minister for Central Australia, Peter Toyne, who wrote to the ACGC in 2002 expressing concern about the lack of servicing and encouraging the council to do something about it. By any standards, the living conditions there are not ideal. Will Sanders and I were requested by the council to assist them in developing a strategy through which they could then respond to the NT Government. Thus, the impetus for the research into the Creek Camp issue was not initiated by the ACGC, but was prompted externally, and we happened to be available to undertake it.

In three reports to the ACGC, produced over a period of a year and a half, we documented the history, mobility patterns and aspirations of the Creek Camp residents, as well as canvassing other Ti Tree residents' perspectives of the place and the possibilities for NT Government action. However, a year and a half since the last of these three reports was delivered there has not been any significant change in the conditions of the place for its residents. Was our work 'rendered invisible' at 'the official and political level?' (Sutton 2001: 142). And how does this official and political level intersect with the level at which the Aboriginal people in this story are operating? Indeed, examining the intersection of our research with these two layers or sites of governance draws out the tensions between them. The contention is that the Aboriginal silence or ambivalence on the issue is, partly, a symptom of powerlessness; silence as 'passive condition' (cf. Rose 2001: 92) as the violent history of the pastoral frontier is recalled. More recently, this history of marginality is reinforced by NT Government policy, as the policy at issue was found to be underpinning the current status quo of Creek Camp. Examining how this policy became manifest as a government rationality was revealed as the research sought out possibilities for change, and in the process realised that these were limited by the policy. This NT Government policy was to the effect that no further Aboriginal urban living areas were to be established within townships.

By examining what has happened to the knowledge produced in the context of the Creek Camp research, the tensions between advocacy, development and research leading to change can be explored. At the risk of sounding 'postmodern', this reflexive gaze can also begin to unpack my own expectations about the outcomes of the research process, in an attempt to consider my own positionality as an anthropologist. The debate between Sutton (2005) and Cowlishaw (2003) on the role of anthropology in policy making and public debate highlights a number of the tensions in the discipline, which are brought to the fore as one engages with the diverse non-Aboriginal ideologically driven interests in the field. Although I do not view 'anthropology ... primarily as a wing or instrument of political activism' (Sutton 2005: 40), as Sutton has suggested Cowlishaw does, it seems to me that solid anthropological research can and should influence policy. The challenge is facilitating and enabling this uptake, as an integral element in the research process. To this end, this research also benefited from an interdisciplinary approach, with Will Sanders as political scientist teaming with myself, as social anthropologist. The different approaches to knowledge construction that both disciplines brought to the enterprise have been valuable for the research and will be considered below.

A reflexive examination of the research method is a key to interrogating knowledge construction. In the case of this project this included realising the value of longitudinal research and relationship building with the research hosts. In our case, as mentioned above, the research hosts and collaborators were the ACGC.[1] And, as will be discussed, each stage of the research into the Creek Camp issue and its potential development was a test of this relationship. It was

---

[1] The ACGC was established in 1993. It incorporated a region that could be broadly understood as Anmatyerr (language group) country; hence the council's name (though note the different and orthographically incorrect spelling of Anmatjere). This council was the first—and remained the only—regional council in desert NT. It incorporated 10 settlements structured on a ward system, incorporating a population of 1,400 predominantly Aboriginal people, and covering a region of 3,631km². See Sanders this volume, Chapter 11.

not to be taken for granted; after all, we as researchers presented ourselves to the council as having something to offer. Thus, we had to show that what we were offering was of some value. Unpacking how this research engagement was negotiated offers a window into the governance of research, as much as the governance processes within this all-Aboriginal council and their engagement with the NT Government over the Creek Camp issue.

When we approached the ACGC in 2004 to ascertain their interest in having us, as researchers, working with them on governance issues, it coincided with the arrival of a new Chief Executive Officer (CEO), who was about to begin a three year tenure. This fortunate timing meant that he was open to our involvement and not at all protective about sharing his new understandings of the current council situation. Ironically, although his initial and ongoing support was in many ways crucial to the development of our research project, his conservative perspective concerning the maintenance of the status quo of the Creek Camp could also, arguably, be perceived as constraining the uptake of the research findings. Yet, as will be examined, the role of the CEO in relation to this issue was only one element in a complex multi-sited government rationality (a concept borrowed from Foucault, discussed below).

As I will elucidate, the value of long term research in one place, allowing ongoing reflection on the research, also enables exploration of the ways in which policy unfolds as truth and tends to reaffirm the status quo. Thus, as this paper revisits the Creek Camp issue, it can continue to explore the dynamics of NT Government agency in terms of a governmental rationality and the ways in which this plays out in policy practice. In my attempt to answer the question 'what is "policy" and where is it located?' I have drawn inspiration from Foucault's (1991) concept of 'governmentality' (or government rationality) and more latterly Rose's (1999) interrogation of this concept. My perhaps simplistic reading of the governmentality concept understands it as a concern with the practices of governing, rather than the structures or institutions of government. How these practices gain legitimation and become mobilised, as they define the parameters of possible conduct and how the truths about these parameters are developed and circulated as discourse, drive a governmentality approach. In this reading, policy is understood as a core device or instrument of the governing rationality. Realising the intimate relationship between knowledge construction and power also permeates this approach to interrogating the governing process.

I suggest in this chapter that if we, as researchers, cannot change the status quo we can at least expose the opaque structural relations of power and the historical legacies that express themselves among the Aboriginal councillors in their ambivalence and division over the future of the Creek Camp. However, before discussing this issue, I will briefly overview the research findings.

Making the concept of governance tangible

The concept of 'governance' is multi-dimensional as it moves between layers of institutions, governments, localities and discourses. To give this concept meaning to the ACGC, and to the then CEO, we took what we called an 'issues' based approach. This approach led us to Creek Camp, as its existence was an 'issue' for the NT Government that required a response from the council. Assisting the ACGC to develop a response to the Creek Camp 'issue' evolved as each period of research and subsequent reporting back opened up further avenues of investigation. The research could be understood as structured by three principal periods of activity. To help make the governance concept real for people, we delivered, verbally and via reports, the findings of each period of research activity in plain English to the council. We ensured that our subsequent visits coincided with a monthly council meeting, where our reports were an item on the agenda. The aim was that this would enable informed discussion about the Creek Camp and canvas potential options for change.

Our first report to the ACGC (June 2005, see Holcombe and Sanders 2007b)[2] provided an overall snapshot of the residential arrangements of Creek Campers in what could be described as a 'survey'. Using both a questionnaire and open ended interviews we ascertained length of residence, camp composition, mobility patterns, the attractions and difficulties of living at Creek Camp, and people's preferred future residence and aspirations. We estimated 102 current and recent residents of the camp, grouped roughly into 13 sub-camps of self-identified Anmatyerr and Warlpiri people. The aspect of these findings that was perhaps the most informative for the Aboriginal councillors was the residential and development aspirations of the Creek Camp residents. Ten of the 13 camps indicated that they sought to remain in Creek Camp in the future and that they would like a minimum of reticulated water and ablution blocks. There was, however, some difference of opinion over the issue of housing. This considerable interest in development of some sort by *all* Creek Camp residents (whether or not they sought to remain there into the future) led the ACGC to ask us to continue on the project by broadening our enquiry beyond the Creek Camp.

The second stage of the research entailed a survey of residents of the roughly 35 houses in the Ti Tree town, and discussions by one of us (Sanders) with senior NT Government officials about their understandings of development possibilities of Creek Camp. As will be discussed, our key government contacts had, until then, been officers in the NT Department of Local Government. In the survey of Ti Tree town residents, other than ascertaining some basic demographic and social characteristics, we specifically asked their perspectives about the potential development of the Creek Camp. Of the 16 people interviewed, only three were

---

[2] The three separately dated reports to the ACGC have since been compiled as a single document in Holcombe and Sanders 2007b.

opposed to any development there. The significant majority were supportive of development of the Creek Camp, including buildings, if that was what people wanted. The perspectives offered by those NT Government officials involved in infrastructure provision, however, had a somewhat different focus. They indicated that Creek Camp's position on 'unallocated vacant Crown land' meant that there was no standard government mechanism through which it could be provided with reticulated services, and that for such servicing to happen an organisation, such as the ACGC, would have to apply for and obtain 'appropriate' title or tenure over the land. They would then also need to find a source of funding for the services. Given these apparent difficulties, the focus of most of the NT Government officials we spoke with was, rather, on ways in which Creek Camp residents could be encouraged to move elsewhere.[3] Finally, we noted in our second report (May 2006) that there seemed to be some basis of support for doing something in Creek Camp among ACGC members, as well as among Creek Camp residents and Ti Tree residents more generally. However, it was clear, as we reported back, that the response from the Department of Planning and Infrastructure (DPI) within the NT Government had not been positive.

The third and final report to the ACGC (July 2006) was brief, as it outlined a new possibility for the development of Creek Camp that emerged as the second report was being circulated to NT Government officials. This possibility (originating from officials in the DPI) suggested that certain basic reticulated services such as water and electricity could possibly be provided under licence or 'permissive occupancy', without the legal complexity of land tenure change. The advantages of such an arrangement were outlined and included a more straightforward way of ensuring that native title was not extinguished, protection of the assets of the organisation providing the services, and the fact that there would have to be a limit on the services provided. In some ways, this final point suited the caution that Creek Camp residents felt about the possibility of the place becoming like a 'town camp'; the perception that with development, greater numbers of people may be attracted, with the associated risk of the place becoming a 'drinkers camp' and thus changing the quiet, spread out nature of the place, one of its key advantages. Nevertheless, although this possibility of a more amenable legal option sounded hopeful and was discussed in our presentation to the council, the issue of whether this path was amenable as a policy option was less certain.

---

[3] One of the most frequently identified options for relocating people was the planned development of aged care housing in the Ti Tree town. This was discussed as an extension of the Aged Care Centre that currently delivered other services, such as food, clothes washing and ablution facilities, to many of the elderly core residents of the camp. However, the funding arrangements for this facility seemed far from settled and, likewise, discussions with potentially affected Creek Camp residents. Our preliminary discussions with aged care staff and the Creek Camp residents who relied on the services suggested that even if funding were forthcoming, such a significant shift in living arrangements may not be welcome to many of them.

Making governance tangible in this research developed as a concern with revealing the legal and (later) policy structures that had the potential to facilitate or hinder change, as much as opening a space for dialogue about the potentials for change.[4]

Research funding as a determinant of methodology

This research, like much research, was (and is) driven by engagement with a broader agenda and set of partners. As part of both an Australian Research Council Linkage Project (the ICGP between CAEPR and Reconciliation Australia, with the financial support of the Western Australian, NT and Federal Governments) and a Desert Knowledge Cooperative Research Centre (DKCRC) project (with 28 research partners), it is compulsory to cultivate relationships with these partners. As such, it is not ivory tower research as it aims to 'make research count on the ground' (Smith 2005: 5) in its applied approach. To do this, as researchers we have a responsibility to engage with government officials and non-government organisations, to both ensure the project is relevant and to disseminate the research findings. There is also a responsibility to work collaboratively with Aboriginal people with whom the research is being conducted. Indeed, through the DKCRC we received monies for collaboration in the field, which I will discuss further below. The Anmatyerr region, with the ACGC as its centre, is developing as something of a research hub for the DKCRC, with several other research projects underway, including desert or outback livelihoods and bush foods projects.

In our project, we discussed the research findings at length with officials in the local government department and in more restricted fashion with other departments, and with the Central Land Council (CLC).[5] After, and sometimes before, each period of field research we held an 'exit interview', which served to brief the attending officers on the major findings of our period of research. In some ways, we were able to offer informed critique of policy implementation 'on the ground' and also offer informed perspective about Creek Camp and associated issues, such as housing supply in the Ti Tree town. Those participating in the local government department discussions tended to be the Community Development Officer for the region and the Regional Manager for Central Australia. Those in the CLC discussions were usually a policy officer and the

---

[4] It is also important to note that although there were three broad stages of the research that sought to canvas different perspectives about the Creek Camp issue, we returned to Ti Tree, and specifically Creek Camp, on at least six other occasions during this time. Each time we were able to gain a greater understanding of the dynamics of the Creek Camp population and the NT Government understandings of the place. We continued to feed this information back to the ACGC and it was also summarised in the reports. Additionally, we spoke separately with many of the councillors about the issue during these visits. In this way, Creek Camp remained an active issue.

[5] The CLC is a representative statutory body under the *Aboriginal Land Rights (Northern Territory) Act 1976* (Cth) (ALRA). It acts as an advocacy organisation for Aboriginal people in relation to land rights, including native title rights, land management and development, and so on.

regional anthropologist. These conversations were of course multi-directional, as we were also returning to our core audience—the ACGC and Creek Camp residents—with updates from these parties.

The collaborative aspect of the research with the ACGC and the Creek Camp residents evolved in a number of ways. Firstly, as we did not arrive with a ready made research topic, the development of the research agenda was itself collaborative. Although it would not be entirely correct to suggest that it was an Aboriginal driven research agenda,[6] given that it was initiated by the NT Government, it was nevertheless a topic of considerable interest to both the Aboriginal councillors and the Aboriginal residents of Creek Camp and Ti Tree. Furthermore, the broadening of the research to include the Ti Tree residents and official possibilities for change was driven by Aboriginal interests.

As neither Sanders, nor myself, spoke Anmatyerr or Warlpiri and neither of us had experience working in that region,[7] we engaged an Anmatyerr and Warlpiri speaker to act as both interpreter and research facilitator. We approached the ACGC for suggestions and a male councillor who lived at the nearby settlement of Pmara Jutunta, and who had training as an interpreter, was appointed. He was paid an agreed rate that equated to the council sitting fees and we bought him lunch each day.[8] One of the challenges in undertaking research with a population that lives outdoors is that there are no doors to knock on. Having a local Aboriginal person introduce us to residents of the various camps was crucial in assisting us to navigate the spatial etiquette that defined the domestic arrangements. When our first 'research facilitator' was unavailable, as happened on our third trip, we were able to engage another female councillor from the same settlement. It was also decided by the ACGC that each interviewee of the Creek Camp should be paid $20 for each questionnaire. We continued this practice in our follow-up questionaries, as it was 'work for the council'. When our research broadened to include residents of the town, however, it was not appropriate to engage Aboriginal research facilitation. Nor did we pay the significant majority of these interviewees.

---

[6] See for instance the CRC for Aboriginal Health (<http//:www.crcah.org.au>) for examples of an Aboriginal driven research agenda.

[7] I had worked as a regional anthropologist for the CLC. However, this work was undertaken many years ago (from 1990–94) and very little of it was spent in this particular region. In fact, the Anmatyerr region had been part of a 'break-away land council' movement and as such there had been relatively little CLC engagement there since the successful land claim over the Ti Tree pastoral lease in 1986 (see Aboriginal Land Commissioner 1987; see also Morton 1994). This has changed more recently, with an active CLC presence in the region.

[8] He also attended a DKCRC workshop in Alice Springs with Sanders and myself, as the first stage of the research was also part of its early 'Governance, management and leadership' theme. The workshop was an update on progress and future directions for the various DKCRC sponsored research projects.

Positionality and 'balance'

As discussed earlier, the nature of the research method was effectively relationship building. We were given a new research task after reporting back from the previous research task at each council meeting. In this way we were being monitored and judgements made as to the ongoing value of the research relationship. This also meant that, perhaps even more than otherwise, we had to be alert to negotiating the diverse interests within and between the ACGC, the township and the NT Government. Within this highly politicised context of research, ensuring that the 'facts spoke for themselves' was crucial. The three reports to the council were exactly that: 'reportage'. They were factual and evidence based with very little interpretive analysis. We were careful to avoid alienating any of our research constituency.

For instance, within the all-Aboriginal ACGC there was a range of views about the Creek Camp. There were councillors who were also Creek Camp residents, one of whom sought only basic reticulated services in the camp—not housing—while the other sought a house within the township. The diverse population profile of the Creek Camp also suggested the need for us to observe a cautious approach. As the majority of the residents were highly mobile—many were regular part time residents from Nturiya, 17km to the west, while other 'residents' were long term visitors from Warlpiri settlements further to the northwest—there was concern that development of the place might make it more attractive for these visitors and change the camp's quiet environment. Thus, there were not only different views about the extent of development that should occur, but there was also a view among some within the council that only those people who worked should be given access to a house.

An approach driven by a straightforward advocacy for equality in mainstream housing and servicing was not appropriate in this context. Nevertheless, balancing an approach that advocates a 'human rights' agenda, which speaks of the rights to basic services, such as running water and sturdy shelter, with the multiple Aboriginal agendas and the agendas of government, has been an especially challenging aspect of the research. Attempts to try to 'get to the bottom' of why the all-Aboriginal council has not brought greater pressure to bear on the NT Government for even minimum servicing of the camp has uncovered not only the multiple views (some of which are canvassed above), but a guarded and uneasy history with their potential advocacy body (the CLC) and a deeper history of a violent colonial frontier.[9] A daily reminder of this 'frontier' is the apparently entrenched 'moral geography' of the Ti Tree township (Rowse 1998: 9), with the Stuart Highway acting as the divide between the camp

---

[9] Possibly the worst massacre in Central Australian settler history occurred at neighbouring Coniston Station in 1928, where between 30 to 100 Warlpiri and Anmatyerr men, women and children were murdered in reprisal for the murder of a non-Aboriginal dingo scalper (see Cribben 1984).

and the more formal residential dwellings. The Ti Tree town is the centralised focus of services within ready reach of the non-Aboriginal population contrasting with the surrounding dispersed Aboriginal population, which is without clinics, schools, or stores. This has been discussed at length elsewhere in terms of the regional colonial history and the subsequent spatialising of social relations (see Holcombe and Sanders 2007a) as Ti Tree became an enclave for settler interests surrounded by Aboriginal land. The point to reiterate here is the consequent embeddedness of this structure of Ti Tree as the centralised service centre and the gradual depletion of resources from the neighbouring settlements from whence many of the part-time Creek Camp residents have come.[10]

Arriving at this research balance of local historical depth, ethnographic insight and the intersections with NT bureaucratic agency has only been possible with an inter-disciplinary approach to the 'Creek Camp issue'. Sanders' method of dealing with the bureaucrats and the ACGC CEO has been to strategically uncover the options for development and then lay out the impediments to this development from within the same structures in a clinical objectivist approach that leaves little room for subjective dismissal (see especially Sanders and Holcombe 2007: 80–2, 84–6). My anthropological approach has been to interrogate the evolution of power relations between the Aboriginal people and the NT Government, and identify both impediments to and spaces for Aboriginal agency in an attempt to grapple with the cultural dimensions of choice in the 'Creek Camp issue'. To achieve this we combined quantitative and qualitative approaches in our discussions with people. Whilst I found it constraining to remain within the bounds of a questionnaire, such standardisation was essential in ensuring a comparative and systematic approach to data generation. It was equally important, however, to range beyond the questionnaires to ensure that the local contexts were grounded in an understanding of genealogical connections between Creek Camp residents, their customary attachments and other biographical details, to paint a fuller picture.

The role and power of 'officials'

In thinking about the governmental structures that acted as nodes in a network of potential change agents, several officials stand out in this research. It has been noted elsewhere that 'the response to altering the status quo [of Creek Camp] has been limited along all links of the decision making chain' (Holcombe and Sanders 2007a: 345). Here I would like to give further consideration to the make-up of this chain. As a multi-sited chain, its links are mobilised across NT Government departments and are at once hierarchical ('change must come from the top') and horizontal in the shared nature of the policy discourse and its emergence as a rationality. Without focusing unduly on the role of any one

---

[10] For instance, the stores closed at nearby Nturiya and Pmara Jutunta in 2002 and 2005 respectively.

official, it seems to me that a policy language developed, which ensured that those officials 'on the front line' spoke in concert. Once this language emerged, there was little shifting it, and the line between what was apparently legally possible and what was policy seemed to become blurred. The officers that emerged in this research at this front line were the ACGC CEO, officers in the local government department and officers in the DPI.

Having finished his contract, the ACGC CEO who began his three year tenure as our research project was beginning has now left. Our research relationship, however, has continued with the council. An integral element of the project is that we ensure that our field research coincides with the monthly council meeting, although it may be every third or fourth meeting that we can attend. However, there had been little or no mention of the Creek Camp issue since we tabled our third and final report to the ACGC in July 2006, although we had suggested a number of ideas for 'action' or 'consideration' from this and previous reports. One idea that developed from our discussions with councillors about the third report was to invite an officer from the DPI to attend an ACGC meeting and discuss the options and issues about potential development with councillors, and the council moved a motion to do so. We then took a back seat and observed that over the next nine months *no* officer from the DPI attended a council meeting. It is unclear whether this was because of reluctance on the part of the DPI or a lack of pushing on the part of the CEO.

Interestingly, the issue of Creek Camp was back on the agenda as an item at the first ACGC meeting that Sanders and I attended with the new CEO in June 2007. One councillor, who is also a Creek Camp resident, stated that 'he would like to see power and water connected to Creek Camp' (ACGC Council minutes, June 2007). This of course was not the first time he had said this, but as noted above, it had not been raised for some time. During our earlier interviews with him, he had made it clear that he sought these essentials, while the issue of housing was not his uppermost priority. However, he had never made so plain a request at any previous council meetings that we had attended.

It is apparent that the issue had lain dormant after our reports had been tabled and that this was not entirely at the discretion of the councillors. Nevertheless, it is pertinent to recall that the ACGC is itself divided and ambivalent as to future development possibilities or options for change at the Creek Camp, and this had not changed over the course of the research. That the new CEO seems to have a slightly different approach to the issue emerged at the same council meeting. She requested an update about possible courses of further action from us and was open to the possibility of formally requesting the attendance of an officer of the DPI to discuss the issue at the following meeting. Time will tell whether a DPI officer attends.

Officers in the DPI report to a different minister than do those in the Department of Local Government.[11] However, as officers in the DPI were the ones who initially identified the legal and financial obstacles to reticulated service at Creek Camp and then the more ready possibilities, as noted earlier, it would seem that they are pivotal in the process of potential change. When the potential for development under licence or permissive occupancy was reported back as a possible option for Creek Camp in a government forum[12] at which Sanders presented, he was informed by another DPI officer that in fact it was not necessarily an option. As was noted elsewhere (see Sanders and Holcombe 2007: 85), this was because of a NT Government policy relating to the establishment of any new Aboriginal 'community living areas', particularly in towns. This policy shift away from Aboriginal urban living areas, which began in the 1980s, has been brought to prominence recently in relation to 'town camps' as 'reverse apartheid' by the then Federal Minister for Indigenous Affairs, Mal Brough.[13] He raised, as a public issue, the sub-standard living conditions of the 19 town camps in Alice Springs. This policy position, away from the establishment of town camps, is primarily evidenced by the lack of structured government support for them, rather than a publicly declared position. Nevertheless, this somewhat opaque policy cannot so readily explain the historical legacy of government inaction over the Creek Camp.

The role that other officials play (such as those in the Department of Local Government) in this chain of rationality is also relevant. When the issue was raised again by the same councillor/Creek Camp resident at the 2007 May ACGC meeting (with the new CEO), the official noted that 'due to the fact that Creek Camp was situated on Crown Land [NT] Power and Water Authority would not provide pipes or services to Crown Land due to legal ramifications'. As examined in some detail above, the position detailed by this officer was indeed underwritten by a policy agenda, as much as legal constraints. Yet, the opacity of the policy position suggests that locating it is indeed a challenge, which may explain why the policy position about town camps was not outlined in this public forum.

It seems that the 'policy' evolved as a shared understanding amongst public service officers, a number of whom were long serving. This front line rationality was effective and presented as an insurmountable hurdle. Yet, we could not

---

[11] The former Minister manages the portfolios of Planning and Lands, and Infrastructure and Transport. The latter Minister, to which the Department of Local Government answers, manages the Local Government and Housing portfolios and 'assists' the Chief Minister with Indigenous Affairs. So, it would seem that the boundaries between ministerial responsibilities in relation to the Creek Camp issue are somewhat blurred.

[12] The 'Southern Regional Executive Coordination Committee', which meets monthly and has senior representation from the various government departments and statutory agencies.

[13] OneNews (New Zealand), 'Aborigines reject land deal', 24 May 2007, <http://tvnews.co.nz/view/page/1148892> [accessed 29 May 2007].

locate any written policy to the effect that leases were no longer being offered for Aboriginal urban living areas within townships. The constraint offered by this policy was able to dominate the discussions and set the parameters of possibilities. As a governmentality, it became authoritative through its common useage. For Foucault, the very activity of governing is conditional on the availability of a certain notion of rationality, which, in order to be operable, needs to be credible to the governed as well as the governing (see Gordon 1991: 48). The credibility of the policy at issue here emerged in the broader milieu of NT Government politics and its intersections with the Federal Government's recent targeting of 'town camps', as discussed above.

Nevertheless, this policy hurdle was really only one element— albeit a key one—in a confluence of factors that include, as mentioned above, a council with diverse views. Another strategic factor is the under resourced CLC who, if they were to push the issue, would be required to take instruction from Traditional Owners (under s. 23 of the ALRA). Preliminary enquiries suggest that at least some Traditional Owners' interests were not found to lie with the interests of Creek Camp residents. Likewise, post the *Native Title Act 1993* (Cth), the development of any new Aboriginal urban living area requires negotiation of an Indigenous Land Use Agreement, which would include a Crown lease for a living area. Again, the CLC would be a key party to such negotiations, as indeed has occurred in other townships. Furthermore, the fact that the township is surrounded by Aboriginal land (Ahakeye Land Trust), where outstation housing currently lies empty for much of the year, had been noted by the previous CEO.[14]

It is apparent, nevertheless, that patience in awaiting opportunities may be an Aboriginal political strategy. Is patience perhaps a form of resistance, a weapon of the weak? Or is this an optimistic way of interpreting passivity in the face of a greater political power? Certainly, a commonly heard phrase is that non-Aboriginal people 'blow in with the west wind and out with the east wind'. Therefore, seizing opportunities to pursue a pre-existing issue of import with a new CEO is standard practice. At any rate, my previous assessment of the lack of action to push for change on the issue as being 'too hard' on the part of councillors (see Holcombe and Sanders 2007a)[15] seems too encompassing on further reflection. It now seems to me that this earlier analysis perhaps underestimated the power relations within the council and the role that policy plays as a rationalising tool of government.

---

[14] The reasons why outstation housing remains unoccupied for much of the year in the ACGC region are numerous. For any individual family, these might include lack of transport and/or high cost of fuel, the death of a relative with whom the outstation is closely associated, and the need to be close to services (e.g. proximity to the clinic, school, store etc.).

[15] I noted then that the context of action is 'framed by the colonial history of marginality and violent subversion and a deeper cultural history that values mobility, family obligations and disregards acquisitive materiality' (Holcombe and Sanders 2007a: 346).

As the councillor raised the Creek Camp issue again, I realised that any set of 'findings', and thus analyses, must be bracketed by the research moment. Ultimately, with the re-emergence of the issue by the councillor/Creek Camp resident, it seems to me that if development of the camp is to happen in some form then it is going to have to be driven by a councillor. Persistence by councillors and the active ear of the CEO may yet lead to change.

Geertz (1988: 147) claims that what anthropology should seek to do is 'enlarge the possibility of intelligible discourse between people quite different from one another in interest, outlook, wealth, and power'. The *possibility* of this has indeed been enlarged by our research project. However, unfortunately, any discourse has been mediated through our reports, verbal and written. As far as I am aware, no non-Aboriginal government or ACGC official has since visited the Creek Camp to discuss any aspects of the research findings or possibilities for change with residents there.[16] The research, however, did 'debunk' certain preconceptions about the motivations of the residents, so at least the discourse between non-Aboriginal officials about the issue was enlarged by the facts. The analysis clearly demonstrated the diversity of the residents' aspirations, histories, affiliations and reasons for residing in the camp. Several of the myths concerning the place, as a drinking camp and as a camp dominated by itinerant Warlpiri, have also been found to be false. Likewise, the fact that a significant number of the core residents have an attachment to the place under Aboriginal customary law, while the depth of attachment for many others is historically located through many generations of dwelling in the location, seemed crucial in adding weight to the residents' rights.

Enforcing marginalisation: what's in a name?

A common reference for informal or unrecognised urban Aboriginal living areas is 'fringe camps', while terms such as 'fringe dwellers' and 'town campers' have commonly been used to describe the residents of these types of places. Yet, both these terms for residents carry different connotations. These definitional problems with finding an appropriate term were detailed in a 1982 report by the Commonwealth Parliament's House of Representatives Standing Committee on Aboriginal Affairs (HORSCATAA 1982). As Sanders (1984: 141) noted:

> the report recounted in detail both suggested terms and descriptions, and objections raised. [For instance] the term 'fringe dwellers' was criticised, because of its lack of currency among Aboriginal [people] and its frequent use by non-Aboriginals as a term of opprobrium to refer to Aboriginal residents of towns and cities who, in the users' view, should not be there.

---

[16] Likewise, I am not aware of the resident Aboriginal councillors holding meetings with other Creek Camp residents about the issue.

The committee eventually decided to use the term 'town campers' because of its less subjective connotations.

These definitional problems are not only indicative of the marginal status of town camping as an Aboriginal urban lifestyle (Sanders ibid.), but it seems that the categorisation of such places as 'camps' is also an attempt to ensure their temporary status by playing into stereotypes of Aboriginal mobility. If these places are labelled as temporary, then it would appear to be the case that the state need not claim responsibility for them. Yet, as we found in the case of the Creek Camp, residential stability emerged as a pattern for a significant number of residents. The implications emerging from this definitional argument could of course equally be applied to the so-called 'town camps' in other towns along the highway, such as Alice Springs, Tennant Creek and Elliot, as they are in fact Aboriginal suburbs. Unlike the Creek Camp, however, these 'town camps' now have some legitimacy as they are on various special purpose leases. Creek Camp is on unallocated Crown land, so the residents are effectively trespassing.

The appellation of 'Creek Camp' to the place at issue in this paper is a non-Aboriginal descriptor, which was not particularly used by Anmatyerr people, although they obviously knew what it referred to. Rather, the place did not seem to be referred to in general terms at all (except in structured contexts of ACGC meetings or this research), but rather was more specifically identified through residences within it, such as 'Old Napurrula's place'. Some older people specifically noted that the Anmatyerr name for the area was *Aleyaw* (Green et al. 2003: 21). This name refers to a 'sacred site' complex to the south of the council building, which represents two Dreamings that moved through what is now the town. The surrounding Ahakeye Land Trust gets its name from one of them (the bush plum). We were shown this place by two male Creek Camp residents and a councillor who was acting as our research facilitator.

Notions of good development

If development of the place was on the agenda for the NT Government—which seems extremely unlikely—the issue of equity of access to housing and associated services poses the challenge of what may be appropriate or demand driven servicing, as opposed to servicing on the basis of equity or by mainstream standards. What might be appropriate development? In other words, if the majority of residents were to be granted their wish of a simple tin shed rather than a house, the moral hazard that the Government is barely addressing, and perhaps perpetuating, is the 'third world conditions' under which the residents currently live. However, building mainstream housing for these people, either in the Creek Camp area or in the township, would actively disregard their right to exercise choice. However, this issue of choice is far from straightforward, as has been noted by Cowen and Shenton (1995: 28): 'choice is as much a precondition of development as its result'. Currently, of course, choices for change are not being offered. In our discussions with residents we were careful to note that we were not in positions of decision making power.

However, I cannot help but feel frustration, a feeling that is shared by at least one Creek Camp resident, who earlier this year asked us in an agitated manner why we were back again, if our work was not going to lead to a change in their living conditions. So, the likelihood that Old Napurrula may not get her tap and that this research may not lead to active change leads me to quote Durkheim: 'because what we propose to study is above all reality, it does not follow that we should give up the idea of improving it'.[17] Hence, the purpose of writing a paper that agitates for an understanding of the constraints imposed on research findings and the contingent possibilities of acting as change agents.

Acknowledgements

I would like to thank Will Sanders and the diligent editors of this monograph at CAEPR for their guidance, especially Janet Hunt and Stephanie Garling. The Desert Knowledge Cooperative Research Centre (DKCRC) also supported this research through funding for travel and community collaboration.

References

Aboriginal Land Commissioner 1987. *Ti-Tree Station Land Claim, Report No. 24*, Report to the Minister for Aboriginal Affairs and the Administrator of the Northern Territory, AGPS, Canberra.

Brady, D. 2004. 'Why public sociology may fail', *Social Forces*, 82 (4): 1629–38.

Cowen, M. and Shenton, R. 1995. 'The invention of development', in J. Crush (ed.), *Power of Development*, Routledge, London and New York.

Cowlishaw, G. 2003. 'Euphemism, banality, propaganda: anthropology, public debate and Indigenous communities', *Australian Aboriginal Studies*, 1: 2–17.

Cribben, J. 1984. *The Killing Times: The Coniston Massacre 1928*, Fontana Books, Sydney.

Foucault, M. 1991. 'Governmentality', in G. Burchell, C. Gordon and P. Miller (eds), *The Foucault Effect: Studies in Governmentality*, Harvester Wheatshaft, London.

Geertz, C. 1988. *Works and Lives: the Anthropologist as Author*, Stanford University Press, Stanford.

Gordon, C. 1991. 'Governmental rationality: an introduction', in G. Burchell, C. Gordon and P. Miller (eds), *The Foucault Effect: Studies in Governmentality,* Harvester Wheatshaft, London.

---

[17] Durkheim, E. *Division of Labor in Society*, 1984: XXVI, cited in Brady 2004: 1630

Green, J. with Ti Tree, Mt Allen and Laramba (Napperby) communities. 2003. *Central Anmatyerr Picture Dictionary*, IAD Press Picture Dictionary Series, IAD Press, Alice Springs.

Holcombe, S. and Sanders, W. 2007a. 'Accommodating difference: the socio-political history of an Aboriginal fringe camp in a small north Australian town', *The International Journal of Interdisciplinary Social Science*, 2 (2): 339–48.

—— and ——2007b. 'Community governance: the Ti Tree Creek Camp study', *Working Paper 10*, DKCRC, Alice Springs, available at <http://www.desertknowledgecrc.com.au/publications/downloads/DKCRC-Working-Paper-10-Ti-Tree-Creek-Camp-Study.pdf>.

House of Representatives Standing Committee on Aboriginal Affairs (HORSCATAA) 1982. *Strategies to Help Overcome the Problems of Aboriginal Town Camps*, Report to Parliament of the Commonwealth of Australia, Canberra.

Morton, J. 1994. The Proposed Anmatjere Land Council: Its Historical Antecedents and an Estimation of Levels of Support, Unpublished report to ATSIC, Canberra.

Rose, D. B. 2001. 'The silence and power of women', in P. Brock (ed.), *Words and Silences: Aboriginal Women, Politics and Land*, Allen & Unwin, Crows Nest, NSW.

Rose, N. 1999. *Powers of Freedom: Reframing Political Thought*, Cambridge University Press, Cambridge.

Rowse, T. 1998. *White Flour, White Power: From Rations to Citizenship*, Cambridge University Press, Cambridge.

Sanders, W. 1984. 'Aboriginal town camping, institutional practices and local politics', in J. Halligan and C. Paris (eds), *Australian Urban Politics*, Longman Cheshire, Melbourne.

—— and Holcombe, S. 2007. 'The Ti Tree Creek Camp study: a contribution to good governance', *Ngiya: Talk the Law*, 1: 72–92.

Smith, D. 2005. 'Researching Australian Indigenous governance: a methodological and conceptual framework', *CAEPR Working Paper No. 29*, CAEPR, ANU, Canberra.

Sutton, P. 2001. 'The politics of suffering: Indigenous policy in Australia since the seventies', Revised version of the Inaugural Berndt Foundation Biennial Lecture, Presented to the *Australian Anthropological Society Conference*, 23 September 2000, UWA, Perth.

——2005. 'Rage, reason and the honourable cause: a reply to Cowlishaw', *Australian Aboriginal Studies,* 2: 35–43.

Part 2: Culture, power and the intercultural

4. Cultures of governance and the governance of culture: transforming and containing Indigenous institutions in West Arnhem Land

Diane Smith

> You can't make people good by Act of Parliament.
>
> (Oscar Wilde, *A Woman of No Importance*, Act 1)
>
> We've had all our meetings and we had to be professional. We had to do our governance properly. We had all that governance training—now we're good! But the government people who pushed that 'good governance' idea; they aren't here. Where are they? They want us to govern, then they should let us govern.
>
> (West Arnhem Shire Transitional Committee member)

Introduction

In the 40 years since the 1967 referendum[1] in Australia, governments have developed legislation, policies, and a multitude of institutional mechanisms in their attempts to govern the Indigenous population and address its entrenched socioeconomic disadvantage. These interventions into Indigenous lives by the state have been primarily predicated on western values, institutions and beliefs about what constitutes 'good governance' and, accordingly, what Indigenous Australians should do to develop it.

Implicit in these government strategies has been a deep-seated lack of confidence in Indigenous 'culture' itself, exacerbated by contradictory underlying assumptions. On the one hand, the hope of policy makers is that if they can only unlock the 'da Vinci Code' of Indigenous culture they will somehow be able to design more 'culturally appropriate' government programs and service delivery, thereby more effectively securing government policy objectives. On the other hand, Indigenous culture is often pathologised by politicians, bureaucrats, the public, and the media. It is viewed as a form of inherited virus that will inevitably contaminate and undermine western standards of 'good governance'. So, 'Acts

---

[1] The 1967 referendum made two changes to the Australian Constitution. These changes enabled the Commonwealth Government to make laws for all of the Australian people by amending s. 51 of the Constitution (previously, people of 'the Aboriginal race in any State' were excluded); and to take account of Aboriginal people in determining the population of Australia by repealing s. 127 of the Constitution (formerly, Indigenous people had been haphazardly included in the census, but not counted for the purposes of Commonwealth funding grants to the states or territories).

of Parliament' and the often unilateral imposition of the state's sovereign powers are deemed to be necessary to 'protect' Indigenous people from the governance disabilities of their own culture. At such times, the Australian state reasserts its own 'culture of governance'—that is, the set of shared values, government institutions, powers, laws, modes of behaviour and norms—in an attempt to direct and mould Indigenous cultures and their systems of governance into its own democratic likeness.

This chapter poses two symbiotic concepts—the 'governance of culture' and 'cultures of governance'—as tools to analyse the nature of the tangled engagement between contemporary Indigenous and non-Indigenous 'cultures of governance' in Australia. Points of interaction focus on the institutional and practice level of governments, and Indigenous communities, their leaders and organisations.

Institutions are the glue of governance; they are the 'rules of the game', the formal and informal ways in which things get done. As such, institutions are pre-eminently about power and who gets to exercise it. In the intercultural context of post-colonial governance in Australia, institutions represent a rich site of visible interaction and contestation between the Australian state and Indigenous peoples.

Employing these two concepts, this chapter first examines how the Australian state attempts, through its policy, statutory and bureaucratic institutions, to govern contemporary Indigenous cultures and their different systems of governance. The same concepts are then used to explore the ways in which Indigenous people use their culturally-based institutions to buffer and reassert the legitimacy of their governance arrangements and decision-making authority. In doing so, Indigenous governance institutions are being re-imagined, recreated, transformed and constrained—both from within and without. But the institutions of the Australian state, in the arena of policy and implementation, are also being affected. Both sets of mutual transformation and containment are investigated.

The analysis focuses specifically on a case study conducted over the last five years in West Arnhem Land. There, Indigenous people (referred to as Bininj in the local Kunwinjku language) and the Northern Territory (NT) Government have been involved in planning the establishment of a regionalised form of local government, for the purposes of delivering essential municipal services and infrastructure to the region as a whole. Some of the Bininj leaders involved are relatives of families with whom I worked over 25 years ago when employed by the Northern Land Council to map land-tenure systems in West Arnhem Land.

In the course of working towards their goal of a strong regional organisation, several Bininj community organisations and their elected leaders have attempted to build elements of a new 'culture of governance'. To do so, they have used a range of techniques and tools to design innovative governance institutions and structures, and to imbue them with practical capability and legitimacy.

In this chapter I examine the design techniques and their points of intersection with government processes, and consider the implications for both the Bininj and government parties. Not all the initiatives and solutions are seen as legitimate or effective by the state, or by some Indigenous community members. How the disjunctions between the two cultures of governance are contested and negotiated forms a large part of the analysis. Whether the process has led to the desired (and different) practical outcomes sought by the Indigenous and non-Indigenous (or *Balanda* in *Kunwinjku* language) participants involved, and whether there has been any growth in their mutual comprehension are considered by way of conclusion.

The research process

The research on which this paper draws is ethnographic, multi-sited, and aims to make both a practical and a policy contribution, and so deserves a brief account. Over a 25 year period I have undertaken sporadic field based research with Indigenous families and groups in West Arnhem Land on their traditional land tenure patterns and social organisation. This work has included mapping clan countries and sacred sites, assessing the socioeconomic impact of mining and other resource agreements, and reviewing the operation and performance of Indigenous organisations. An integral part of the research has been analyses of the wider government policy, legal and funding environment within which Indigenous rights, interests and institutions have been recognised or limited.

My research frequently ventured into the cultures of government bureaucracy and departments. Most recently, between 2003 and 2006, I was engaged as a part-time policy researcher by the NT Government's Department of Community Development, Sport and Cultural Affairs (DCDSCA) under contract with my employer, the Centre for Aboriginal Economic Policy Research (CAEPR) at The Australian National University. During that period, I provided research analysis, evaluation and advice to the Department regarding the effectiveness of government policy, projects and implementation regarding Indigenous governance, community development and regionalisation.

In 2004, I was invited by two of the department's Community Development Officers (CDOs) to work with them on planning and implementation for a specific regional local government initiative in West Arnhem Land. Shortly after, I was asked by the Indigenous members of the newly-formed West Arnhem Land Regional Authority (WCARA) Interim Council representing the communities and organisations involved, to continue this work with them and attend their meetings. This, in turn, further engaged me in departmental (as well as inter-agency and cross-government) meetings about the local government reform over 2004–06.

In late 2006, after my contract with the Department had finished and I returned to my university, the Interim Council requested that the WCARA process become part of the national Indigenous community governance research that I was jointly involved in conducting. Subsequently, I have continued to work in the capacity of researcher and 'special advisor' to the Indigenous members of this West Arnhem regional committee.

These overlapping professional roles enabled me to experience first hand the different government, bureaucratic, and Indigenous culturally-based perspectives, strategies and agency at play in the regional initiative. Whilst it was by no means inclusive of all the parties involved, and on occasions problematic, the multi-sited research generated an unusually broad set of insights into the complex and rapidly changing intercultural process.

Seeing governance like a state

> Perhaps no people ever had more rudimentary rules of law and government than those savages … with hardly any government over the wandering clan except the undefined authority of the 'bully' of the tribe.
>
> (Tylor 1894:150)
>
> … in many Aboriginal communities, social organisation has completely broken down. The people have shown they are incapable of governing themselves. There is no point in consulting them about the creation of authority; authority has to be created for them. Their lives will then better match our own.
>
> (Hirst 2007)

How we see governance makes a difference. As the commentators above suggest, from colonial settlement through to today, Indigenous governance has often seemed invisible, unknowable, and underdeveloped to non-Indigenous Australians. It has been treated as a kind of *'gubernare nullius'*,[2] a *tabula rasa* onto which could be written the language, norms and institutions of western liberal statecraft and control.

In *Seeing Like a State*, James Scott (1998: 3) argues that efforts to permanently settle highly mobile sub-populations like nomads, gypsies, vagrants, and

---

[2] The word 'governance' is derived from the Latin word 'gubernare' meaning 'rudder', conveying 'the action of steering a ship'. The word was first used in 12th century France, where it was a technical term designating the administration of a bailliage (the jurisdiction or district of a bailiff; bailiwick in English). From France, it crossed the channel and in England came to designate the method of organising feudal power (see de Alcantara 1998; Kooiman 2003; and Plumptre and Graham 1999 for a definitional autobiography of the concept). Just as the British legal concept of *terra nullius* was used to usurp control over the lands of Indigenous Australians, the related idea that they had no government, no chiefs, and no enduring form of authority, law and order was used to justify the imposition of British jurisdiction and the common law over Indigenous lands and people.

hunter-gatherers has been a perennial project of the modern state, underwritten by strategies to standardise and simplify 'what was a social hieroglyph into a legible and administratively more convenient format'. In Australia, British colonists similarly went to considerable lengths to make the alien social and institutional 'hieroglyph' of Indigenous governance and leadership legible to themselves.

In the early days of the colony, Indigenous groups were perceived to be acephalous, lawless and unruly. Metal 'kingplates' and 'queenplates' were bestowed on favoured elders—hung around their necks to make them visible to the British authorities. People were often forcibly relocated from their lands and centralised into artificial communities where 'councils of elders', 'chiefs', 'kings' and 'queens', 'princes' and 'headmen' were created by missionaries and government reserve managers as part of an arsenal of techniques to govern and immobilise people. This naming of Indigenous governance was about state surveillance and control.

Today, western democratic concepts, structures and governance institutions continue to be imposed through such devices as legislative and policy frameworks that require the incorporation of social groups into organisations; the ordering concepts of democratic elections and voting systems; the asserted primacy of individual citizenship over collective rights; and via the statutory naming of newly-created categories of people on whom are bestowed specified decision-making rights, responsibilities and authority by the state.

The allocated mark of condoned authority is still used by governments. There are now legal categories of people—such as 'traditional owners', 'authorised claimants' and 'native title holders'— who have to be registered and certified, and 'councillors', 'chairpersons', 'bodies corporate' and 'governing boards' who are required to operate under legal and constitutional guidelines.[3]

Government's own 'culture of governance' in Indigenous affairs is based on institutionalised forms of policy, program and grant funding that are supported by the tools of financial compliance and accountability, service delivery outcomes, administrative review, and technical audits. These tools are activated by the ever-changing face of government departments, agencies and committees, which work to defend their relative influence, functional 'territories' and budgetary power.

---

[3] This categorisation for the purposes of making Indigenous people visible and susceptible to external control is not restricted to governance. It is especially apparent in the history of the census enumeration by Australian governments, where people are renamed and so transformed into 'households', 'household reference person', 'nuclear families', 'visitors' etc. (see Morphy 2007). In resource negotiations with private sector companies, people are renamed and transformed into 'stakeholders', 'land owners', 'historical peoples', 'beneficiaries', 'affected groups' etc. (see Holcombe 2005; Howitt and Suchet 2004; Smith 1995). In the social security system they are renamed and reconstituted as 'sole parents', 'welfare dependents', and people 'in breach' (see Smith 1992).

Aligned to departmental territories are vast bureaucratic networks where influential senior officers formulate policy frameworks and devise implementation strategies for government consideration. In doing so, they create their own internal language for the operation of Indigenous affairs.[4]

For most public servants, the face of Indigenous governance is incorporated community organisations, of which there are an estimated 5000 across Australia. Even in the most well-intentioned policy approaches, the governance of Indigenous organisations is invariably made subservient and overwhelmed by the workload of mundane bureaucratic procedures and financial reporting that they are required to undertake.

As public servants are increasingly centralised and work behind the key-coded locked doors of departmental offices, they become further distanced from the practical realities of Indigenous community governance. The overall effect has been a growing field-based disengagement of bureaucrats from Indigenous communities, and a widening misalignment between government policy and departmental practice.

For Indigenous communities and their organisations, the state does not exist 'up there', at a disembodied remove from them. The sovereign governing power of the state is plain for Indigenous people to see on a daily basis. They experience it in the form of visiting public servants, the ever-changing rules of service delivery and funding, the deluge of information gathering by governments, and the burdensome routine of meetings and consultations.

In the local interaction between the state and Indigenous people, there are mutual blind spots where government policy rationales and decision-making processes are just as opaque and confounding to Indigenous people, as Indigenous governance processes and institutions are to governments and their officers.

But amongst the spaces of mutual unintelligibility of each other's 'social hieroglyphs' (cf. Scott 1998), some individual government field officers do make the room to develop personal relationships of trust with leaders and organisations, and so are better able to negotiate with them, provide credible advice, and undertake community development work. Similarly, some Indigenous leaders and organisations look for room to build relationships with particular public servants and, through them negotiate the conditions under which they can better exercise their own authority, make decisions and mobilise action. They do so, however, in an environment of seemingly constant policy change and containment by the state. In the process they occasionally transform aspects of

---

[4] In contemporary Indigenous Affairs, public servants have created powerful policy names such as 'coordination', 'whole-of-government', 'joined up government', 'mainstreaming', 'normalisation', 'transparency', 'mutual obligation, 'partnership' and so on.

their own governance cultures, and subvert the techniques and institutions by which the state seeks to govern their culture and deny their self-governance.

This institutional interplay between 'cultures of governance' and the state's goal of 'governing Indigenous culture' is fully evident in the West Arnhem Land process of regionalising local government.

The NT view of governance

Northern Territory Government discussions with Indigenous leaders from West Arnhem Land about establishing a regional local government began in late 2002 under the reform agenda of the *Building Stronger Regions, Stronger Futures* (BSRSF) policy. Since then, the progress of the West Arnhem initiative has been subject to a constantly changing policy environment within the NT Government. The impacts of this have been exacerbated by equally tumultuous policy reforms at the national level.

The collaborative phase

The BSRSF policy was one in the long line of efforts by both the NT and Australian Governments to create various kinds of representative and administrative 'regions' over the Indigenous population.[5] In the NT, its antecedents lay in the previous Government's policy initiative known as the *Reform and Development Agenda* (RADA). This policy sought to amalgamate the existing 65 local governing bodies[6] into around 20 'larger and more sustainable' councils, 'ideally representing and delivering services to at least 2000 people'. A key goal of RADA was the creation of 'Indigenous governments with legitimate authority' (Coles 2004).

The BSRSF policy similarly sought the voluntary amalgamation of community councils into large-scale local governments, which were to be called Regional Authorities, with 20 expected to be established. The policy vision was to enact 'a radical transformation in the method of service delivery and regional Indigenous governance' (Ah Kit 2002; see also Ah Kit 2003: 2–3) in collaboration with community councils and their leaders.

The rationale was the perceived parlous state of local government councils in the Territory, characterised by one NT Minister as constituting a 'stark crisis' of governance that included widespread 'organisational bankruptcy',

---

[5] See Behrendt et al. (2007), Sanders (2003, 2004) and Smith (1995, 1996, 2007) for a review of some of the different phases and forms of regionalism in Indigenous affairs.

[6] These include six municipal councils, 31 community government councils that are incorporated under NT legislation, and 28 association councils that are constituted under Commonwealth legislation. Approximately 80 per cent of these councils are situated on Aboriginal inalienable freehold land and so must operate within the statutory context of the *Aboriginal Land Rights (Northern Territory) Act 1976* (ALRA), which provides protection and recognition for the rights and interests of traditional owners in matters of land access, use, planning, and management.

'institutional incapacity', 'ineffective service delivery, fraud and corruption by staff and leaders, a high turnover of key non-Indigenous staff', and an 'historical legacy of poor governance' (Ah Kit 2002: 1).

Evidence for that view came not only from lurid media accounts, but also from DCDSCA audits and compliance reviews of community councils. Those reported indicated that close to 50 per cent of local government bodies were either 'highly dysfunctional' or 'at risk' in terms of their financial management, service delivery and governance.

A critical factor underlying this failure rate has been the issue of scale. The average population serviced by Indigenous community and association councils is 670 persons (Local Government Association of the Northern Territory (LGANT) 2003: 4). In other words, many small, isolated community councils simply do not have the population size, economies of scale, resources, administrative systems, personnel or management expertise to adequately meet either their existing or potential service delivery obligations (Tapsell 2003).

In launching the BSRSF policy, the NT Government argued that 'effective and legitimate frameworks for regional governance [would be] the foundations for any regional development strategy that will be sustainable over time' (Ah Kit 2003). The policy intention was that regional authorities would:

- have jurisdiction and powers as regionalised forms of local government under the *Local Government Act 1978* (NT)
- be established by 'voluntary agreement' between councils and require a 'substantial majority of residents in favour'
- be able to undertake 'regional decision making to determine priorities, establish service delivery policies and allocate resources', and
- 'provide for decision-making structures that meet the needs of the communities to be governed and, where applicable incorporate strong relationships with cultural decision-making arrangements and particularly traditional owners' (Ah Kit 2003).

The policy emphasis was to be on the flexibility of structures and timeframes, and the development of culturally-based representative and electoral arrangements.

A review of the *Local Government Act 1978* (NT) was proposed to provide a better statutory foundation for regionalised local government.[7]

In mid 2004, at the end of the policy's first year of implementation, the Australian Government abolished the Aboriginal and Torres Strait Islander Commission

---

[7] This review was never carried out. A new *Local Government Bill* was eventually introduced to the NT Legislative Assembly in February 2008; it was debated in the mid year sittings and enacted in the second half of 2008. The Bill implements the radically changed 'New Local Government' policy that was commenced in 2007, not the BSRSF policy launched in 2003.

(ATSIC). ATSIC had been a statutory-based national forum for Indigenous Australians, based on the election of representatives from every state and territory. Its abolition, and the attendant dismantling of the regional council structure, left a major representative vacuum in the NT, as elsewhere. So, while one form of statutory regionalism was being abolished, the proposed regional local governments came to be seen as a possible alternative in the eyes of some in the NT and Australian Governments, and of some former ATSIC regional councillors as well.

To cement what became a fortuitous convergence of policy directions, support for regional authorities was included in a bilateral *Overarching Agreement on Indigenous Affairs* negotiated between the NT and Australian Governments in mid 2005. A schedule to the agreement set out shared goals for the two Governments, which included working together to ensure:

- 'effective and legitimate representation';
- that 'the establishment of Regional Authorities involves voluntary amalgamations of community councils based on extensive and effective consultation to ensure constitutions reflect local aspirations, and have cultural legitimacy'; and
- that the 'amalgamation of community councils into Regional Authorities effectively addresses current problems of scale, improves service delivery, reduces staff turnover and ensures greater coordination and continuity of interest in community economic and social development' (see Schedules 1 and 2.3 to the *Overarching Bilateral Agreement on Indigenous Affairs*, 2005).[8]

However, little more than 18 months later, in late 2006, the BSRSF policy framework was dramatically reformed by the NT Government and replaced with what was named the New Local Government policy.[9]

What had happened? The sudden demise of the BSRSF policy owed much to the ideological dissatisfaction and implementation difficulties experienced by government bureaucrats in trying to accommodate Indigenous ideas about 'regions' and representation for local government, and their consensus modes of decision making about these matters. Discussion and decision making took time, internal negotiation and sensitive facilitation—all of which challenged the capacity, commitment and resources of both the NT and Australian Governments. The political imperative for fast results chaffed at the more measured pace of voluntary regionalisation, and in the meantime, several NT community and

---

[8] The *Overarching Agreement On Indigenous Affairs Between the Commonwealth of Australia and the Northern Territory of Australia 2005–2010* and associated schedules are available at <http://www.facsia.gov.au/internet/facsinternet.nsf/via/indigenous/$file/IndigenousAffairsAgreement.pdf> [accessed 5 May 2008].
[9] See 'Local Government Reform' on the DLGHS website at: <http://www.localgovernment.nt.gov.au/new> [accessed 5 May 2008].

association councils had collapsed owing to poor financial administration and governance.

Reverting to coercion

The New Local Government policy framework attempted to contain the inherent slipperiness and flexibility of Indigenous governance institutions and decision-making processes. The policy did away with any formal recognition of culturally-based processes for determining local government regions, and effectively turned a blind eye to the potential for using Indigenous governance systems and issues of cultural geographies as the basis for the shire model.

Regionalisation was still the goal, but it was to be mandatory and meet government-imposed deadlines. To signal this major policy turnaround, Regional Authorities were renamed 'Shires'. There were to be only nine in total, and their boundaries would be determined by government.

Indigenous input was corralled into newly-formed 'Transitional Committees' created by government to provide it with 'advice' about the establishment of each shire. Government, private sector and non-Indigenous stakeholders were able to participate on these committees, widening the range of parties and views. An 'Advisory Board' was established to support the implementation process and provide recommendations to the Minister for Local Government. Its members and the Chair (an experienced Indigenous leader) were appointed by the Minister.

The new policy proposed that the shires:

> will be democratically elected by the people, just like everywhere else in Australia. All councils including the municipals will have a minimum of six and a maximum of twelve councillors ... [and that] All Territorians who are registered on the electoral roll will have a say in who will represent their community by voting at the council election (DLGHS 2007).

A 'one-size fits all' approach was applied. The shires would have a single common governance structure, each with the same cap on the total numbers of representatives, and each sharing a single model constitution designed by the DLGHS and Parliamentary Counsel. All would deliver the same mandatory set of 'core' local government services, to be identified by government and set out in the new legislation.

In the early days of this NT policy reversal, in June 2007, the Australian Government responded to a damning report on child abuse in NT Indigenous communities (Anderson and Wild 2007) and, without notice to the NT Government, initiated a unilateral intervention to takeover the administration of some 60 remote Indigenous communities, including those in the West Arnhem region.

As part of the intervention, the Australian Government would compulsorily acquire leaseholds for discrete Indigenous settlements for an estimated minimum period of five years. All communities located on Aboriginal inalienable freehold land under the *Aboriginal Land Rights (Northern Territory) Act 1976* (Cth) (ALRA) would have their permit systems revoked, and legislation was drafted and passed to enact changes to this Act.

Australian Government administrators (to be called 'government business managers'), answerable to the Emergency Response Taskforce comprising Australian Army and Department of Families, Community Services and Indigenous Affairs and other government officials, were placed into 'priority' communities. Their job was to oversight mandatory health checks on children and to coordinate the intervention requirements in each community.

In late 2007, national elections were held and the Labor Party was elected as the Australian Government. In the early phase of its first term, it committed to evaluate the implementation of the NT intervention, whilst continuing with its basic strategies.

Regionalisation in West Arnhem Land

In the context of this hyperactive policy environment—with its extreme swings from collaboration to coercion and intervention—the Indigenous organisations and leaders involved in the West Arnhem initiative were forced to cope with several major, imposed changes of direction.

The collaborative phase

Indigenous leaders from West Arnhem community organisations became involved in the regionalisation process in mid 2003 as part of what was referred to as the 'Top End Triangle' (TET), comprising representatives from the Pine Creek, Coomalie, Kunbarllanjnja, Warruwi, Minjilang, and Jabiru local government councils. In December 2003, at a meeting of TET representatives, members of the Minjilang, Warruwi and Kunbarllanjnja Community Councils split from the other representatives in the TET group. They perceived there to be a lack of communal purpose between the Bininj and *Balanda* organisations, and felt that priorities were weighted to the latter.

The West Arnhem Land representatives began to see the potential for an 'Indigenous Regional Authority' and to work towards the establishment of what they eventually called the 'West Central Arnhem Regional Authority' (WCARA).[10] At this stage, the nearby Jabiru Council stayed out of the process, and the Coomalie and Pine Creek Councils decided to proceed together in a separate initiative.

---

[10] See Smith (2007) for a more detailed account of the West Central Arnhem regionalisation process during the WCARA phase, and the traditional patterns of land-tenure and social organisation involved.

The initial leaders of the WCARA process were Bininj elected representatives from three community councils and two outstation resource organisations, including:

- Kunbarllanjnja Community Government Council;
- Warruwi Community Incorporated;
- Minjilang Community Incorporated;
- Demed Outstation Resource Association Incorporated; and
- Jibulwanagu Outstation Resource Association Aboriginal Corporation.

Together with their Chief Executive Officers (CEOs), up to three representatives from each organisation began meeting every six to eight weeks and, in August 2004, formed the WCARA Transitional Council with the goal of progressing discussions about amalgamation into a single regional authority. Representatives from the Local Government Association of the NT (LGANT) and the Commonwealth Office of Indigenous Policy Coordination also attended these meetings.

Interim Council members initially talked about the regionalisation policy both as an opportunity to secure greater authority and control for Bininj people over the things that mattered to them, and to exercise greater influence over government funding and service delivery to the region:

> We will get to say what we want in our communities, we will set the priorities ... We have control over this project ... We will create policies and strategies that achieve more local employment and better services ... We will have a much stronger voice speaking as one to government ... The government always has a hidden agenda; we want our say from the word go (Members of the WCARA Interim Council).

The proposed area for the regional authority was approximately $25,000km^2$—all of it inalienable Aboriginal freehold land under the ALRA. The area encompassed several inter-related language and landowning groups, three large discrete community settlements (two of which were on islands), and numerous small dispersed outstations (see Fig. 4.1).

The process was substantially facilitated by DLGHS and particularly through the efforts of two of its CDOs. From 2003 onwards, this male/female team travelled extensively throughout West Arnhem Land, disseminating information and holding discussions with community leaders and organisations about the BSRSF regionalisation policy. In doing so, they developed a large network of contacts with senior leaders and family groups, and built up strong relationships and considerable personal trust with local Indigenous residents. Through this community development approach, they facilitated the formation of the Interim Council and subsequently were asked to act as the secretariat for their meetings.

Fig. 4.1 The proposed region for the West Central Arnhem Regional Authority, under the BSRSF policy

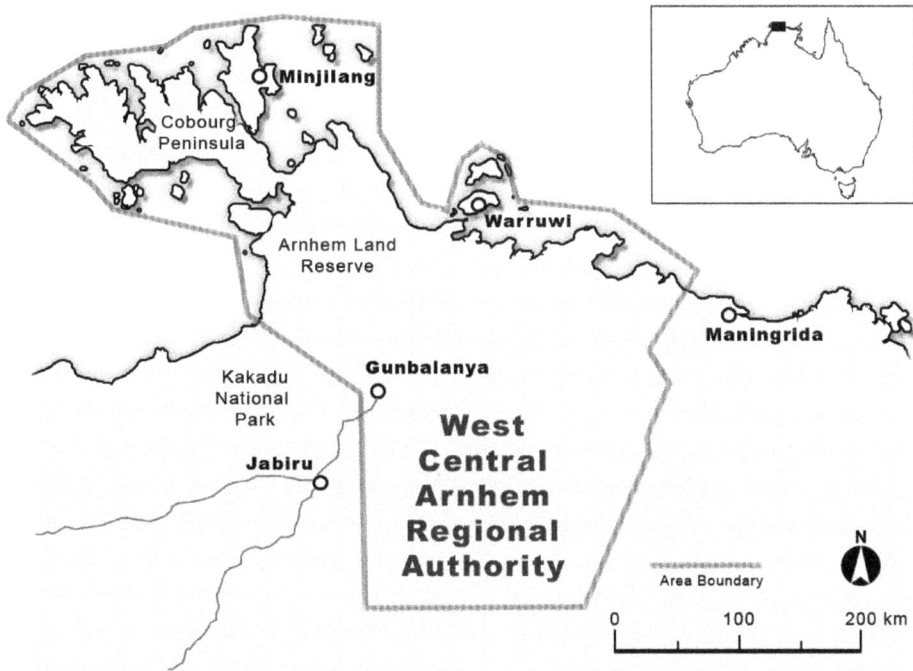

In mid July 2005, a 'Memorandum of Understanding' signed between the Department of Local Government, Housing and Sport (DLGHS) and the participating organisations formally committed all parties to support the decision-making work of the Interim Council to establish a regional authority for West Arnhem. A timeframe of December 2005 was proposed for its establishment.

Over that early period there was scepticism amongst community residents and Interim Council members about the extent of the NT Government's commitment to full Indigenous participation in regionalisation. Fears were expressed that the Government would simply impose a solution rather than negotiating with residents and their elected representatives.

Despite these reservations, the WCARA Interim Council met regularly between 2004–06. The workload was intensive for both the members and the departmental officers involved, as they navigated a complex organisational and legal transition. The proposed regional authority structure meant that the three existing community councils would have to be entirely dissolved as local government organisations.[11] New election processes would also have to be designed and held for regional councillors, and the local government assets, functions, staff and administrative systems of the separate councils would have to be transferred across to the new authority. The BSRSF policy sought cost-sharing and resource efficiencies, so a rationalisation of some staffing positions was also proposed.

During this phase, the WCARA Interim Council made a number of collective decisions about the authority's governance and organisational structure, administrative arrangements, business planning, its system of representation, external boundaries, election procedures, headquarters, and service delivery roles (see Fig. 4.2).

Fig. 4.2 Proposed representative structure for the West Central Arnhem Regional Authority

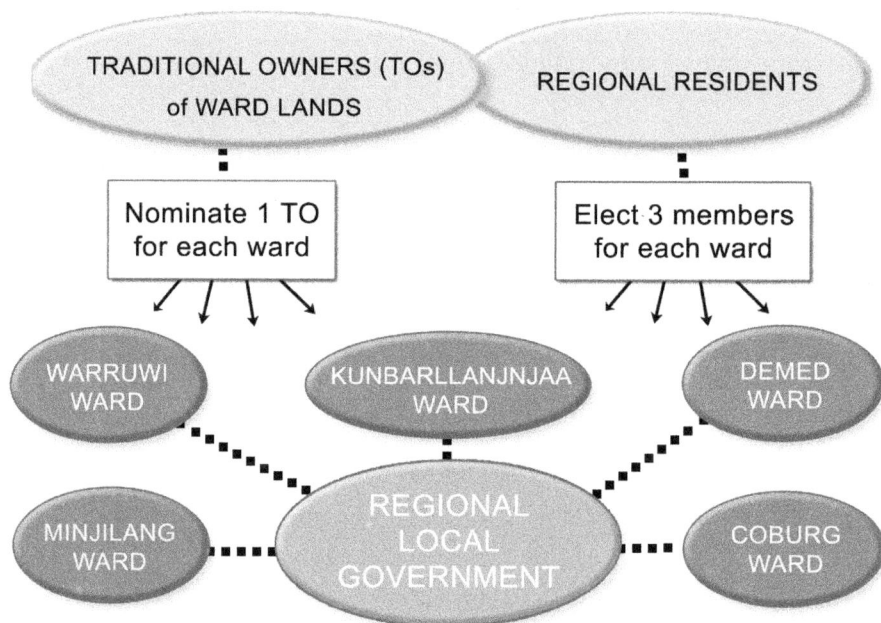

During 2005–06, the Interim Council participated in regular governance capacity-building sessions at their meetings, and spent considerable time developing a culturally-based constitution with a unique Preamble. A vision

---

[11] Kunbarllanjnja is a local government under the *Local Government Act 1978* (NT) and so will be entirely dissolved; whereas Warruwi and Minjilang are Association Councils that are treated as if they are local governments by the NT Government for the purposes of receiving relevant government funding. They can maintain their organisational incorporation for other community purposes, but must transfer their local government type functions and funding to the new authority. Note that Kunbarllanjnja spelling was chosen by the Community Local Government Council as its name; Gunbalanya is the older form of spelling for the entire settlement.

statement for the regional authority aimed: 'To develop safe communities for families, provide real jobs for local Indigenous people, and promote economic development through strong legitimate governance'.

Considerable work was involved in developing this constitution, designing a ward system for voting that was based on a Bininj cultural geography, and documenting a business plan for the authority. The process required considerable time and commitment from senior government bureaucrats, extensive community development work, as well as legal, funding and administrative support from both the NT and Australian Governments. To coordinate Government efforts, the DCDSCA convened a Project Management Group with officers from the NT and Australian Governments and LGANT. This inter-departmental group met every six to eight weeks over 2005–06.

But after the NT Labor Government was re-elected in 2005, its restructuring and renaming of the DCDSCA (which became the DLGHS) had significant consequences for the regionalisation process. In particular, the participation of government officers changed frequently on the Project Management Group for WCARA. Nevertheless, the group drafted a transitional funding framework for the region, considered mechanisms for streamlining the transitions to regional programs, and held interviews to employ a Transitional Manager to steer the administrative amalgamation of staff and community council resources.

Over three years had passed since the TET group first met. The Interim Council anticipated the establishment of the regional authority within just a few months. In late 2006, however, rumours abounded that the NT Government was contemplating changes to the BSRSF policy. In early 2007, a New Local Government policy was fully formulated by DLGHS and a detailed implementation plan put to the NT Cabinet for consideration. It required several NT Cabinet meetings in the first half of 2007 for the new policy to be officially endorsed. The policy was immediately implemented by DLGHS.

Coercive implementation

What did this mean for the WCARA Interim Council and participating community organisations, perched, as it were, on the brink of establishing their own authority?

First, the WCARA Interim Council was told by the Department that it would now be required to include Maningrida community and Jabiru township. The new 'region' was thereby extended to cover approximately 32,200km^2 and an estimated total population of some 5000–6000 people (see Fig. 4.3).

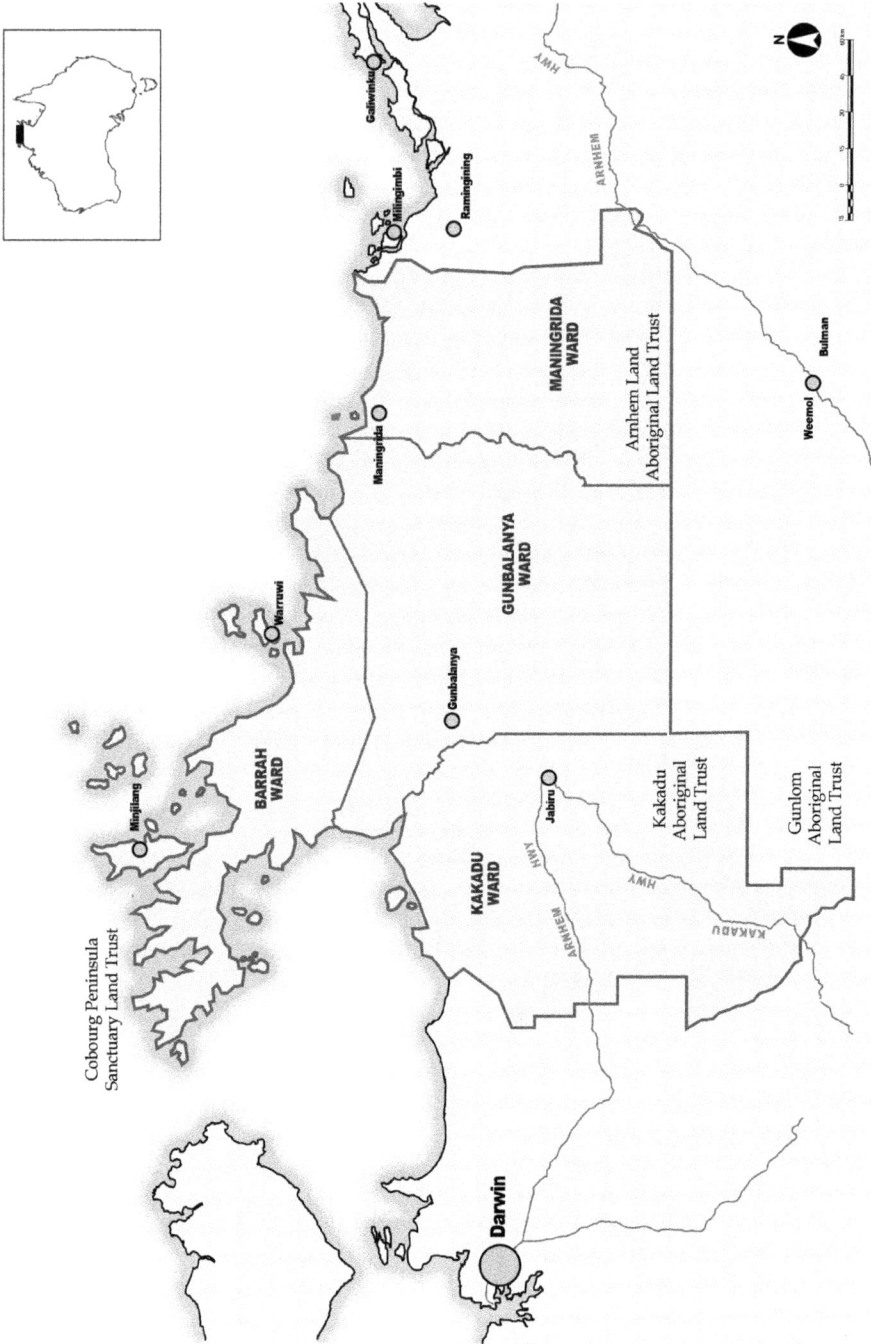

Fig. 4.3 The required region for the West Arnhem Shire under the New Local Government policy

This larger shire involved an even more complex set of organisational and governance transitions. Like Kunbarllanjnja, the Maningrida Community Council is a local government under the *Local Government Act 1978* (NT), and so would have to be entirely dissolved as a local government organisation and its relevant functions transferred to the new shire. Additional discussions would be needed with the Bawinanga Aboriginal Corporation, which provided services to numerous outstations, and with Jabiru town and its Council.

The mandatory inclusion of Jabiru confronted the WCARA Interim Council with a challenging issue—until then the proposed regional organisation included only Bininj communities and organisations, and covered inalienable Aboriginal freehold land. Jabiru's inclusion extended the region beyond the boundaries of Indigenous-owned land, which meant the Indigenous members of the Interim Council would have to accommodate a non-Indigenous town, its residents and elected representatives, and its different cultural values and priorities. In other words, a very different kind of regional local government was being proposed under the new NT policy.

Second, Interim Council members were extremely angry that their collective decision-making role had been usurped. They were told by the Department that they would henceforth be referred to as a 'Shire Transitional Committee' and have an identified consultation and advisory role. They would be required to provide their suggestions to the Advisory Board that serviced the NT Minister for Local Government, who would make all the final decisions about their organisational structure.

Decision-making power about the management, staffing, financial status and business plans of the new shire was abruptly reclaimed by government bureaucrats. A CEO was hired for them through a DLGHS process in which the new Transitional Committee had little involvement. A Transitional Shire Manager, who was an officer from the Department appointed by the Minister, became the legal face of the shire delegated to act as its decision-making Council, until such time as members were elected.

One committee member summarised the impact of the changes in these terms:

> the NT Government is thinking ahead of us before we get to make our own decisions. It's running ahead of us. It's not even talking to us first about these things—so we are just talking about things that the government has already decided. We are already cooked—the cake has already been cooked by the government. We're not involved in making that cake; the government has made the decisions ahead of us (WCARA Interim Council Member).

Third, the Council was no longer seen by government to be 'representative' owing to its requirement that members from Maningrida and Jabiru should be included. A West Arnhem Shire Transitional Committee (WASTC) replaced the WCARA Interim Council, and a cap was put on the total membership by the Department. This meant that the number of representatives on the old Interim Council had to be cut down in order to include new members. Consequently, it was a smaller core of senior leaders from the Interim Council who moved across to the new committee.

Maningrida and Jabiru were initially unhappy to be told to enter into a regional process in which, until then, they had chosen not to participate. Not surprisingly, it took their representatives some time to familiarise themselves with the issues and decisions already made. Initially, they felt marginalised from what had become a very united team of representatives on the WCARA Interim Council.

From the point of view of the Interim Council members, they felt they were being told to start all over again, having to reconsider issues and decisions that they had already considered and made. They also realised that it would mean a considerable delay in the establishment of the new organisation.

Fourth, the culturally-based institutions that the WCARA Interim Council had designed, such as their constitution and preamble, were effectively thrown out. Also tossed aside was their solution for ward representation, which had sought to balance a Bininj nomination process for the single traditional-owner representative, alongside *Balanda* election procedures for three other representatives.

The overall effect was to relegate the Interim Council and its new Transitional Committee guise to a consultative, advisory role. The sense of disempowerment was felt keenly by all members:

> Those foundations [for the regional authority] were built four years ago, and then they just get knocked from under us by the government. The horse hobbles are still there on us. That government just like a stockman sitting on the fence, they put the hobbles on us to keep us tied down. We've been put in the paddock and we've eaten every bit of grass. When our hobbles get rusty and we look like we might get out and free to eat some new green grass, someone just comes in and puts a new set of hobbles on us (WCARA Interim Council member).

But what was extraordinary at this point was that the WCARA Interim Council members decided to continue to participate in the process. The fact that they did is testimony to the significant headway they had made in working together as a team, and the effort they had put into designing their own governance institutions and making consensus decisions. As a consequence of this, they had developed a strong commitment to each other and to a shared vision of a future regional forum through which they hoped to exercise greater self-governance. They had also developed a significant sense of trust in the two CDOs working with them, whom they felt would continue to provide them with frank and robust advice about the new policy demands of government.

In order to stay engaged in the radically reshaped process, the Indigenous participants had to use every opportunity to strategically and persistently reinsert their own governance priorities and goals. This has included grappling with a non-Indigenous culture of governance within their meetings and negotiating a space for the development and exercise of their own institutions and values.

Re-imagining Indigenous governance

The Bininj leaders involved in this regional governance process have used their traditional rules, values and system of social organisation to re-imagine their contemporary governance needs and solutions. An important driving force behind this has been the desire to create a regional organisation that will better reflect Bininj cultural values and institutions: 'We will have a council that respects and works with our culture'.

Some of this re-imagining has been highly formalised; some has been spontaneously informal. Meetings of the Interim Council (and then the WASTC) were an important catalyst for designing workable governance structures and institutions, and highlighted the differences between Bininj and government expectations and concepts.

The 'glue' (cf. Cornell and Kalt 2000) of Bininj governance lies in its institutions; that is, in its own 'rules of the game', the way things should be done. These give legitimacy to practice, and include laws, kinship and marriage systems, behavioural and gender norms, family values, religious beliefs and moral system, principles of land ownership, ceremony and ritual, and so on (see Kesteven and Smith 1984; Smith 2007). Not surprisingly then, the creation and transformation of governance institutions became a focus for innovation, containment and contestation by Bininj and government bureaucrats alike.

Constructing the region

The tools and concepts employed by the state to construct the new local government 'region' diverged greatly from those of Bininj. The NT Government emphasised the need for an 'efficient' scale of population for local government and to have boundaries precisely mapped:

> Half of the existing Territory councils are too small to provide and pay for the services that communities should expect to receive. Many of the councils are too small to attract experienced senior staff to run the services ... The shires will be big enough to negotiate with the Territory and Federal Governments on behalf of their communities (McAdam 2007).

Rather than employing the cultural-community blocs recommended by the WCARA Interim Council, voters were to be congregated by requiring them to officially register against their place of residence as the basis for voting in particular wards. In the early phase of the BSRSF policy framework, Bininj leaders employed a 'cultural geography' in their construction of the new region. Their primary criteria for creating the external regional boundary was about 'who' should be included and excluded from the new region, on the basis of dense layers of traditional land-owning relationships and networks. In other words, the region and its boundary was, first and foremost, a negotiated interpretation by leaders of who legitimately constitutes the regional Bininj 'self'.

In the second policy phase of regionalisation, this internal reading of the cultural boundaries of relatedness was forced to expand as a result of the above-mentioned mandatory inclusion of the Maningrida and Jabiru communities—neither of whom was initially included under Bininj criteria for the proposed region.

To this extent, the new, larger shire boundary has been an evolving compromise between Bininj concepts of what is the culturally relevant geography for the region, and the NT Government's consideration of what constitutes the best scale to secure its goal of greater cost and service delivery efficiency. In this instance, the legal and policy powers of the state enforced a major constraint on the re-imagined Bininj regional 'self'.

Nevertheless, throughout the process, Bininj leaders continued to generate a correlation between their core cultural metaphor of 'one family' and the proposed region:

> We need to stick together and look after each other ... It [the committee and proposed regional shire] has brought families together in the region ... We have had to work hard and we have become one big family (WCARA Interim Council members).

The overarching Bininj metaphor of 'one family' denotes a core institution that underlies individual and kin-group identity. It has been used frequently by members of both the WCARA and WASTC to invoke the values of mutual support and reciprocity, loyalty, and shared work efforts that are seen to lie at the heart of Indigenous 'family' life. Its use in the regional context seeks to imbue the proposed shire and its governance arrangements with the cultural legitimacy derived from the concept of 'family'.

This metaphor also has a domesticating power. The leaders on the earlier WCARA Interim Council have continued to invoke it during WASTC meetings in order to extend the 'ties that bind' to the newly included communities of Maningrida and Jabiru. Their purpose has been to ease the transition of the new committee members from the status of 'strangers' or 'outsiders' to being part of the close family that is forming a new 'collective self' for regional local government.

At every point of engagement in this convoluted and complicated process, the Bininj leaders have denied the ordering power of the NT Government's approach to creating boundaries for the region and its composite wards. During a discussion about the newly imposed external boundaries, one leader succinctly expressed an opinion that was common within the earlier Interim Council:

> In the *Balanda* word that will be a boundary there. But it's just a service line. It's just a line for the government. You see this line? It's not there. We're not going to trip over that boundary line when we're walking out on our country. This line is local government, it's not for traditional owners' land—we know our own land, every little place; long time, from start' (WASTC member).

The Bininj members of the Council/Committee are themselves traditional owners and have consistently argued that regionalised local government should not impinge on their cultural and legal rights under the ALRA. From the start, they have been keen to ensure their decisions do not undermine those primary rights, or exacerbate tensions over land ownership. For that reason, they initially decided there should be no mapped internal boundaries for the proposed electoral wards. These were to be kept deliberately *invisible* so that they could continue to be managed under the Bininj system of knowledge and control of country. However, the current policy requires that all shire internal ward and external regional boundaries be mapped and made visible.

In the Bininj-government interplay that continues over the issue of boundaries, the Bininj representatives continue to reinforce the importance of locally relevant cultural geographies as the foundation for their governance solutions. They strategically use this ordering mode to resist the externally imposed institutions of government, which work to re-group and re-order Bininj people into neatly bounded geographies:

> We said to people [out in communities] don't be worried about that line out there. That's a service line. They think it will cut them off from everyone else. But it's not a line for Bininj land. Your right cannot be disturbed by that idea (WCARA Interim Council member).

Seeing the pattern of Indigenous governance

The pattern of traditional Bininj governance, visually reproduced in much of their art, ceremony and ritual can be understood as a 'nodal network'. This type of network is formed by the interconnectedness and interdependence of essentially autonomous units and actors (each constituting 'nodes'), where the constituent linkages can facilitate or inhibit the functioning of the overall system.

A 'governance network' then refers to the interconnected distribution and exercise of a group's decision making and leadership to achieve their collective goals.

Bininj governance networks in West Arnhem Land comprise clan groups, inter-related by complex webs of kinship, land-ownership identities, marriage systems, historical alliances and ceremonies (see Kesteven and Smith 1984; Smith 2007). In these networks there are 'nodes' or points of individual agency and decision making, where particular male and female leaders who have respect and influence are able to mobilise people and resources to create order and collectively get things done. In highly decentralised systems of social organisation like those in West Arnhem Land, governance nodes such as leaders and organisations enable decision making to coalesce and be implemented. In this system, nodal leaders constitute the circuitry of governing order and authority that enables things to be achieved over time.

Bininj networked governance in West Arnhem can be deciphered, although it is often invisible to outsiders. It has its own culture or world view—a way of thinking about the matters that need to be governed, and ways of reproducing the patterns of interconnectedness that underlie the networks needed for governance. It has a set of technologies, powers and processes for exerting influence and power, and for prompting action amongst people. It is able to marshal resources via nodal leaders and organisations. And it employs a set of institutions, or rules, which enable nodal leaders to legitimately activate governance networks.

The Bininj members of the WASTC are part of nodal leadership networks that stretch across West Arnhem and well beyond. They have striven to create a representative structure for the regional authority, and now the shire, that is based on their governance culture of nodal networks. Much of their effort and motivation has not been immediately intelligible to *Balanda* in the region, or to government officers. And when they have become intelligible, Bininj proposals are not always acceptable to *Balanda*, who have different ideas of what constitutes 'good', 'effective' and 'legitimate' governance.

The NT Government and its departmental officers insist that a democratic standard be applied to the future number and election of shire representatives. Representation, they assert, should properly be based on the total population of each constituent ward in the region: 'Under New Local Government, councils will be democratically elected by the people, just like everywhere else in Australia'.[12]

As one NT Government officer stated at a WASTC meeting:

---

[12] See DLGHS website, 'Governing', <http://www.nt.gov.au/localgovernment/new/ministers_update/governing> [accessed 5 May 2008].

The next complexity factor for us [government] is, this is a democracy and everyone should have a vote—one person, one vote. Another challenge is remoteness and the dispersed nature of the population, plus the cultural groupings of small communities. These can't be the basis for wards and representation. We don't want loose cultural groupings, but we want bigger wards so that we keep the total number of representatives to ten or twelve.

Bininj members of the committee see this interpretation of democracy as being fundamentally at odds with their own governance institutions. They feel it to be unfair and unequal. From their perspective, representatives are seen as:

people who have got picked by their communities and elders in their area. They didn't just come for nothing. It's each council and elders who picked those people to represent their people. When we first started off we wanted everyone to be equal (WASTC member).

The Bininj view of 'equal' is based on each main cultural-community bloc having an equal number of representatives for each ward, irrespective of the population or geographic size of the ward:

Our main issue is that it is 'all equal', so we don't upset people. We have to be very careful. Every person out there knows we are working together on this—we got a jury out there. When we go back to our community we have to behave properly and make our decisions properly so people in our communities can see us paying respect and behaving properly.

… We decided we wanted three reps for each ward because they are the right people; not on a population basis. Remember we talked about that [i.e. representation] three years ago, and we said each ward should get 'equal vote', 'equal number'; that's fair for everyone' (WASTC members).

There is disquiet about this view of equality amongst some *Balanda* CEOs on the WASTC who work for councils in the communities that have a large population. They too stress the democratic benchmark of 'one person, one vote'. But at several committee meetings about the issue, the Bininj members—including those from the communities with large populations—reconfirmed their strong preference for having an equal number of representatives for each ward. They also pointed out to government officers that the Bininj approach was in fact similar to that of the Australian Senate in its representative arrangements.

Bininj leaders continued to apply the same logic of 'all equal' to representation for the proposed shire; that is, each major community with its participating council and outstation organisation would have an equal number of representatives regardless of population size (see Fig. 4.4).

Fig. 4.4 The proposed representative structure for the West Arnhem Shire under the proposed New Local Government policy

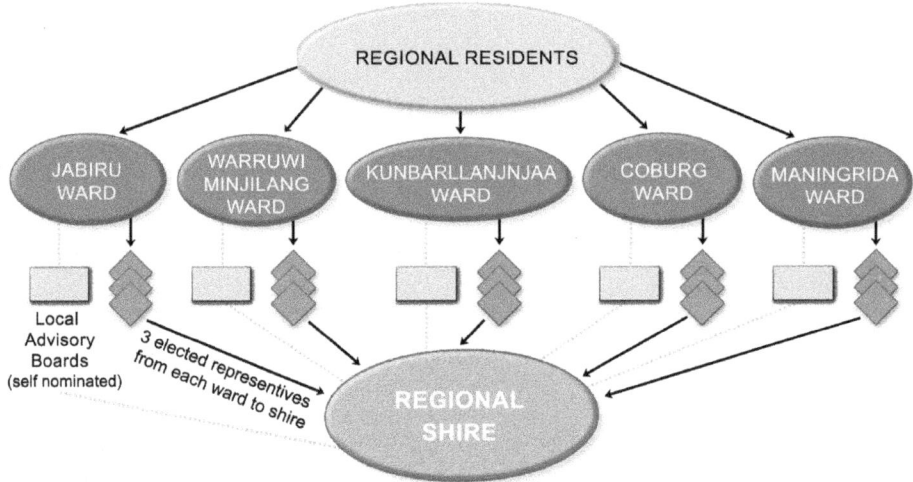

Negotiations about this are continuing between committee members and departmental officers. The Advisory Board is attempting to operate as a go-between for the WASTC, putting their views forward to the Minister and supporting the value of their cultural logic.

This is an important issue for committee members who are attempting to reconcile the two different cultures of governance operating in the process, at the same time as striving to arrive at a culturally legitimate solution that will gain the backing of their community members. Bininj members prefer to take major governance issues back to their communities for further consideration. This has meant considerable discussion and negotiation within the committee and the participating organisations.

Governing 'two-ways'

An early activity of the Bininj committee was to design a logo[13] for the WCARA. The logo is a visual map of the regional Bininj 'self' (see Fig. 4.5). It depicts two turtles—one saltwater, the other freshwater—to indicate the inclusion of people from the coastal and island communities, as well as the inland communities of West Arnhem. The turtles allude to the ancient interaction between two mythological creatures, and 'the two coming together' to resolve their differences. The logo also depicts Bininj and *Balanda* hands clasped together, to symbolise

---

[13] The logo for the WCARA was chosen from a regional design competition. The winning design was created by Mr Ahmat Brahim, an Indigenous man with traditional ties to the region, and whose father has been a member of both the WCARA Interim Council and the WASTC. The transitional committee later affirmed their choice of the logo for its new shire.

the two collaborating for the benefit of all residents of the region. This vision was expressed by one committee member as 'working two-ways'.

Fig. 4.5 The proposed logo of the West Arnhem Shire Transition Committee and the former regional authority

The WASTC readily adopted the logo as being a positive symbol of how Bininj and *Balanda* could work together as a shire. As one senior member of the committee explained:

> This is how we are working two ways. We are using our *Arrarrakpi* [Bininj/Indigenous] concept and using it with this *Balanda* concept.

The WCARA constitutional preamble drafted by the Interim Council also embedded this 'two-way' approach, stating that:

> This Preamble is grounded in the traditional Aboriginal law, language and systems of self-governance for the region. It brings this view to the implementation of local government administrative systems that provide service delivery to all peoples of our area.

The WASTC adopted the preamble, confirming their intention to continue to use Bininj traditional systems of culture and governance in order to:

> strengthen the legitimacy of the Regional Authority [shire], and use the [shire] to strengthen traditional systems of governance. Through this vision and commitment we seek to maintain observance and respect for traditional values, and to join the responsibilities and structures of traditional authority with those of local government to achieve a high quality of life and a wide range of opportunities and choices ... We are developing our own rules that include our culture. In our own culture

we have our own rules that are very strong and we are bringing this into the [regional local government].

The logo and preamble subsequently became important devices for positively accommodating Jabiru Town Council and its largely *Balanda* population. As one committee member noted: 'It's [the logo] a good one because the handshaking now takes in Jabiru as well. It includes *Balanda* as well'.

The principle of 'working two ways' to develop governance solutions for the new shire has, at its core, a Bininj process of innovation and active adaptation. A consistent benchmark has been the Bininj committee members' need to ensure that the process has internal cultural legitimacy.

This process was contested by government. For example, a component of the new policy was the NT Government's requirement that all shires adopt a single common constitution. This effectively meant that the WCARA preamble and constitution were no longer relevant. Over several meetings, however, the newly formed WASTC Council negotiated through the Advisory Board that the preamble could become part of the shire's business plans (which were being developed by departmental officers). They also began compiling a Governance Reference Manual of their draft policies and decisions to guide future elected shire representatives and managers. They subsequently gained departmental agreement to have the preamble and governance manual included as an official document in the shire's strategic development plan. These were significant breakthroughs.

Transforming institutions

Over the four-and-a-half years of their operation, a number of formal and informal governance institutions (rules) have been generated by the Interim Council and Transitional Committee. This 'rule innovation' often occurred in the course of their meetings. It was there that members attempted to create workable solutions to some of the challenging problems caused by the disjunctions that kept arising between the two cultures of governance.

The litmus test at meetings was that Bininj-generated rules needed not only to be seen as culturally legitimate, but to be immediately useful. If they were, then committee members adopted them quickly. For example, in the middle of one committee meeting when new members had arrived, the chairperson announced to all participants:

> I don't like to say people's name. Bininj way, I can't say that name. So when you move and second a resolution can you please say your name out loud yourself so you can have your name put down on the minutes.

The chairperson effectively resolved what might otherwise have been an awkward situation for himself by designing an impromptu procedural rule that enabled him to continue directing the passage of resolutions in the formal *Balanda* style, without having to forgo his observance of an important Bininj etiquette rule that restricted his public use of people's personal names. The new rule was immediately acted upon as everyone could see its practical benefits for themselves as well as for the chairperson.

At the beginning of another meeting, before the commencement of business, a committee member made an announcement:

> Before we start with that agenda I just want to say something about my cousin sister's boy over there [referring to a young man sitting across the table who had recently been chosen by his community council organisation as a representative on the committee]. Well, Bininj way, that boy can't look at me or talk to me—nothing. He shouldn't be sitting here in this room. I talked to his mother last night and we decided that for these meetings he can talk to me and he can speak up. He comes here, he's got to do his job. That means he might have to talk to me and I gotta listen to him talking about his idea. But Bininj way he would get into trouble if he does that. So, just for these meeting here, we making a new rule: he can talk and look at me. But only here, not for outside; that still Bininj way out there.

In response to this statement, the other committee members at the meeting (both Bininj and *Balanda*) made supportive comments and agreed to the new rule.

In this instance, a senior leader and his close relative had designed a new rule that had the hallmarks of the cognitive tool of compartmentalisation. This process enables people to organise things (ideas, events, relationships) into discrete units or categories, each of which has its own properties of boundedness and isolation, at the same time as having some form of limited or controlled relation with the other parts (see Spiro and Jehng 1991; Strauss and Quinn 1997). Cognitive compartmentalisation is a particularly useful tool in intercultural contexts. It means that seemingly contradictory ideas or behaviours can be observed and held, without either being undermined or elevated over the other.

In the example above, a new rule was created for a specific context, which addressed a widely recognised kin-based behaviour that required certain kinds of avoidance and deferential behaviour to be observed between two classes of relatives. Failure to observe the avoidance rule would incur family and public censure, and perhaps, retribution. The new rule enabled the WASTC members who stood in such a kin relationship to each other to effectively suspend the accepted customary rule of kin avoidance and so behave differently in the meeting. Outside the room, at breaks in the meeting, the norm of avoidance behaviour quietly reasserted itself.

By compartmentalising this 'meeting behaviour' under a new rule, the potentially negative consequences were not only ameliorated for the individuals concerned, the new behaviour was also disambiguated. That is, it was made collectively comprehensible to all the other members of the committee, and able to be assessed by them as being culturally legitimate owing to the fact that it was a derivative of the more fundamental customary norm. This became an accepted process of rule transformation at the meetings.

An important effect of this process of cognitive compartmentalisation is that the cultural authority of underlying customary institutions is buffered from the potentially negative impacts of contradictory new rules by those contradictions being contained and nullified. Compartmentalisation also enables the Bininj worldview of the continuity and inalienability of their laws to be maintained, at the same time as allowing condoned institutional innovation to occur.

Other examples of rule innovation have occurred at meetings in the more formal context of governance capacity development and training sessions. These sessions have been conducted with Bininj representatives from the very beginnings of the regional initiative, and have been provided by the same male and female team of CDOs from the DLGHS, with personal input from my governance research (see Evans, Appo and Smith 2006; Smith 2007).

The training sessions focused on a wide range of governance issues including governing roles and responsibilities, the concept of separation of powers, systems of representation, organisational models to support regionalisation, policies for codes of conduct and conflict of interest, meeting procedures, human resource management and employment contract conditions, communication with community residents, and so on.

In each session, the Bininj committee members discussed the non-Indigenous concepts and values, alongside their own. They raised a range of cultural issues that might potentially undermine the legitimacy and enforcement of new governance rules. They tested proposed rules against potential community and cultural scenarios, and revised them to enhance their workability and legitimacy.

Members often shared ideas about how they might collectively and individually enforce their governance policies and rules. Each session culminated in the committee drafting new governing institutions, for example, in the form of written policies, agreed procedures and resolutions. Through this process, the Bininj leaders on the committee steadily developed a growing confidence in their capacity to work together as a team, and to make and enforce collective decisions, policies and other rules.

In these situations, committee members have been creating shared meanings about their expected and actual behaviour, roles and responsibilities, which then provide the groundwork for forming new governing rules. The rules that work most effectively are those which appear to fit four fundamental criteria.

First, they give priority to people's pre-existing cultural knowledge, norms, systems of authority, and experiences. Second, they have been designed collectively and in a practical governance context. Third, they can be put to immediate practical use; and fourth, they can continue to be adapted to suit changing governance needs.

As Spiro and Jehng (1991: 163–205) have noted, this calls for considerable cognitive flexibility at both an intra- and inter-personal level. It suggests that a Bininj culture of governance is created and maintained through interaction and practice. This enables nodal leaders to act as instigators of new and old meanings, and to mobilise consensus and action around those. That is, nodal leaders are able to tailor concepts and social value to create new institutions in ways that have legitimacy in the eyes of the rest of the network. Importantly though, Bininj innovation and practice are firmly located within an intercultural frame. Legitimacy and effectiveness are judged and shaped as much by the concepts and institutions of the state as those of Bininj people.

Conversely, when governance institutions are imposed from the outside and have no grounding in the pre-existing meanings and experience of Bininj culture, those rules have a weak hold on people's values and behaviour. Such externally generated rules cannot be easily compartmentalised and so can undermine existing cultural institutions of governance. They also tend to have less cognitive flexibility and therefore cannot easily be customised or reassembled by Bininj to meet changed circumstances.

Conclusion

In the second phase of its policy reform agenda, the NT Government sought to reassert its own culture of governance in an attempt to contain, mould and rename Indigenous systems of governance and their attendant institutions, and in an effort to hasten the process of regionalisation. In the course of working to achieve their goal of a strong regional organisation, Bininj community organisations and their elected leaders have attempted to design elements of a new 'culture of governance'. To do this, they have used formal and informal techniques and tools to create innovative governance institutions and structures, and imbue them with legitimacy and practical capability.

At its heart, the intercultural contest occurring within the West Arnhem initiative is over power and authority itself:

> They don't trust us to make our own decisions. There has been a lot of terminology that has been used in the history of this shire, and that term is democracy. Can you define what democracy is for us? We keep hearing about it, but we don't get to do it. We don't get to make our decisions about these things.

... I don't see any democracy—you just get told what to do: lump it, or do it ... What kind of message do we take to our people? Do we just tell them that in two years down the track we will have the power *maybe*; that sometime in the future we will get to make the decisions? Poor bugger blackfella that's what we are (WASTC members).

Committee members overwhelmingly see this intercultural contestation as more than just a struggle for regionalised local government. It is a process by which they hope to secure greater self-governance and control over the longer term. It remains to be seen whether regionalised local government delivers on its promises and expectations in West Arnhem. In the meantime, there is much that can be learned from the process to date.

The new NT Government policy framework states that its:

intention in seeking [its latest] fundamental reform of local government is to create certainty and stability through strong regional local governments that will have a similar capacity to that of the municipal councils ... The need is for orderly transitional and implementation arrangements (McAdam 2006).

But policy implementation has been anything but orderly. This is more than simply a consequence of the real world complexities of implementation catching up with the policy vision. The local government reform process has been wracked by problems created by the institutional failings of the government's own culture of governance, including differences of political opinion within the government and cabinet. Several NT Ministers have appeared reluctant to commit to the New Local Government policy, preferring the more flexible and culturally-inclusive approach laid out in the BSRSF.

In 2008, erratic government commitment to its own policy led to the NT Cabinet allowing non-Indigenous residents in the Litchfield region west of Darwin to opt out of regionalisation, while still requiring Indigenous residents in other regions of the NT to continue. As a consequence, some of the Indigenous communities who were told in early 2007 that they had to amalgamate into larger regions are now questioning why they should continue to be involved, or why they need to rush to meet a government-imposed deadline of the middle of 2008.[14]

Another recent Government decision to set an unusually low cap on the rate payments from pastoralists and the mining sector caused considerable disquiet

---

[14] A media release by LGANT (2008) noted that following this decision 'other councils are asking about the Government's processes and timetable for bringing in the reforms ... The Government's action in abandoning the Top End Shire proposal has set a precedent which is leaving councils with an emerging feeling of mistrust, of being led to believe one thing only to find it has changed dramatically to something else. They say they are losing faith in the Government's plan since the resignation of the previous Minister and since the change was introduced'.

within the bureaucracy and amongst several members of the WASTC.[15] In this highly charged environment, in mid 2008, the NT Minister responsible for oversighting the New Local Government policy and two senior departmental officers resigned. These officers were centrally involved in the West Arnhem Shire process.

The WASTC has not been surprised by the erratic governance of government, with all its policy reversals, changing implementation rules, and rapid turnover of bureaucratic faces at their meetings. The nub of contention for committee members has consistently focused on whether they actually have genuine decision making powers or not. This issue has especially arisen in the context of departmental reassertion of its decision making powers under the New Local Government policy. Consequently, implementation of that policy has been transformed and contained by its engagement with persistently asserted Indigenous governance institutions and agency.

Today, a growing number of Indigenous Australians are re-imagining what constitutes legitimate representation, decision making and leadership for their community governance arrangements. They are doing this at different societal scales and experimenting with models of governance. More specifically, the West Arnhem case study describes the ways in which principles of networked governance, nodal leadership, institutional innovation, and the cognitive tools of compartmentalisation are being used—both consciously and unconsciously—by Bininj people as interpretative instruments with which to design new governance arrangements that suit larger scale cultural geographies and retain cultural legitimacy.

Indigenous leaders play a pivotal role in mobilising deep-seated cultural understandings and imperatives in order to do this. When their transformations and experiments have resonated with their peer network of leaders and with their members (their 'jury'), and are judged to be 'fair' and 'equal' in Indigenous terms, then the new rules and structures have gained internal legitimacy. In this way, it has been the nodal leaders and their networks who have created an internal culture of governance, but it is the 'governed' (the 'jury' of community members) who have enabled new governance institutions to be implemented and sustained.

To be imbued with legitimacy, new governance institutions have to be tested and proven useful in the real world. If new rules and ways of looking at governance prove workable and legitimate—not only in the Indigenous arena, but in the wider intercultural arena of government policy—then they may receive endorsement within the policy implementation processes. But if

---

[15] LGANT estimates that the regional local governments in the NT will lose between $14–18 million in foregone rates from pastoral and mining industry as a result of the NT Government decision.

governance rules are imposed by external agents, or if they cannot be enforced without damaging fundamental Indigenous cultural values and ways of behaving, then those governed will inevitably deliver a verdict of failure and resist the application of the rules.

There are limits to the extent to which Indigenous Australians can currently transform and reassemble their institutions of governance. One set of constraining factors lies within Indigenous cultures of governance themselves. In West Arnhem Land, the Indigenous cultural drive towards localism and small-scale autonomy acts to impose social limits to political aggregation. When internal legitimacy and trust waver, the group to be governed tends to default back to small localised networks of close kin.

As a consequence, there can be significant difficulties in sustaining the horizontal social spread of new governance institutions. Indigenous networks—especially those of leaders—can facilitate this horizontal extension, in particular to the regional level. But transforming and deepening the legitimacy of Indigenous institutions to enable larger scale cultural geographies of governance requires time, facilitation and ongoing discussion in order to generate the wider consensus and support needed at the local levels.

New governance institutions that appear to preference the rights and interests of some groups or individuals over others, or which diminish valued group norms, do not generate sufficient cognitive or cultural traction to sustain their ordering power. Nor will they be sustained if they are unable to accommodate the layered and networked nature of power and decision making in Indigenous societies. Institution building that is based on the flexible reassembly of pre-existing Indigenous norms and ideas about what is 'equal', 'proper' and 'fair' appears to have greater effectiveness, both in meeting the challenge of new situations and in winning the support of the members of a community or organisation.

Another significant factor limiting Indigenous transformation of governance institutions arises from the external environment. Contemporary Indigenous governance initiatives are embedded in, not separate from, the institutions and power of the state and its culture of governance. In Australia, the state exercises overwhelming jurisdictional, institutional and financial powers through which it governs Indigenous culture and seeks to make Indigenous governance and people 'good' in western terms. As one member of the WASTC summarised this relative power imbalance:

> We Bininj have small power, only little backstop, just one backstop. Whitefellas, government, got plenty backstop behind them. They can come in any time and tell us what to do. They got the power.

But Indigenous processes of institutional transformation have the power to subvert, contain and modify the agenda of the state's own culture of governance and its efforts to govern Indigenous culture. This partly explains why, in Australian Indigenous affairs, policy implementation inevitably becomes disorderly and uncertain, leading to processes and outcomes on the ground that are often entirely different from those originally intended. This has been the case in West Arnhem Land.

Indigenous societies do not exist frozen in time as outdated 'cultural museums' (cf. Vanstone 2005). They have a long history of highly sophisticated innovations in their governing institutions. Furthermore, Indigenous leaders are often adept at connecting into non-Indigenous policy, bureaucratic nodes and political networks in order to achieve their own priorities. Astute government officers who pay attention to, and build relationships of trust into, those networks are themselves better able to act as intermediaries between the two cultures of governance, and to carry out community development work to support governance initiatives at local and regional levels.

From this it is clear that in order for contemporary institutional transformation of Indigenous governance to be effective and sustainable a number of conditions must be met. First and foremost, new governance institutions must be initiated by Indigenous people themselves on the basis of their informed consent. Second, the role of trusted and respected leaders is critical to institution building. Third, it must be undertaken in ways that resonate with community members' views of what is considered to be culturally legitimate and practically workable. Fourth, external coercion and the imposition of governance institutions have little traction in changing behaviour or building commitment and responsibility. And fifth, the facilitation and community development work of trusted government officers can make a major contribution to the implementation of enabling policies about governance.

But it appears that in these matters the state is a slow learner; or rather, in the case of West Arnhem regionalisation, its desire to retain decision making power and control appears to have inhibited its learning and outcomes. In some ways, the state has been less innovative than Bininj in designing effective institutions to carry out its governance objectives. In the end, the state seems to have failed to recognise the value and benefits of Bininj decision making, to see that Bininj leaders can resolve complex governance problems with innovative strategies, and that their solutions can actually facilitate government policy implementation. In the end, it may well be that regardless of the power differential the Bininj understanding of the state's governance culture is greater than the state's comprehension and control of Bininj governance culture.

Acknowledgements

I would like to take this opportunity to thank the management and staff of the DCDSCA and the restructured DLGHS, who provided me with collegial support and engaged in robust debate over many Indigenous policy and local government issues. I would especially like to thank Leanne Evans and Harry Appo, the two Community Development Officers, for the opportunity to work alongside them over five years. Their considerable professional knowledge and practical expertise in community development, built up over many years working with Indigenous leaders and community organisations, contributed enormously to my work and insights. Needless to say, the analysis presented here is my own and does not reflect the official position or opinions of DLGHS or any of its officers.

The opportunity to work with the Indigenous members of the WCARA Interim Council, and then the Indigenous and non-Indigenous members of the West Arnhem Land Transitional Committee, has been especially rewarding for me. I would like to thank them all for their ongoing friendship, support, openness, humour, and critical feedback on my ideas, and for the opportunity to participate in their challenging Bininj discussions.

In regard to this paper, I would like to thank the ICGP research team for their feedback during a workshop we specifically convened to discuss contributions to this edited volume. I also greatly appreciate the insightful comments from Janet Hunt, Sarah Holcombe, Stephanie Garling and Neil Westbury, as well as the very useful critique made by anonymous referees.

References

Ah Kit, J. The Hon. 2002. 'Ministerial statement', delivered as Minister assisting the NT Chief Minister on Indigenous Affairs, 7 March, Northern Territory Parliament, Darwin.

——2003. 'Building stronger regions—stronger futures', Speech as NT Minister for Community Development to the Local Government Association of the Northern Territory, 14 May, Alice Springs, available at <http://www.lgant.nt.gov.au/lgant/layout/set/print/content/download/248/749/file%20Speech.pdf?PHPSESSID=5a3aa6c5c2599f135f6271b1a4461c16> [accessed 15 May 2008].

Anderson, P. and Wild, R. 2007. *Ampe Akelyernemane Meke Mekarle—Little Children Are Sacred, Report of the Northern Territory Board of Inquiry into the Protection of Aboriginal Children from Sexual Abuse*, Report to the Northern Territory Government, Darwin, available at <http://www.nt.gov.au/dcm/inquirysaac/>

Behrendt, L., McCausland, R., Williams, G., Reilly, A. and McMillan, M. 2007. 'The promise of regional governance for Aboriginal and Torres Strait

Islander communities', *Ngiya: Talk the Law, Governance in Indigenous Communities*, 1: 126–66.

Coles, D. 2004. 'Representative Authorities: Towards representative structures and service delivery to meet the Northern Territory's needs', Unpublished paper presented to the *Sustainable Economic Growth for Regional Australia* conference, 6–8 September, Alice Springs.

Cornell, S. and Kalt, J. P. 2000. 'Where's the glue? Institutional and cultural foundations of American Indian economic development', *Journal of Socio-Economics*, 29 (5): 443–70.

de Alcantara, C. H. 1998. 'Uses and abuses of the concept of governance', *International Social Science Journal*, 155: 105–13.

Department of Local Government, Housing and Sport (DLGHS) 2007. 'Governing', New Local Government Fact Sheet, Northern Territory Government, available at <http://www.localgovernment.nt.gov.au/new/community_engagement/fact_sheet_updates> [accessed 15 May 2008].

Evans, L., Appo, H. and Smith, D. E. 2006. 'Community development practices and principles in the development of the West Central Arnhem Regional Authority', Unpublished paper, Department of Community Development, Sport and Cultural Affairs (DCDSCA), Northern Territory Government, Darwin.

Hirst, J. 2007. 'The myth of a new paternalism', *The Australian*, 26 June, available at <http://www.theaustralian.news.com.au/story/0,20867,21966257-7583,00.html> [accessed 24 April 2008].

Holcombe, S. 2005. 'Luritja management of the state', Oceania Monograph Special Issue, *Figuring the Intercultural in Aboriginal Australia*, M. Hinkson and B. Smith (eds), 75 (3): 222–33.

Howitt, R. and Suchet, S. 2004. 'Rethinking the building blocks: Management and Indigenous epistemologies', Paper presented in the 'Processes for Cross-Cultural Engagement—Remote Regions/Northern Development' session of the *Western Regional Science Association Meeting*, 26–29 February, Wailea Marriott Resort, Maui.

Kesteven, S. and Smith, D. E. 1984. Contemporary Land-Tenure in Western Arnhem Land: An Investigation of Traditional Ownership, Resource Development and Royalties, Report to the Australian Institute of Aboriginal Studies and the Northern Land Council, Darwin.

Kooiman, J. 2003. *Governing as Governance*, Sage Publications, London.

Local Government Association of the Northern Territory (LGANT) 2003. 'Submission to the Standing Committee on Legal and Constitutional Affairs into an Examination of Structural Relationships in Indigenous

Affairs and Indigenous Governance within the Northern Territory',
Darwin.

——2008. 'Storm front brewing for local government reform', Media Release,
20 February, available at <http://www.lgant.nt.gov.au/lgant/content/
view/full/1930>.

McAdam, E. The Hon. 2006. 'Minister's Speech' as Minister for Local
Government, *Local Government Association of the Northern Territory
(LGANT) Conference*, 11 October, Alice Springs, available at
<http://www.localgovernment.nt.gov.au/new/minister/ministers_speech>
[accessed 15 May 2008].

——2007. 'New Local Government', Message from the Minister, DLGHS
brochure, Northern Territory Government, available at
<http://www.localgovernment.nt.gov.au/__data/assets/pdf_file/0005/9698/
Local_Govt_Brochure_web.pdf> [accessed 5 May 2008].

Moran, M. 2002. 'The devolution of Indigenous local government authority in
Queensland: Opportunities for statutory planning', *Australian Planner*,
39 (2): 72–82.

Morphy, F. (ed.) 2007. *Agency, Contingency and Census Process: Observations of
the 2006 Indigenous Enumeration Strategy in Remote Aboriginal Australia*,
CAEPR Research Monograph No. 28, CAEPR, ANU E Press, ANU,
Canberra.

Plumptre, T. and Graham, J. 1999. *Governance and Good Governance: International
and Aboriginal Perspectives*, Institute On Governance, Canada.

Sanders, W. 2003. 'Participation and representation in the 2002 ATSIC elections',
CAEPR Discussion Paper No. 252, CAEPR, ANU, Canberra.

——2004. 'Thinking about Indigenous community governance', *CAEPR
Discussion Paper No. 262*, CAEPR, ANU, Canberra.

Scott, J. 1988. *Seeing Like a State–How Certain Schemes to Improve the Human
Condition Have Failed*, Yale University Press, New Haven.

Smith, D. E. 1992. 'The cultural appropriateness of existing survey questions
and concepts', in J. C. Altman (ed.), *A National Survey of Indigenous
Australians: Options and Implications*, CAEPR Research Monograph No.
3, CAEPR, ANU, Canberra.

——1995. 'Representative politics and the new wave of native title organisations',
in J. Finlayson and D. E. Smith (eds), *Native Title: Emerging Issues for
Research, Policy and Practice*, CAEPR Research Monograph No. 10,
CAEPR, ANU, Canberra.

——1996. 'From cultural diversity to regionalism: The political culture of difference in ATSIC', in P. Sullivan (ed.), *Shooting the Banker: Essays on ATSIC and Self determination*, North Australia Research Unit, ANU, Darwin.

——2007. 'Networked governance: Issues of process, policy and power in a West Arnhem Land regional initiative', *Ngiya: Talk the Law, Governance in Indigenous Communities*, 1: 24–52.

Spiro, R. J. and Jehng, J. 1990. 'Cognitive flexibility and hypertext: Theory and technology for the non-linear and multidimensional traversal of complex subject matter', in D. Nix and R. Spiro (eds), *Cognition, Education, and Multimedia*, Erlbaum Press, Hillsdale, New Jersey.

Strauss, C. and Quinn, N. 1997. *A Cognitive Theory of Cultural Meaning*, Cambridge University Press, Cambridge.

Sutton, P. 1995. 'Atomism versus collectivism: The problem of group definition in native title cases', in J. Fingleton and J. Finlayson (eds), *Anthropology in the Native Title Era*, Proceedings of a workshop conducted by the Australian Anthropology Society and the Native Title Research Unit of AIATSIS, 14–15 February, Canberra.

Tapsell, T. 2003. 'Learning from local government reform: The lessons from other Australian jurisdictions', Unpublished paper presented to the *Building Effective Indigenous Governance Conference*, 4–7 November, Jabiru, NT, available at <http://www.nt.gov.au/cdsca/indigenous_conference/web/html/papers.html> [accessed 15 May 2008].

Tylor, E. 1894. 'On Tasmanians as representatives of Palaeolithic man', *The Journal of the Anthropological Institute of Great Britain and Ireland*, 23: 141–52.

Vanstone, A. The Hon. 2005. 'Beyond conspicuous compassion: Indigenous Australians deserve more than good intentions', Address as Minister for Immigration and Multicultural and Indigenous Affairs to the Australia and New Zealand School of Government, 7 December, ANU, Canberra, available at <http://epress.anu.edu.au/anzsog/policy/mobile_devices/ch03.html> [accessed 15 May 2008].

5. Whose governance, for whose good? The Laynhapuy Homelands Association and the neo-assimilationist turn in Indigenous policy

Frances Morphy

> Originally, I set out to understand why the state has always seemed to be the enemy of 'people who move around' … Efforts to permanently settle these mobile peoples … seemed to be a perennial state project—perennial, in part, because it so seldom succeeded (Scott 1998:1).

Introduction

The Laynhapuy Homelands Association Incorporated (Laynha for short) is an Indigenous organisation that was incorporated under the Northern Territory's (NT) *Associations Incorporation Act 1963* in 1984.[1] Its headquarters are at Yirrkala in northeast Arnhem Land, from where it acts as the resource centre for a group of nearly 20 surrounding outstations or homeland settlements across a region of some 6500km[2] in extent.[2] Yirrkala and the Laynha homelands are in the most easterly area of the Yolngu-speaking bloc (see Fig. 5.1), where varieties of Yolngu-matha are still the first languages of close to 100 per cent of the Aboriginal population.[3] The 2006 Census recorded just under 6300 Indigenous people in

---

[1] This Act was superceded in 2004 by a new *Associations Act* (NT). Laynha is now incorporated under the new Act.

[2] The terms 'outstation' and 'homeland', which are interchangeable in this context, are both problematic for different reasons. 'Outstation' carries the connotation that such places are peripheral to neighbouring larger settlements, which does not reflect the perspective of their inhabitants. 'Homeland' has become problematic because of a recent book (Hughes 2007) that deliberately conflates the meaning of this term in the Australian context with its meaning in the South African context, to support the spurious argument that Australian 'separatism' (to use the author's terminology) is analogous to the former apartheid regime in South Africa. The area given is the estimated extent of the Laynhapuy Indigenous Protected Area, the boundaries of which are not precisely coterminous with those of the Laynha service area (see Fig. 5.2).

[3] Yolngu is the term for (Aboriginal) person in the majority of Yolngu-matha dialects. Since the 1970s, it has become the most commonly used term to refer to the Yolngu-speaking peoples as a whole, but did not originally have that meaning. In the earlier anthropological literature the most well known alternatives are Murngin (Warner 1958), Wulamba (Berndt 1951, 1952, 1962) and Miwuyt (Shapiro 1981). The Yolngu-speaking people of northeast Arnhem Land are one of the most intensively studied Aboriginal societies in Australia. Roughly in chronological order according to when the authors undertook their fieldwork, major studies include: Warner (1958), Thomson (1949, 2006), Berndt (1951, 1952, 1962), Shapiro (1981), Peterson (1986), Williams (1986, 1987), Reid (1983), H. Morphy (1984, 1991, 2007), Keen (1994, 2003) and Macgowan (2007). The complex, asymmetrical Yolngu kinship system was the subject of the 'Murngin controversy' that occupied much space in anthropological journals in the 1960s (see Barnes 1967; Maddock 1970).

discrete Indigenous communities in the Yolngu region of northeast Arnhem Land, and Laynha itself services a fluctuating population of between 600 and 800 people. The majority of the Laynha homeland settlements are on or near the coast. Inland, they tend to be near large rivers. They vary from large, permanently occupied settlements of well over 100 people to those that are only intermittently occupied and/or have small populations (fewer than 20 people). Several are inaccessible by road during the wet season, and all are inaccessible at the height of a 'big' wet. The most distant homelands are about three hours' drive from Yirrkala (during the dry). They mostly have all-year airstrips, although one or two do not.

Over the years since its incorporation, Laynha has become increasingly dependent on government—largely Commonwealth Government—grant funding. In 2006, some 87 per cent of its income was derived from government grants and one-quarter of its income from the Community Development Employment Projects (CDEP) program alone (including CDEP wages and associated costs) (Tallegalla Consultants 2006). Grant funding fuels its core service delivery functions of housing (building and maintenance), infrastructure and health, and its large CDEP program of around 300 participants. The Yirralka Rangers program, with over 40 rangers employed on CDEP wages, is also part of the organisation. It operates in the Laynhapuy Indigenous Protected Area (IPA) which was officially established in 2006 after several years of preparatory planning (Fig. 5.2). Until kava importation was summarily banned in June 2007 by government fiat, Laynha's major source of discretionary income was kava wholesaling and distribution.[4] It also derived some income from civil works contracts such as road grading undertaken by its operations department, and from a small proportion of the royalty equivalents from the Alcan (now Rio Tinto) bauxite mining operation on the Gove Peninsula near Yirrkala. The separately incorporated air service, Layhna Air (or more formally Balamumu Mungurru Aviation Pty Ltd), runs a break-even charter service between Gove airport and the Laynha homelands.

---

[4] The term 'discretionary' is applied here to income derived from other than government grant funding. This is the only portion of the organisation's funds that it is at liberty to spend or distribute entirely according to its members' priorities.

Fig. 5.1 The Yolngu region

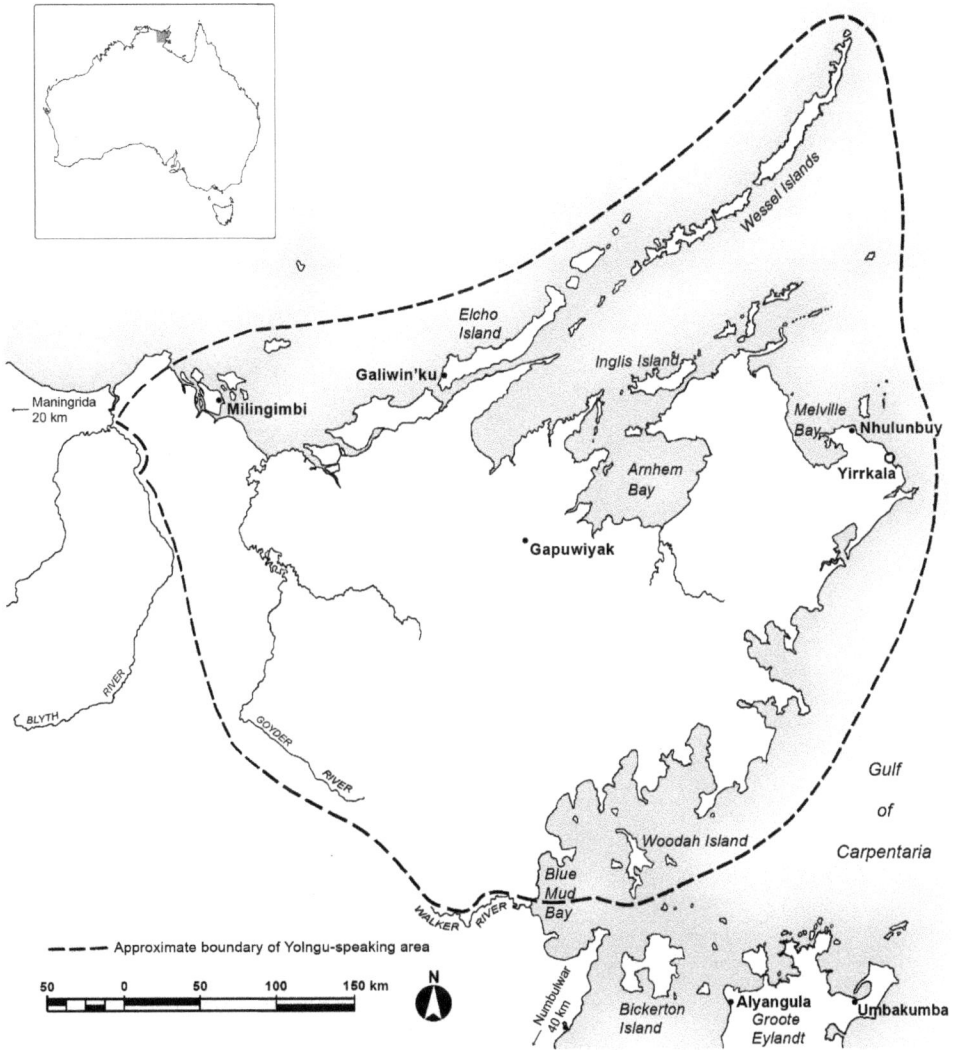

Fig. 5.2 The Laynhapuy Homelands Association homelands and the Laynhapuy Indigenous Protected Area

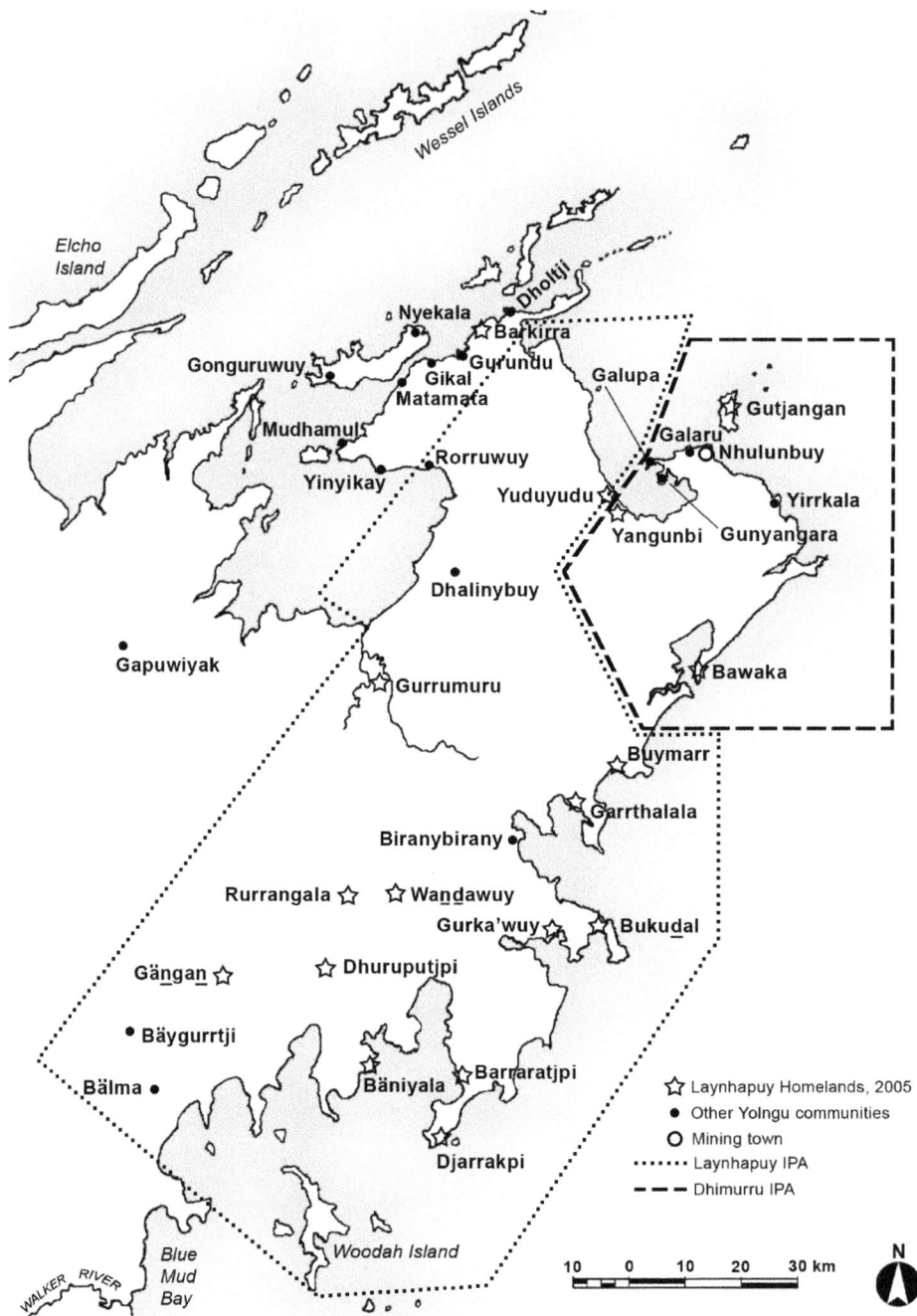

Wessel Islands

Elcho Island

Nyekala
Dholtji
Barkirra
Gonguruwuy
Gurrundu
Gikal
Matamata
Galupa
Gutjangan
Mudhamul
Galaru
Nhulunbuy
Rorruwuy
Yinyikay
Yuduyudu
Yirrkala
Yangunbi
Gunyangara

Dhalinybuy

Gapuwiyak
Gurrumuru

Buymarr

Garrthalala

Biranybirany

Rurrangala
Wandawuy
Gurka'wuy
Bukudal

Gängan
Dhuruputjpi

Bäygurrtji

Bälma
Bäniyala
Barraratjpi

Djarrakpi

☆ Laynhapuy Homelands, 2005
● Other Yolngu communities
○ Mining town
········· Laynhapuy IPA
━ ━ ━ Dhimurru IPA

WALKER RIVER
Blue Mud Bay
Woodah Island

10 0 10 20 30 km

N

But Laynha did not start out that way. Its origins were in the Yolngu homelands movement of the 1970s, and it is necessary to understand these origins in order to understand certain characteristics of the contemporary organisation. The title of this chapter alludes to its major structuring theme: who 'owns' the organisation—its Yolngu members or its government paymasters? It will be argued that until recently it was not necessary for Yolngu to confront this question directly, and this had certain consequences for the way in which the governance of the organisation developed over the years.

There is currently abroad a mythical but influential view (epitomised in Hughes 2007) of 'homelands' people as passive victims of the misguided and failed policies of past governments. It is arguably true that Yolngu and other Indigenous Australians have been victimised through state neglect, but this does not automatically make them victims in any simple way. On the contrary, the Yolngu of the Laynha homelands have been able to maintain and elaborate a locally distinct domain of action and value precisely because the state's gaze was intermittent and largely directed elsewhere. Among those values are ones relating to governance—values that Yolngu bring with them into the organisation as members of its board and its staff.

A colonial history?

To understand the governance of Laynha it is necessary first to understand that the Yolngu and the encapsulating settler society have very different views of the relationship between the Yolngu and the state. The state views Yolngu unambiguously as 'citizens', albeit ones who have a unique historical relationship to the state. They are 'Aborigines'—descendants of the colonised original inhabitants of the continent. Colonisation, in the settler state view, is a fait accompli—Australia is a post-colonial, post-enlightenment liberal democracy, in which all citizens have both responsibilities and rights. How these rights and responsibilities are actively construed varies according to the political ideology currently prevailing in government circles, but the essential elements of the framework for governance are a given. The state view will be discussed in more detail below. It is necessary first to review, briefly, the local version of the colonial encounter and its impact on the Yolngu domain, as a background to elucidating the Yolngu view.

The incursion of the pastoral frontier[5]

The pastoral frontier, pushing from the south and west, ground to a halt at Florida Station on the southwestern fringes of the Yolngu region in 1885 (Berndt and Berndt 1954: 98–9). In the area around that station, Yolngu groups suffered depopulation in the 1890s, but the rest of the Yolngu region was substantially

---

[5] This summary draws substantially on the account of contact history found in H. Morphy (2003).

unaffected. There were sporadic incursions further into Yolngu country by prospecting expeditions (ibid. 93). During this period, Yolngu gained the reputation of being dangerous and unpredictable 'wild blacks' (Morphy and Morphy 1984). In the early 1900s, according to Yolngu oral history that is backed up in some cases by written accounts, a series of punitive expeditions were mounted into Yolngu territory. From the Yolngu perspective these expeditions were arbitrary acts of violence perpetrated by hostile invaders.

It was not until the 1930s that three interrelated events precipitated the 'pacification' of the Yolngu region (Berndt and Berndt 1954; Dewar 1992; Egan 1996). These were the killing of some Japanese pearlers at Caledon Bay in 1932, and of two white men, Fagan and Traynor, in 1933 in the vicinity of Woodah Island, and finally the spearing of Constable McColl on Woodah Island.[6] In Yolngu oral history, all these killings happened as a result of the behaviour of the victims.

The reaction in the southern States at first was to send in a punitive expedition to avenge the deaths and 'teach the wild blacks a lesson'. Wiser council prevailed, however; the missionaries who were by now established on the fringes of Yolngu territory to the south and west and on Groote Eylandt, offered to intercede, and so too did the anthropologist Donald Thomson.[7]

'Mission times'

Methodist missions were established in the Yolngu area during the 1920s at Milingimbi, and then later in the 30s and 40s at Yirrkala and Elcho Island (Galiwin'ku). The Yolngu did not perceive this as an act of colonisation. Thomson reported to the Commonwealth Government in 1937 that Aborigines in Arnhem Land 'believe they are still living under their own laws, and that they have no reason to recognise a new regime has taken over their affairs' (cited in Attwood 2003: 116). And Williams (1987: 20) comments that '[f]rom a Yolngu perspective it was Mawalan, as head of the land-owning Rirratjingu clan, who granted permission to Chaseling, as agent of the "mission" to establish the station at Yirrkala [in 1935]'. The missionaries were few in number and came with peaceful intent, and early superintendents, such as Wilbur Chaseling at Yirrkala, showed respect for Yolngu culture and took a syncretic attitude to the introduction of Christianity that did not seek to eradicate the Yolngu belief system.[8]

---

[6] McColl was a member of the police expedition sent into the area from Roper Bar to investigate the killing of the Japanese.

[7] Thomson never produced a major monograph on his fieldwork among the Yolngu, and his work did not have the impact that it merited within his lifetime. See H. Morphy (2002), and Nicolas Peterson's compilation of his most significant writings (Thomson 2006). The latter, the second edition of the work, contains many of Thomson's superb photographs of Yolngu life on country in the mid 1930s.

[8] The superb Yirrkala Church Panels, that once stood on either side of the altar in the church at Yirrkala and are now housed at Buku-Larrnggay Mulka, are a testament to the attitudes of the missionaries in this period. See Kleinert and Neale (2000: plates 31 and 32, opposite p. 70).

The missionaries did seek to centralise the population in the mission settlements through the provision of rations and schooling for the children (the latter was valued by Yolngu from the outset), but there was no coercion or forced removal of people from their lands. Not all Yolngu went into the missions to live; some groups stayed out on their clan estates, coming into the mission from time to time for supplies or medical attention. Others lived at the missions most of the time, but returned regularly to their country, particularly during school holidays. Many members of the southern clans of the Blue Mud Bay area went south to Numbulwar (then Rose River) or to Umbakumba on Groote Eylandt rather than north to Yirrkala.

From the perspective of the senior Yolngu generations of today, this period, which lasted until the early 1960s, was something of a Golden Age. Interaction with outsiders, mediated through the missionaries, was sporadic and usually peaceful, and while sedenterisation on missions created some strains and tensions the Yolngu social fabric was not shattered, and the Yolngu were not dispossessed and alienated from their country.

The most senior living generation of today's Yolngu leaders spent their formative years in this era. Many of them, through the efforts of the missionaries, received a good western-style education; several went south or to Brisbane for further education. The Yolngu of this generation have never fully acceded to the proposition that their sovereignty over their clan estates has been eclipsed by the process of colonisation; they see themselves as encapsulated, but not colonised, as living in 'two worlds' (F. Morphy 2007b).

Mining and land rights

In the late 1950s, Yolngu became aware of prospecting activity on the Gove Peninsula, and discovered shortly afterwards that mining leases had been taken out over considerable areas of Yolngu land. There had been no consultation with Yolngu. Their response, in 1963, was to send a petition framed in bark to the Federal Parliament, demanding, among other things, the recognition of their rights in land and sea. It is significant that from the very beginning of the struggle against the coming of the mine the local clans whose land was affected received active support from the other Yolngu of the region.

The events that followed are well known and well documented, and will not be detailed here (see Attwood 2003; Wells 1982). The Yolngu were ultimately unsuccessful in their efforts to block the development of the mine and the building of the mining town of Nhulunbuy. Yolngu leaders asked for Nhulunbuy to be a dry area, foreseeing all too clearly what the effects of the introduction of alcohol would be, but in this too they were unsuccessful. Nevertheless, the Yolngu struggle to protect their rights was ultimately a significant factor in the advent of land rights and the passing of the *Aboriginal Land Rights (Northern Territory) Act (1976* (Cth) (ALRA). The irony is not lost on the Yolngu.

The homelands movement and the origins of Laynha

The move out of Yirrkala and back to permanent settlements on the homelands was precipitated by the social trauma that followed the building of the mining town and the introduction of alcohol to the area. But it was also motivated by a positive desire to protect clan estates from further incursion, to demonstrate to outsiders that northeast Arnhem Land was not an uninhabited 'wilderness'. In the beginning, people received very little support—opinion among local missionaries, who had been very supportive in the struggle against the mine, was divided. With the logistic help of just a very few people, most notably the Fijian lay missionary Jonetani Rika, Yolngu groups began to go back to their country in 1971–72. At first they lived in bush shelters and had no reliable food supply apart from that obtained through hunting and gathering. Overland access was difficult—over a network of rough tracks that were impassable during the wet season—and there were very few vehicles. People cleared their airstrips by hand.[9]

This homelands movement was thus a Yolngu initiative (Morphy and Marika 2005: 1), and began before there was any official support from government for such movements. It predated the era of 'self-determination' ushered in by the first Whitlam Government, and it predated the ALRA. Subsequent policy settings certainly supported the movement both financially and logistically, but to suggest that it was a 'socialist experiment' perpetrated on Yolngu (see Hughes 2007) is a distortion of the historical record.

In the early 1970s, the Uniting Church ceded the administration of Yirrkala and its outstations to the Dhanbul Association—a Yolngu council that was incorporated under the NT's *Associations Incorporation Act 1963*. At first, the servicing of the homelands was part of Dhanbul's responsibility. As the homelands grew in number, the perception also grew among homelands people that their interests were regarded by Dhanbul as secondary to those of the clans who were the traditional owners of Yirrkala and the area covered by the mine. In 1984–85 Laynha was established as a separate association, also under the NT's *Associations Act*. The separate establishment of Marngarr, as the governing body of the settlement of Gunyangara (Ski Beach) on Gupa Gumatj clan land nearer to the mine's processing plant, soon followed.

---

[9] See Ian Dunlop's *Narritjin at Djarrakpi* (motion picture) 1980, Part 1, one of a series of films that he made for Film Australia's Yirrkala Film Project. Dunlop's Yirrkala series provides a unique documentary record of many aspects of homelands life from the beginning of the homelands movement in the 1970s through to the mid 1990s.

In many ways, what was happening was a dissolution or weakening of the alliances between the groups who had joined forces to fight the Gove case, and who had been gathered together under the polity of the mission. The splits that occurred reflect the spheres of interest created by missionisation and the coming of the mine, lying, as it were, over the top of pre-existing, intra-Yolngu nodes and networks of political interaction. In the case of Laynha, an additional impetus to separate incorporation came from the Blue Mud Bay clans' involvement in the homelands movement, since they had never been a significant part of the Yirrkala mission polity.

The young adults who followed their parents back home and did most of the hard labour in the early days are now the senior generation living on the homelands. For them the homelands are the bastions of Yolngu identity, where people have the power to filter the influences of the outside world. They recognise that they are now inextricably linked economically to the wider society, but they wish to have control over the nature and intensity of those links. Today, they see the need for economic development on the homelands to provide meaningful employment that will keep the younger generations from drifting to the bigger settlements and the influences of the mining town. They are also keen to see improvements in the health, housing and infrastructure of their communities and in the education of their children.

The Yolngu 'world'

In writing of the theorisation of relationships between Aboriginal people and the state, and of understanding continuity and change in that context, Merlan (1998: 180–1) contrasts three views. She argues that both Sahlins (1993) and Cowlishaw (1988) have a 'vision of indigenous cultural production as autonomous', the former framing change as an adaptive process and the latter as opposition or resistance. She characterises her own theoretical position in terms of the intercultural: 'the contemporary Australian scene … cannot be fundamentally understood in this way [in terms of autonomous production] … That scene is not one of autonomy, but of still unequal, intercultural production'.

The Yolngu themselves (as might be predicted from the previous section, and from their espousal of the 'two worlds' view) would favour the Sahlins view, with perhaps a dash of Cowlishaw, particularly in relation to their response to the incursion of the mine. Yet another analytic framework (H. Morphy 2007) posits the *relative* autonomy of systems of cultural production, each with its own properties and trajectory through time. This approach privileges neither 'adaptation' nor 'resistance' as modes of interaction with other systems, and allows such interactions to have effects on a system and on its trajectory without compromising its relative autonomy.

Such a model captures the Yolngu view and seems more relevant from an analytic point of view to the facts of the Yolngu case than a model that portrays everything as 'intercultural'. The relative lateness of the colonial incursion into northeast Arnhem Land, and its partial and predominantly peaceful nature, spared the Yolngu from the more devastating consequences of colonisation experienced by Aboriginal people in most other parts of the continent, including the area that is the focus of Merlan's analysis. It is possible to mount a cogent argument for the relative autonomy of the Yolngu system.

Where the Yolngu view and the analyst's view might diverge is in the analysis of the effects of interaction between the Yolngu system and that of the encapsulating settler state. The 'two worlds' view has been effectively unchallenged by the state until recently. In hindsight, however, it has proved to be a source of vulnerability as well as strength, for it has perhaps concealed from the Yolngu the extent to which their 'world' depends for its space to exist and follow its current trajectory upon institutions of the encapsulating state (Morphy and Morphy 2007). For more than a generation, two of the most important of these institutions—the fee simple status of Aboriginal land under ALRA and the CDEP program—had seemed permanent, and were taken-for-granted features of the social landscape. All this was to change between 2005 and 2007.

Rom and *gurrutu*: the foundations of Yolngu governance

The foundation of the Yolngu social system and system of governance is *gurrutu*—the complex networks of kinship that link individuals and groups to each other. Underlying *gurrutu*, and anchoring the human groups that are linked by *gurrutu* to their land and sea estates, is *rom*. Often translated as 'law', *rom* is a much more encompassing concept. It is nothing less than the Yolngu way of being, conceived as having been set down in the time of *wangarr* (creation) by beings who are still present in the landscape, and whose substance each Yolngu person shares through the conception spirit that enters their mother and gives life to the physical substance of the baby.

A person belongs to the *bäpurru* of their father. In one meaning of the term, *bäpurru* are the groups in which the ownership of land and sea estates is vested, and the meaning encompasses not just the living representatives of the group but also its spiritual essence located in the clan estate, the product of *wangarr* activity. Clan members are *wänga-watangu* ('place-belongs to' [people]; i.e. those to whom the place belongs, and who belong to the place) with respect to their clan's estates. In the anthropological literature, *bäpurru* are termed 'clans' (H. Morphy 1984, 1991, 2003; Williams 1986, 1987), 'patrifilial descent groups' (Keen 1994, 2003) or 'patri-groups' (Keen 2006), and Yolngu themselves often use the English word 'tribe' to describe them.[10] The Yolngu universe is divided into two exogamous patrimoieties called Dhuwa and Yirritja.[11] Each clan and its estates and creator *wangarr* beings belong either to one moiety or to the other. By definition then, clans are also exogamous.

In the Yolngu marriage system (see Fig. 5.3) a man marries his matrilateral cross cousin—his mother's mother's brother's daughter's daughter (MMBDD) (*galay*). A woman marries her patrilateral cross-cousin (*dhuway*). A man and his sister must therefore take spouses from different groups. The clans involved in the marriage of a man are: his mother's mother's clan (his *märi*), who bestow on him a mother-in-law (*mukul rumaru*) (his MMBD); his own clan; his mother's clan (his *ngändi*); and his wife's own clan (which may be the same clan as his own mother belongs to, but need not be). The marriage of the man's sister involves a different (but often overlapping) chain of linked clans.

Viewed over time, the Yolngu marriage system constructs long-term relationships of bestowal and marriage that link groups of both moieties. The relationship between a person and their mother's clan (of the opposite moiety) is some times referred to as *yothu-yindi* (child-mother). Just as a person is *waku* to his/her mother and her brother, so he/she stands in a *waku* relationship to his/her mother's (*ngändi*) clan. *Waku* have special responsibilities to their *ngändi* clan. In fulfilling these responsibilities they are termed *djunggayarr* (or *djunggayi*), often translated into English as 'manager' or 'caretaker' or sometimes 'policeman'. In essence, they have a duty of care to their mother's estate, and this involves helping—or sometimes ensuring that—the *ngändi* clan members look after their country properly, both in mundane and ceremonial contexts.

An equally significant relationship is constructed between two clans of the same moiety who stand in a relationship of *märi* (MM) and *gutharra* (DD) to one another, because over time the *märi* clan bestows mothers-in-law on members of the *gutharra* clan.[12] This structure is illustrated in Fig. 5.4. The *märi-gutharra* connection between two clans is central to the Yolngu system of governance.

---

[10] The differences in terminology reflect the authors' different conceptualisations of these groups. *Bäpurru* may also be used to refer to a set of clans linked ceremonially by the travels of particular *wangarr* beings, reflecting a Yolngu modelling of the social world that privileges connections over boundaries when considering the relationship between groups. Further discussion of this issue falls outside the scope of this chapter.

[11] A patrimoiety is one in which a person inherits their membership from their father. An exogamous group is one that does not allow marriage between its members.

[12] That is, a man bestows his daughter as mother-in-law, and therefore his daughter's daughter as wife, to his sister's daughter's son. A man calls both his mother's mother and her brother *märi*, and they call him (and his sisters) *gutharra*.

Fig. 5.3 Kin relations in the Yolngu marriage bestowal system

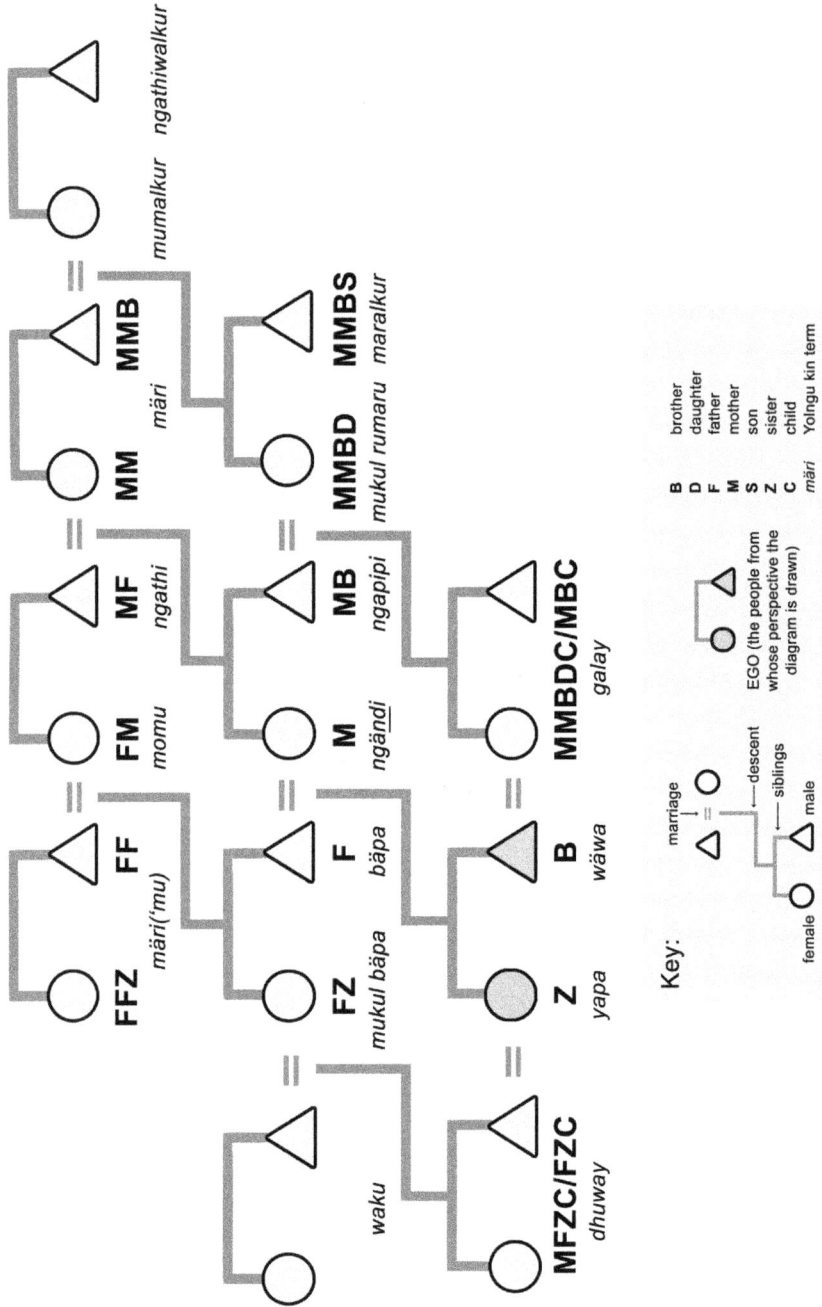

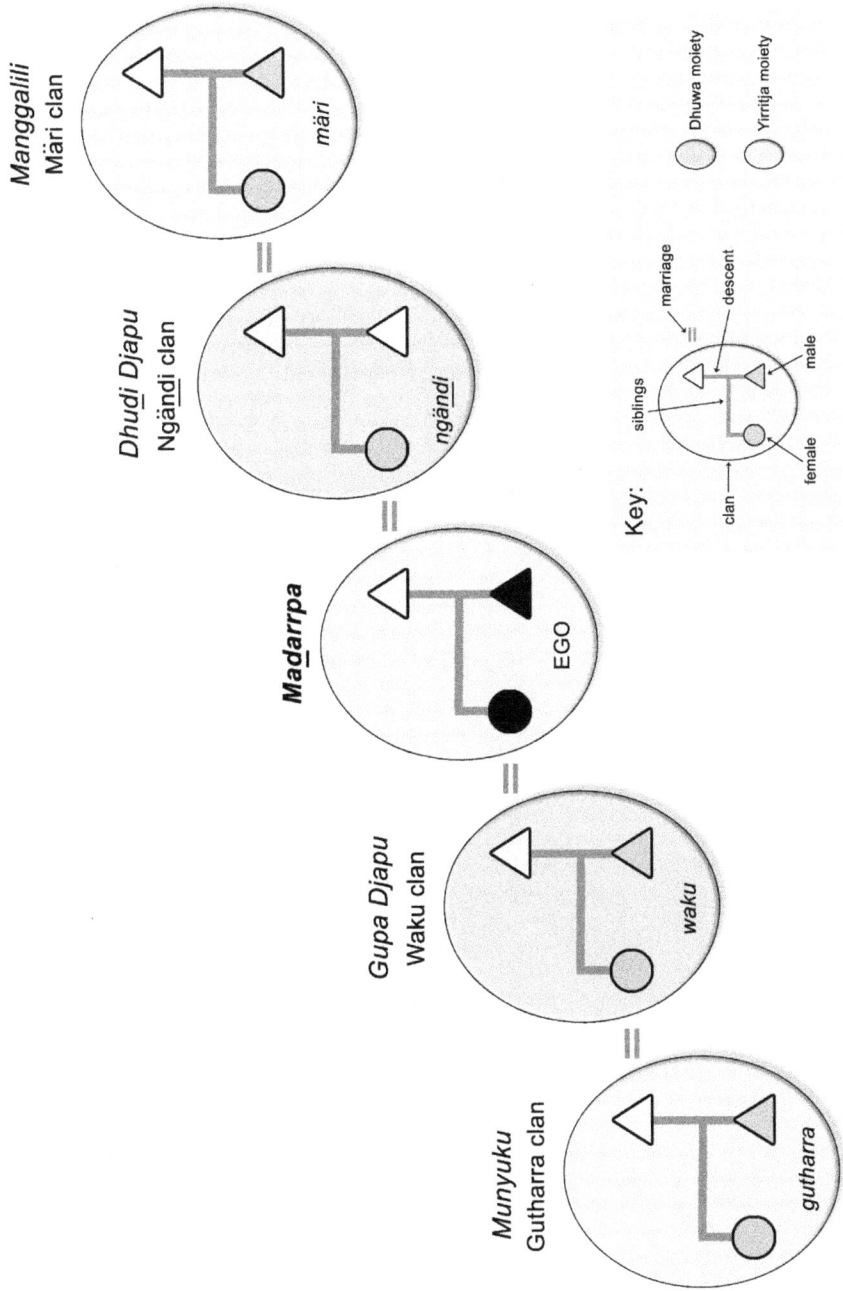

Fig. 5.4 The märi–gutharra and ngändi–waku relationships between clans, from the perspective of a Madarrpa sibling pair

Manggalili
Märi clan

märi

Dhudi Djapu
Ngändi clan

ngändi

Madarrpa

EGO

Gupa Djapu
Waku clan

waku

Munyuku
Gutharra clan

gutharra

Key:

marriage

descent

siblings

clan

male

female

Dhuwa moiety

Yirritja moiety

In the past, and to a considerable extent still in the present, most marriages tended to take place between members of geographically neighbouring clans, and so over time 'connubia'—that is, regional groupings of clans that are linked in sets of marriage relationships—tend to emerge. In the northern Blue Mud Bay area, for example, the Manggalili clan provides mothers-in-law to the Madarrpa clan, and the Madarrpa in turn provide mothers-in law to the Munyuku (see Fig. 5.4). The clans from which wives come (i.e. the clan into which the mother-in-law is married) are, for the Madarrpa, predominantly the Dhudi Djapu and the Marrakulu clans, and for the Munyuku, predominantly the Gupa Djapu. The Dhudi Djapu clan, in turn, provides mothers-in-law to the Gupa Djapu.

The existence of connubia is not merely statistical—they are not simply an emergent property of the local system of kinship and marriage. They are recognised by Yolngu as a social fact. Connubia are often associated with regional names.[13] For example, the northern Blue Mud Bay clans are the Gindirrpuyngu 'people of the floodplains' or Djalkiripuyngu 'foot(print) people'.[14] These cultural properties of connubia are a factor in their reproduction over time.

Connubia are nodal networks rather than bounded groups. Their networks intersect with those of other similarly constituted connubia. For example the *märi* for Manggalili are the Yarrwidi Gumatj, and this links Manggalili to the Laynhapuy connubium that is focused around Caledon Bay to the north. These networks of individuals may stretch out beyond the connubium in which other members of their clan are embedded. In the Blue Mud Bay area, for example, there is another *märi-gutharra* chain that links some members of the Madarrpa clan, through marriage, to groups on Groote Eylandt, and other individuals are linked to groups to the south and inland, again through their marriages.

Despite the challenges posed by colonisation and its aftermath, the underlying principles of the Yolngu *gurrutu* system are largely intact. As a system it can be said to exist in a state of relative autonomy: not untouched or uninfluenced by its contact with settler Australian society, but, nevertheless, with structures and systems of value that have their own trajectory. The system was always flexible and adaptive, and it has continued to be so in the face of the changes ensuing on the colonial process. The demography of small groups is rarely stable; some groups decline in number over time while others expand. The Yolngu system was flexible enough in the past to deal with such contingencies, and it had

---

[13] The Yolngu naming of groups at various levels is an extremely complex issue. The pioneering (and most comprehensive) study is Schebeck (2001). Williams (1986: 57–74) also has an extended discussion of names and their meanings.

[14] *Djalkiri*, ('foot', 'footprint') like many Yolngu terms for body parts, is entangled in a complex metaphorical universe (see also Tamisari 1998). It may also refer to an 'ancestral imprint on the landscape', and it is sometimes translated as 'foundation'—that is, 'the origin of law and identity'. In the name 'Djalkiripuyngu' it refers ostensibly to footprints in the mud of Blue Mud Bay, but may also carry the connotation that these groups are the 'foundation' people with respect to *rom*.

mechanisms for succession when individual clan groups declined to a point where they could no longer partake fully in the system. In brief, if a clan becomes depleted or extinct a *gutharra* clan that shares the same *wangarr* inheritance will (ideally) first assume responsibility for looking after that clan's estate, and, if extinction follows, it will assume ownership of it (H. Morphy 2003). There is no reason to suppose that connubia were ever static entities with bounded memberships. Both political and demographic factors work over time to shift the nodal foci.

Mobility in the midst of stability

Since mission times, with sedentarisation, a certain fixing of connubia has been taking place. Today, they tend to be associated with groups of geographically contiguous homelands, situated on the clan estates of the constituent clans. Djambawa Marawili (pers. comm., 4 October 2007) draws an analogy between a group of connubially-linked homelands and a town, with each homeland being a 'suburb'. The spatial relationship between clans and their estates, and between clans within a connubium on neighbouring estates (see Morphy and Morphy 2006), is thus reinforced by the physical presence of settlement infrastructure. But at the same time, the Yolngu lifestyle is characterised by high levels of mobility. Short-term, localised mobility is fuelled by both social and purely logistic considerations. Only one of the Laynha homelands has a store, and so it is necessary for most homelands dwellers to go either to Nhulunbuy or Yirrkala to shop for food and other necessities. People also have to travel to meetings, for training, for medical appointments, and even on occasion further afield for such things as art exhibition openings in metropolitan centres. Ceremony, particularly in the context of funerals and boys' initiation rites, is a major and frequent cause of short-term mobility (see F. Morphy 2007a, 2007c). Visiting kin in other communities is also a factor, particularly during school holidays. People tend to be more mobile at certain times in their lives—many young adults, particularly young men who have not yet married and 'settled down', are highly mobile in the medium term. They are referred to as *dhukarrpuyngu* ('people of the track'), and move frequently between households and communities where they have kin. In the longer term—but here we enter the realm of speculation since no reliable research exists on the extent, trajectory and nature of outmigration—are those who are 'economic' migrants to places where there are 'real' jobs, or even medical migrants.[15] If one sits at a particular homeland in any particular week, the impression can be one of constant flux and movement

---

[15] As in other parts of Indigenous Australia, kidney failure as a consequence of diabetes is unfortunately becoming common. Until very recently, there were no facilities for dialysis in Arnhem Land. Yolngu suffering from renal failure had to live semi-permanently in Darwin to avail themselves of the facilities there. There was a bucket of money from the NT Department of Health (delivered through Laynha) to support them and their families to live in Darwin, but no bucket in the Health Department's hospital budget to pay the technicians necessary to maintain a dialysis facility in Nhulunbuy Area Hospital.

as vehicles and planes come and go. Yolngu are still very much 'people who move around'.

Leadership in the Yolngu world

Gurrutu continues to be the Yolngu 'governance environment' par excellence. The domain of governance is the management of relationships, both mundane and ceremonial, between groups at various levels of articulation from the very local to the regional.[16]

At the level of the clan, primogeniture and gender are the most important determinants of ascribed leadership status, but there are quite effective checks to the automatic ascription of power to people in powerful structural positions. Personal autonomy is highly valued and may be strongly asserted (sometimes by avoidance of situations in which the power of others can be exercised). Ultimately a 'good' leader is a person to whom other people will listen, and who can create and maintain consensus—a sense of *ngayangu wanggany* 'one feeling' or *mulkurr wanggany* 'one mind' (see F. Morphy 2007c). Thus, leadership is conferred conditionally and has to be constantly earned. It is a process rather than an ascribed position in a hierarchy, although some people do start with structural advantages. Whereas English-speakers tend to talk about the 'head' of a family or organisation, the predominant Yolngu metaphor is *ngurru*—'nose, prow of canoe'. The English metaphor implies a view of a leader as the apex of a vertical hierarchy, whereas the Yolngu metaphor implies a view of a leader as someone who carries others behind him.[17]

On the Laynhapuy homelands, the Yolngu system of governance still operates according to these principles. It has adapted to the circumstances of small settlement life. It still depends on the same mix: 'good' leaders are those who can lead through consensus and, all things being equal, they tend to be the first-born sons of the leaders of the preceding generation. And the system is still grounded, in the sense that homelands settlements tend to cohere around the senior male members of the estate-owning clan (see Barber, forthcoming).

'Fairness', 'equality' and 'democracy', the cornerstones of 'good' governance in western liberal democracies, are not salient to this system. There is nothing 'fair' or 'equal' about male primogeniture—all people are not created equal, and leaders are not 'elected' on democratic principles. But this system has its own set of checks and balances (or mechanisms of accountability): leaders who lead

---

[16] For an extended analysis of Yolngu leadership in relationship to land, and particularly in relation to religious aspects that fall outside the scope of this paper, see Williams (1986, 1987).

[17] The term *ngurru* is not generally applied to women in the context of clan leadership, but if a woman happens to be the first-born person in her generation (*malamarr*), and if she is a person with a strong personality, she may sometimes take on '*ngurru*-like' roles. On one famous occasion in the 1970s, the female *malamarr* of a large clan, a formidable woman, led a party of her clansmen to do battle with another group.

by consensus are constrained by the need to reproduce consensus. Disaffected 'constituents' can 'vote with their feet', withdraw their support, and align themselves with another leader (or become one themselves if they can garner the support).

At a regional level, affairs are ordered by groups of senior leaders according to the same principles. There is no fixed hierarchy or fixed membership of such groups, but once again certain individuals will be regarded as pre-eminent because of their knowledge (mundane and sacred), seniority, and/or the size and structural position of their clan within a regional system.

Gender and leadership

In Yolngu society, there is not the same strict separation of male and female domains that is found, for example, in some desert societies. Nevertheless, power relations and the expression of power are gendered. Women are not excluded from power and influence, or from positions of leadership, except in certain restricted ceremonial contexts, but they do not generally attempt to exert their authority overtly in public contexts in the same way that men do. At public meetings, men tend to sit centre stage, with the most senior men in the most central positions, and women sit on the periphery. It is mostly men who speak, but women monitor proceedings carefully, and senior women interject comments into male 'performances' or sometimes take the floor if they feel that the discussion is not going as it should. If male leaders fail to achieve the consensus of senior women, then it is unlikely that whatever decision they make will take effect.

For some time, women have been taking positions of power and authority in certain intercultural contexts, particularly education. The head teacher of the school at Yirrkala was until recently a Yolngu woman, and the head teacher at Gapuwiyak is also a Yolngu woman. At Laynha, following the recent departure of the non-Yolngu Chief Executive Officer (CEO), his successor is a Yolngu woman.[18]

Laynha as an intercultural zone

In adopting a framework that privileges relative autonomy it is possible to view organisations like Laynha as sites of intercultural production, using Merlan's term in a more restricted sense. Such sites are 'border zones' (Clifford 1997) where two relatively autonomous systems meet and interact to create hybrid or intercultural forms.[19] Mattingly (2006: 495) characterises such zones as places

---

[18] Women have also become increasingly prominent as artists since the 1970s.

[19] Cornell and Begay's (2004) concept of 'culture match' also addresses the idea of intercultural forms, but with an important difference. True 'culture match', as envisaged by Cornell and Begay, can only take place in a context where actors from an encapsulated society have freedom to choose, pragmatically, between alternatives. In practice, this means that the encapsulating culture refrains from using its power

where 'culture emerges more vividly as a *space of encounter than of enclosure* ... This sort of cultural world is characterised by *politically charged*, difference-making exchanges among actors' (emphasis added). As Merlan rightly notes (see above), in a situation where one system is the encapsulating state and the other is a localised system of a minority group, the power relationship between the systems is unequal.

The Laynha constituency: connubia and 'membership'

Laynha's constitution, as an organisation incorporated under the NT's *Associations Act*, stipulates that the organisation must maintain an up-to-date list of members. The Act, as an instrument of settler society, assumes that membership of an association is a bounded category. Laynha does maintain such a list, but it is essentially an artefact of the intercultural space rather than a true reflection of the organisation's Yolngu constituency.

The region serviced by Laynha is partly a construct of the colonial past, reflecting the former sphere of influence of Yirrkala Mission. It contains (parts of) the estates of the clans of three large contemporary connubia: the Djalkiripuyngu centred around Blue Mud Bay; the Laynhapuyngu, whose clan estates stretch down the east coast and its hinterland from south of the Gove Peninsula to south of Caledon Bay; and the Miyarrkapuyngu to the west of them and to the north of the Djalkiripuyngu. There is a dynamic tension in the governance of Laynha between two connubia—the Djalkiripuyngu of Blue Mud Bay and the Laynhapuyngu, which is dominated numerically (in the context of the Laynha homelands and the Association) by the senior lineages of the large Gupa Djapu clan.[20] The sources of tension are complex—Gupa Djapu at one time (still within the memory of the parents of the oldest people still now alive) were part of Djalkiripuyngu, and have moved their sphere of influence northwards, with certain lineages forging alliances through marriage with the clans of the Yirrkala

---

to impose particular socio-cultural forms: 'the issue of culture match is about power ... what matters for governance legitimacy and effectiveness is that the process of culture match be under Indigenous control' (Hunt and Smith 2006: 18). It could be argued that in the period of 'self-determination' such conditions obtained to some extent in Australia, but that this became less and less true during the neo-assimilationist regime of the Howard Government.

[20] As with connubia, there is now a certain fixing of clan identity taking place. Gupa Djapu is a very large clan of over 350 people, all descended from a single ancestor who had over 20 wives. It is unlikely that in the past such a large clan would have continued to exist as a 'corporate' entity. Evidence from the period around missionisation (and from the memory of the oldest people still living) suggests that fission of large groups occurred, usually along lines of marriage. In these circumstances, the existing clan estate would have become two, or one of the subgroups would have taken over the clan estate of a small or extinct *märi* group, first in caretaker mode, but over time becoming seen as the primary owners for that country with a separate clan identity. This tendency is visible in the Gupa Djapu case, where certain lineages are more closely associated with the Laynhapuyngu connubium and other lineages with the Djalkiripuyngu or Miyarrkapuyngu, through their marriages into clans of those connubia. However, with the advent of certain fixing processes such as the written record and the introduction of clan 'surnames' the further process of fission is frozen. What we are seeing is the influence of one system on the trajectory of another.

area. They are now thought of principally as Laynhapuyngu, although they have strong connections to all the connubia of the area. Today's Djalkiripuyngu, on the other hand, are the group with the least strong history of association with Yirrkala Mission. In 'mission times' many of their senior leaders and their families went south or to Groote Eylandt rather than to Yirrkala. Their return to the orbit of Yirrkala was prompted by the start of the homelands movement, which was initiated by the senior lineage of the Gupa Djapu. Today, many Gupa Djapu live at Yirrkala, and of the Yolngu office staff at the Laynha headquarters the majority are Gupa Djapu. Gupa Djapu is the only clan with more than one homeland settlement on its clan estate, and Gupa Djapu men are the senior leaders at two other settlements.

The Laynha 'community'

In geographical, organisational and political terms, Laynha fits the 'centralised hub and spokes' model described by Hunt and Smith (2006: 88, Fig. 7; reproduced here as Fig. 5.5), but with added complexities. The organisation is physically located in the 'hub' community of Yirrkala, but is not under the jurisdiction of the local council. It is in, but not institutionally part of, Yirrkala's community of governance.

Fig. 5.5 The hub and spokes model

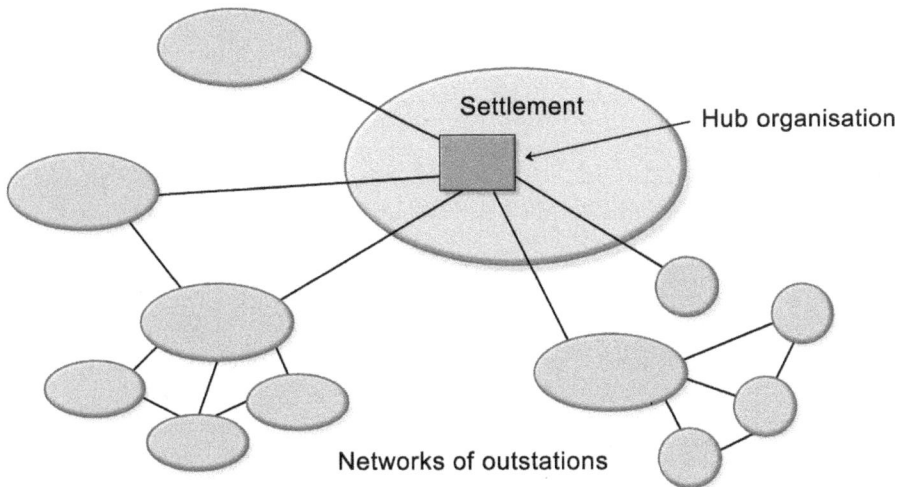

Networks of outstations

Laynha does not service a 'community', but rather a group of outlying homelands settlements. The people who live on these homelands are interlinked both with each other and with the people who live in the wider region (see Fig. 5.1), including Yirrkala, through the complex web of kinship, ceremonial and political interests described above. Although Yirrkala is the service 'hub', it is not the 'hub' of socio-political relationships for many Laynhapuy homelands dwellers.

Many do have strong kin connections to Yirrkala, but others, particularly those who live in the southern outstations around Blue Mud Bay, are oriented as much to Groote Eylandt and/or Numbulwar, or to Gapuwiyak and its homelands. Some of the northern homelands have strong kinship and ceremonial links to the Gumatj-dominated community of Gunyangara (Ski Beach) and its homelands (one of which, Biranybirany, is physically located inside the Laynhapuy area), and/or to communities further west such as Galiwin'ku and the Marthakal homelands. This can be seen, for example, in the pattern of people's movements to funeral ceremonies in the region. Although some people reside on a long-term basis at a particular homelands community, others shift over time—sometimes in and out of the ambit of the Laynha homelands—according to particular life circumstances and their kinship connections. Some people who are considered to be Laynha members in fact reside principally at Yirrkala. They are members because their clan identity ties them to one or other of the homelands settlements.

It is therefore not a straightforward matter to define the 'membership' of the association. The notions of 'community of identity' and 'community of interest' (cf. Hunt and Smith 2006: 5) have some application, but only if these 'communities' are understood as being somewhat unbounded in nature. The notion of 'administrative community' also only fits partially. In terms of health services, Laynha services homelands that are not otherwise part of the service population, and the recently declared Laynhapuy IPA covers some homelands that are outside the Laynha service area and excludes some that are inside it. Finally, the artists of the Laynha homelands are serviced by Buku-Larrnggay Mulka at Yirrkala, which is under the umbrella of the Yirrkala Dhanbul Association.[21]

The 'community' that Laynha services can best be conceptualised as a nodal network (a set of localities that receive the full range of Laynha services) and a penumbrum of other homelands that are connected to the organisation in particular ways but peripheral to it in others. The lack of clear boundaries around 'membership' constitutes a 'problem' for policy makers who want to deliver services to bounded entities with sedentary populations (see F. Morphy 2007d). However, it should not be assumed a priori that lack of boundedness is a problem for Yolngu themselves, or for the governance of their organisations. Indeed, in many respects the structure of the Laynha 'community' mirrors the networked and unbounded nature of Yolngu polities of kinship. And it shares with them

[21] At least this was the case until the Federal Government's 'intervention' in the NT. Like many other community owned businesses in 'prescribed' communities, the future ownership of Buku-Larrnggay Mulka and its assets is currently uncertain. Art production and sale is a significant component of the local economy, with around 100 homelands artists dealing regularly with the art centre, and another 150 or so on a less regular basis (Andrew Blake, pers. comm., 21 December 2007). From time to time Laynha has contemplated starting its own art centre, but has never pursued this option. Established originally in the 1970s, Buku-Larrnggay is one of Australia's most successful Indigenous arts centres, and in face of that, setting up in local competition would make very little sense.

another property—that of a relative stability over time which is not merely an emergent property of the system but a social fact.[22] And if Laynha is conceptualised as a set of localities—the hub and the homelands—it shares yet another property of the Yolngu system. Whereas the localities are fixed in space, the individuals in the populations associated with them are mobile to varying degrees and over varying timescales.

Leadership in the Laynha context

Laynha's constitution currently provides for the election of a 12-person board at the Annual General Meeting (AGM). Those nominated must have a proposer and a seconder. Election is through a secret ballot of the membership, and the system is 'first past the post'—the first 12 people with the most votes are elected.[23] Once elected, the board members then decide among themselves who the office holders will be for that year. On the surface, this appears to be a standard democratic process conducted according to settler notions of good governance.

In practice, because of distance and expense, it is impossible for the entire membership of Laynha to attend an AGM. A meeting is quorate if 24 members are present, and on average an AGM has an attendance between 30 and 50. Very often, there are no more than 12 people nominated, although this was not the case in 2007. The resulting composition of the board is remarkably similar over the years, with each of the major homelands having at least one member, and the largest usually having two. Those elected tend to be drawn from the ranks of middle-aged leaders.[24] The distribution over the three connubia also tends to reflect their relative prominence, with the Laynhapuyngu and Djalkiripuyngu usually having roughly equal numbers of board members and the Miyarrkapuyngu having fewer than either. Within the Laynhapuyngu contingent, the Gupa Djapu usually predominate. This process is democratic, but not according to the 'one vote, one value' model that the constitution enshrines. In the hands of the Yolngu membership, what emerges is more like

---

[22] From time to time particular communities shift in and out of the orbit of Laynha membership, in a way that parallels shifts in the composition of connubia. During the fieldwork period, one large homeland that had once been a 'full' member of the Laynha constituency, but which had transferred to Marngarr following a disagreement (not with Laynha as an organisation but with the leaders of one of the clans that is central to Laynha), decided that they wanted to return to the Laynha fold. They were welcomed back, and this was a sign of the resolution of tension between the two parties. Also during this period, the Gumatj homeland of Biranybirany, which is geographically surrounded by Laynha homelands but is primarily serviced by Marngarr, decided that it would become part of the Laynhapuy IPA.

[23] This is the number under the current constitution, which was put in place in 2006. The board has replaced the 10-member council that operated under the previous constitution.

[24] Middle-aged here designates people between the ages of approximately 35 and 55. A few homelands have more elderly leaders still living, but it is rare for these people to seek nomination. Power is ostensibly delegated to the next generation.

a system of proportional representation that achieves a balance between the different kin networks and regional interests of the membership.

Thus, both in terms of the membership and of the leadership structure of the organisation, Laynha conforms on paper to the 'norms' of 'good' governance as laid out in the legislative framework provided by the settler state. Yet it actually operates in a way that is heavily imbued with Yolngu principles of governance.

Power, accountability and value

This study began with quite a different research focus from that which has emerged during the course of fieldwork. As a linguistic anthropologist who had worked with Yolngu—but not with their organisations—since 1974, I was initially interested primarily in Yolngu conceptualisations of governance and how these translated into the organisational environment. I anticipated that there would be differences between Yolngu conceptualisations and those of non-Yolngu staff (see F. Morphy 2007c), and wanted to investigate how the space between these two sets of views was negotiated in the context of the organisation. Was some form of 'cultural match' (Cornell and Begay 2004) in place, and if not, was it attainable? Although I was conscious of something called the 'wider governance environment' within which the organisation sat, I did not then see it as a major focus of the research.

But it happened that my fieldwork took place during a period (2005–07) when that wider environment was undergoing a radical transformation. Early on, it became clear that the increasing pace of change in government policy and in the manner of its implementation, both at the Territory and Commonwealth levels, was putting the organisation under strain.[25] The tension between Yolngu conceptualisations of the nature of the organisation and those of its government paymasters had reached a point where its causes had to be examined and addressed if the organisation was to survive. In effect, I was witnessing a struggle between the Yolngu 'world' and the state over exactly what kind of organisation Laynha is, and what it exists for.

In his introduction to *Seeing Like a State*, James C. Scott (1998) describes the project outlined in the epigraph to this chapter as 'the road not taken'. He came to see efforts at sedenterisation as but one type of action in the more general project of the modern state—that of making society 'legible', the better to control and administer its subject-citizens. This chapter is framed partly in terms of Scott's original, more narrowly defined research question. In the case of an Indigenous organisation whose members live 'radically uncontained' mobile lives (F. Morphy 2007d), but which is heavily dependent on funding from a

---

[25] During most of the field research period, the NT Government's plans to reorganise local government remained in a preliminary stage, and it was hard to gauge the implications for organisations like Laynha. Ultimately, they may be far-reaching, but are outside the scope of this paper.

state that has in recent years become increasingly inimical to such a lifestyle, the governance of the organisation has to be seen as the site of a political struggle—rather than merely a site of engagement—between incommensurable sets of values and objectives. In such a context, 'good' or 'effective' governance is not, as it is so often portrayed, a matter to be contemplated as if it were a politically neutral matter. The question to be asked here is: when considering the governance arrangements of an organisation like Laynha, who is this governance for, and for whose good? This is partly a question about power—how it is exercised by the powerful, and resisted, circumvented or accommodated by the relatively powerless—and partly a question about value. The focus of this chapter, then, is on the struggle over value that I witnessed, rather than on the details of Laynha's governance arrangements per se.

Central to the question of 'good' governance is the notion of accountability. In this case, government, the holder of the purse strings, has much more power than the other partner in the arena—the encapsulated and locally isolated minority Indigenous population, as represented by local organisations like Laynha. Elsewhere I have argued (F. Morphy 2007c) that having a system of checks and balances—in other words a system of accountability that is bidirectional—is a universal of good governance arrangements.[26]

Drawing on the work of O'Donnell (1999) and Schedler (1999), Schacter (2000: 1) distinguishes 'vertical' accountability 'of the state to its citizens' from 'horizontal' accountablility 'by the state to its own public institutions of accountability'. He points out that:

> Governments are more likely to bind themselves through institutions of horizontal accountability under circumstances where citizens will punish them for failing to do so. Horizontal accountability must therefore be buttressed by strong vertical accountability (Schacter 2000: 1–2; emphasis in the original).

The Howard Coalition Government, in its relationship to Australia's Indigenous peoples, began quite early on to systematically diminish their ability to hold the government to vertical account, starting with the abolition of the national representative system embodied in the Aboriginal and Torres Strait Islander Commission (ATSIC). The attrition of horizontal accountability followed inexorably, and reached its apogee when the government gained control of the Senate in 2006. Its 'National Emergency' intervention into the NT and the passing of the legislation that legitimated it were the actions of an unaccountable government—it seemed to feel no need either to address the recommendations

---

[26] For an extended analysis of reduced political accountability in Indigenous affairs in the last two decades and its effects see Sullivan (forthcoming, 2008).

of the report[27] that was the purported catalyst for the intervention (Behrendt 2007: 15) or to put in place measures to evaluate its effectiveness (Hinkson 2007: 2–3).

Two contrasting conceptualisations of Laynha as an organisation

Having now set the framework for the analysis, outlined some relevant characteristics of the governance principles that Yolngu and the state bring to the intercultural space, it is now time to look at that space itself in more detail. Figures 5.6 and 5.7 attempt to capture in graphic form the differences between the state view of the organisation—or rather a particular version of the state view promulgated by a neo-assimilationist government—and the Yolngu view.

The view of the neo-assimilationist state

In late 2005, the then Minister for Indigenous Affairs, Amanda Vanstone, characterised small homelands communities as 'cultural museums' (Vanstone 2005). This trope designates Indigenous worlds as static repositories—they cannot, in this view, be a valid field of social action and value. In such a view, the Laynha homelands are merely a particular kind of (remote, expensive, 'dysfunctional') service population encompassed within the state, and Laynha is their service provider. If the ongoing existence of the 'other culture' as a system of action and value is denied, then so too, by definition, is the intercultural nature of Indigenous organisations. In Fig. 5.6, then, Laynha is shown as fully incorporated in a state system that is arranged in a vertical hierarchy.

The Howard Government did not have a coherent view of remote homelands as functioning communities, and indeed, as Fig. 5.7 suggests, it did not have a coherent view of organisations like Laynha. Following the demise of ATSIC, funding for programs had been increasingly provided by a series of mainstream departmental silos; Yolngu individuals were perceived as partible—as consumers of health care, CDEP participants, units requiring housing, and so on. Laynha is also partible, viewed by one government department as an Indigenous Housing Organisation, by another as a CDEP provider under contract, by another as a local heath service provider, and by yet another as the management support for an IPA. This is not a particularly unusual circumstance in the government machinery of large nation-states like Australia. Settler Australian citizens are accustomed to such partibility and compartmentalisation, viewing them as

---

[27] This was the *Little Children Are Sacred* report, of the Northern Territory Board of Inquiry into the Protection of Aboriginal Children from Sexual Abuse (Anderson and Wild 2007). Among other things the report strongly advocates a detailed process of consultation with affected communities and individuals in addressing the problem of abuse, whereas the intervention took place with no prior consultation with those affected.

'normal' (if sometimes regrettable) features of governance arrangements. The failure to recognise the Yolngu 'world' as an encapsulated social field, and the failure to see that Laynha is a complex organisation with multiple functions that interrelate to support its material base, is what is at issue here.[28]

Fig. 5.6 The intercultural space from the state's point of view

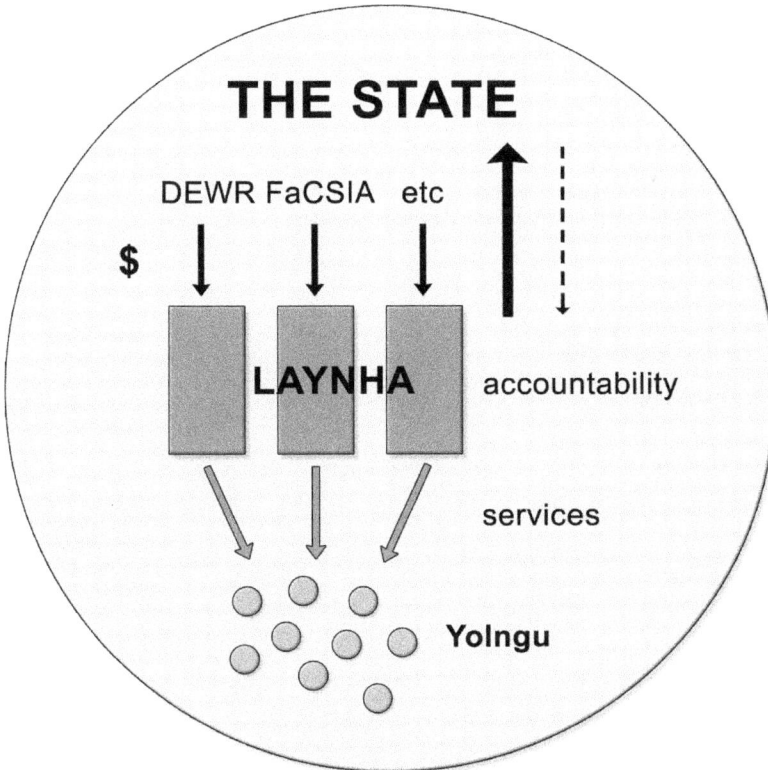

---

[28] It could be argued that the Howard Government did attempt in various ways to take a more 'holistic' approach to Indigenous affairs. They instituted the Council of Australian Governments (COAG) trials, they set up Indigenous Coordination Centres (ICC) as 'one-stop shops', and instituted the Shared Responsibility Agreement regime. None of these initiatives has been successful, however. The failure of the COAG trials is well-documented (in a series of evaluation reports that the government failed to release for many months; see Department of Families, Housing, Community Services and Indigenous Affairs (FaHCSIA) website at <http://www.facsia.gov.au/internet/facsinternet.nsf/indigenous/publications.htm>). The shortcomings of the ICCs lie, ironically, in their localness. Like the organisations with which they interact, they are small and distant from the centre of power. Many individual public servants who work in ICCs do have good local knowledge and an understanding of the complex role of organisations like Laynha. But their own role is to act as conduits for (and enforcers of) the policies of central government. Because of the power of the silos at the centre it is also often not possible for the ICC to act as a 'one-stop shop'. Individual public servants are accountable to their department first and to the ideal of 'whole of government' second (see Dillon and Westbury 2007: 60).

Theoretically, in such a model accountability goes both ways, but in practice there is a great deal of upward accountability and very little in the other direction. This is a function of the power relations that obtain between the small, local, funding-dependent organisation and the national state as paymaster. Upward accountability is especially burdensome because of the fractured way in which funding is delivered. Because government has no coherent overview of the local organisation, it fails to acknowledge the level of the burdens that it imposes, and fails to understand, or is indifferent to, the consequences for the organisation of abrupt and unsignalled changes in policy.[29]

Because government has no clear view of the Yolngu system and of accountability structures within that system, and no clear view of the organisation as an intercultural institution where different systems of accountability have to be reconciled, it also has no clear view of the burdens of downward accountability that the organisation sustains with respect to its constituency. When 'training' for governance is provided to Yolngu board members it is mostly about helping them to be upwardly accountable within the framework of government requirements (F. Morphy 2007c). To government, a 'good' organisation is a compliant organisation that delivers programs according to government guidelines on budget and on time. To the extent that the intercultural nature of the organisation is recognised at all, it is perceived as a problem, as bits of 'museum culture' that keep getting in the way of 'good' governance.

The Yolngu view, 2005

The first point of contrast between the Yolngu view and that of the government and its agencies, a point not captured in Fig. 5.7, is that for the Yolngu, Laynha has a history, and it is part of their history. It has been a constant in their institutional landscape for over 20 years.[30] In the years of 'self-determination', Laynha was felt to be unambiguously a Yolngu organisation. As well as having a Yolngu council, there was a tradition of having a Yolngu manager. There was

---

[29] A classic example of this towards the end of the Howard era was the summary and unsignalled banning of kava imports, removing more or less at a stroke Laynha's major source of discretionary income. The Federal Government was either indifferent to or ignorant of the consequences, not only for Laynha as an organisation but for the homelands that depend for the moment on the continuing existence of Laynha for services and infrastructure. The desirability of kava use is not the issue here; rather, it is the manner and the timing of the ban.

[30] In the past, the public service allowed and even encouraged certain of their staff to specialise in areas like Indigenous affairs, and some people developed detailed and long term local knowledge of particular regions as a result. There are ex-public servants who have an understanding of the history of organisations like Laynha, and some of them rose to senior positions, taking that knowledge with them to the centre. However, very few of them are there now, and the younger generations operate in a very different public service culture, where accumulation of such expertise and long-term association with particular regions is neither encouraged nor, it seems, particularly valued. As Dillon and Westbury (2007: 61) state: 'government disengagement has meant that over the last thirty years, there has been a significant diminution in the intellectual capital available within government to implement programs effectively in remote Australia'.

usually a non-Yolngu second-in-command who managed day-to-day business and also the interface with funding agencies. In Fig. 5.7, the state is represented as a black box to reflect the general level of Laynha members' knowledge about and interest in the sources of Laynha funding. The 'upwards accountability' arrow is much less prominent than in Fig. 5.6, and originates in an underspecified zone of the oval representing the organisation, signalling that the Yolngu membership, including the council members, did not have a clear view of the burden of accountability demanded by the state, nor of the mechanisms of accountability.

Fig. 5.7 The intercultural space from the Yolngu point of view

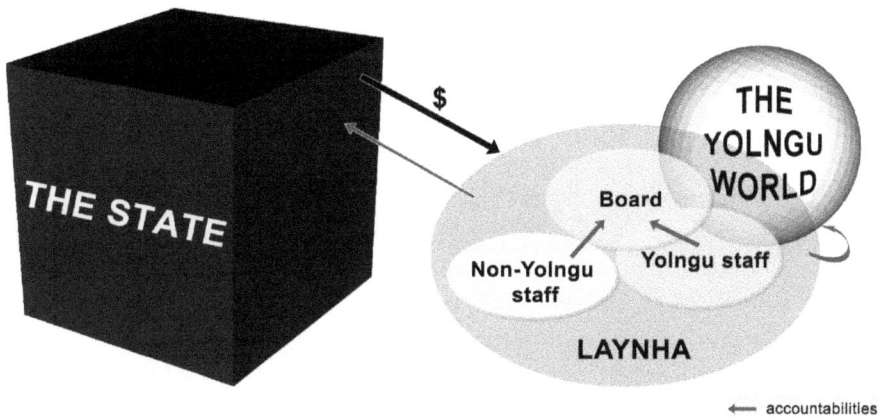

In the post ATSIC period, the membership of the organisation, including its council, continued to hold the view of Laynha as 'their' organisation, even as the policy ground began to shift under their feet. This is represented in Fig. 5.7 by the lack of overlap between the state and Laynha. The question is, why had they not noticed or understood the implications of 'grant creep', whereby Laynha now depended for its continuing existence on the state?

By and large in this period, particularly in the days of ATSIC, government was broadly supportive of the aims of organisations like Laynha, and the homelands communities that they represented and serviced. The membership could take for granted the continuing existence of their homelands, Laynha, and CDEP, and they did. One might think at first glance that in its governance arrangements Laynha achieved a kind of cultural match in this period. It complied with the conditions of its funding to the extent that it did not attract unfavourable attention to itself in the relatively benign wider governance environment. It grew and developed in a relatively organic way, with response to contingencies rather than long-term planning as the main driver of change. It did not have a linear hierarchy of management or tightly demarcated areas of responsibility (with certain exceptions—health and Laynha Air were clearly separated from the rest of the functions of the organisation), and the decision-making processes of the council (and later the board) were characterised by fluidity and open-endedness. These characteristics are represented in Fig. 5.7 by a set of overlapping ovals (the board, and the Yolngu and non-Yolngu staff of the organisation) that are in no clear structural relationship to one another with respect to the governance of the organisation. In one sense, this is not surprising, because they do not represent its governance structure per se, but rather the Yolngu 'two worlds' view of Laynha as an intercultural space. Laynha is conceptualised as a zone between the two 'worlds', with different sets of actors positioned along a continuum of inclusion and exclusion. The board, and the Yolngu staff members overlap with the Yolngu 'world' (and with each other), and the non-Yolngu staff sit between the periphery of that world and the state.

In such a conceptualisation there is an implicit general principle of governance: it is the role of Yolngu to manage relations with the Yolngu world and the role of non-Yolngu staff to manage relations with the state, for the benefit of Yolngu. While the state holds a partible view of the organisation's functions, the Yolngu view is holistic. Yolngu living on the homelands do not have a clear appreciation of funding streams and their associated conditions and constraints. In the past, Laynha has frequently used its income from kava to supplement government programs, for instance by providing assistance to members to act as escorts for sick relatives, and by contributions to the funding of capital projects such as the building of the ranger station at Yilpara. It has also initiated its own projects, such as building and equipping offices on the homelands. The power and water systems on the homelands have also been substantially funded from kava income. Laynha's contributions from kava income to the expenses of funerals and other ceremonies have had a significant impact on the trajectory of Yolngu ceremonial life, and on the process of intergenerational cultural transmission.[31] Such aspects of the organisation's role are not given any kind of official recognition by the state.

Culture mismatch?

In 2005, at the beginning of the research period, the differences between these two conceptualisations of the organisation were taking their toll on the governance of the organisation and on the morale of its staff. Council was not truly in control. The locus of power and decision-making was with certain non-Yolngu members of staff who mediated the flow of information between the organisation and its members (as represented by the council), and between the organisation and the state. Other non-Yolngu staff members were uneasy about the lack of hierarchy and the lack of defined areas of delegated

---

[31] For a fuller account of the uses of kava income see Laynhapuy Homelands Association Inc. (2007: 23–5).

responsibility, and the ad hoc nature of much decision-making. There were chronic points of tension between non-Yolngu staff and both Yolngu staff and members—over the 'proper' use of Laynha vehicles and perceived inequities in the distribution of staff time and Laynha resources, to name but two. It was an organisation not fully attuned to the wider governance environment and how its role was viewed in that environment, and it was ill-prepared for the neo-assimilationist turn in government policy.

Meeting the neo-assimilationist challenge, 2005–07

In the last years of the Howard Government, Laynha and other organisations of its kind found themselves thrust into crisis mode. There was a lot of change during this period. Some of it was pre-emptive on the part of the organisation, in anticipation of the need to prepare itself for engagement with an increasingly interventionist regime. Some of it was enforced—to resist would have meant loss of funding and threatened the viability of the organisation.

The catalyst for change was the transfer of the CDEP program from ATSIC to the Department of Employment and Workplace Relations (DEWR). In 2005–06, changes to the CDEP program were put in place from the centre, which appeared to take no account of the realities of the local economies of, and the state of the labour market in, remote Aboriginal Australia, nor of the 'job-readiness' of the majority of the working-age Indigenous population. Laynha was told that it had 12 months to create one business and exit 15 individuals off CDEP and into 'real' employment. By dint of transferring some Yolngu staff of the organisation off CDEP wages onto 'real' wages paid from Laynha's discretionary income, the organisation almost succeeded in meeting the 'employment' target, but clearly this was not a sustainable strategy over the longer term. The organisation did not have the capacity or the resources to start a business within a 12-month timeframe, and there was no coherent support from government to help them achieve this. It was almost as if government was wanting organisations like Laynha to fail, and not surprisingly, Laynha was told at the end of the year that it had performed 'poorly'. For the next year it was told that it had to employ a CDEP co-ordinator as a condition of receiving the Laynha CDEP contract and that it had to undertake a capacity building plan against which its achievements would be measured as a condition for future funding. It was set another (higher) job creation target, and told it had to create two businesses. The CDEP guidelines for 2006–07 also had major implications, potentially, for other aspects of the organisation's governance. Under '6.1.1 Governance', the following appeared:

> To ensure commercial effectiveness CDEP organisations are also encouraged to have Board or Governing Committee members who have accounting, legal and/or business qualifications … As an initial step DEWR requests that wherever possible CDEP organisations work towards a goal of no more than 50 per cent of their Board or Governing Committee

be [sic] active participants, supervisors, coordinators or managers of the organisation by the end of 2006–07 (DEWR 2006).

Or, in other words, by the end of the year the Laynha council would, in the government's mind, be replaced by a board with 50 per cent non-Yolngu membership.

During the next year, Laynha commissioned a review of its structure (Tallegalla Consultants 2006), appointed a CDEP co-ordinator and, for the first time in its history as an organisation, a non-Yolngu CEO who was charged with improving the internal governance of the organisation. It also revamped its executive arrangements, including providing a stipend for the Chair of the newly constituted board of directors so that this position was no longer filled by a CDEP participant. All this was not achieved without internal struggle. Appointing a non-Yolngu CEO required a substantial change to the culture of the organisation, and the new CDEP arrangements, once the co-ordinator was in place, began to have perceptible effects that were not always welcomed by participants. For example, the continuing requirement to create jobs quickly meant a continuing emphasis on jobs at Yirrkala rather than on the homelands, and the stricter reporting requirements for CDEP participants began to have an effect on people's abilities to fulfil their cultural obligations. The Yolngu board found themselves in the position of having to participate in social engineering, for example by reducing financial and practical support for funeral ceremonies, thus adding a new dimension to Yolngu 'politics'.[32] And the organisation was to receive two further body blows: the summary banning of kava on which it depended for valuable discretionary income, and the summary abolition of CDEP, now fortunately averted.

All this was taking place in a context of accelerating change in Commonwealth Government policy, in which the very existence of homelands, and therefore of the organisations that support them, began to be at issue. Also, as the NT Government's planning for the new shire structure began to gather pace, questions over the future role of organisations like Laynha in the delivery of services have begun to be raised (but not as yet answered). Thus, despite making great efforts to comply with government requirements, to the extent of compromising the Yolngu view of the role of Laynha as an organisation, at the time of writing the future of the organisation seems very uncertain.

The strains placed on the staff of the organisation in the last two years have been very considerable. Staff vary in their perceptions of their role, and these

---

[32] This question is examined in detail in Morphy and Morphy (2007). For very different reasons, both DEWR and elements of the local Yolngu leadership consider the hypermobility occasioned by funerals, and the amount of people's time that they occupy, to be problematic. So, in a sense the government's new strictures provided certain Yolngu leaders with an opportunity to make changes that would have been difficult to implement otherwise.

differences have been exacerbated by the increasing ambiguity of Laynha's role. Few of the non-Yolngu staff see the two 'worlds' as separate in the way that Yolngu do. Some subscribe to a government-like view of the position of the organisation. Others struggle to maintain a sense that they are working in a Yolngu organisation for the Yolngu members, while being conscious that they are implementing policies that are inimical to varying degrees to the Yolngu world view.

Conclusion: towards a negotiated and empowering system of governance in the intercultural space

If Laynha is to survive as an organisation, it is clear that it is going to have to change its roles and functions—yet again. Until the new shire arrangements are in place, it will be difficult to know precisely what the reactive changes will have to be. But organisations like Laynha ought to survive, for two reasons. First, they are a locus of representation for homelands Yolngu in the interface with the encapsulating society. Second, until governments can improve their own capacity, this is the only level in the governance structure of remote Australia where a view of Yolngu society as a complex, functioning whole is consistently maintained. Given the right assistance and support, organisations like Laynha can institute proactive change and become the drivers of sustainable economic development in their constituent communities—in an economy that envisions more options for Yolngu than migration to unskilled or semi-skilled jobs in towns and on mine sites (at best), or unemployment and fringe-camp dwelling (at worst).

The Yolngu people who are the constituents of Laynha, and for whose benefit the organisation exists, bring to their interactions with the Australian settler state a set of local and culturally distinctive ideas about what constitutes 'good governance' (F. Morphy 2007c). As an institution of the 'intercultural space' or 'border zone', Laynha is a site of contestation over value, where Yolngu and settler Australian (represented by state bureaucratic) ideas of 'good governance' presently meet head on. This is often an uncomfortable—and sometimes untenable—place to be, for both Yolngu and non-Yolngu staff of the organisation, and it is not conducive to effective governance arrangements. The way in which the settler state has recently sought to exercise power and authority over Aboriginal people and their organisations has exacerbated this struggle over value, and it is wasteful of time and energy, to the extent that 'good' governance is compromised—not only the governance of organisations but also of government itself.

Sidestepping the struggle over value—over what constitutes 'good' governance—involves two distinct steps. First, both the state and the Yolngu have to come to an understanding that there are two systems of value at play in the intercultural space, and that both systems are complex.

Yolngu principles of governance tend towards the production of fluid, open-ended situations. 'Boundaries are to cross' (Williams 1982), in that nearly everything is potentially negotiable and subject to iterative negotiation, so long as correct principles are followed and values adhered to. Although there are ascribed aspects to the creation of leaders, leadership is defined and maintained through process rather than fixed hierarchies of authority. There are separations of duties and responsibilities, as in the roles of *wänga-watangu* ('land owner') and *djunggayarr* ('manager') with respect to clan estates, but there is no absolute separation of powers. Actors are always socially positioned in a particular social context, even when taking mediating stances in a particular interaction (e.g. in dispute settlement). Indeed, not being so positioned is viewed negatively. One of the worst things a person can say of a fellow Yolngu is that they are *gurrutumiriw* ('self-interested', lit. '[behaving] without [regard to] kin'). All of these characteristics of the Yolngu polity and its principles of governance are antithetical to the western ideal of 'good' governance, with its emphasis on boundedness and closed categories, fixed hierarchies, planning, risk management, and 'neutral' professionalism.

The Yolngu system is founded in a view of the world that sees its ancestral underpinnings as eternal and unchanging, but life on the surface, in the everyday, as governed by contingency. In such a world planning happens, but more often than not contingencies will intervene to disrupt the plans. Adaptability, fluidity and creative negotiation are seen as valuable and necessary in such a world, and are valued as integral to planning. A border zone can be viewed as a space of contestation, but also as a space for creativity in which complex contingencies are at play. And some of those contingencies, it seems, include abrupt and un-negotiated shifts in government policy.

In the world view of the governments and bureaucrats of western state systems, on the other hand, contingency is seen as something that can be contained through planning—one can 'manage risk' and even plan for contingencies, after all. The illusion of control is achieved by setting up bounded categories and controlling the enclosed space (either physical or conceptual). If that fails, if what is contained threatens to overflow the boundary, one simply shifts the boundary ('reviews the plan'). Most of the time this is such a 'normal' process that it goes unremarked—indeed it is the very stuff of governance. But sometimes the shift is very noticeable, and momentarily the solidity of the boundary disappears. When that happens, one speaks of 'moving the goalposts' or, more cerebrally, of a 'paradigm shift'.

Other evidence of this worldview is seen in the power of silos—government departments that, in effect, create arbitrary boundaries that cut across the continuities of everyday life. In this context it is interesting that the state seems to have difficulty in conceptualising where Indigenous people fit. For many years they were treated as a bounded category, and given their own department. Sometimes they were bundled with 'culture' (tourism and the arts), sometimes with the 'other' (immigration and ethnic affairs). Today it seems they are partible just like everyone else, although also categorised through the continuing existence of Indigenous-specific programs or sub-offices within the mainstream departments. Added to this is a fundamental lack of clarity over which 'bits' of Indigenous affairs are the Commonwealth's responsibility, and which the NT's. It is little wonder that many Indigenous people experience the workings of government as impenetrable and essentially contingent and arbitrary in nature.

Compartmentalism may be the only way in which such a large and complex system as a state can be managed. The problem comes with the attribution of value—this may be an *effective* worldview *for its purposes*, but is it *good* in some absolute moral sense and therefore always desirable? If so, it would be an effective view in all circumstances, and it would appear that this is not the case. For example, in such a view a border zone is an anomalous space. Where does it belong? Is it in this container or that one? Or does it somehow complexify the boundary, thus causing a 'problem' for governance? These questions and this problem are of the world view's making, not properties of the boundary zone in itself, for it is possible to take a very different view—the Yolngu view. It is also arguably a very ineffective view at the local level, since it results in very small communities and very small organisations having to bear onerous burdens of accountability, and deal constantly with the consequences of uncoordinated directives and actions from the centre.

Systems of value are just that—*systems*—not simply collections of ideas thrown together in some random and arbitrary fashion. For the moment, agents of the state seem blind to the Yolngu system, seeing Aboriginal people as having 'gaps' in their 'capabilities', as half-full vessels that can be filled by somehow pouring western ideas about governance in on top of what is already there (or in the neo-assimilationist version, by tipping out the current contents and replacing them wholesale, holding the vessels under state control until the process is complete and they are fit to govern themselves). Government agencies and trainers in 'capacity building'—consciously or unconsciously—constantly counterpose settler Australian notions of 'good governance' to a 'deficit' view of Aboriginal modes of governance.

While this remains the case, they will always meet with resistance or avoidance—whether conscious or unconscious—from Yolngu. For few Yolngu are likely to respond positively to a view which holds that the Yolngu way of doing things and the Yolngu system of value are deficient. The Yolngu system is not going to go away, and people are not vessels that can be emptied of one set of ideas and values and refilled with another, at least not without taking measures that are unacceptable in a liberal democracy.[33] Moreover, as I have argued elsewhere (F. Morphy 2007c), to the extent that Yolngu have a theory of the value system of the encapsulating society, they do not particularly like what they see. In their view, *that* is the deficient system.

Having recognised that different systems can and do exist, the next step is to come to an agreement in principle to respect difference rather than viewing it as deficit—and this applies to both parties. Respect involves a suspension of the attribution of positive value to one system but not another. A respectful, informed and honest debate about pragmatics can then follow—what are the local goals in sight, whose goals are they, and what are the most effective (as opposed to 'best') strategies to achieve them in a negotiated space between the two 'worlds'. Where the two systems seem incommensurable, what compromises are possible that will best help to achieve the intended goals? This is, in fact, a debate about cultural match, where both parties—not just the weaker party—are willing to consider making changes to their way of doing things. The willingness and capacity of government is as much at issue here as the 'capacity' of Indigenous people and their organisations, for it involves a radical change in perspective, in which Indigenous peoples' local aspirations and goals take precedence over the state's impulse to socially engineer Indigenous lives from the centre, 'for their own good'.

Acknowledgements

My first and most important debt is to the board and staff of Laynhapuy Homelands Association, past and present, for allowing me to undertake the governance study during what turned out to be a rather tumultuous period in the organisation's long history. It has been a privilege to work with them, and I hope that I have contributed something positive in return. My especial thanks to Sally Wagg for her generous hospitality in giving me a home away from home on so many occasions. I thank Janet Hunt, Howard Morphy, Rebecca Morphy and two anonymous reviewers for their constructive comments on various drafts of this chapter. Any remaining errors of fact and interpretation are my responsibility.

References

Anderson, P. and Wild, R. 2007. *Ampe Akelyernemane Meke Mekarle—Little Children Are Sacred, Report of the Northern Territory Board of Inquiry into the Protection of Aboriginal Children from Sexual Abuse*, Report to

---

[33] Such as, for example, removing children from their parents on the basis of their 'race', or instituting dormitory systems where children and parents have very limited access to one another, and the children are punished for speaking their own language. A more current example is the quarantining of people's welfare income on the basis of race in the NT.

the Northern Territory Government, Darwin, available at
<http://www.nt.gov.au/dcm/inquirysaac/>

Attwood, B. 2003. *Rights for Aborigines*, Allen & Unwin, Sydney.

Barber, M. forthcoming. 'A place to rest: dying, residence, and community
stability in remote Arnhem Land', in M. Tonkinson, Y. Musharbash, K.
Glaskin and V. Burbank (eds), *Dealing with Death: Essays on Funerals
and Mourning in Indigenous Australia*, Ashgate, London.

Barnes, J. 1967. 'Inquest on the Murngin', *Royal Anthropological Institute
Occasional Paper No. 26*, Royal Anthropological Institute, London.

Behrendt, L. 2007. 'The emergency we had to have', in J. Altman and M. Hinkson
(eds), *Coercive Reconciliation: Stabilise, Normalise, Exit Aboriginal
Australia*, Arena Publications Association, North Carlton.

Berndt, R. M. 1951. *Gunapipi*, Cheshire, Melbourne.

——1952. *Djanggawul*, Routledge and Keegan Paul, London.

——1962. *An Adjustment Movement in Arnhem Land*, Mouton, Paris.

——and Berndt, C. 1954. *Arnhem Land, its History and its People*, Cheshire,
Melbourne.

Clifford, J. 1997. *Routes: Travel and Translation in the Twentieth Century*, Harvard
University Press, Cambridge, MA.

Cornell, S. and Begay, M. 2004. 'What is cultural match and why is it so
important? Lessons from 14 years of the Harvard Project', Paper
presented at the *Building Effective Governance* conference, Jabiru, NT,
5–7 November 2004.

Cowlishaw, G. 1988. *Black, White or Brindle*, Cambridge University Press,
Melbourne.

Department of Employment and Workplace Relations (DEWR) 2006. *CDEP
Guidelines 2006–07: Community Development Employment Projects (CDEP)
Program*, DEWR, Canberra.

Dewar, M. 1992. *The 'Black War' in Arnhem Land: Missionaries and the Yolngu
1908–1940*, North Australia Research Unit, ANU, Darwin.

Dillon, M. C. and Westbury, N. D. 2007. *Beyond Humbug: Transforming
Government Engagement with Indigenous Australia*, Seaview Press, West
Lakes, SA.

Egan, T. 1996. *A Justice All Their Own: the Caledon Bay and Woodah Island
Killings 1932–1933*, Melbourne University Press, Melbourne.

Hinkson, M. 2007. 'Introduction: in the name of the child', in J. Altman and M. Hinkson (eds), *Coercive Reconciliation: Stabilise, Normalise, Exit Aboriginal Australia*, Arena Publications Association, North Carlton.

Hughes, H. 2007. *Lands of Shame: Aboriginal and Torres Strait Islander 'Homelands' in Transition*, The Centre for Independent Studies, St Leonards, NSW.

Hunt, J. and Smith, D. 2006. 'Building Indigenous community governance in Australia: preliminary research findings', *CAEPR Working Paper No. 31*, CAEPR, ANU, Canberra.

Keen, I. 1994. *Knowledge and Secrecy in an Aboriginal Religion: Yolngu of North-East Arnhem Land*, Clarendon Press, Oxford.

——2003. *Aboriginal Economy and Society on the Threshold of Colonisation*, Oxford University Press, Melbourne.

——2006. 'Ancestors, magic, and exchange in Yolngu doctrines: extensions of the person in time and space', *Journal of the Royal Anthropological Institute*, 12 (3): 515–30.

Kleinert, S. and Neale, M. (eds) 2000. *The Oxford Companion to Aboriginal Art and Culture*, Oxford University Press, Melbourne.

Laynhapuy Homelands Association Inc. 2007. Submission to Senate Standing Committee on Legal and Constitutional Affairs Inquiry into the Appropriation (Northern Territory National Emergency Response) Bill (No. 2) 2007–2008, Laynhapuy Homelands Association Inc., Yirrkala, NT.

Macgowan, F. 2007. *Melodies of Mourning: Music and Emotion in Northern Australia*, James Curry Publishers, Oxford.

Maddock, K. 1970. 'Rethinking the Murngin problem: a review article', *Oceania*, 41: 77–87.

Mattingly, C. 2006. 'Pocahontas goes to the clinic: popular culture as lingua franca in a cultural borderland', *American Anthropologist*, 108 (3): 494–501.

Merlan, F. 1998. *Caging the Rainbow: Places, Politics, and Aborigines in a North Australian Town*, University of Hawai'i Press, Honolulu.

Morphy, F. 2007a. 'Mobility and its consequences: the 2006 enumeration in the north-east Arnhem Land region', in F. Morphy (ed.), *Agency, Contingency and Census Process: Observations of the 2006 Indigenous Enumeration Strategy in Remote Aboriginal Australia*, CAEPR Research Monograph No. 28, ANU E Press, Canberra.

——2007b. 'Performing law: the Yolngu of Blue Mud Bay meet the native title process', in B. R. Smith and F. Morphy (eds), *The Social Effects of Native Title: Recognition, Translation, Coexistence*, CAEPR Research Monograph No. 27, ANU E Press, Canberra.

——2007c. 'The language of governance in a cross-cultural context: what can and can't be translated', *Ngiya: Talk the Law*, 1: 93–102.

——2007d. 'Uncontained subjects: "population" and "household" in remote Aboriginal Australia', *Journal of Population Research*, 24 (2): 163–84.

——and Marika, W. 2005. 'Laynhapuy IPA and Yirralka Ranger Program: a new initiative for a venerable homelands association', *Community Governance*, 1 (4): 1–2, Occasional newsletter of the ICGP, CAEPR, ANU, Canberra.

—— and Morphy, H. 2007. '"Soon we will be spending all our time at funerals": Yolngu mortuary rituals in a time of constant change', Paper presented at the 106th Annual Meeting of the American Anthropological Association, *Difference, (In)equality and Justice*, 28 November–2 December, Washington, D.C. (In preparation for publication in 2008).

Morphy, H. 1984. *Journey to the Crocodile's Nest*, Australian Institute of Aboriginal Studies, Canberra.

——1991. *Ancestral Connections: Art and an Aboriginal System of Knowledge*, University of Chicago Press, Chicago.

——2002. 'Thomson, Donald Finlay Fergusson (1901–1970)', *Australian Dictionary of Biography*, 16: 385–7.

——2003. An Anthropological Report on the Yolngu People of Blue Mud Bay, in Relation to Their Claim to Native Title in the Land and Sea, Unpublished draft report prepared at the instruction of the Northern land Council, December 2003, Northern Land Council, Darwin.

——2007. *Becoming Art: Exploring Cross-Cultural Categories*, Berg, Oxford.

—— and Morphy, F. 1984. 'The myths of Ngalakan history', *Man*, 19 (3): 459–78.

—— and ——2006. 'Tasting the waters: discriminating identities in the waters of Blue Mud Bay', *Journal of Material Culture*, 11 (1–2): 67–85.

O'Donnell, G. 1999. 'Horizontal accountability in new democracies', in A. Schedler, L. Diamond and M. F. Plattner (eds), *The Self-Restraining State: Power and Accountability in the New Democracies*, Lynne Rienner Publishers, Boulder.

Peterson, N. (in collaboration with J. Long) 1986. *Aboriginal Territorial Organization: a Band Perspective*, Oceania Monograph No. 30, University of Sydney, Sydney.

Reid, J. 1983. *Sorcerers and Healing Spirits: Continuity and Change in an Aboriginal Medical System*, Australian National University Press, Canberra.

Sahlins, M. 1993. 'Goodbye to tristes tropes: ethnography in the context of modern world history', *Journal of Modern History*, 65: 1–25.

Schacter, M. 2000. 'When accountability fails: a framework for diagnosis and action', *Policy Brief No. 9*, Institute on Governance, Ottawa.

Schebeck, B. 2001. *Dialect and Social Groupings in Northeast Arnheim* [sic] *Land*, Lincom Europa, Munich.

Schedler, A. 1999. 'Restraining the state: conflicts and agents of accountability', in A. Schedler, L. Diamond and M. F. Plattner (eds), *The Self-Restraining State: Power and Accountability in the New Democracies*, Lynne Rienner Publishers, Boulder.

Scott, J. C. 1998. *Seeing Like a State: How Certain Schemes to Improve the Human Condition Have Failed*, Yale University Press, New Haven.

Shapiro, W. 1981. *Miwuyt Marriage: the Cultural Anthropology of Affinity in Northeast Arnhem Land*, ISHI, Philadelphia.

Sullivan, P. Forthcoming 2008. 'Reciprocal accountability: assessing the accountability environment in Australian Aboriginal affairs policy', *International Journal of Public Sector Management*, 21.

Tallegalla Consultants. 2006. *A New Direction for Laynha: a Report on a Review of the Organisation*, Tallegalla Consultants Pty Ltd, Brisbane.

Tamisari, F. 1998. 'Body, vision and movement: in the footprints of the ancestors', *Oceania*, 68: 249–70.

Thomson, D. F. 1949. *Economic Structure and the Ceremonial Exchange Cycle in Arnhem Land*, Macmillan, Melbourne.

——2006. *Donald Thomson in Arnhem Land* (2nd edn, compiled and introduced by N. Peterson), Melbourne University Press, Melbourne.

Vanstone, A. The Hon. 2005. 'Beyond conspicuous compassion: Indigenous Australians deserve more than good intentions', Address as Minister for Immigration and Multicultural and Indigenous Affairs to the Australia and New Zealand School of Government, 7 December, ANU, Canberra.

Warner, W. L. 1958. *A Black Civilization*, Harper and Row, Chicago.

Wells, E. 1982. *Reward and Punishment in Arnhem Land 1962–1963*, Australian Institute of Aboriginal Studies, Canberra.

Williams, N. M. 1982. 'A boundary is to cross: observations on Yolngu boundaries and permission', in N. M. Williams and E. S. Hunn (eds), *Resource*

Managers: North American and Australian Hunter-Gatherers, Australian Institute of Aboriginal Studies Press, Canberra.

——1986. *The Yolngu and Their Land: A System of Land Tenure and Its Fight for Recognition*, Australian Institute of Aboriginal Studies Press, Canberra.

——1987. *Two Laws: Managing Disputes in a Contemporary Aboriginal Community*, Australian Institute of Aboriginal Studies Press, Canberra.

6. Regenerating governance on Kaanju homelands

Benjamin Richard Smith

Introduction

Across Australia, the complexities of Indigenous governance are increasingly recognised. These complexities are apparent in intercultural engagements between Aboriginal people and the Australian 'mainstream', but they are also a feature of what is often described as the 'Aboriginal domain'. This chapter explores governance in central Cape York Peninsula—focusing on the upper watersheds of the Wenlock and Pascoe Rivers—where these two sets of complexities are deeply interwoven and are now manifest as aspects of a single, heterogeneous *field of governance*.

Kaanju people, who consider the upper Wenlock and Pascoe Rivers to be their traditional country, have recently sought to reestablish their presence there through the development of 'outstations' or 'homelands'. These outstations are small kin-based communities whose populations continue to move between homeland camps and larger communities, including the township of Coen (Smith 2004). Kaanju people have also regained some measure of control of their homelands through land claims and through the development of organisations concerned with the environmental and economic management of their 'country'. These organisations are the basis of Kaanju people's attempts to develop sustainable futures, by facilitating their involvement in political processes and through generating economic benefits from homelands-based projects. Given the growing number of projects currently based in Kaanju homelands—many of which include a potentially significant economic component—these organisations have, not surprisingly, become the subject of increasing contestation among the Aboriginal people involved with them.

In addition to contestation over governance arrangements between local Aboriginal people, the contemporary field of governance has also been shaped by a number of non-Indigenous or 'outside' organisations. These include various State and Federal government agencies and a series of non government organisations (NGOs) concerned with Aboriginal socioeconomic development and natural resource management. These organisations—and key individuals working within them—have responded to the reoccupation of Kaanju homelands by supporting homelands-based development. Development projects have been supported in a manner intended to lead to a rapprochement between the aspirations of various Kaanju people and what those working in these organisations regard as viable or sustainable forms of Indigenous social and economic development.

The resulting interplay between various local and 'outside' interests has produced a field of governance marked by ongoing tensions. In particular, there are tensions between Aboriginal aspirations for what might broadly be described as 'self-determination' and forms of support that remain conditional on working within frameworks determined by local and regional organisations and by government agencies. The resulting tensions focus on three key areas of contestation:

- the relationship between homelands-based, sub-regional and regional 'Aboriginal organisations' (as well as between these organisations and government agencies)
- the relationship (both putative and enacted) between contemporary forms of Aboriginal law and custom ('Indigenous governance') and 'mainstream' forms of governance and government, and
- the relationship between different forms of Aboriginal identity—in particular in the articulation of Aboriginal groups of various kinds at various social scales.

Whilst the first of these sets of relationships (between various formally-constituted organisations) involves relatively discrete kinds of social institution, careful examination of the various relationships constitutive of Indigenous community governance suggests that Aboriginal and 'mainstream' aspects of governance are now deeply interwoven in a single—albeit complex—field. This is the case despite continuing Aboriginal and non-Indigenous claims to the contrary. Further, despite marked continuities from pre-colonial Aboriginal sociality, it seems that contemporary articulations of Kaanju identities and interests at various scales are now deeply embedded within this contemporary field of governance. In the contemporary region, Aboriginal identities, as well as the field of governance and its constituent institutions and practices, are now markedly *intercultural*.

The Aboriginal domain, the mainstream and the intercultural field

A number of anthropologists have recently emphasised the intercultural character of Aboriginal life-worlds across northern and central Australia (see Hinkson and Smith 2005a). The empirical and theoretical accounts presented by these scholars move away both from a previous anthropological distinction between an 'Aboriginal domain' and a (socially if not culturally dominant) Australian 'mainstream'. This parallels the distinction prevalent in the popular imagination between the life-worlds of Aboriginal people living in very remote areas and the norms, values and practices that predominate elsewhere in Australian life—a distinction that underlies much Indigenous policy.

Such a distinction—also commonly made by many Aboriginal people themselves—has found more nuanced expression in various anthropological accounts of the 'Aboriginal domain'. This domain is understood to exist variously as a space in which social closure acts as a form of Aboriginal resistance to non-Indigenous dominance (e.g. Trigger 1986, 1992) or a set of practices (von Sturmer 1984) in which:

> the dominant social life or culture is Aboriginal, where the system of knowledge is Aboriginal, where the major language is Aboriginal; in short where the resident Aboriginal population constitutes the public (von Sturmer 1984: 219).

Both in these anthropological accounts, and (often with less nuance) in popular understandings and the 'administrative imagination' (cf. Rowse 1992), this Aboriginal domain, space or life-world is contrasted to a putative 'mainstream', broadly taken to indicate the commensurate dominance of social life and cultural production[1] by 'white', 'European', 'Anglo-Celtic', 'modern' or 'Australian' forms of knowledge, language ('Standard English') and a predominantly non-Indigenous public.[2]

Conceptualising a distinct Aboriginal domain differentiated from this 'mainstream' has proved useful in treating ethnographic accounts of social interactions and hegemonic relations in remote majority Aboriginal settlements. In his discussion of Aboriginal governance, for example, Keen (1989: 21) notes the usefulness of 'treating the Aboriginal domain as a conceptual isolate ... distinguishing it from its [wider social and political] environment'. But the increasing interpenetration of Aboriginal and 'mainstream' life-worlds in places like central Cape York Peninsula means that this kind of treatment now provides only a partial account of the character of Aboriginal governance.

For this reason, when writing about the central Peninsula I have reservations in treating 'Indigenous Community Governance' in terms of a central core of informal and formal aspects of Aboriginal governance, located within a surrounding 'governance environment' (Hunt and Smith 2006a: 39–42; and compare Keen, *passim*). Rather, whilst there are spaces, spheres of thought and styles of behaviour (Trigger 1986: 99) in the central Peninsula that are readily identifiable as constitutive of an 'Aboriginal domain', a more even-handed

---

[1] I follow Merlan's (1998, 2005) use of the term 'cultural production' to indicate the continuing reproduction and recreation of cultural categories, understandings and modes of practical action within day-to-day social life.
[2] Although beyond the scope of the present paper, this discussion could usefully engage with the recent development of anthropological consideration of the nature of 'publics' and 'public culture'.

analysis of governance—in its fullest sense—must account for these as moments within a broader social field.

The concept of the social field has a relatively long history in social anthropology. It is perhaps most closely associated with the work of Max Gluckman and the 'Manchester School' (e.g. Gluckman 1968), whose work included accounts of interethnic relations in the context of governance in sub-Saharan Africa. More recently, the term has been taken up by anthropologists working in Aboriginal Australia (e.g. Smith 2007; Sullivan 2005).

Following Gluckman, it is possible to understand events and institutions associated with a particular 'domain' as part of a wider social field. Such an understanding entails the analysis of:

> [a] set of social institutions … and their 'intermesh' [in which] … [e]vents emerging from the operation of one institution may intervene in the operation of another institution in a manner that is haphazard as far as the systematic interdependencies of the recipient institution are concerned. [Further,] [e]xternal events from quite different areas … may intrude into the field under analysis, again in what, from the point of view … of systems, is a haphazard manner (Gluckman 1968: 223).

Nonetheless, more careful examination of such events and interactions may well reveal:

> that institutions and wider social fields have a marked tendency to endure, that they and/or their parts are resistant to both unintended and deliberately attempted changes, though radical changes will, after some period of time, occur. We might therefore say that an institutional system, or a field of institutional systems, will tend to develop, and even hypertrophy, along the main facets of its organisation, until conditions make it quite impossible for the system to continue to work (ibid.).

In the analysis that follows, I take up Gluckman's model of a social field in relation to Indigenous community governance as it has developed in the central Peninsula, but with some qualifications.

My first qualification is that Gluckman's use of the term 'institution' should be read here as inclusive both of formal and informal social institutions *and* of instituted forms of behaviour, knowledge and the like; in what follows, I understand 'institutions of governance' to form parts of a *socio-cultural* field. Secondly, I understand Gluckman's use of the term 'haphazard' to indicate, on one hand, the relatively open trajectories of socio-cultural *production* in fields marked by the interplay of originally distinct (Aboriginal and settler) socio-cultural forms. On the other hand, the term 'haphazard' also marks the unexpected results of interventions by those within this shared field. In particular, I am thinking of the interventions of non-Indigenous agencies, the 'haphazard' results of which often seem unpredictable to those working within these agencies. Lastly, I am reticent to discuss the endurance of those 'institutions' that together mark the 'Aboriginal domain' in terms of their 'parts'. Notions of 'parts and wholes' as they are often applied to Aboriginal socio-cultural production are extremely problematic (cf. Strathern 1992). Indeed, the imposition of notions of parts and wholes marks one of the principal ways in which non-Indigenous socio-cultural production forces radical changes within the field of Indigenous community governance, such that it is near impossible for aspects of the Aboriginal domain to persist within this wider field.

This last point concerns a key problem within the wider field of Indigenous governance in the central Peninsula—the contrasting (and culturally-shaped) expectations and enactments of leadership in relation to governance arrangements involving wider sets (or 'groups') of Aboriginal people. Again, I am reticent to use the language of 'groups' here because—as Keen (1989) insightfully argues—although 'leadership' is clearly identifiable within those parts of the field of governance that we might identify as the 'Aboriginal domain', within that domain, leadership does not operate in relation to a social structure of pre-given 'groups'. Instead, such leadership is linked to a more fluid or processual articulation of 'social networks and fields' (Keen 1989: 26). However, in recent years it has become increasingly apparent that, despite their incommensurability, originally exogenous ('outside') understandings of Aboriginal social life (ideas about 'tribal groups' for example) have folded back onto Aboriginal people's own reckonings of sociality and governance within the region's shared social field. The result is commonly what Gluckman (1968: 223) describes as the haphazard outcome of the intervention of one institution 'in the operation of another institution … as far as the systematic interdependencies of the recipient institution are concerned'. Put more simply, the folding back of such reckonings of sociality into local usage leads to a problematic—and often antagonistic—articulation of the socio-cultural modes of the Aboriginal domain and those introduced from the 'mainstream' within the shared field of governance.

The manner in which these differing conceptualisations of leadership, social networks, groups and the like come to affect each other indicates the cultural complexities of the contemporary field of governance. The ongoing interplay of originally distinct Aboriginal and settler socio-cultural forms has led to this field now possessing a profoundly *intercultural* character. Whilst the character of this field remains heterogeneous, the intermesh of its various social and cultural 'institutions' is such that even seemingly autonomous aspects of Aboriginal cultural production are, in fact, deeply shaped by their exposure to aspects of the 'mainstream'.[3] For this reason, the field of governance is intercultural in the sense that this term is used by Merlan (2005).[4] That is, the various 'institutions' and forms of thought, action and personhood which together constitute this field are deeply interwoven, but are by no means heterogeneous. Rather, the interweaving or 'mutual exposure' (Smith 2007) through which this field is constituted is marked by ongoing forms of socio-cultural difference, similarity, and mutual engagement and transformation. And, as Gluckman's earlier analysis of social fields suggests, such intercultural fields are marked by ongoing changes, reconfigurations and realignments.

In order to better understand how such an intercultural field has developed, its contemporary complexities, and the changes that continue to be enacted within it, I now turn to relationships of governance within a particular area of the central Peninsula—the homelands of the Kaanju people of the upper Wenlock and Pascoe rivers. More particularly, what follows focuses on the history of decentralisation—the reoccupation of homelands or 'outstations'—and the forms of governance that developed in relation to this 'outstation movement'.

Kaanju homelands

Kaanju homelands (*ngaachi*)[5] stretch from the township of Coen in the centre of Cape York Peninsula to around the former Moreton Telegraph Station to the north (Fig. 6.1), covering the headwaters of the eastern and western-flowing river systems that run off the Great Dividing Range. The Aboriginal people of this area spoke and owned[6] the Kaanju language, which they considered to have been emplaced in their 'country' through the actions of mythological, ancestral hero figures (called 'Stories' in the region's Aboriginal English). However, neither this area, nor the Kaanju-speaking people who owned and occupied it, were considered as a homogenous group. Rather, particular Kaanju people identified with places and areas within the wider Kaanju bloc, and exercised particular rights with regard to such places on the basis of these identities. These identities were in turn based upon the actions of the 'Stories', which shaped or left various

---

[3] Likewise, despite the continuation of hegemonic relationships between local Aborigines and 'outside' agencies, the local operations of these agencies are inexorably shaped by their involvement with particular Aboriginal people. Not least because, as Scott (1998) insightfully argues, the operations of state (and state-like) agencies depends on the enactment of otherwise lifeless schema in particular local life-worlds.

[4] For other accounts of the 'intercultural' in Aboriginal Australia, see Martin (2003); Smith (2007); Hinkson and Smith (2005b); Sullivan (2005).

[5] I use italics throughout this chapter to denote words from the Kaanju language and other Indigenous language varieties (except for proper names, which are not italicised). Words and phrases in the region's Aboriginal English are not italicised, but are placed in inverted commas.

[6] Aboriginal language varieties in the central Peninsula are understood to be substantially connected to land or 'country' through the actions of mythological beings ('Stories'). These languages are further understood to be jointly owned by all those whose country is connected to a particular language in this manner (see Rigsby 1999; see also Merlan 1981; Rumsey 1989). This is despite the previous lack of any formal social organisation at the (language-named) 'tribal' level.

named 'Story-places' across the regional landscape. Several such places—along with other named sites—were considered the joint property of sets of close kin. Anthropologists often identify these sets of people as 'clans', but they were locally identified by the use of the suffix *–thampanyu* ('associated with'—see Thomson 1933; Chase 1980) attached to the name of a place, an associated totem, or another signifier of conjoint place-based identity. These *–thampanyu* identities formed the basis of a regional system of property rights. They were also closely tied to other aspects of regional Aboriginal governance, which was enacted primarily between sets of senior men from across the region.

This regional system of land-ownership and governance—and the associated use of Kaanju 'country' by hunter-gatherer bands—was disrupted by the arrival of white settlers in the central Peninsula in the late 19th century. Following the discovery of gold at several locations in the wider region, miners flooded into the central Peninsula, followed by pastoralists who took up large cattle runs to supply the miners and the townships that they established. Kaanju people experienced considerable social and cultural impacts following the establishment of the township of Coen—at the southern limit of Kaanju country—and the mining fields and camps near Birthday Mountain and on the upper Wenlock River (then called the Batavia River), which were also established on their homelands (Fig. 6.1). In addition, a number of cattle stations—including Mt. Croll, Pine Tree, Rokeby, Merluna and Batavia Downs—were established on Kaanju homelands, with the majority of Kaanju country being taken over for the running of cattle. Displaced from their hunting grounds and subject to disease, malnutrition and settler violence, Kaanju people were forced to live in fringe camps close to the major centres of white settlement, or to move to the mission stations on the land of their coastal neighbours at Lockhart River, Weipa and Mapoon. As the cattle industry grew, increasing numbers of Kaanju people worked on cattle stations on their own homelands or in other parts of the Peninsula. Significant numbers of Kaanju people—including a number of mixed-race children—were also removed[7] to the missions and penal settlements at Cherbourg, Woorabinda, Yarrabah and Palm Island. Those so removed (and their descendants) have subsequently formed part of the Peninsula's Aboriginal diaspora or 'stolen generations' (Smith 2000a, 2006).

---

[7] Under the regime of state control legislated for by the Queensland Government's *Aboriginals Protection and Restriction of the Sale of Opium Act 1897* and subsequent legislation.

Fig. 6.1 Central Cape York Peninsula outstations map

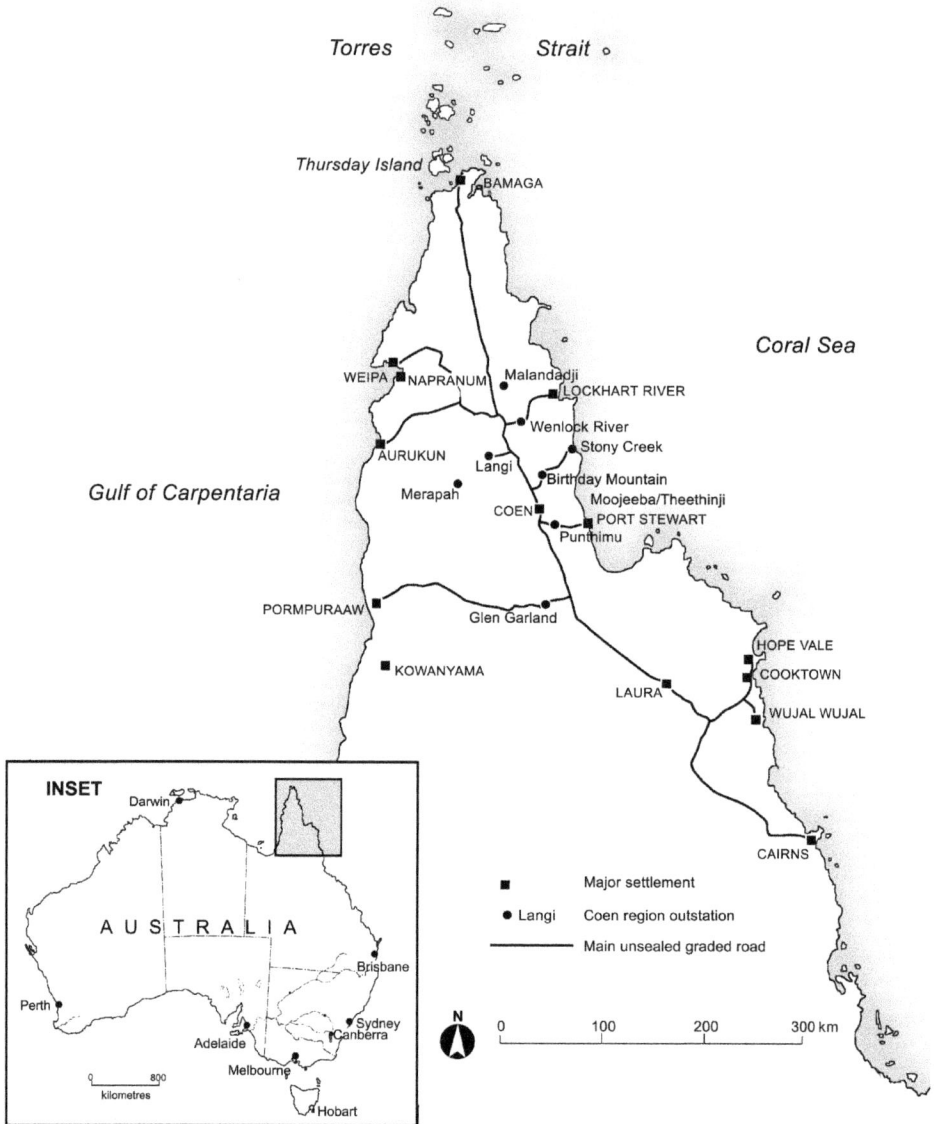

In the late 1960s and early 1970s, a decline in pastoral employment was exacerbated by the recognition of Aboriginal citizenship and the granting of award wages. As a result, Kaanju people living in the central Peninsula found themselves centralised in places like Coen, a small township in the centre of the Peninsula, as well as at discrete Aboriginal settlements like Lockhart River and other former mission or government settlements. This situation persisted until the late 1980s, when the establishment of a series of Aboriginal corporations in

Coen, and the increasing possibility of access to traditional land through claim, transfer and purchase processes, allowed Kaanju people to re-establish permanent living spaces on their country.

Kaanju outstations (1989–96)

In the late 1980s and early 1990s, two distinct groups of Kaanju people sought to establish 'outstations' on their homelands, and to regain control of their country through land claims. The first of these groups was centred on an extended family[8] whose forebears' clan country lay just to the north of Coen, around Birthday Mountain (Watharra).[9] The second group, which included a number of closely related members of several extended families, sought to re-occupy country on the upper Wenlock River.

For this latter group, the desire to return to country was complicated by the character of mainstream land tenure on their homelands. The principal 'boss' of this group in the 1980s, M_, a Kaanju woman then in her forties, had a particular connection to a stretch of the Wenlock River focused on the Lightning Story-Place, Malantachi. However, this Story-Place, along with much of M_'s father's country (with which she primarily identified), was occupied by an 'experimental farm' run by Queensland's Department of Primary Industries.[10] The only available land for the establishment of an outstation lay further upstream, close to the Frill-Neck Lizard Story-Place called Chuulangun (Dusty Lagoon), on the upper Wenlock River just inside the Deed of Grant in Trust (DOGIT) lands of the Lockhart River Aboriginal community.

In order to establish the Wenlock River outstation, M_ needed the support of other Kaanju people with closer ties to the country around Chuulangun. In part, this support was needed to gain the formal permission of Lockhart River Council to establish the outstation within the DOGIT. But M_'s primary consideration appears to have been the 'informal' permission she required, in accordance with local Aboriginal Law, to undertake the establishment of an outstation on an area somewhat removed from her father's principal country. To this end, she sought the support of two senior Kaanju men, T_ (her cousin) and S_ (her classificatory uncle). Both of these men had close connections in the vicinity of Chuulangun. T_'s principal ties were to the nearby Eagle-Hawk Story-Place called Nantanchi, and S_'s connections centred on the 'Tommy-Round Head Lizard' Story-Place at Mula at the headwaters of the Pascoe River. In partnership with these two senior Kaanju men, M_ was able to develop the Wenlock River outstation with funds administered by an Aboriginal corporation in Coen, whilst simultaneously

---

[8] Here, and throughout this paper, my use of the term 'family' indicates what Sutton (2003: 206–9), following the common Aboriginal use of the term 'family', identifies as 'families of polity'.
[9] See, Land Tribunal 1995.
[10] This farm had previously been a pastoral lease, which was the subject of compulsory purchase by the Queensland Government.

seeking support for regaining control of her own country around Malantachi, where she also hoped to establish a camp.

At this early stage in the development of the outstation, the complex interplay between 'informal' aspects of governance within the Aboriginal domain and 'formal' Aboriginal organisations and councils was already apparent. On the one hand, M_'s establishment of the outstation at Chuulangun depended upon a negotiation of particular interests in Kaanju country distributed among a set of senior men and women (including T_ and S_, as well as M_ herself). These more localised interests together coalesced into a wider 'countryman' (Chase 1980) grouping of Kaanju people from the upper Wenlock and Pascoe river systems, who jointly re-established and utilised the Wenlock outstation camp.

But these localised and countryman identities—key aspects of governance within the Aboriginal domain—articulated with more formal aspects of the region's field of governance. These more formal aspects of governance included the Lockhart River Aboriginal Shire Council, whose permission was needed to allow the establishment of the outstation on the DOGIT. They also included several Aboriginal corporations based in Coen,[11] where M_ and T_ both lived.

Importantly, the manner in which Kaanju governance was articulated in the formal governance arrangements at Coen and Lockhart River varied both in scale and style from the manner in which Kaanju governance was enacted within the Aboriginal domain. In Coen, for example, Kaanju people were formally represented as members of two discrete groups—the 'Northern Kaanju' (who included M_ and the other Kaanju people from the Wenlock and Pascoe rivers) and the 'Southern Kaanju', a term taken to identify Kaanju people from the more southerly Archer River system, but which in practice was near-synonymous with the Coen-based Kaanju family from Watharra (Birthday Mountain).

The principal cause of the emergence of this formal 'Northern' and 'Southern Kaanju' distinction seems to have been the development of a land claim (under Queensland's *Aboriginal Land Act 1991*) over the Birthday Mountain area. In developing this claim, C_, the senior member of the Wathara-associated family group, sought to limit the claimant group to his own 'clan' or 'family'. As the claim process developed, however, the claimant group was broadened to include all 'Southern Kaanju' families. But the claim continued to exclude the 'Northern Kaanju' group, an exclusion based on linguistic and social distinctions between Kaanju people from the Archer River and the Wenlock and Pascoe river areas.

Sutton (1996) has outlined the expansion of the Birthday Mountain claimant group, an event whose concern with social scale in relation to traditional

---

[11] These included the Moomba and Malpa Kincha corporations, established in the late 1980s, and their successor, the Coen Regional Aboriginal Corporation, established in 1993 (see Smith 2000b).

ownership is of relevance to understanding the field of governance in the central Peninsula:

> It is sometimes the case that people maintain proximate entitlements to small areas such as classical [clan] estates as well as an identification with more widely cast landed entities such as language groups … Such a situation may lead to conflict. In the Birthday Mountain land claim … this particular distinction came to a head when the claim was lodged solely on behalf of a small descent group … Other southern Kaanju people lodged a subsequent claim over the same land … [Later] the two sets of claimants came to a signed settlement to the effect that … the southern Kaanju as a whole had traditional affiliation to the claimed land [but] the small descent group were the owners of the land under Aboriginal tradition … Here was a case in which an assertion of autonomy by a group holding proximate title failed, not completely, but partially, and as a result of the assertion of interests by those speaking for a wider group that included them (Sutton 1996: 24).

Comparable forms of contestation by 'groups' of various scales has occurred in relation to 'Northern Kaanju' country, although—as I argue below—the language of 'groups' may not be the best way to apprehend the articulation of differing interests in such cases.

At the same time that the 'Southern Kaanju' group was engaged in the Birthday Mountain land claim, the newly formed Coen Regional Aboriginal Corporation (CRAC) reserved places for 'Northern Kaanju' and 'Southern Kaanju' representatives on its Board of Directors, alongside representatives of several other Coen-based 'tribes' and a set of people whose primary identity was as a 'town mob' (Smith 2000b). But despite the obvious attempt by CRAC to produce a 'culturally appropriate' form of representation—by way of reserved places for the region's various 'tribal' factions—there was a clear difference apparent between the notion of representation that underlay the development of the CRAC board (that a senior man or woman could speak for an amalgamated 'tribal' group) and the carefully negotiated politics of 'speaking for country' apparent between M_ and other senior Kaanju people. Further, the reified 'Northern' and 'Southern Kaanju' 'tribal' groups—presumed by CRAC to exist as principal sociopolitical conglomerations within regional Aboriginal governance—were also at odds with a more localised emphasis on country within the region's Aboriginal domain. Nonetheless, rather than a distinction between 'Aboriginal' and 'formal' governance arrangements, the late 1980s and early 1990s instead saw ongoing attempts at an accommodation between informal Aboriginal values and processes, and formal representation within CRAC.[12] In this way, reified constructs like the 'Northern Kaanju' identity acted as place-holders for M_ and her relations' engagements with outsiders, whilst the flow of resources that enabled the development of the Wenlock River outstation reinforced the reproduction of a conjoint 'countryman' group of Kaanju people with shared interests in the Wenlock River outstation and surrounding areas of Kaanju country.

Development of Chuulangun (late 1990s–present)

A number of changes occurred in the regional field of governance in the late 1990s. These included changes in the Kaanju people acting as the focal men and women for 'business' involving homelands on the upper Wenlock and Pascoe rivers, and a growing set of organisations becoming involved in the governance of these homelands.

Fig. 6.2 Kinship relations of the Wenlock outstation 'mob'

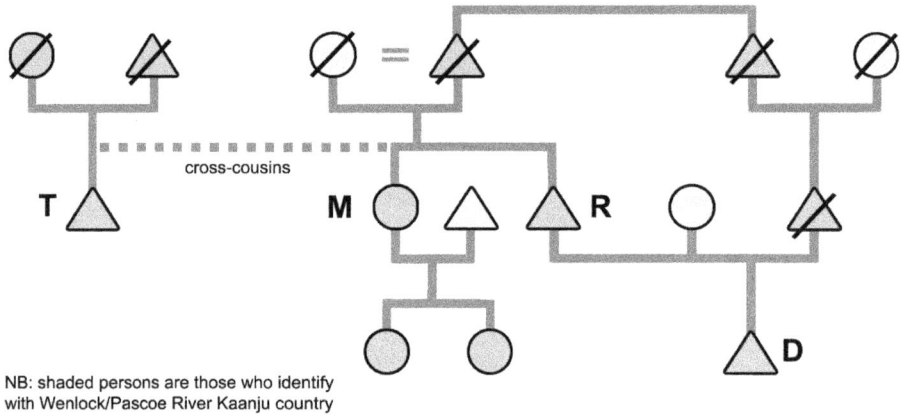

NB: shaded persons are those who identify with Wenlock/Pascoe River Kaanju country

In the mid 1990s, the set of men and women primarily involved in Aboriginal decision making for Kaanju homelands on the upper Wenlock and Pascoe rivers changed following the death of S_ and the increasing involvement of M_'s brother R_, who had returned to the central Peninsula in the intervening years (see Fig. 6.2). R_ and his wife V_ had taken up residence at the Wenlock River outstation, and took primary responsibility for the day-to-day running of the camp, which had become the focus of R_'s intention to develop a cattle property on Kaanju land. T_ continued to move between the outstation and Coen, while M_ resided principally in Coen but maintained her position as the principal

---

[12] Such formal representations were determined, in part, by the expectations and requirements of 'outsider' administrators, consultants and organisations, ranging from the first 'project manager' to regional Aboriginal and Torres Strait Islander Commission officers.

'boss' for the outstation, in part due to R_'s disinclination towards taking such a role.

The Wenlock River camp had also attracted a number of other people as occasional residents, including the family of A_, a senior Kaanju woman whose principal connections to country lay further upstream. A_'s family had become extremely influential at Lockhart River, where they usually resided, and had also become more involved with the outstation. A number of stolen generation Kaanju people had also begun to express increasing interest in 'business' pertaining to Kaanju homelands, although they lived in the settlements to the south of the Peninsula to which their forebears had been removed.

This shifting set of focal individuals was further shaped by the increasing prominence of D_, M_'s nephew, who began to move into a more active role in the late 1990s. Over time, D_ and his wife succeeded to control of the Wenlock outstation, whilst R_ and V_ (D_'s mother) shifted their principal place of residence to Coen. D_ consolidated his focal role at the Wenlock camp following the deaths of T_ and M_ in the early 2000s.

As the new boss of the Wenlock camp, D_ moved to place what he understood to be 'proper Kaanju governance' at the heart of homelands' business. The crux of D_'s attempts to regenerate 'proper' Kaanju governance was his establishment of a formal structure—the Chuulangun Aboriginal Corporation (CAC). The corporation was based at the Wenlock River outstation, but purported to represent and to 'manage' a wide area of Kaanju land on the upper Wenlock and upper Pascoe rivers.

In part, D_ sought to establish CAC in response to other governance arrangements, which he understood to be inappropriate. The CRAC, for instance, was seen as taking an improper 'sub-regional approach' to governance, instead of a form of governance 'from the inside out', based on homelands and directed by traditional owners living there. D_ also established the CAC in reaction to an increasing 'regional' approach to governance, led by a series of organisations based in Cairns, as well as new governance arrangements based at Lockhart River.

The new Lockhart River arrangements were a source of considerable concern for D_. Despite the ongoing focal role of Kaanju people living between Chuulangun and Coen, the outstation remained situated within lands managed from Lockhart River. The new Lockhart-based Mangkuma Land Trust (hereafter Mangkuma)—established following the 'handover' of the former Lockhart DOGIT to traditional owners (who include a number of coastal 'Sandbeach' people, as well as both 'Northern' and 'Southern Kaanju')—now vied with the more localised CAC for the control of the relevant part of the DOGIT. D_'s dissatisfaction with Mangkuma was further intensified by the appointment of a stolen generation man, L_, as its chairperson. L_ asserted a Kaanju identity, and regarded himself as able to 'speak for' the country purportedly controlled by CAC. But L_'s understanding—and enactment—of Kaanju law and custom was at odds with D_'s. As a result, the conflict between the two men—and the formal bodies that they controlled—had also become a conflict over the definition of 'proper' governance within the Aboriginal domain. This conflict was exacerbated by D_'s parallel conflict with A_ and her family, which also focused on competing interpretations of Kaanju law and custom.

In this way, the conflicts over the appropriate forms of governance for Kaanju homelands involved disputes both over 'informal' governance, based in traditional law and custom and the 'Aboriginal domain', and competing claims between a series of organisations established at various scales of representation and with different mandates and styles of governance. But rather than being separate issues, these aspects of the field of governance were increasingly interwoven.

More recently, this interweaving of the Aboriginal domain and various local and regional Aboriginal organisations has been further intensified by a series of partnership arrangements between these organisations and a series of NGOs, researchers, and commercial operators. The resulting flow of resources for homelands-based projects has intensified the conflicts between the various factions, organisations and individuals involved. But alongside such conflicts, a series of crosscutting ties and partnerships between these organisations has also emerged. D_, for example, is currently a CRAC Director, despite his vocal criticisms of this corporation, and he has more recently become the Deputy Chairperson of Mangkuma (taking up the role following L_'s resignation as chairperson). He is also engaged with various Cairns-based 'regional' organisations, despite simultaneously seeking to lessen their influence on the governance of Kaanju country. More than ever, governance of Kaanju homelands is vested in a complex field of governance that simultaneously allows for conflict and competition, and for shifting partnerships and alliances.

Discussion

The field of governance in central Cape York Peninsula involves three sets of contested relationships that are constitutive of this field and its inherent complexities. Firstly, this field involves the articulation of homelands-based, 'sub-regional' and 'regional' Aboriginal organisations, in addition to the role played by State and Federal government agencies. Secondly, the region's field of governance involves both putative and enacted relationships between contemporary forms of traditional Aboriginal law and custom, and 'intercultural' and 'mainstream' governance processes. Lastly, the region's field of governance is marked by various forms of conjoint Aboriginal identity, articulated at different social scales.

The relationship of homelands-based, 'sub-regional' and 'regional' Aboriginal organisations with one another, as well as their engagements with State and Federal government agencies, represents the first set of contested relationships constitutive of this field. The past two decades have seen the establishment of a range of such organisations, including a series of Aboriginal corporations in Coen and Mangkuma at Lockhart River, Cairns-based 'regional' organisations such as the Cape York Land Council and several homelands-based corporations like CAC. This proliferation of formally incorporated bodies recalls Sanders' (2004) suggestion that, rather than marking a 'failure' of Indigenous governance, the development of a complex and contested series of incorporated organisations meets particular socio-cultural and political requirements. The development of such representative structures may well mark a successful indigenisation of governance rather than a failure in the development of governance arrangements.

This recalls Gluckman's (1968: 223) suggestion, as mentioned above, that institutions and wider social fields have a tendency to endure, such that 'a field of institutional systems ... will tend to develop, and even hypertrophy, along the main facets of its organisation, until conditions make it quite impossible for the system to continue to work'. As Sanders suggests, a hypertrophic tendency—a tendency to enlarge and increase in complexity—is widespread in Indigenous community governance. The establishment of a range of organisations at different scales should not be regarded as accidental, but rather as an expression of the different ways in which both Aboriginal and non-Indigenous agents seek to enact governance.

Further, the fact that focal men and women like D_ dispute the operation of Indigenous governance at certain scales, whilst remaining involved with organisations operating at those scales, should not be taken simply as capitulation to pre-established conditions. Rather, the organisational structures, institutions and procedures of the central Peninsula's field of governance are themselves often partly driven by Indigenous relationships and systems (Hunt and Smith 2006a). This is one aspect of the increasing interweaving of formal and informal aspects of the regional field of governance. The resulting ability of Aboriginal people like D_ to activate formalised relationships of governance across various scales demonstrates the continuing existence of styles of Aboriginal politics within the contemporary field of governance surrounding Kaanju homelands.

Thus, as well as the interaction of formal Aboriginal organisations, the region's field of governance includes relationships between contemporary forms of traditional Aboriginal law and custom and formal structures and processes of governance. These relationships have been treated elsewhere in terms of 'cultural match' and 'legitimacy' (see e.g., Hunt and Smith 2006a).

Questions concerning 'cultural match' are important in relation to Kaanju homelands, not least because they are a focus of current disputes between various focal men and women and the organisations with which they are aligned. Here it is important to note the high degree of heterogeneity of the 'preferred contemporary values, norms and conceptions of how authority should be organised and leadership exercised' (Hunt and Smith 2006b: 2). This heterogeneity implies that it may not be possible to discover a single governance arrangement best suited or most appropriate to this region. Rather, outside observers—and those entering into partnerships with Kaanju people in homelands-based projects—would do better to understand Aboriginal assertions about 'culture', 'law' and 'custom' as aspects of the shifting articulations of identity that remain deeply interwoven with Aboriginal politics. Likewise, issues of scale of representation or styles of decision making are deeply interwoven with the shifting field of relationality, autonomy and encompassment that lies at the heart of Aboriginal political life. To presume that there is a fundamentally legitimate cultural form or social scale that can be the basis of appropriate governance is to privilege one moment within the dynamic processes that constitute the regional field of governance.

For this reason, formal institutions of governance are deeply interwoven with less formal aspects of governance—in particular, the relational politics of the Aboriginal domain. This interrelationship problematises the idea of 'culture match'. In the central Peninsula, one cannot simply expect to 'match' an institution to an underlying social order. Rather, the various 'institutions' (whether formal or informal) that together constitute the field of governance are marked by ongoing processes of inter-relation and contestation. In generating a complex institutional field, local Aboriginal styles of governance have not been 'matched'. Rather, Aboriginal organisations have been accommodated within an existing field of governance, resulting in a hypertrophic series of organisations that extends the informal complexities of Aboriginal politics.[13]

The complexities of these local Aboriginal styles of governance include the articulation of various forms of Aboriginal identity at different social scales—particularly in relation to intra-Aboriginal politics. What Hunt and Smith (2006a: ix) call a 'continuum of localised and regionalised scales of population and land ownership' lies at the heart of the region's complex field of Indigenous governance. Here, rather than the 'groups' on which most attempts at formal Indigenous governance are based, what is apparent is the constantly shifting presentation of various conjoint identities as the basis of political action. As in the contested history of 'Southern Kaanju' people's involvement in the Birthday Mountain claim, 'Northern Kaanju' involvement in the governance of their homelands makes it clear that any attempt to identify a basic level or form

---

[13] Conversely, the originally exogenous political formations and styles of the state have become intermeshed with local Aboriginal forms of governance, leading to the development of an intercultural field of governance.

of Aboriginal governance obscures the inherent indeterminacy of the identities through which Aboriginal social and political life is enacted. Indeed, any such attempt at formalisation of Aboriginal 'groups' is likely to result in a reactionary projection of interests at a smaller or larger scale, again revealing the dynamic of 'autonomy and relatedness' (Martin 1993; Myers 1986) that lies at the heart of Aboriginal sociality.[14]

Issues of leadership and succession are similarly embedded in the negotiative, contested and fractious domain of Aboriginal political identities. Following the death of several of the region's focal men and women, succession in relation to Kaanju homelands 'business' was marked by the emergence of an intercultural representative politics, and by a move away from an emphasis on negotiative interrelation with an 'as of right' model of representation being asserted by at least one local 'leader'. But both of these phenomena were undercut by a continuing emphasis on a negotiative form of relational politics among Kaanju people. This negotiative character weakened the effectiveness of both CAC and Mangkuma, whilst those controlling these organisations avoided seeking widespread political support. L_'s recent resignation and D_'s concurrent move to engage a wider set of Aboriginal people in his projects suggest a realignment of both organisations towards the involvement of a wider range of 'countrymen'. This move may prove vital to these organisations in continuing to garner support from 'outside' organisations, support that remains essential to successful homelands development.

Despite their earlier shift away from the negotiative style of Aboriginal politics, both CAC and Mangkuma were previously managed to generate homelands-based development projects. But these projects were hampered by continuing inter-organisational and inter-personal conflicts, and by growing questions amongst the employees of partnering governmental and non-governmental organisations concerning the legitimacy of their operations. Whilst both organisations could claim some successes in relation to particular development projects on homelands, it seemed likely until recently that internal tensions and external caution might eventually have hindered the sustainability of such development.

The manner in which the relational style of Aboriginal politics has undermined organisations like CAC and Mangkuma recalls Hunt and Smith's (2006a) insistence that the governance environment can enable or disable. Certainly, it seems that where focal men and women exceed the support of their wider set of countrymen, the organisations for which they are responsible can face considerable difficulties.

---

[14] Interestingly, all of the region's focal men and women—despite continuing disputes over the articulation of regional and local identities—recognise a wider level of regional connectedness. But exactly how this regional connectedness relates to Indigenous governance arrangements is a key aspect of the contested and cross-cutting articulation of politicised identity across the region.

But I am not convinced that we can presume that such disabling effects are necessarily negative from local Aboriginal perspectives, even where they impede economic development. As anthropologists working with (former) hunter-gatherers have argued (see e.g., Woodburn 1982), these peoples—who commonly have a strongly acephalous political orientation—are often resistant to political formations that do not satisfy their interests, even where they will suffer material losses as a result. Although it is difficult to even consider such ideas within the current climate of Aboriginal affairs in Australia, it is vital to consider whether the disabling of governance arrangements may, on balance, be viewed as desirable by many Aboriginal people where these arrangements do not meet with their approval and support.

Conclusion

Rather than understanding Indigenous community governance in the central Peninsula in terms of incorporated organisations and an informal 'Aboriginal domain', both located within a wider 'governance environment', it can be best understood in terms of a complex regional field. Within this field, what Hunt and D. Smith (2006a: 76) have identified as 'four layers or dimensions of governance'— individual, entity, inter-relationships and 'environment'—can all be recognised. But disentangling these 'layers' in this manner involves the reification of aspects of a complex field, which can lead to both analytic and practical complications.

One important problem inherent in the notion of a surrounding governance environment is that it masks the substantial interweaving of the 'Aboriginal' and the 'mainstream', and the intercultural character of Indigenous community governance. This is analytically inaccurate—as the concept of the field of governance makes clear, 'outside' agencies and their interventions are very much a constitutive aspect of such fields. But any masking of this social, cultural and political interweaving also limits possibilities of an effective rapprochement between the various interests—Aboriginal and otherwise—at play in such fields.

Acknowledgements

This paper is based on research supported by the Australian Research Council, the Leverhulme Trust, the Australian Institute of Aboriginal and Torres Strait Islander Studies, the Emslie Hornimann Fund and the University of London. I am grateful to Kaanju people from the Wenlock and Pascoe rivers, and to the other families of central Cape York Peninsula, for their ongoing support of my research. I owe a particular debt to members of the Moreton/Nelson family, without whose ongoing support this paper could not have been written. I am also grateful to the two anonymous referees for their useful comments. Any errors of fact and analysis that remain are mine.

References

Chase, A. 1980. Which Way Now? Tradition, Continuity and Change in a North Queensland Aboriginal Community, PhD Thesis, The University of Queensland, Brisbane.

Gluckman, M. 1968. 'The utility of the equilibrium model in the study of social change', *American Anthropologist*, 70 (2): 219–37.

Hinkson, M. and Smith, B. R. (eds) 2005a. *Figuring the Intercultural in Aboriginal Australia*, Special Issue, *Oceania*, 75 (3).

—— and ——2005b. 'Introduction: conceptual moves towards an intercultural analysis', in M. Hinkson and B. R. Smith (eds), *Figuring the Intercultural in Aboriginal Australia*, Special Issue, *Oceania*, 75 (3): 157–66.

Hunt, J. and Smith, D. E. 2006a. 'Building Indigenous community governance in Australia: preliminary research findings', *CAEPR Working Paper No. 31*, CAEPR, ANU, Canberra.

—— and ——2006b. 'Ten key messages from the preliminary findings of the Indigenous Community Governance Project, 2005', ICGP, CAEPR, ANU, Canberra, available at <http://www.anu.edu.au/caepr/ICGP_publications.php #resreports> [accessed 9 October 2007].

Keen, I. 1989. 'Aboriginal governance', in J. C. Altman (ed.), *Emergent Inequalities in Aboriginal Australia*, Oceania Monograph No. 38, University of Sydney, Sydney.

Land Tribunal 1995. *Aboriginal Land Claims to Vacant Crown Land in the Vicinity of Birthday Mountain*, Land Tribunal, Queensland Government, Brisbane.

Martin, D. F. 1993. Autonomy and Relatedness: An Ethnography of the Wik People of Western Cape York Peninsula, PhD Thesis, ANU, Canberra.

——2003. 'Rethinking the design of indigenous organisations: the need for strategic engagement', *CAEPR Discussion Paper No. 248*, CAEPR, ANU, Canberra.

Merlan, F. 1981. 'Land, language and social identity in Aboriginal Australia', *Mankind*, 13: 133–48.

——1998. *Caging the Rainbow: Places, Politics, and Aborigines in a North Australian Town*, University of Hawaii Press, Honolulu.

——2005. 'Explorations towards intercultural accounts of socio-cultural reproduction and change', in M. Hinkson and B. R. Smith (eds), *Figuring the Intercultural in Aboriginal Australia*, Special Issue, *Oceania*, 75 (3): 167–82.

Myers, F. 1986. *Pintupi Country, Pintupi Self: Sentiment, Place and Politics Among Western Desert Aborigines*, University of California Press, Berkeley.

Rigsby, B. 1999. 'Aboriginal people, spirituality and the traditional ownership of land', *International Journal of Social Economics*, 26 (7/8/9): 963–76.

Rowse, T. 1992. *Remote Possibilities: The Aboriginal Domain and the Administrative Imagination*, North Australia Research Unit, ANU, Darwin.

Rumsey, A. 1989. 'Language groups in Australian Aboriginal land claims', *Anthropological Forum*, 6 (1): 69–79.

Sanders, W. 2004. 'Thinking about Indigenous community governance', *CAEPR Discussion Paper No. 262*, CAEPR, ANU, Canberra.

Scott, J. C. 1998. *Seeing Like a State: How Certain Schemes to Improve the Human Condition Have Failed*, Yale University Press, New Haven.

Smith, B. R. 2000a. 'Local and diaspora connections to country and kin in Central Cape York Peninsula', *Native Title Research Unit Issues Paper 2(6)*, Native Title Research Unit, AIATSIS, Canberra.

——2000b. Between Places: Aboriginal Decentralisation, Mobility and Territoriality in the Region of Coen, Cape York Peninsula (Australia), PhD Thesis, Department of Anthropology, London School of Economics and Political Science, University of London, London.

——2004. 'The social underpinnings of an "outstation movement" in Cape York Peninsula, Australia', in J. Taylor and M. Bell (eds), *Population Mobility and Indigenous Peoples in Australasia and North America*, Routledge, London.

——2006. '"More than love": locality and affects of indigeneity in Northern Queensland', *The Asia Pacific Journal of Anthropology*, 7 (3): 221–35.

——2007. 'Towards an uncertain community? The social effects of native title in Central Cape York Peninsula', in B. R. Smith and F. Morphy (eds), *The Social Effects of Native Title: Recognition, Translation and Coexistence*. CAEPR Monograph No. 27, ANU E Press, Canberra..

Strathern, M. 1992. 'Parts and wholes: refiguring relationships', in A. Kuper (ed.), *Conceptualizing Society*, Routledge, London.

Sullivan, P. 2005. 'Searching for the intercultural, searching for the culture', in M. Hinkson and B. R. Smith (eds), *Figuring the Intercultural in Aboriginal Australia*, Special Issue, Oceania, 75 (3): 183–94.

Sutton, P. 1996. 'The robustness of aboriginal land tenure systems: underlying and proximate customary titles', *Oceania*, 67 (1): 7–29.

——2003. *Native Title in Australia: An Ethnographic Perspective*, Cambridge University Press, Cambridge.

Thomson, D. F. 1933. 'The hero cult, initiation and totemism on Cape York', *Journal of the Royal Anthropological Institute*, 63: 453–537.

Trigger, D. 1986. 'Blackfellas and whitefellas: the concepts of domain and social closure in the analysis of race relations', *Mankind*, 16 (2): 99–117.

——1992. *Whitefella Commin'*, Cambridge University Press, Cambridge.

von Sturmer, J. R. 1984. 'The different domains', in Australian Institute of Aboriginal Studies, *Aborigines and Uranium: Consolidated Report on the Social Impact of Uranium Mining on the Aborigines of the Northern Territory*, AIAS , Canberra.

Woodburn, J. 1982. 'Egalitarian societies', *Man*, 17 (3): 431–51.

Part 3: Institutions of Indigenous governance

7. Different governance for difference: the Bawinanga Aboriginal Corporation

Jon Altman

This chapter focuses on the organisational history and governance development of the Bawinanga Aboriginal Corporation (BAC) from its establishment in 1979 until late 2007. BAC is located in the Aboriginal township of Maningrida in north-central Arnhem Land in the Northern Territory (NT). It was incorporated under the Commonwealth *Aboriginal Councils and Associations Act 1976* as an outstations resource organisation. Its original objects were to provide services to its members, most of whom resided at small dispersed outstation communities in the Maningrida hinterland of around 10,000km². BAC, however, has always been more than just a resource agency for outstations. From its formation it has also administered a significant Aboriginal arts centre, Maningrida Arts and Culture (MAC), and so has provided services to artists both at outstations and at Maningrida. Even before its formal incorporation, key Aboriginal and non-Aboriginal personnel subsequently associated with BAC were engaged in advocating for land rights, outstation development and ultimately regional Aboriginal self-determination. BAC has always been a progressive organisation advocating for appropriate forms of development for its membership.

BAC's organisational life path can be seen in three phases. The first, which dates from the early 1970s to 1989, is as an outstation resource agency (ORA) and Aboriginal arts centre. The second, from 1989, saw the transformation of BAC as it evolved into a major Community Development Employment Projects (CDEP) organisation. The start of the third phase, which saw BAC expand into a regional development agency, is more difficult to precisely demarcate. This phase probably dates from 1996, when BAC established its first Maningrida-based business and was subsequently recognised by the Australian Government as an organisation with sufficient capacity to administer major programs.

The Maningrida region is culturally heterogeneous and administratively complex. Maningrida was established as a government settlement some 50 years ago, during an era when the assimilation of Aboriginal people into mainstream Australian society was official colonial settler state policy. From 1957, there were political tensions between local Aboriginal land owners and other Aboriginal groups; and between Aboriginal people and white administrators operating with very different social norms and notions of accountability, and with highly differentiated political power. While BAC was established in the immediate post-colonial period, when self-determination became official government policy, it has had to operate in a complex intercultural environment. While ostensibly

BAC has a key role brokering on behalf of its membership with the Australian state, it also faces the complex challenge of mediating the diverse interests of its membership. These diverse Aboriginal interests are dynamic, transforming, and difficult to unambiguously demarcate—they are influenced by a complex system of land ownership, language (or multi-language), personal and group identity, shifting locational and family affiliations, and associated local political alliances.

The principal aim of this chapter is to explain how BAC has managed to effectively and simultaneously manage governance tensions between Aboriginal and non-Aboriginal social norms and within its Aboriginal membership. This explanation is provided by tracing BAC's organisational history and its transformative, intercultural form of governance. The analytic explication seeks to identify some of the factors that have been critical to the governance and development success of BAC in effectively managing the tensions between western market-based and Indigenous kin-based social norms.

While history matters greatly in the BAC story, the focus here is primarily on the years since 1999. This is the time when formal governance emerged as a growing organisational issue. It is also a period in which the broader national Indigenous affairs environment has undergone some major transformations, with the abolition of the Aboriginal and Torres Strait Islander Commission (ATSIC) in 2004 and the sudden declaration of the NT National Emergency Response in June 2007. These recent events provide an interesting book-ending of the nearly 30 year organisational existence of BAC.

The corporation was established to meet the emerging needs of the Maningrida region's growing outstations population. Today, those same needs exist, but the policy proposals announced in 2007 to abolish the two programs that have provided core funding to BAC by 30 June 2008 placed its future at considerable risk. This is a timely juncture to consider the vulnerability of a structurally dependent Aboriginal organisation (in what Rowse [2002] has termed 'the Indigenous sector') to the vagaries of policy change, irrespective of impressive performance, robust governance or the aspirations of membership. This in turn raises broader questions about the asymmetry of power relations in Australian society, the recent intolerance of the neoliberal state to cultural difference, and the extent that community governance and advocacy really matter for vulnerable Indigenous organisations.

A brief regional, social and historical background

The governance of Indigenous discrete communities is significantly influenced by their particular colonial histories and subsequent decolonisation experiences. The history of the Maningrida region needs some explication if we are to understand the background and operations of BAC. There is quite a significant literature about this region with key publications including Hiatt (1965), Meehan (1982), Altman (1987) and Gurmanamana, Hiatt and McKenzie (2002).

The Maningrida region is loosely demarcated by a region bounded by the Liverpool River to the west, the Glyde River to the east and the Arnhem Land escarpment to the south. It is estimated to cover 10,000km^2 of tropical savanna. The regional population estimated in the 2006 Census is about 3,000, 162 being non-Aboriginal.[1] The region is extraordinarily linguistically diverse, with at least 10 distinct Aboriginal languages still in common usage in the region, besides Aboriginal English. And regional diversity is not just limited to languages. There are also variations evident in local and social organisation, religion and ritual, customary economies, art styles, and so on.

The region is extremely remote, even by Australian standards, located 500km east of Darwin and with only seasonal overland access. It is for this reason in part that it was colonised by the Australian state relatively late (Altman and Hinkson 2007). The region is in the middle of the vast Arnhem Land Aboriginal Reserve with entry limited by the *Aboriginals Ordinance No. 9* (Cth) from 1918 onwards. A trading post was established in Maningrida in 1949–50 by the Native Affairs Branch of the NT Administration—to repatriate and keep Aboriginal people from the region out of Darwin—but then abandoned. In 1957, a government settlement was established at Maningrida, and only in 1963 was a bush track 'blazed' between Oenpelli (also known as Gunbalanya) and Maningrida by staff of the now renamed Welfare Branch of the NT Administration.[2] Some people from outlying inland areas only moved to Maningrida at that time.

Significant effort and public funding was expended on the development of Maningrida from 1957. Under the policy framework of assimilation, the aim was to centralise, sedentarise and 'civilise' or Europeanise Aboriginal people in the region, a state project that proved extremely costly and unsuccessful, and which was abandoned in 1972. This failure of assimilation is an aspect of policy history that current neo-conservative writing conveniently overlooks (see e.g., Hughes 2007). Even before 1972, there was a people's movement in the region that saw families return to live in small decentralised groups on their traditional lands. In doing so, they were rejecting the particular form of 'modernisation' offered at externally-controlled settlements and missions, and moving to live remotely

---

[1] The 2006 census enumerated 1904 Aboriginal and 156 non-Aboriginal people at Maningrida; 355 Aboriginal and six non-Aboriginal people at outstations; and a total regional population of 2345, including those who did not state their identity. An estimated resident population for Maningrida and outstations is not provided by the Australian Bureau of Statistics, but it is estimated that Territory-wide there is an undercount of 19 per cent. Assuming that this undercount is consistent across the NT (which it is not), the regional Aboriginal population can be factored up by 1.19 to just fewer than 3000, of which about five per cent is non-Indigenous. It is possible that the undercount was actually greater in the Maningrida region than elsewhere in the NT because of the large hinterland and dispersal of the population to outstations and seasonal camps during the dry, when census enumeration is undertaken.
[2] Before then, Maningrida was supplied by sea.

with minimal support from the state. A conservative reading of history erroneously sees this decentralisation as just a product of the permissive and progressive shift to self-determination and land rights from 1972, whereas this social movement preceded these policy developments (Coombs 1974). Decentralisation certainly accelerated as policy settings changed, but it may have happened anyhow owing to the failure of centralisation and the associated social tensions and extreme poverty experienced in Maningrida.

Fig. 7.1 Maningrida regional map

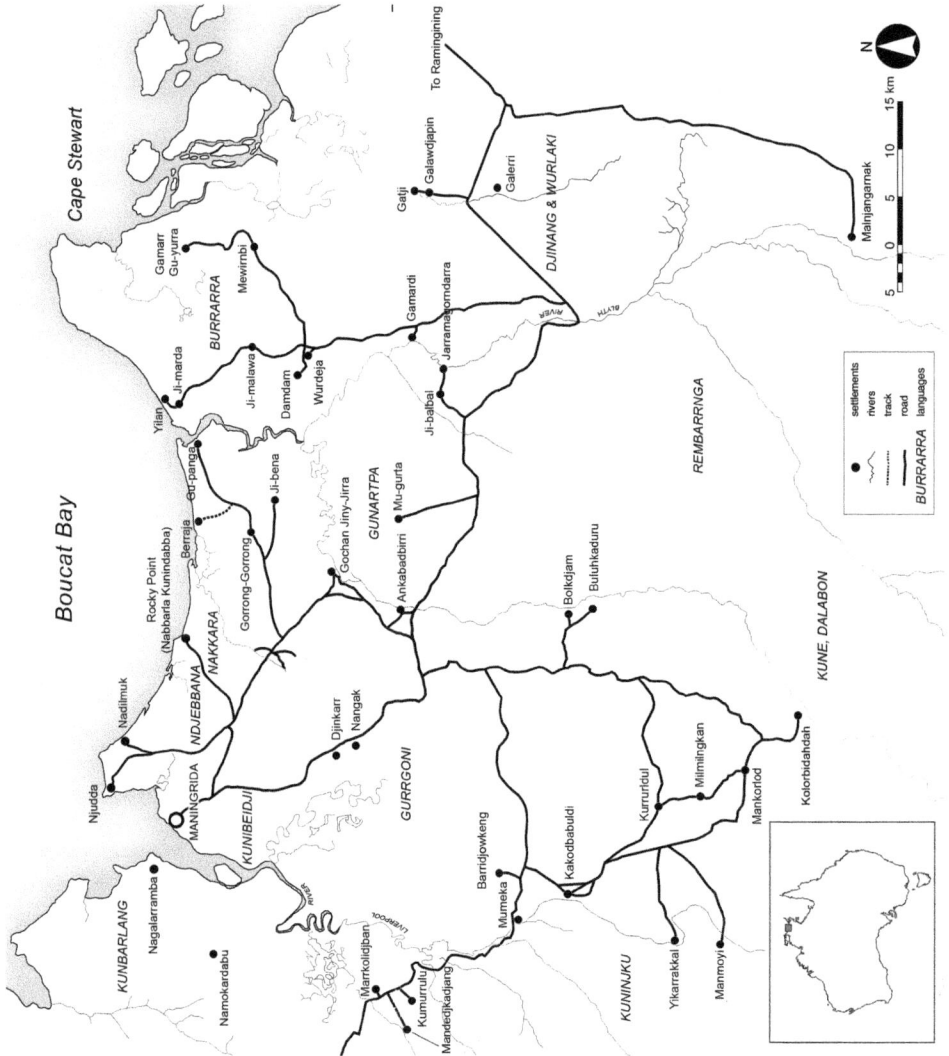

Elements of colonial discourse and associated ambiguities that remain today are notions of decentralisation and the term 'outstation', both of which are rarely used by Aboriginal people. Even the more modern terms, such as 'homeland communities' and 'return to country' (Blanchard 1987), suggest that people left, voluntarily or involuntarily. An outstation conjures up a notion of an outpost from a settlement, whereas in reality, for the residents it is just a locality on the land that they either own or to which they have rights of residence owing to kinship or other customary criteria. Local Aboriginal people just use the place name for an outstation locality as in Fig. 7.1, although when talking to outsiders generally prefer the term 'outstation' that I use here.

Maningrida was established because it was an administratively convenient locality near a fresh water spring at the mouth of the Liverpool River, on the land of the Dukurrdji clan. It is now, some 50 years on, a well-established township where the Dukurrdji land owners are greatly outnumbered. Outstations, by contrast, are small and generally located near perennial sources of fresh water and other natural resources. Outstations now have infrastructure and telecommunications that facilitate articulation with the wider administrative world, while maintaining a physical distance from Maningrida. Outstations have changed little in function from the 1970s (see Council for Aboriginal Affairs (CAA) 1976). Today, an outstation locality generally consists of a few houses, a source of year-round reticulated water, a Telstra pay phone, a bush airstrip or helipad, seasonal road access, and sometimes a small school building, usually with a residence for a visiting teacher (see Altman 2006).

Theory, methods and caveats

There is a dominant theoretical supposition in the governance and development literature that good governance at the local level is imperative to poverty reduction and development more generally (Grindle 2004: 525). This proposition has been theoretically and empirically examined in the Harvard Project on American Indian Economic Development (Cornell and Kalt 1995), which has greatly influenced the Indigenous Community Governance Project (ICGP) in Australia.

From 1979, I have observed and then collaborated with BAC, but it was nearly 20 years on before I belatedly started asking the fundamental question, does governance really matter? Initially, I did this in a very partial way, focusing only on parts of BAC's operations. In 1998, I examined BAC as an ORA as part of a national review (Altman, Gillespie and Palmer 1999); in 1999, I produced a business development plan for Maningrida Arts and Culture (Altman 1999); and in 2000, I collaborated in a review of BAC as a CDEP organisation, but again focusing somewhat narrowly on the efficacy of this program (Altman and Johnson 2000).

My specific interest and direct involvement in BAC governance issues escalated in 2003 when I was engaged as an advisory consultant by Dan Gillespie of Tallegalla Pty Ltd in the development of the first strategic plan for BAC for the triennium 2004–06 (Tallegalla 2003). In 1999, as part of a consultancy to revise BAC's constitution, Gillespie (1999) had undertaken a diagnostic assessment of the organisation, which identified the need for a strategic plan as a high priority. This planning exercise was undertaken in 2003 and involved consultation with members of BAC, its Executive Committee, senior management and staff—it was explicitly sought and funded by ATSIC.

Despite Gillespie's (1999) earlier recommendation, strategic planning was externally driven. This reflected a certain organisational antipathy to formal planning and governance processes. There was a degree of organisational comfort with a historically stable status quo based largely on relations of trust between senior managers and members, and an organisational preference for informal processes. An analysis in 2003 of BAC's strategic weaknesses and threats identified governance as a major planning and operational issue (Altman and Gillespie 2003: 10). In the subsequent strategic plan, governance was elevated to the first 'Key Result Area' priority (Tallegalla 2003: 12). The strategic planning exercise was a turning point for BAC, in belatedly recognising active engagement with formal notions of governance as an organisational priority.

The research reported here is mainly informed by visits made to Maningrida between 2005 and 2007 under the research umbrella of the ICGP. The field research visits have been quite short, so in a sense only provide governance 'snapshots'. But owing to long-standing research relationships, BAC's senior managers and executive have been welcoming, transparent and inclusive. For example, I was invited to all formal meetings of the executive that occurred during my visits, and was also able to participate, sometimes on a daily basis, in the informal meetings of members of BAC executive in the 'smoko' room, sometimes with BAC senior staff, sometimes without.

Participant observation in the smoko room critically influenced my views about BAC governance when I was finally able to recognise it as an 'informal' institution. The smoko room is a part of the BAC office, but has no windows, only security mesh so that passers-by can see in and chat with those inside—it is very transparent. It is popular with both Aboriginal staff and the executive because it is a place where one can relax, have a cup of tea, and, importantly, smoke. There is a great deal of communication and social interaction, both between members of the executive and between the executive and other BAC members and their families, constantly occurring in this place. This happens in various communication styles, in a mix of the numerous local languages and in Aboriginal English. Social interactions in the smoko room are often theatrical, humorous and extremely difficult to follow. But they constitute an institution where the rules of the BAC game (to paraphrase Leach, Mearns and Scoones 1999) are debated and explicated. Governance encompasses notions like power sharing, making legitimate decisions about actions and resources, sharing information, accountability, making policy, and having rules and norms that determine such actions. This all happens informally in the smoko room.

The smoko room is an informal institution (to be differentiated from the more formal executive meetings held to accord with western incorporations law) because distinctly Indigenous social norms and codes of behaviour dominate in this setting. This institution is of crucial importance to BAC's sound governance. This is especially the case when local Aboriginal elites, with ascribed power based on seniority and customary authority, interact with the 'neo-elites' whose power is mandated through modernising processes (see Collman 1988). A long time ago, Bagshaw (1977: 28) referred to the latter as *balanda marringi* (in the Burarra language), literally 'understanding whiteman' to be contrasted with *gala marringi*, the non-cognisant.[3] I labour this point to highlight that the smoko room provides opportunity for these two groups to interact productively. It is also noteworthy that outsider snapshots of such Aboriginal governance processes can be inadequate if they do not observe such informal institutions at work, although they can be difficult to interpret.

Finally, it is important that my earlier interests in the activities and governance of BAC are clearly stated to transparently address the issue of potential conflict of interest. While I am recognised by BAC as a long-term 'friend', both the governing committee and senior management have historically allowed me unfettered access to material and have been open to research findings, even when critical. Another source of potential conflict of interest is my early residence in 1979–81 at an outstation called Mumeka, whose residents are members of the Kuninjku language community. Arguably (and this argument has been made by local Aboriginal people themselves), my take on BAC has always been a little over-influenced by a Kuninjku-centric view of the regional polity. I do not deny this possibility, but note that this old allegiance has abated somewhat as more and more research is undertaken with individuals from other language communities.

A potted history of BAC's organisational evolution

In the early 1970s as the outstations movement gathered momentum in central Arnhem Land, Aboriginal people were increasingly empowered to return to live on their traditional lands. The exodus from Maningrida was one of the most significant from the NT's centralised Aboriginal settlements in population terms (see CAA 1976; Meehan 1982; Altman 1987). Government policy at that time supported decentralisation and this in turn required organisational support, especially in the delivery of basic services: fortnightly delivery of social security

---

[3] In recent communications, Bagshaw notes that the grammatically more correct terms in Burarra would be *marngi balanda gun-nika rom aburr-ni* and *gala marrngi balanda gun-nika aburr-ni* (pers. comm. 5 November 2007).

cheques and commodities from the Maningrida store; assistance with basic external communications and the marketing of arts and crafts; and assistance with establishing rudimentary water reticulation in some situations. In those days, there were no standard western housing or ablution facilities at outstations.

Initially, this basic support was provided by the Department of Aboriginal Affairs, then by the Maningrida Progress Association, and then from 1976 by a branch of the Maningrida town council, called the Maningrida Outstation Resource Centre (see Gillespie, Cooke and Bond 1977). The resource centre was staffed by three non-indigenous men—Dan Gillespie, Peter Cooke and David Bond— assisted by a number of local men, some now deceased. Gillespie and Cooke had lived in the region for some years and were strong advocates for land rights, the outstations movement and Aboriginal self-determination. At that time, a political dispute emerged within the Maningrida Council between these white staff of the resource centre dubbed 'progressives' and other 'conservative' senior staff of the Maningrida Council. While this division was between *balandas* (non-Aboriginal people) and was along party political lines, it also reflected a tension in the region between the township and outstations, and between those adhering to the old 'assimilation' regime that still had considerable influence in the township and those committed to the new 'self-determination' policy introduced in 1972.

The political rift within the Maningrida Council came to a head in 1978 when, on the advice of the Department of Aboriginal Affairs, the Minister for Aboriginal Affairs, Ian Viner, ordered the sacking of key members of both factions and the revocation of their permits, an action that he was empowered to make as Maningrida township was not yet part of the Arnhem Land Aboriginal Land Trust. Subsequently, Gillespie, Cooke and Bond challenged the Minister's decision in the NT Supreme Court and his decision was judged illegal and overturned. It is noteworthy that there was strong community support for Gillespie, Cooke and Bond, and after the decision Cooke and Bond went back to again work to support outstations. An insightful account of this episode is provided by MacCallum (1978).

As a consequence of this episode, there was recognition by the Department of Aboriginal Affairs that a separate incorporated entity was needed to support outstations, and so BAC was established as a purpose built ORA during 1979 by its inaugural executive officer, Ian Hughes. BAC was incorporated under the *Aboriginal Councils and Associations Act 1976* (Cth) in October 1979. The name Bawinanga was a composite of three language names from the hinterland, as then spelt: **Ba**rada (Burrarra) in the east, Gun**win**ggu (Kuninjku) to the west, and Rembarr**anga** (Rembarrnga) to the south.

BAC operated successfully as an outstation service delivery organisation, both from the perspectives of funding agencies and its membership, from 1979 to the late 1980s. It was mainly funded by the Commonwealth Department of Aboriginal Affairs because, under a Memorandum of Understanding between the Commonwealth and a self-governing NT, the Commonwealth agreed to meet this responsibility (see Altman 2006). BAC gained a sound reputation as an efficient service delivery agency that was effective in supporting a population in the bush. Some of this status was linked to BAC also running Maningrida Arts and Culture (then Crafts) as a high profile Aboriginal arts centre that operated for both township and outstations artists. This was an important service, which provided BAC with some experience in running a cultural enterprise that made a significant difference to local people's livelihoods. From late 1980, David Bond took over as chief executive officer of BAC and remained with the organisation in that capacity until 2005; Peter Cooke ran Maningrida Arts and Crafts from 1979 to 1982, and subsequently retained strong personal and professional links with BAC.

From 1989, BAC expanded to also become an organisation that administered the CDEP scheme. The growth of BAC as a CDEP organisation has been covered in some detail elsewhere (Altman and Johnson 2000). This was an historic moment that marked a fundamental change in the nature of BAC for a number of reasons. First, while its early CDEP engagement was limited and mainly oriented to provide income support to outstation residents, its corporate robustness meant that this role expanded rapidly. This was especially the case after 1997 when BAC was invited by ATSIC to take over the Maningrida Council's CDEP scheme participants, owing to Council problems with maladministration at that time. Running CDEP meant that BAC had to rapidly expand its administrative and project management capacity, especially when it took over administering township based participants. Second, CDEP provided BAC with discretionary administrative and capital resources that it incrementally invested in developing a number of business and service arms. As a consequence of both these developments, BAC attained a far more visible Maningrida profile. Its earlier reputation as a best practice resource agency was now matched by a high reputation as a CDEP organisation, with associated external bureaucratic and political support.

From the late 1990s, about a decade after it gained access to the CDEP scheme, BAC entered another phase as a regional development agency. This phase is less easy to demarcate because it was linked to a gradual expansion of the organisation, which was largely overseen by a senior project officer, Ian Munro, appointed in 1991. Munro subsequently became BAC's deputy Chief Executive Officer (CEO) and from August 2005 its CEO. An analysis of BAC's consolidated financial accounts shows fairly marked increase in organisational turnover in the late 1990s, including in the administration of some significant grants for housing and infrastructure development at outstations, as well as a steady increase in the proportion of total income from trading activities (as distinct from CDEP grants from ATSIC). Organisational scale appears to have taken BAC onto a new level after its income exceeded $10 million in 1997–98 and then expanded by another 50 per cent by 1999–2000.

The fundamental changes in organisation were recognised in 1999 with a modification of its constitution to provide greater emphasis not just on service delivery functions, but also to support Aboriginal cultural priorities, promotion of the management and sustainable use of Aboriginal-owned lands and resources, the welfare of its members, and business opportunities and economic independence.

Recently, BAC (2005a: 4) defined its mission in accord with its constitution in the following terms:

> At the regional level we act as a force for the political integration and representation of the interests of over 100 regional land owning groups [members of patrilineal clans] of our members ...

> As a service delivery agency BAC provides cultural and natural resource management programs, essential municipal and social services and labour market and economic development opportunities to its members in Maningrida and surrounding outstation communities.

The maintenance of land, language(s) and culture, the sustainable use of natural resources and the creation of viable enterprises employing Aboriginal people are central themes in all of BAC's activities.

Its mission statement demonstrates that BAC recognises its evolution into an organisation that serves members living in both Maningrida and outstations, and often residing flexibly between the township and various locations in the hinterland. This in turn makes its goal of acting as a force for political integration highly problematic, as the basis, authority and contexts for such a role are largely undefined, and the political interests of its membership are highly variable.

Even at an organisational level, BAC is diverse and complex for an Aboriginal entity as Fig. 7.2 illustrates. BAC has 20 formal business and service arms, with many combining the provision of services with a focus on commercial objectives and economic development possibilities.

A quick summary of BAC's published annual reports and audited financial statements for the last three years, 2004–05 to 2006–07, indicates that BAC employs over 500 CDEP participants—making it one of the country's largest CDEP organisations—and engages over 50 mainly non-Aboriginal salaried staff. Its turnover exceeds $25 million per annum, with well over 50 per cent generated from trading income and the balance coming from a number of external grants, the most significant being for the operation of CDEP (see BAC 2005a, 2005b, 2006a, 2006b, 2007a, 2007b).

Fig. 7.2 BAC organisational structure and business units

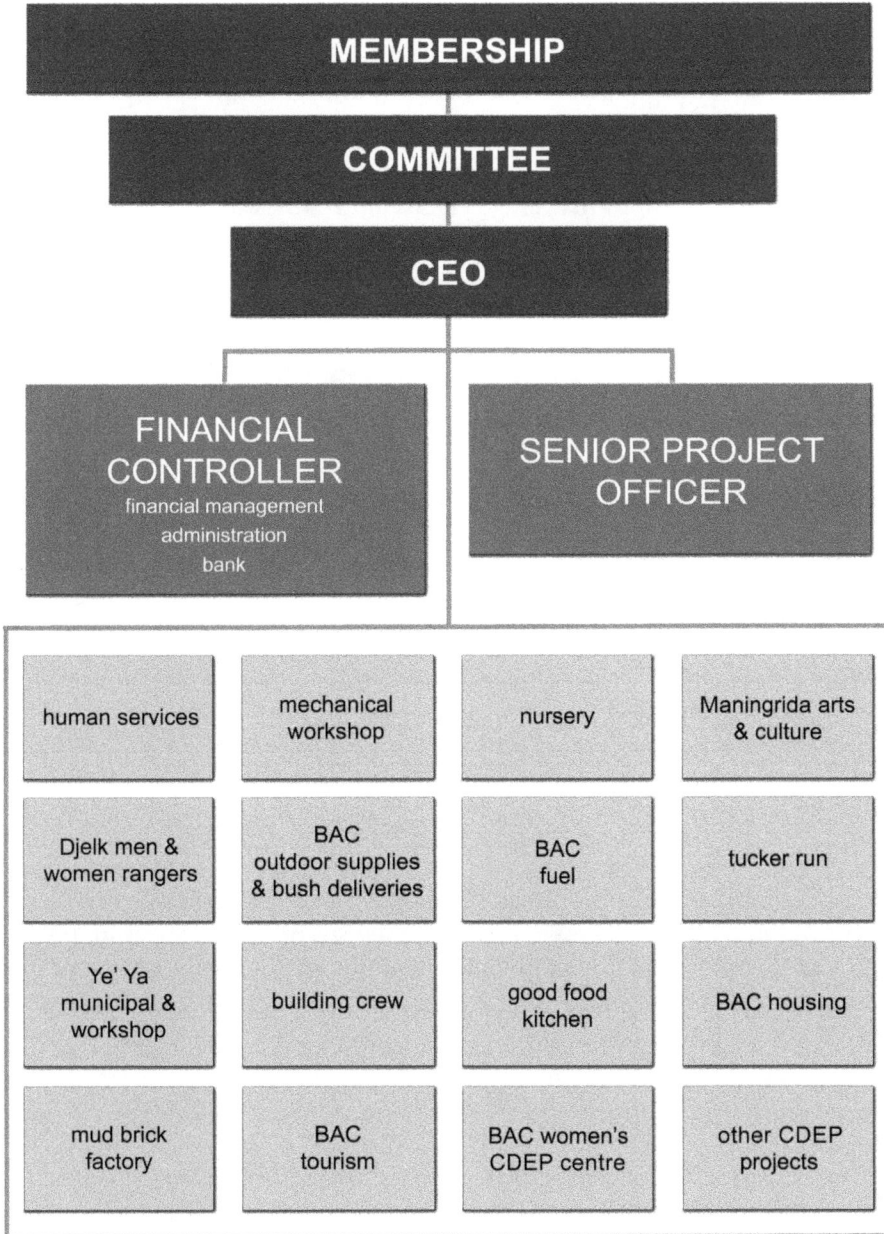

Source: Fogarty and Paterson 2007

Governance challenges

BAC is a distinctive form of organisation that is intercultural: its organisational governance has to accommodate both western legal requirements and Indigenous social norms and external and internal accountability. In BAC's case, this governance interculturality is further complicated by the scale of the organisation, its history and its transformations over time, from a focused ORA to a mixed and more diverse organisation that also operates as a CDEP organisation and development agency. These complexities are further complicated again by the extraordinary cultural and linguistic diversity of its Indigenous constituency, by differences between the needs and aspirations of members who reside in town and country, and by long-standing territorial disputes (some of which had their genesis in the 1970s) with other Maningrida organisations. Many of these governance challenges and tensions are not unique to BAC. In this section, I focus on just a few of a myriad of governance challenges that BAC faces.

A first-order issue for BAC is the challenges that its all-Aboriginal executive face. This executive is elected by secret ballot at the annual general meeting, with the chairman being the nominated candidate who attracts the most votes. There is invariably a change of chairman from one year to the next and regular turnover in the composition of the executive. This makes executive decision making—which varies from the mundane to the multi-million dollar—difficult. This diversity of business is not unusual for committee-run organisations. For example, the executive has to be heavily involved in setting rules for CDEP, the dominant every day business, as well as in making investment decisions in relation to enterprises, and decisions about forms of new grant funding to be sought and new projects to pursue.

Two key challenges emerge here. First, the level of expertise needed to understand and oversee the operations of this complex conglomerate (see Fig. 7.2) is significant. In a community like Maningrida there is a relatively small pool of Aboriginal people who have the requisite educational qualifications and understanding of business and corporate governance to undertake this task. Arguably, this is an indictment of the Maningrida education system, but also of the lack of opportunity for on-the-job education and training at BAC given its organisational longevity. The few who have such skills face pressures to participate on other boards, placing them in actual or potential conflict of interest and under considerable workload pressures. As BAC's constitution requires an annual spill of executive positions, it is unusual for any executive members to be consistently re-elected. This, as noted later, reflects the aspirations of members to share both the benefits and responsibilities of office among numerous regional interest groups. Consequently, new executive members need to be familiarised with corporate decision making processes on an annual basis and there is limited growth of capacity and ongoing executive expertise over time. Board training and induction takes time and the legal requirements facing members are onerous.

This in turn means that senior management has far greater knowledge about the running of BAC than the executive. In BAC's case, the divergence between the Aboriginal executive and the non-Aboriginal management expertise has been exacerbated by high turnover of executive membership and low turnover of senior management: BAC has only had three chief executive officers since 1979. Historically, this has resulted in a degree of executive apathy in actively engaging in organisational governance and BAC being vulnerable to the external perception that it is only governed by senior management rather than the Aboriginal executive. BAC's organisational complexity and the past reluctance of the executive to be actively involved in governance also pose a major challenge to management in finding the right balance between executive and member consultation, and a focus on implementation and action. In the past this resulted in too much governance by management, something that is in the process of changing.

BAC is incorporated under Australian law and so has requirements to comply with western, formal modes of governance as set out in incorporations statute. As a general rule, incorporations law requires that members of the executive operate impartially without vested interest and to meet the objectives of the corporation for the benefit of its membership. Gerritsen and Straton (2007: 166) refer to this western incorporations requirement as a 'weberian rationality of impersonal distribution'. Such modes of governance are very different from Aboriginal modes of governance that prioritise kin-based obligations and sectional interests. In the BAC case, these sectional interests are diverse and fluid, comprising members of one's household or extended kinship group, or members of one's language community or totemic cluster, or outstation co-residents. Aboriginal social norms see pressure continually applied to executive members to respond to demands of particular sectional interests.

There is an ongoing tension between senior managers, who more readily ascribe to western modes of governance and are highly aware of external accountability requirements, and Aboriginal executive members, who have variable understandings of external accountability, but are acutely aware and constantly reminded of internal accountability to the sectional interests and the Aboriginal priorities that they represent. Finding the right balance between corporate compliance and appropriate responsiveness to member priorities is a continual governance challenge. This challenge is exacerbated if non-Indigenous staff do not understand Indigenous kin-based social norms and fundamentally appreciate the nature of Aboriginal connections to, and responsibilities for, country.[4]

---

[4] Understanding the actual content, not just the kin-based form, of local Aboriginal activities and priorities can be very difficult for non-Aboriginal staff. It is for this reason that Aboriginal people

Choosing which governance approach to emphasise implicates a process that Bagshaw (1977: 27) referred to as 'jural selectivity'. While BAC's objects are broadly defined to allow compliance with Aboriginal priorities, like ceremonial participation, there is an ongoing tension in making the resource allocation between competing priorities, while complying with external bureaucratic and internal membership accountability.

Within BAC's membership and generally within the elected executive, there is a mix of elites: those who enjoy status on the basis of Aboriginal customary criteria and those who gain status on the basis of western knowledge, Bagshaw's 'balanda marringi'. The poor outcomes from the Maningrida education system mean that there are relatively few with the requisite English literacy to be members of the neo-elite. While this relatively small cadre is now actively involved in organisational governance, as noted above a number are simultaneously members of several Maningrida-based (and external) organisations. Historically, BAC has under-invested in corporate governance training for its executive, in part because of high executive turnover and in part because suitable governance training has not been locally available. This in turn resulted in member apathy and disinterest in what was often (erroneously) viewed as 'balanda business', because of the way the organisation had been structured and run in the past.

Invariably, the BAC executive includes a mix of the customary elite and the more western-familiar neo-elite. Informal processes see cross-cultural tensions between western and Indigenous modes of governance being constantly played out, often in executive committee meetings or in the less formal 'smoko room' context described earlier. Western modes of governance require strict adherence to corporations law and external accountability, at least in principle.[5] The BAC executive neo-elites partially understand this, while Indigenous modes of governance require accountability to immediate family, broader kinship networks, language communities, ritual allies, co-residents and a myriad of other obligations with which executive members are encumbered. On occasion, an executive member belongs to both elites, and on other occasions elites and neo-elites form alliances in executive decision making.[6]

Organisational metamorphosis has presented BAC with new governance challenges. BAC's original *raison d'etre* was as an outstations support agency,

---

consistently seek to bridge this cultural gulf by inviting key *balandas* onto their country and into ceremonies.

[5] I say 'in principle' because of the historically high rate of corporate non-compliance (and associated potential for fraud and embezzlement) that has bedeviled Aboriginal organisations, especially in very remote localities.

[6] This essentially heuristic distinction between elites and neo-elites overstates the relative roles and statuses of the two categories. The very use of the term neo-elite is a heuristic categorisation that is potentially problematic as it is contextually constituted in relation to both *balandas* and Aboriginal people, 'countrymen'.

but as noted elsewhere (Altman and Johnson 2000), its success first as a CDEP organisation and then as a development agency has provided more and more employment opportunities to its membership in Maningrida. Five-yearly census data indicate some drift of outstation residents into Maningrida over time, and while the reasons for this re-centralisation are complex, BAC's success is certainly one contributing factor.

This in turn has generated a new set of governance challenges. For example, BAC increasingly needs to maintain good patronage relations with the Dukurrdji traditional owners of Maningrida on whose lands its growing numbers of enterprises are located. This challenge has been addressed by the payment of lease rentals. Ultimately, BAC's success may offer too much opportunity for its membership in Maningrida (where all enterprises are located) rather than in the bush—a centralisation chain in-migration may result as kinship and sociality draw in the relatives of those finding opportunity in town. The logical consequence of this process is the abandonment and undermining of the culturally differentiated outstation communities in favour of a single culturally homogeneous (in relative terms) Maningrida population, whose younger members will become increasingly attenuated from their own lands and traditions. This will increasingly require BAC members to have multiple allegiances to both BAC and other Maningrida organisations that provide housing and other services. This creates challenges, as such multiple allegiances, mixed with notions of egalitarianism and risk minimisation, can create some ambivalence about BAC's regional dominance. In interview, two members of multiple boards emphasised to me that they did not want BAC to get 'too big'. It is also contrary to the original aims of the outstations movement.

From the outstations perspective, BAC has clearly become less of a resource agency, although it remains supportive of outstation needs. Outstation residents for their part have loosened their identity links with BAC alone and now also patronise other Maningrida organisations. The issue of servicing outstations in the Maningrida region is becoming increasingly complex, especially in the context of discussions about the amalgamation of townships and outstations into regional authority 'shires' (see D. Smith this volume, Chapter 4), and the proposed withdrawal of Commonwealth support of outstations from 1 July 2008. Any potential to resolve such issues appears to have been placed in temporary abeyance by the unfolding of dramatic 'national emergency' policy events in June 2007 discussed further below.

Adaptively managing governance tensions

The critical focus of my research is on understanding how western (incorporated) and customary (kin-based) forms of governance have been balanced in the operations of BAC. At one level, there has clearly been a successful mediation of these two quite different governance approaches. This is evidenced by the longevity of BAC, its growth and its success. At another level, historically there has been ready deferral to non-Aboriginal management, at least until recent times, which might suggest abrogation of governance responsibilities. What is remarkable about the BAC case is how these identified governance tensions have been astutely accommodated over a long period of time, while the organisation has experienced impressive growth and performance. In this section, I focus more specifically on the period since 2005 and what I have observed.

As noted earlier, the rapid growth of BAC in the 1990s was not matched by sufficient investment in organisational development. Between 2005 and 2007, there has been a rapid increase in focus on formal governance issues and a growing membership participation in governance. Historically, BAC management had been a little reluctant to embrace formal governance capacity building for its membership in part, because there was some reluctance to tamper with an organisational model that was working. A number of factors challenged and ultimately changed this view, including: external review and active participation in strategic planning in 2003; a change of organisational leadership in 2005; and a willingness by the executive and senior management to participate in the ICGP from 2005. A parallel process of governance training within the broader Maningrida community, sponsored by the Office of the Registrar of Aboriginal Corporations (ORAC) and delivered by the Maningrida JET Centre, a registered training organisation, also highlighted BAC's deficiencies in this area and provided some opportunity for governance training.

The new CEO, while a member of the senior management team since 1991, has embraced a greater focus on formal governance and has encouraged greater executive participation in the overall decision making for BAC. The strategy to change the governance balance to ensure greater membership participation has gained momentum. From 2004, BAC senior management moved to systematically address organisational deficiencies highlighted during strategic planning and incorporated in an action plan. In particular, executive committee members have been paid sitting fees and are expected to attend all meetings; the executive are involved more actively in agenda setting; more detailed records of meetings are maintained; and a number of members have participated in governance training. A survey of senior managers of four Maningrida-based organisations undertaken in mid 2005 suggested that they had all observed benefits from this governance training by the initial cohort of trainees—it provided participants with some understanding of corporate governance and financial management issues. Unfortunately, this training has only been provided on a sporadic basis owing to high staff turnover at the training centre, and in 2007 this training program was suspended.

Overall, in formal governance terms, BAC has adopted a far more transparent organisational culture in recent years: it has published annual reports of activities since 1999–2000, developed an Induction Manual (Johnson 2004), and has provided cross-cultural training for its non-Indigenous staff since 2004. There is no doubt that at a formal level BAC is regarded highly by ORAC, and in 2004–05 it rated special mention as a best practice Indigenous organisation (ORAC 2006: 37). BAC's formal processes are sound, financial audits are invariably unqualified, and the overall financial performance of the organisation is probably without parallel in a remote Indigenous community context.

What is equally important is to understand how intercultural checks and balances have been maintained, or how the apparent incommensurability between western and customary social norms have been mediated. This has occurred in three interdependent ways.

First, the annually elected executive comprises between 11 and 15 representatives affiliated with different outstations and language groups. Turnover of executive members ensures that there is no dominance by one section of the regional membership and this is recognised as beneficial to the entire membership. The executive is invariably made up of members of the elite and the neo-elite, and in executive meetings and through informal institutions such as meetings in the 'smoko' room, consensus is reached on key policies and decisions like the allocation of new housing. It is not uncommon for non-executive members to attend such meetings as observers, in accord with customary decision making processes.

The position of chairman is important as this is a salaried position that also provides access to a highly valued chairman's vehicle (when one is available). This prestigious position is invariably rotated on an annual basis, even though it is based on a secret ballot and is generally shared equitably between a number of language communities. In July 2006, the incumbent chairman identified the rapid turnover of his position as a potential problem for BAC and indicated a desire to possibly seek re-election, but this did not eventuate.

Second, there is careful negotiation of the tensions between customary obligations and legal compliance between non-Indigenous senior managers and members of the Indigenous executive. Much of BAC's corporate success and sound governance can be sheeted home to the stability of its non-Indigenous senior management and seamless succession. Effectively, after the first executive officer established BAC in 1979–80, there have been only two more: one from 1980 to 2005, and the next from September 2005 (who was appointed after 14 years with the organisation since 1991). Such continuity and succession is extraordinarily important, especially in a corporate environment where the Indigenous executive is only appointed for a period of 12 months at a time. BAC's organisational history and culture has ensured that senior managers have been appropriately attuned to the aspirations of BAC's membership. Importantly, as BAC's organisational scale and capacities have grown, there have been sufficient numbers of senior managers to ensure checks and balances on management decision making. As noted earlier, BAC is not averse to extra-regional scrutiny and constructive criticism, much of which emanates from a healthy organisational engagement with external, at-arms-length, independent research bodies.

Third, BAC executive and senior managers in particular retain an open-door policy whereby individuals have good access to discuss personal, family and outstation issues and priorities. This approach makes an important contribution to ensuring that governance is transparent and facilitates early detection and correction of any policy errors or misallocations. While this open-door approach is demanding and often appears time inefficient, it is something BAC has made into a virtue. As a general rule, there is an expectation that senior staff are prepared to commit to this governance mechanism.

None of this is intended to suggest that BAC's operations are either tension or error free. From time to time, the social norms of customary governance take precedence and there have been disputes over unauthorised vehicle use and inappropriate use of order books, usually associated with ceremonial or funeral expenses. But as a general rule, these incidents are relatively rare; they are sometimes resolved by adapting existing procedures and usually by ensuring repayment of any outstanding advances. It is not unusual for the informal institution of public shaming to be invoked when excesses occur among members of the executive. Similarly, tensions can erupt between managers of business units, for they too need to compete for an equitable share of BAC resources. At times these can be mediated and resolved, at other times a manager may resign or be dismissed. The governance of an intercultural organisation like BAC is difficult and systems can break down. Over time, and especially in recent years, BAC has ensured that the fiscal bottom line is maintained, while enterprise innovation and associated risk is encouraged.

A critical, and at times highly problematic, challenge that has been highlighted is that long-term managerialism has probably inhibited Aboriginal executive decision making. It is too easy to highlight BAC's success and longevity as a 'business enterprise' and to overlook its lack of success in genuinely representing and empowering its Aboriginal membership. The particular form of governance that operates at BAC is intercultural and hybrid. To retain its historic success as an organisation it will need to be increasingly adaptive and creative as it continues to address the re-alignment challenges posed by its need to operate effectively between western and Aboriginal worlds.

Recent external threats

BAC has operated successfully for nearly 30 years in a remote and difficult context where governance is influenced by competing western and Indigenous social norms. It provides an exemplary case of how such competing social norms can be negotiated and managed.

Yet in the last three years since the abolition of ATSIC in 2004, BAC faced a series of threats from the now defeated Howard Government. At one level, these threats were linked to changed Commonwealth policy emphases and BAC's dependence on Commonwealth programs, especially CDEP and the Community Housing and Infrastructure Program (CHIP), which funds municipal services for outstations. At another level, these threats were highly political, with federal politicians and bureaucrats seeking to determine, in accord with the ideological fashion of the day, what was best for BAC and its membership even if this was in direct opposition to the aspirations of BAC's elected executive and members. Elsewhere, I have termed this approach 'remote managerialism' (Altman 2005a).

There are at least two paradoxes apparent in the Commonwealth's approach since 2005. First, despite the dominant rationale peddled by the Australian Government that ATSIC was ineffective in delivering support to remote Indigenous communities, BAC's relations with ATSIC were robust and constructive. Indeed, in large measure it was ATSIC that encouraged and funded the processes whereby BAC embraced greater emphases on formal governance and strategic and succession planning. Just as these requirements were all being implemented and as my governance research began in 2005, relations between the Australian Government and BAC soured. This is paradoxical because as the central terms of Indigenous affairs policy swung to mutual obligation and shared responsibility, BAC and its successful CDEP operations and robust governance should have been viewed as a flagship example of achievement. Instead, the complex issue of mainstreaming, with its multiple meanings, has loomed large. This placed BAC at loggerheads with some powerful federal agencies, especially the Department of Employment and Workplace Relations (DEWR), which administered CDEP from 2004.

In 2005 and 2006 these strained relations mainly focused on divergent interpretations about the CDEP scheme's objectives: DEWR, as an employment agency, unilaterally redefined it as a program to transition participants to mainstream employment, while BAC remained focused on its historical intent to provide a mix of community development, employment creation, enterprise subsidy and income support.

This tension resulted in what was locally termed 'the CDEP wars', which ended in a stalemate in 2005 and 2006 because BAC acquiesced to sign externally imposed and unrealistic performance targets (see Altman 2005a). At the heart of this dispute were radically different views about the appropriate economic future for BAC's membership. The unrealistic view from Canberra was that mainstream employment, so called 'proper jobs', should be the long-term goal for all in the Maningrida region. BAC's objects, on the other hand, emphasise a different notion of development that is realistic and grounded and incorporates the high degree of flexibility that matches its members' aspirations—BAC has quite proactively adopted the 'hybrid economy' model (Altman 2001, 2005b) as encompassing its approach.

A syndrome marked by unnecessary tension seems to pervade relations between the bureaucracy and successful Aboriginal organisations, which goes beyond the current neoliberal hegemony. On the one hand, the bureaucracy relies on organisations like BAC to deliver the limited successes that have been achieved in Indigenous development in the last three decades. On the other hand, there is a palpable feeling of enmity toward successes like BAC at many levels of the bureaucracy. Success seems to attract criticism, increased scrutiny, and cynicism rather than praise and championing.

The announcement of the NT National Emergency Response and its associated measures by the Howard Government on 21 June 2007 constituted the greatest external threat to date to BAC's existence. These measures, enshrined in legislation in August 2007, provided the Australian Government legal instruments to strip BAC of its considerable fixed assets, while an externally-appointed bureaucrat, the Government Business Manager, was given absolute authority over democratically-elected executives like BAC's. Furthermore, as part of this emergency intervention, on 23 July 2007 the Australian Government announced that it would abolish the CDEP scheme throughout the NT (Hinkson 2007). BAC was informed in late 2007 that its CDEP support, which totalled just on $9 million in 2006–07 (BAC 2007a: 29–31), would cease from March 2008. Its CHIP municipal funding of $400,000 in 2006–07, which funds outstations support, would end on 30 June 2008. However, with a change of government on 24 November 2007 with a commitment to retain CDEP, this decision has now been reversed, although the CHIP municipal funding decision still stands. But in a Memorandum of Understanding signed between the Australian and the NT Governments in September 2007, $20 million has been provided to underwrite the CHIP municipal funding for outstations, which BAC may well access in the future.

It is clear that without its considerable asset base, without funding for outstations support, and without a CDEP workforce of 550 and associated administrative resourcing, BAC would cease to exist as the significant regional development agency it has become. BAC's (2007a, 2007b) most recent audited financial statement and annual report indicate that it is a profitable $27 million per annum organisation. All this was to be jeopardised by the Australian Government's emergency intervention and new draconian laws. However, the change of government appears to have given BAC a reprieve, at least in the immediate term.

Governance for difference: analytic explication

There is a considerable literature in Australia that highlights the ambiguity embedded in the notion of an Indigenous jurisdiction (Collman 1988; Rowse 1992, 2007; Sullivan 1996) and how the very notion of Aboriginal self-determination is often bounded by the legal requirements of western incorporations law. There is a dominant perception of incongruity between western and Aboriginal notions of governance. Yet what I argue here is that an organisation in the Indigenous sector is successfully engaging with both western and Aboriginal notions of governance via a particular form of interculturality. In this section, I briefly engage with two alternate views about governance in Maningrida, before providing my own analytical explication for why BAC has succeeded for nearly three decades.

Bagshaw (1977) analysed local government in Maningrida. Bagshaw's focus was on the Maningrida Council at the time when the outstation resource centre was one of its branches. Bagshaw (1977: 69) observed a degree of 'cross-cultural incongruity' between European economic-based and Aboriginal kin-oriented governance. Ultimately, he observed that European political forms and objectives were imposed on Aboriginal social life and that this took away any discretionary power from Aboriginal councillors. This dominance by European management resulted in Aboriginal people feeling politically impotent and generally disinterested in what was perceived of as *'balanda* business'. At the same time, he noted that local Aboriginal people, who in relative terms understood European ways, practised what he termed 'jural selectivity' (1977: 27) as a means of coping with the ambiguities inherent in post-colonial township living. Jural selectivity involved choosing between traditional Aboriginal law and European law to cope with any given social situation. As a Nakkara informant put it to Bagshaw: 'now we have two ways … *angugalia* [Aboriginal] and *balanda* [European] to fix our problems'. Bagshaw's was an early expression of the notion that was later termed interculturality, which can be understood as the complex processual manifestations of difference and inter-influence in situations of transformation (Hinkson and Smith 2005: 160).

Recently, and again referring to Maningrida (but no particular organisation), Gerritsen and Straton (2007: 166) highlight an apparent incongruence between what they term 'the weberian rationality of impersonal distribution' that dominates western governance and Indigenous kin-based competitiveness. They suggest that policy makers provide funding to Aboriginal organisations with the mistaken belief that Aboriginal social norms ensure egalitarian sharing. Their perspective recognises a mix of 'traditional culture' and 'western power and logic' in Maningrida, but nevertheless focuses only on intra-Aboriginal tensions in heterogeneous communities marked by hierarchy, divisions and competition that precludes the likelihood of social cooperation. Gerritsen and Straton's (2007) analysis can be juxtaposed with Bagshaw's. For Bagshaw, state intervention and control resulted in Aboriginal participation being crowded out by the domination of white management, while white management does not even figure in Gerritsen and Straton's analysis.

Writing about central Australia and using a Foucauldian framework, Batty (2005) focuses on the effective working relationships that have emerged between Aboriginal and non-Aboriginal people involved in the state project of self-determination. In his analysis, Batty highlights that these partnerships develop into sites of administrative and cultural mediation that accommodate the aspirations of both Aboriginal people and the state. Batty (2005: 220) suggests that one of the unintended consequences of the policy of self-determination was the formation of a 'more or less permanent class of white advisers whose position and effectiveness depended almost entirely on partnerships with Aboriginal people'.[7] Elsewhere (Altman 2005b: 129), I have broadly concurred with Batty's partnership framework, but construe it a little differently in the BAC case. Here there are a series of partnerships: *between* white management and Aboriginal executive; *within* the senior management team, to provide the checks and balances that will militate against possible excesses often associated with monopoly management; and *within* the elected executive, which needs to constantly negotiate a degree of accommodation between diverse Aboriginal township and regional interest groups.

The analysis undertaken here recognises the tension between kin-based and market-based (or indigenous and western) governance orders and traces how creative organisational adaptations have been made to address such apparent structural incongruity.

Part of the explanation of BAC's success is the long-term relationships that have formed between a small number of trusted senior white managers, who have stayed for long periods and have understood Aboriginal social norms based on kinship obligations, and constantly churning Aboriginal executives. The annual changes in the composition of executives have ensured that no one sectional interest in the Maningrida region has been politically dominant, while the longevity of white management has facilitated administrative and cultural mediation between western and customary social norms.

Another important element is the particular history and politics of the organisation. From the outset, BAC was established to support Aboriginal aspirations to live on their country, to gain access to state income support and to pursue market opportunities compatible with remote outstation living. The culture and associated governance of BAC has always been politically allied to

---

[7] An alternative and possibly more accurate term here, also from central Australia, might be Collman's (1988) notion of 'mutual patronage'.

a particular section of the regional population: outstation residents. The white staff of BAC (and its predecessor) championed Aboriginal self-determination and emphasised practical aspects of meeting such Aboriginal aspirations. From the outset, BAC has been structured to accommodate diverse Aboriginal aspirations and differences, the commercial and the cultural. BAC has also been a thoroughly intercultural organisation, accommodating from the outset both western and Aboriginal social norms, while providing space for effective management by trusted whites. The ability of Aboriginal people to retain key *balandas* for long periods of time is fundamental to its success.

BAC effectively facilitates livelihoods that are dependent on the customary or non-market sector, on state support, and on successful engagement with the market (see BAC 2007b). BAC also recognises that its members might participate in all three sectors of the hybrid economy and the interdependencies between these sectors that are mainly underwritten by the CDEP scheme. BAC delivers a local form of 'cultural match' that allows its membership to readily move between outstation and township living, while actively engaging in different forms of livelihood possibilities. Over time, BAC has evolved into a hybrid intercultural organisation (Altman and Cochrane 2003) whose objects and actions clearly recognise the highly flexible nature of local hybrid economies (Altman 2001). The parallels between this hybrid institutional framework and the hybrid economy are at the heart of BAC's success.

A final reflection

It would be nice to conclude this chapter here because it seems that, as an organisation, BAC has strengthened its institutional capacities and its adaptively managed governance is robust. In a policy sense, BAC is an important case because it is a clear success in a broader narrative of Indigenous failure dominant in recent years. Yet, as noted above, each of its core organisational components—outstations, CDEP and appropriate development that accords with local aspirations—are currently under threat from the NT intervention and the new state project of normalisation. Unfortunately, BAC has remained dependent on the state and hence it is highly vulnerable to changes both in policies and in laws. For nearly 30 years, BAC has provided its membership effective 'governance for difference', but this has been threatened in recent times by the Howard Government's attempts to impose 'governance for sameness'. The BAC case shows that it is possible to govern to meet both western and Aboriginal requirements—cross-cultural congruence is possible. However, if cultural difference is not tolerated by the state, then power asymmetry can undermine and ultimately destroy intercultural projects, irrespective of their success. Or can it?

In early 1978, just five years after self-determination became official Commonwealth policy, the federal Minister for Aboriginal Affairs in the Fraser

Coalition Government intervened to revoke the permits of three non-Indigenous staff working for outstations, despite the protestations of local Aboriginal people. At that time, recourse to the Supreme Court of the NT was available to challenge the Minister's decision, which was judged illegal and overturned. These people were empowered by the Australian legal system to return to Maningrida.

As this chapter is being completed, BAC is a joint plaintiff (with Maningrida traditional owners Reggie Wurridjal and Joy Garlbin) in an action in the High Court of Australia, which is challenging the authority of the Commonwealth to seize its assets without just terms compensation and so to undermine its organisational viability. The Commonwealth has always been empowered to terminate BAC's access to the CDEP scheme, despite its obvious success in administering this program since 1989. The change of Federal Government on 24 November with an election commitment to retain the CDEP scheme will see a reversal in some recent destructive policy proposals and in BAC's fortunes. Ultimately, the demise or survival of BAC might always be determined by wider ideological and political processes. But it says a great deal for the robust intercultural governance of BAC that its membership, executive, management and staff have effectively taken the fight up to the Australian state during the last three years to fight for its survival, in the name of 'governance for difference'.

Acknowledgements

I would like to thank my very many Aboriginal and non-Aboriginal collaborators in Maningrida for their assistance and support over many years. There are just too many to name individually so I will just select Ian Munro, the CEO of BAC, and Peter Danaja, the BAC public officer, for special mention. In completing this chapter I thank Geoff Bagshaw, Mike Dillon, Bill Fogarty, Dan Gillespie, Melinda Hinkson, Will Sanders and two anonymous referees for incisive and challenging comments.

References

Altman, J. C. 1987. *Hunter-Gatherers Today: An Aboriginal Economy in North Australia*, Australian Institute of Aboriginal Studies, Canberra.

——1999. Maningrida Arts and Culture: Business Development Plan 2000–2002, Unpublished report prepared for the Bawinanga Aboriginal Corporation, CAEPR, ANU, Canberra.

——2001. 'Exploring sustainable development options on Aboriginal land: the hybrid economy in the 21st Century', *CAEPR Discussion Paper No. 226*, CAEPR, ANU, Canberra.

——2005a. 'The governance of outstations in the Maningrida region, north-central Arnhem Land, and the challenges posed by the new arrangements', *ICGP Occasional Paper No. 11*, ICGP, CAEPR, ANU, Canberra.

——2005b. 'Economic futures on Aboriginal land in remote and very remote Australia: hybrid economies and joint ventures', in D. Austin Broos and G. Macdonald (eds), *Culture, Economy and Governance in Aboriginal Australia*, University of Sydney Press, Sydney.

——2006. 'In search of an outstations policy for Indigenous Australians', *CAEPR Working Paper No. 34*, CAEPR, ANU, Canberra.

—— and Johnson, V. 2000. 'CDEP in town and country Arnhem Land: Bawinanga Aboriginal Corporation', *CAEPR Discussion Paper No. 209*, CAEPR, ANU, Canberra.

——and Cochrane, M. 2003. 'Sustainable development in the Indigenous-owned savanna: innovative institutional design for cooperative wildlife management', *CAEPR Discussion Paper No. 247*, CAEPR, ANU, Canberra.

——and Gillespie, D. 2003. Strategic Planning Project for Bawinanga Aboriginal Corporation, Progress Report 1, Unpublished report to BAC, Tallegalla Consultants Pty Ltd, Brisbane.

—— and Hinkson, M. 2007. 'Mobility and modernity in Arnhem Land: the social universe of Kuninjku trucks', *Journal of Material Culture*, 12 (2): 181–203.

——, Gillespie, D. and Palmer, K. 1999. *National Review of Resource Agencies Servicing Indigenous Communities, 1998*, Aboriginal and Torres Strait Islander Commission, Canberra.

Blanchard, C.A. (Chairman) 1987. *Return to Country: The Aboriginal homelands movement in Australia*. Report of the House of Representatives Standing Committee on Aboriginal Affairs, Australian Government Publishing Service, Canberra.

Bawinanga Aboriginal Corporation (BAC) 2005a. *Bawinanga Aboriginal Corporation, Annual Report 2004/05*, BAC, Maningrida.

——2005b. Bawinanga Aboriginal Corporation, Annual Financial Report 30 June 2005, BAC, Unpublished audited financial statements dated 21 September 2005.

——2006a. *Bawinanga Aboriginal Corporation, Annual Report 2005/06*, BAC, Maningrida.

——2006b. Bawinanga Aboriginal Corporation, Annual Financial Report 30 June 2006, BAC, Unpublished audited financial statements dated 29 August 2006.

————2007a. Bawinanga Aboriginal Corporation, Annual Financial Report 30 June 2007, BAC, Unpublished audited financial statements dated 25 September 2007.

————2007b. *Bawinanga Aboriginal Corporation, Annual Report 2006/07*, BAC, Maningrida.

Bagshaw, G. 1977. Analysis of Local Government in a Multi-Clan Community, BA (Hons) Dissertation, Department of Anthropology, The University of Adelaide, Adelaide.

Batty, P. 2005. 'Private politics, public strategies: white advisers and their Aboriginal subjects', *Oceania*, 75 (3): 209–21.

Collman, J. 1988. *Fringe Dwellers and Welfare: The Aboriginal Response to Bureaucracy*, University of Queensland Press, St Lucia.

Coombs, H. C. 1974. 'Decentralisation trends among Aboriginal communities', *Search*, 5 (4): 135–43.

Cornell, S. and Kalt, J. P. 1995. 'Successful economic development and heterogeneity of government form on Aboriginal Indian reservations', *PRS 95-4*, Harvard Project on American Indian Economic Development, Malcolm Weiner Center for Social Policy, John F. Kennedy School of Government, Harvard University, Cambridge, MA.

Council for Aboriginal Affairs. 1976. *Report on Arnhem Land*, Commonwealth of Australia, Canberra.

Fogarty, B. and Paterson, M. 2007. Constructive Engagement: Impacts, Limitations and Possibilities During a National Emergency Intervention, Unpublished report for BAC, PIA Consultants, August 2007, available at <http://www.aph.gov.au/Senate/committee/legcon_ctte/nt_emergency/submissions/sub03.pdf>.

Gerritsen, R. and Straton, A. 2007. 'Coping with a tragedy of the Australian Aboriginal common', in A. Smajgl and S. Larson (eds), *Sustainable Resource Use: Institutional Dynamics and Economics*, Earthscan, London.

Gillespie, D. 1999. Report to Bawinanga Aboriginal Corporation, Maningrida NT—Strategic Planning Issues for the Corporation, Unpublished report, Tallagella Pty Ltd.

————, Cooke, P. and Bond, D. 1977. *Maningrida Outstation Resource Centre, 1976–77 Annual Report*, Milingimbi Literature Production Centre, Milingimbi.

Grindle, M. S. 2004. 'Good enough governance: poverty reduction and reform in developing countries', *Governance: An International Journal of Policy, Administration and Institutions*, 17 (4): 525–48.

Gurrmanamana, F., Hiatt, L. and McKenzie, K. 2002. *People of the Rivermouth: The Joborr Texts of Frank Gurrmanamana*, Aboriginal Studies Press, Canberra.

Hiatt, L. R. 1965. *Kinship and Conflict: A Study of an Aboriginal Community in Northern Arnhem Land*, ANU Press, Canberra.

Hinkson, M. 2007. 'Introduction: in the name of the child', in J. C. Altman and M. Hinkson (eds), *Coercive Reconciliation: Stabilise, Normalise and Exit Aboriginal Australia*, Arena Publications, Melbourne.

—— and Smith, B. 2005. 'Introduction: conceptual moves towards an intercultural analysis', *Oceania* , 75 (3): 157–66.

Hughes, H. 2007. *Lands of Shame: Aboriginal and Torres Strait Islander 'Homelands' in Transition*, Centre for Independent Studies, Sydney.

Johnson, V. 2004. Bawinanga Aboriginal Corporation Induction Manual: A Guide to Newly Arrived Staff, Unpublished report, BAC, Maningrida.

Leach, M., Mearns, R. and Scoones, I. 1999. 'Environmental entitlements: dynamics and institutions in community-based natural resource management', *World Development*, 2 (2): 225–47.

MacCallum, M. 1978. 'Viner muscles in on Maningrida', *Nation Review*, 27 April–3 May, p. 13.

Meehan, B. 1982. *Shell Bed to Shell Midden*, Australian Institute of Aboriginal Studies, Canberra.

Office of the Registrar of Aboriginal Corporations (ORAC). 2006. *Yearbook 2004–05*, ORAC, Canberra.

Rowse, T. 1992. *Remote Possibilities: The Aboriginal Domain and the Administrative Imagination*, North Australia Research Unit, ANU, Darwin.

——2002. *Indigenous Futures: Choice and Development for Aboriginal and Islander Australia*, UNSW Press, Sydney.

——2007. 'The national emergency and Indigenous jurisdictions', in J. C. Altman and M. Hinkson (eds), *Coercive Reconciliation: Stabilise, Normalise and Exit Aboriginal Australia*, Arena Publications, Melbourne.

Sullivan, P. 1996. *All Free Men Now: Culture, Community and Politics in the Kimberley Region, Western Australia*, Aboriginal Studies Press, Canberra.

Tallegalla Consultants Pty Ltd. 2003. Bawinanga Aboriginal Corporation, Strategic Plan 2004–2006, Unpublished report, Tallegalla Consultants Pty Ltd, Brisbane.

8. The business of governing: building institutional capital in an urban enterprise

Diane Smith

> In the wider community, people who have a business idea and the means to develop their idea can develop their own enterprise at their own initiative. It is not as straightforward in Aboriginal communities. This is because Aboriginal people are invariably members of wider family groups and communities, and individuals are not completely free to undertake private enterprise ... Similarly, opportunities are frequently seen as communal assets—belonging to clan groups or to communities, not to individuals ... Indigenous social and cultural imperatives often result in the creation of decision-making and ownership structures that make enterprise ownership and management inefficient, unwieldy, impossible ... Indigenous decision-making structures are about social and political representation, whereas optimum business decision-making should be about expertise, experience, knowledge and talent.

(Ah Mat 2003: 6)

> The notion that all indigenous communities are the same is another of the myths or misunderstandings that has made its way into the policy and psyche of successive governments. Indigenous communities are diverse ... Diversity is not only in terms of language groups, clans or country, it goes further. Some communities may see economic growth as their primary goal, while others may accord more importance to cultural richness and taking care of country. It is important that differing indigenous traditions and values be recognised and accommodated in a way that contributes to building strong communities rather than undermine them.

(Armstrong 2007: 75–6)

Introduction

Behind the interest in Indigenous community governance lies a concern for the improved socioeconomic well being of Indigenous people. International research has found that there is a 'development dividend' (see Kaufmann 2005) attached to what is commonly referred to as 'good governance', and that it applies to quite poor countries and Indigenous societies (see Cornell and Kalt 1990; Kaufmann, Kraay and Mastruzzi 2005). In Australia, Indigenous communities are familiar with the cycle of business and economic development failures, and there is evidence that weak governance capacity is a contributing factor (Hunt and Smith 2006, 2007). In other words, Indigenous economic development is a governance issue.

The prime issue addressed in this chapter is whether there are particular kinds of organisational governance that might facilitate Indigenous economic success. The governance factors that impede Indigenous economic success have been extensively documented in Australia, to the point where there appears to be a public fixation on a deficit model of Indigenous economic development (see Dodson and Smith 2003 for a summary). This chapter focuses on the forms of organisational culture, governance representation, institutional frameworks and decision-making that facilitate rather than undermine economic success. This concern goes to the heart of 'who' should be the relevant Indigenous actors in the governance of economic initiatives, and the extent to which 'governing for business' should reflect Indigenous cultural values, relationships and systems of authority.

In Australia, these are hotly contested matters. The Indigenous commentators whose quotes open this chapter highlight one of the biggest challenges for Indigenous Australians in their governance arrangements today—namely, mediating the considerable tensions, expectations, and contemporary myths surrounding the role of 'community' and 'family' in Indigenous societies and their economic development. Many stakeholders agree with Richard Ah Mat above, that the social and cultural imperatives which are part of Indigenous family and community life are problematic for the kind of governance that is thought necessary for generating successful businesses and other economic development outcomes. Others identify 'family' and 'community' as potential sources of social and cultural capital, but ones that need to be strategically managed and 'balanced' within an organisation's governance arrangements and business objectives.

Indigenous organisations attempting to operate businesses seem to be particularly vulnerable. Their viability as businesses can be quickly eroded, not only by divisive conflicts created by community and family politics, but also by the unrealistic demands of government and the private sector, which hold their own ideological views about the role that 'community' and 'family' should and should not play in governance and economic development. For urban organisations and leaders engaged in business enterprises, key areas of vulnerability and challenge include:

- negotiating what constitutes 'the community' and 'family' in the light of historical resettlement, ongoing high rates of mobility, and the often tangled web of urban relationships and land-ownership rights;

- negotiating processes of representation and decision making that support their economic goals, at the same time as building the internal and external legitimacy of their governance;
- responding to the diverse views and cultural values that Indigenous people have about their community, families and their governance needs;
- balancing Indigenous calls for more inclusive 'community' participation in, and access to, the services and benefits provided by organisations, alongside the hard-headed decision making and corporate governance required for economic success;
- responding to government pressure for 'whole-of-community' participation and representation, in circumstances where the community may be heterogeneous or fragmented; and
- negotiating the funding labyrinth of governments, and their underlying assumptions that 'urban communities' have 'easier' access to mainstream services, infrastructure, employment and economic opportunities.

This chapter looks at the establishment and operation of an urban Indigenous organisation in Newcastle—the Yarnteen Aboriginal and Torres Strait Islanders Corporation (YATSIC)—and how it has tackled the challenges of 'governing for business' within a complex community and economic setting. Yarnteen Corporation has a reputation for outstanding business and service delivery success that has been sustained over a 20 year period. Its Indigenous leaders have instigated specific strategies in respect to 'family' and 'community' when designing a governance model for the organisation. The paper proceeds by first unpacking the two social institutions of 'family' and 'community'—in both their broader Indigenous and Newcastle specific contexts—and then examines the corporation's governance solutions to these.

Importantly, Yarnteen's leaders have consciously constructed an internal governance culture and institutional environment to support its economic functions and goals. The organisation's economic success is directly related to these strategies. Specifically, Yarnteen has built up a foundation of institutional and governance capital that invests it with resilience, practical capacity, and business flexibility that is 'paying a development dividend'. It appears to have done this without forsaking its cultural identity as an 'Aboriginal organisation in the Newcastle community'. This is a considerable achievement given the difficulties highlighted by Richard Ah Mat, which seem to have contributed to the failure of so many other Indigenous community organisations and businesses.

The problem with 'community' and 'family'?

The concept of the 'Indigenous community' remains fuzzy and confusing. It continues to be associated with discrete geographical settlements, where it evokes ideas of a shared, idealised culture and a unity of purpose and action among its members (see Peters-Little 2000). In this way, 'community' and a homogeneity of culture and interests have come to be conflated in the public mind.

But this is not the case. A 'community' can be defined as a network of people and organisations that are linked together by webs of relationships, cultural identity, traditions, rules, shared histories, or simply common interests and goals (Hunt and Smith 2006, 2007). Indigenous communities are diverse in their cultures, historical experiences, governance histories and location. In Indigenous Australia, communities include not only discrete remote locations and rural settlements (of which there are over 1000; see Taylor 2006) but also 'communities of identity' whose members share a common cultural identity but are residentially dispersed across a region or set of locations. There are also Indigenous 'communities of interest' comprising different groups who unite for a common purpose, but may have different cultural identities and rights (see Hunt and Smith 2007: 4; Smith 2005: 24–5).

Today, approximately three-quarters of Indigenous Australians live in urban areas, with 30 per cent residing in major cities (Taylor 2006). While some are permanent residents of particular towns, many others are periodic urban dwellers who travel between towns and their hinterland rural communities, where they make use of a series of 'usual residences'. The high population turnover associated with this pattern of movement between cities and rural communities 'is such that Indigenous people in the city are not just similar to those in country areas—to a large extent they are the 'same' people spatially displaced at different stages of their lives' (Taylor 2006: 3). In other words, reference to 'urban Indigenous communities' needs to be qualified in terms of their mobility, cultural heterogeneity and contemporary social complexity.

Many Indigenous Australians have built up strong historical attachments to particular urban residential 'hubs',[1] which have become an integral part of their contemporary identities. The resident Indigenous 'community' in such locations is not homogenous. More often, it comprises a mixed constituency of large extended families and related individuals, who come and go. These families form social networks within their urban location that stretch outwards to connect to other family members and 'communities' in surrounding regions (see Macdonald 2000; Peters-Little 2000: 412; Smith 2000; Sutton 1998). As a consequence, there are usually many 'communities' within a community, and extended families invariably form the foundations for these.

The governance of these fluid and compositionally complex urban communities is extremely challenging. A contributing factor has been the tidal wave of organisational incorporation that has occurred over the past 30 years. Today,

---

[1] Sometimes these 'hubs' are discrete communities. But they also include pastoral stations, fringe camps, and suburbs and neighbourhoods within towns and cities that have a long historical association by particular Indigenous groups and families.

there are an estimated 5000 incorporated community and regional organisations across Australia, with an estimated (minimum) 30 000 governing board members at their helm.[2] To some extent, this growth has been the result of a large number of government agencies taking an interest in Indigenous corporate affairs and socioeconomic outcomes. However, it has also been the product of Indigenous agency and choice, as small urban Indigenous groups, and more recently regional alliances of urban organisation and communities, have sought greater autonomy and control in the conduct of their community affairs, delivery of services, and business and enterprise development.

While there have been important practical, political and funding advantages to incorporation, some organisations have become silos of factional power in communities, competing with each other for members and local legitimacy, as well as scarce funds, resources and staff. The well documented result is that community organisations can find themselves subject to debilitating internal conflict, poor governance and financial management, and are sometimes at odds with their own membership and each other.

This situation has been exacerbated by the lack of national policy clarity about who these urban organisations are supposed to represent and how they are to be governed. Are different governance arrangements needed for organisations that deliver community services, as opposed to those operating business enterprises? As Leah Armstrong highlights in the opening quote to this chapter, an overly simplistic view of 'community' has become entrenched in government policy, program and funding frameworks, where it is equated with the expectation that there should be a collective, community-wide basis to service delivery and the distribution of any benefits flowing from government funding. This has flowed through to expectations about the governance of organisations which have been tagged by governments as being 'community organisations'. These are subject to idealistic expectations that they will have 'community representation', 'community participation', engage in 'community consultations' and so on.[3]

Governments and the private sector commonly prefer to deal with local organisations that are 'representative' in this manner. They then look to these organisations to speak for and make decisions on behalf of 'the community', when this is invariably a highly fluid, mixed set of sub-groups. Even

---

[2] Approximately 2500 Indigenous organisations are incorporated under the *Corporations (Aboriginal and Torres Strait Islander) Act 2006* (CATSIA), each of which is encouraged to have a maximum of 12 directors (see Office of the Registrar of Aboriginal and Torres Strait Islander Corporations 2007). In addition, there are approximately an equal number of Indigenous corporations incorporated under state and territory incorporations laws.

[3] See for example, the long list of reports from government reviews and inquiries over the last three decades; perhaps most prominently set out in various reports by the House of Representatives Standing Committee into Indigenous Affairs.

organisations set up to represent a specific location, or sub-group within a location, are still expected to treat their members as a community of like-minded people with similar interests, goals and priorities. Under such institutional conditions, governments have promoted the 'community' as a benchmark for fair representation, equitable distribution of resources and benefits, proper consultation, the source of legitimacy, and the rightful recipient of 'downwards' accountability.

Hand in hand with the murky concept of community goes that of 'family'. While the important role of extended families in the domestic economies and social systems of Indigenous communities is well documented (see Finlayson 1991; Macdonald 2000; Smith 2000; Sutton 1998), it is not clear to what extent (or how) they might provide a positive basis for governance and economic development. Indeed, it is commonly asserted that Indigenous family relationships are highly problematic for good organisational governance and undermine economic development outcomes. The family is viewed according to a dysfunctional, deficit model, not as a form of contemporary social and economic capital.

Yet the notion of 'family' has long been the central ordering principle within Indigenous Australian societies, both in their traditional and contemporary modes. Invoked in almost every context and in every discussion, 'family' is the core unit, at both an actual and conceptual level, in Indigenous social and economic life (see Smith 2005; Sutton 1998). In particular, the extended family is the primary residential form, with each individual's investment in family relationships widely distributed across expanding networks of relatedness.

Today, families of polity (cf. Sutton 1998) form the backbone of Indigenous communities and many local organisations, thereby linking an extended family group identity to organisational identities and forms of political representation. In this manner, extended families not only have a form of internal governance, they are also embedded into other layers of governance at community and regional levels, and outwards.

So, why is it that family participation in governance and the business arena is seen so negatively? Increasingly, Indigenous families in communities have come to be associated with images of organisational nepotism and corruption, disputation and violence, debilitating factionalism, self-interested decision making, insular thinking and low business expertise. The transformation of the Indigenous family from a positive to a negative symbol has a long history in Australian colonialism.[4] In recent times, its image has further deteriorated under

---

[4] See Edmunds (1990) for an account of the impacts of colonisation on Indigenous family life and socialisation practices; Smith (1991: 5–6) for a summary of some of the key colonial interventions in Indigenous families and the increasingly negative portrayal of family life and relationships; and also

public and media criticism of family violence and dysfunction in some communities, and their role in poor organisational management and governance. In regard to the latter, a report by the Office of the Registrar of Aboriginal Corporations (ORAC)[5] found that:

> The matter that Indigenous people make the most complaints to ORAC about is 'nepotism' within Indigenous corporations. Unmanaged nepotism has many adverse consequences, including high disputation, and will undermine an otherwise functioning program and corporation. It is a risk that funding agencies need to manage well. A key to managing it is understanding what it means and agreeing when action by the funding agency is necessary. Nepotism is widely understood to mean advantages obtained through family relationships, and is not necessarily illegal (ORAC 2004: 19).

The involvement of families in enterprise and commercial projects is seen as especially problematic. The Indigenous family lies at the heart of values of reciprocity, mutual responsibility and obligation. Because of this, it is argued that these institutional rules of family life cannot be trusted in the world of capitalism, business management and profit making. The family has thus become positioned as the antithesis of accountability, transparency and fairness; a form of 'cultural virus that infects economic development' (Ah Mat 2003: 3). For many stakeholders, 'community' is posed as the preferable unit for a more legitimate, inclusive form of governance, and for generating economic development.

There is certainly a plethora of evidence documenting the negative impacts of family politics on organisational governance, community life, and business success. But is that the whole story? Does family involvement in economic development initiatives and governance arrangements have to operate as a deficient cultural institution? Do core Indigenous values and relationships have to be entirely excluded from the governance of economic development initiatives in order for them to be successful? Can the two be reconciled? The experience of Yarnteen Corporation provides evidence for some alternative conclusions and options.

Community and organisational governance in Newcastle

With a population of 146 000, the industrial town of Newcastle on the central coast of New South Wales (NSW) is the second largest town in the state. According to 2006 Census results, around two per cent of its residents are Indigenous. The Aboriginal 'community' largely comprises families who resettled

---

Daly and Smith (2003), in which the 'deficit' and 'asset' views of families are considered in respect to their impact on the well-being of Indigenous children.

[5] As of 1 May 2008, this Australian Government office is now called the Office of the Registrar of Indigenous Corporations (ORIC).

in the town several decades ago, who have strong, continuing cultural ties both to the town itself and to surrounding rural communities and families across NSW (Ball 1985; Hall and Jonas 1985; Jonas 1991; Smith 1996, 2005). There is also a small group of Torres Strait Islanders living and working in the town, who have links to Islander communities in northern Queensland and the Torres Strait. An early survey of Indigenous households in the town carried out in the mid 1980s by the local Awabakal Cooperative reported that 75 per cent of those households were from outside the area (Hall and Jonas 1985). This movement into Newcastle created an estimated 700 per cent increase in the city's Indigenous population over the twenty years between 1971 and 1991 (Arthur 1994).

Importantly, amidst this flow of people there is a stable core of family members who have called Newcastle home for over four decades. These 'immigrant' families were instrumental in establishing the early Aboriginal service delivery organisations and local Aboriginal land councils in the town and surrounding region. Recent assertions of a local native title claim by an Indigenous family in the town, as well as the proliferation of traditional owner groups in the larger Newcastle-Hunter Valley region in recent years, have inserted issues of 'land ownership' versus 'historical' residence into the wider community dynamics. To date, there has been no native title land returned in the Newcastle town area.

The Aboriginal 'community' of Newcastle is therefore compositionally complex, comprising numerous extended family groups who have their Indigeneity in common, but who have family histories and relationships that link them to different resettlement phases, different cultural identities, and different regional communities. The so-called Newcastle 'Indigenous community' is in fact a network of dispersed nodes of governance in the form of organisations, senior leaders and key families. Some strands of the network are more closely connected than others.

It is not surprising then that there is no single 'community' governing body. Rather, the Indigenous residents in Newcastle are represented by an extremely large number of organisations based in the town and surrounding Hunter Valley region.[6] Some organisations are required to be widely representative under their statutory rules, while others are associated with particular families or service needs. There are community tensions that occasionally erupt into disputes over services and the governance of organisations, and which spill into attempts by different groups to 'take over'. At the same time, there are also positive relationships between a number of the families and organisations whose senior leaders meet regularly at forums and community events, forming an influential

---

[6] The Arwarbukarl Cultural Resource Association Inc (which operates out of Yarnteen) recently produced a 'Directory of Indigenous Organisations and Government Services in the Hunter' that listed over 60 different Indigenous service delivery organisations, see <http://www.arwarbukarl.com.au/default.aspx?id=27>.

peer network in the town. A number have worked for decades at regional, state and national levels on Indigenous political, governance and policy issues.

The formation of the Awabakal[7] Aboriginal Co-operative Ltd in 1976 was a pivotal event in creating a sense of Aboriginal identity in Newcastle. 'The co-op' was established as a response to the unmet service and employment needs of the growing number of Aboriginal people who had migrated to the town in the 1960–70s. It focused on community development initiatives and started several long-standing housing, health, welfare, economic and training initiatives.

The co-op also played an extremely important role as the incubator of other organisations that play an important role in the town today. Because some 'younger' organisations have been incubated out of older, apical organisations there is, in effect, a 'genealogical connection' between groups of organisations who support each other's work and goals. Yarnteen is an influential node in this urban network.

Yarnteen—a quiet economic success

Yarnteen Corporation has a long-standing reputation for both its business success and community development outcomes on several fronts. It successfully runs a major bulk warehousing and bagging facility for grains, protein meal and fertiliser—Port Hunter Commodities—which commenced trading in 1994. This venture commenced with one warehouse and bagging plant, and now has three state-of-the-art warehouses with storage capacity for 70 000 metric tonnes. It succeeded in gaining accreditation from the Australian Quarantine Inspection Service to conduct 'cleaning' of non-compliant imports, making it the only warehousing operation to do so in the port area.

In 1992, the corporation was one of the first urban organisations to operate a Community Development Employment Projects (CDEP) scheme, and it provided a range of social and cultural services and economic development opportunities for Aboriginal and Torres Strait Islander residents of the town and the wider Hunter River region (Smith 1996). It was one of a small number of CDEP organisations to subsequently participate in 2001–02 in the Australian Government's Indigenous Employment Centre trial,[8] successfully placing 20 people into full-time work and then going on to become a fully-fledged Indigenous Employment Centre.

---

[7] 'Awabakal' is the spelling of the name for the traditional land-owning group of the Newcastle area, which was used by the founding leaders of the co-operative when it first formed in 1976. At that time, it was thought that no representatives of the original traditional group remained. The leaders of the co-operative adopted the name as a mark of respect for the traditional lands and culture of that group. Recently, a native title claim has been made by extant members who are asserting traditional ownership, and a contemporary linguistic orthography has developed that spells the same name as 'Arwarbukarl'.
[8] See Champion (2002) for an account of these employment trials.

Subsequently, Yarnteen received a CDEP 'Achievement Award for Innovation' from the Australian Government in recognition of the advances it made in the use of technology to network CDEP organisations.[9] More recently, the organisation has consistently been on the front foot in responding to the recent radical changes to the CDEP scheme.

From the beginning, an integral part of its economic and employment initiatives has been the provision of in-house training, professional development and case management support to individuals. The corporation recently established the Indigenous Creative Enterprise Centre. This enterprise addressed the 'digital divide' by offering the Indigenous community in Newcastle access to computers and technology for skills and small business development. It has provided financial support and professional mentoring to the Arwarbukarl Cultural Resource Association. This is a dedicated cultural organisation whose main activities are 'protection and continual practice and teaching of our culture and the revival of the local Awabakal language' (YATSIC 2005). More recently, Yarnteen has expanded activities into small business training functions.

In 2006, Yarnteen extended its business portfolio by opening a car wash business in Port Macquarie. It aimed to capitalise on the growing demand to conserve water in areas under restrictions and provide a customer friendly car wash service. It sought the most recent technology—this time from the United States of America—to develop 'green' water recycling processes.

Yarnteen Pty Ltd was also created to operate as a property investment vehicle that enables the corporation to build an asset base for future investments. It currently owns land and warehouses at the Newcastle Port, 100 acres at Wollombi that it operates as a cultural and conference camp accessible to all Newcastle's Indigenous residents, and major residential property and buildings in town and interstate.

Yarnteen's governance history

Different institutional elements (such as norms, values, policies, regulations and routines) evolve as a product of the unique governance history of each organisation. These internally sourced institutions govern the behaviour of an organisation, its leaders and staff.

Not surprisingly, the governance history of Yarnteen Corporation has both urban and rural influences. Like many other Aboriginal organisations in the Hunter region, Yarnteen had its beginnings in the Awabakal Co-operative. An early internal review by leaders of the co-op led to several of its functional programs being 'farmed out' to organisations that were set up to take on the program roles.

---

[9] Under a prestigious partnership it negotiated with Microsoft Australia, Yarnteen developed an innovative website to assist networking and best practice exchange between CDEP organisations.

These organisations were incubated and mentored by the co-op until they became independent service delivery organisations in their own right.

Yarnteen was one such incubated organisation, becoming incorporated in June 1991. The leadership of the Awabakal Co-op stayed closely involved in mentoring the early development of Yarnteen and its emerging leadership. This process of organisational mentoring and incubation has in turn become a signature feature of Yarnteen's development.

While the corporation's purpose and objectives evolved over the years in keeping with its growth, there has always been a strong focus on economic development at the heart of its operations. Reflecting back on the organisation's governance history, Yarnteen leaders identify several 'key factors that influenced [its] governance structure' right from the beginning (pers. comm.; see also YATSIC 2005). The two founding leaders (one Aboriginal, the other Torres Strait Islander) say they were particularly keen to make an enduring change for the better in the economic circumstances of their families. They wanted greater economic independence for their own families and, in that way, to act as an economic role model for the wider Indigenous community: 'From the first, our organisation stressed its desire to become a full agent in our own development' (YATSIC 2005).

In order to do this, the leadership felt strongly that:

> the governance structure was ... an important strategy to achieve the long-term objectives and economic self sufficiency of the organisation. Our number one priority was to have a governance structure that was sensitive to and compatible with the culturally [sic] diversity and interests of our community, but importantly that offered stability and contributed to good governance rather than undermining it (Armstrong 2003).

> In particular, we aimed to create a balance between economic and social obligations for greater community capacity building ... Our goal to empower Indigenous individuals and organisations to achieve self-determination is being achieved through our governance structure (YATSIC 2005).

From the beginning, a first-order consideration in designing Yarnteen's organisational governance was a recognition amongst the founding Awabakal and corporation leaders 'that the Indigenous community around Newcastle area is made up of many different family and clan groups ... who have resettled in the region in search of better employment opportunities' (YATSIC 2005). They wanted to avoid the problems that other organisations had experienced with open-ended, amorphous community participation leading to unwieldy representative structures, and to focus on a core group of families with whom they had well-established connections. They had also witnessed first hand the debilitating effects of community politics on the governance of earlier NSW co-operatives and Local Aboriginal Land Councils. These organisations were regarded as having 'lost' valuable financial assets and economic ventures because of factionalised disputes over membership, representation, and community access to benefits.

The organisation's leaders also wanted to create 'a balance between economic and social obligations for greater community capacity building'. However, they also 'held the view that focusing only on the social aspects of people's lives may not produce lasting changes to individual families or communities' (YATSIC 2005). They clearly 'recognised the importance of business in supporting a healthy community' (cf. Jonas 1991: 12).

This positive assessment of the potential role of family, in tandem with their reservations about a 'whole of community' approach to business, and a desire to secure a strategic balance between cultural, social and economic goals, has set the tenor of Yarnteen's governance and institutional operations since 1991.

Yarnteen's governance model

Yarnteen's founding leaders believed that culturally-based decision making processes could form an effective basis for governing arrangements, but within a tight representative model. The leaders identified a core set of large extended families with long-term ties to Newcastle as the organisation's main membership group. They proceeded to establish the organisation's system of governing representation, decision making and membership around this particular subset of the wider community.

Given the problems, expectations and misunderstandings associated with the notion of family representative models in organisational governance, it is useful to examine how Yarnteen managed the potential negative impacts and built upon the positives in its governance for economic development. And furthermore, how it addressed the external pressure for wider community participation and access to its economic success.

The organisation stresses that it does not purport to represent the whole Aboriginal community of Newcastle. It did not feel bound to seek its board representatives from across the diversity of groups residing and travelling through the town. It did, on the other hand, see itself as having a broad community development remit in many of its service delivery functions, several of which are accessible to all Indigenous residents. These functions are not seen as necessitating the inclusion of the whole community into its representative structure. As a senior leader on the board noted: 'It's ok to have one group of people cooking the cake, if everyone else eventually gets a slice of it'. Yarnteen's leaders saw their commitment to deliver particular cultural, employment and training services to the wider community as part of their ability to spread some of the benefits of their economic success more widely, but without jeopardising their business viability.

These seemingly contradictory strategies—the one business, the other community/cultural—have been operationalised within the organisation's governance and institutional environment. In 1991, a Yarnteen Management Committee was established which represented four major extended family groups who had resettled in the Newcastle-Hunter region and 'adopted' the town over several decades. At that time, the organisation acknowledged that the traditional landowners of the region were the 'Awabakal', even though when it was first established none were thought to remain. The Management Committee started with 10 members, and is now called the Yarnteen Board. New representatives on the board are nominated and selected from the core member families. The board oversights the business and some of the cultural initiatives of Yarnteen, but these functions are differently structured.

The corporation's governance model for board representation and 'membership' for its economic ventures is tightly circumscribed to the core group of extended families. Its community development initiatives, on the other hand, are more inclusive and focus on its wider community 'constituency', which is the wider Newcastle Indigenous population. These residents can access and benefit from a range of 'community' initiatives and services provided by the organisation. The 'community' services operate out of separately incorporated organisations, under the umbrella of Yarnteen Corporation. The boards of these organisations also have a wider set of representatives on their governing boards.

In effect, Yarnteen's leadership designed separate approaches to its 'membership' and its 'constituency'. The organisation's *members* are the core families, and they stand at the heart of board membership and are the beneficial members of the economic ventures. Its *constituents* are drawn from the wider community, and are the people to whom cultural, employment, training and other social services are directed. This distinction appears to have been extremely beneficial in helping to quarantine the economic arm of the organisation from its other functions.

However, as a consequence of the tight governing structure created for its business ventures, the organisation has been seen in some quarters of the Newcastle Indigenous community and by some government departments as being 'exclusive', unrepresentative and 'not a community organisation'. But in light of its transparent governance strategy for economic success and its diverse delivery of community services, this is clearly not the case. However, these assertions highlight the considerable pressure that governments can apply to Indigenous business organisations to be 'whole-of-community' and how they equate this with 'good governance'. It also highlights the pressures that arise from within the wider Indigenous community when some groups feel that a local organisation should distribute its economic benefits more widely to all residents of the community. Neither of these expectations is applied to non-Indigenous private sector businesses in Newcastle.

The tight family representative model appears to have directly contributed to remarkable stability within the governing board. Eight out of the current 10 people are foundation members of the organisation. There have been significant benefits for the organisation as a result of this representative stability. One important advantage appears to be the creation of considerable governance 'capital'. For example:

- board members have been able to build a strong shared commitment to the organisation's long-term economic vision;
- the board is seen to have considerable legitimacy in the eyes of its members and staff;
- a solid foundation of trust and openness has been progressively developed within the board;
- there is a collegial relationship of partnership and honesty between the board and senior management (many of whom are also long-term employees of the organisation);
- a decision-making process has developed over time that is familiar and reliable; and
- board members can fall back on their history of consensus-building and experience of having resolved problems.

Stability is not only a feature of the governing board, but also of management and staff. Several senior staff members have been employed for as long as the original board members. Of the 37 people employed full-time in 2003–04 (YATSIC 2005), 29 were Indigenous and eight non-Indigenous, which is evidence of a very high level of Indigenous participation and employment. This figure includes 24 males and 13 females—with women represented in management as well as office staffing areas.

With such stability of leadership and staff an organisation could easily settle into a convenient comfort zone in its governance and business initiatives. Yet Yarnteen seems to have been able to avoid the associated pitfalls of insularity, narrowing expertise, failing performance, and resistance to change. It has also designed a set of effective buffers against potential family factionalism, disputes and self-interested decision making, which have been evident in other organisations with tight family-based representative models. The implementation of a four-pronged strategy appears to have been influential in achieving these outcomes, and includes the development of:

- structural flexibility and diversification;
- a strong, internal governance culture;
- diverse and deep institutional capital; and
- accountable, professional leadership.

Structural flexibility and diversification

Over the years as Yarnteen has grown, it has retained operational flexibility by routinely reviewing its strategic direction and diversifying its structure to respond to changing economic and commercial conditions. The corporation adopted an 'incubation strategy' to facilitate the establishment of offshoot organisations, which have taken over specific functional parts of its operation.

For example, in 2004, Yarnteen undertook an internally instigated review of its governance, organisational structure and functions. As a result, it decided to minimise possible risk to its business enterprises, whose assets were identified as being open to potential 'social stripping' by broader community constituents, and to the risk of the potential failure of any of the organisation's more community oriented services. As a result of that review, the corporation set up two separately incorporated organisations with their own boards—Youloe-ta Indigenous Development Association and Yamuloong Incorporated Association—to deliver their community-based employment and training services.

Youloe-ta now manages the original Yarnteen CDEP scheme and operates the Indigenous Employment Centre. It also runs a conference facility, an Aboriginal bush foods centre for school groups, and training and employment mentoring services. At one stage, along with Yamuloong, it was a wholly-owned subsidiary of Yarnteen.

Yamuloong Association was established as an Aboriginal Registered Training Organisation to provide nationally accredited training in business administration, small business mentoring, and information and technology training. It was subsequently re-incorporated into Youloe-ta after another Yarnteen-initiated review determined that it required better corporate support.

These separately incorporated bodies have continued to retain close links with the corporation. This group of organisations refer to themselves collectively as the 'Yarnteen family of organisations' or 'the Yarnteen group' (see Fig. 8.1) and includes Port Hunter Commodities Pty Ltd, Riverside Car and Boat Wash, Indigenous Creative Enterprise Centre, and Yarnteen Pty Ltd as wholly-owned subsidiaries, plus the incubated offshoots.

Fig. 8.1 The 'Yarnteen family' of organisations

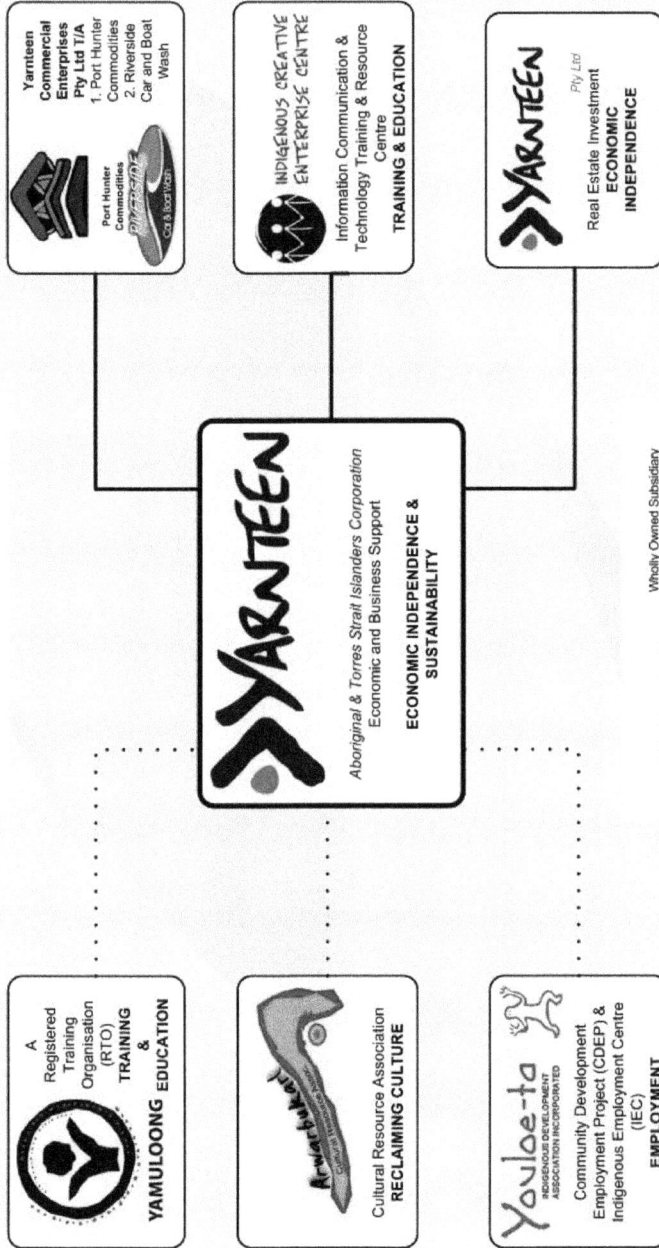

Source: Yarnteen Aboriginal and Torres Strait Islanders Corporation

Over the course of its operations, Yarnteen has also assisted Newcastle Aboriginal residents with business start up, operational advice and mentoring. These incubated enterprises have included: an Indigenous housing construction company, a transport company, cultural tourism accommodation, and a plumbing business. These operate as self-employed businesses.

This alliance of organisations comprises a networked governance model. Yarnteen Corporation acts as a 'hub', maintaining a valued relationship of mentoring, management support and financial advice for the incubated offshoots. At the same time, as mentioned above, it has legally quarantined its economic ventures from potential financial liability and stripping by retaining them as wholly-owned subsidiaries. The incubated organisations have separate boards on which there is representation from the Yarnteen Board, but a majority of other community members.

This strategy of 'planned organisational devolution' and 'strategic incubation' reinforces the demarcation of Yarnteen's economic pursuits alongside its partnership approach to community service-delivery and cultural goals.

It is noteworthy that the cultural metaphor of 'family' has been used as a model for developing this form of devolved, networked governance. A major advantage of this model lies in its flexibility, its tolerance of a diversity of identities, its capacity to extend close working relationships to new components, and the benefits of inter-dependency—in much the same way as extended families do in Indigenous communities.

The relationship between the incubated organisations and the 'mother' corporation is seen by both staff and leaders as being flexible and egalitarian. The groups cooperate for particular purposes, but each regards itself as undertaking valued functional roles and responsibilities over which it has autonomy. This type of networked governance operates like a close coalition of autonomous parts and appears to be well suited to undertaking business in parallel with separate community functions.

A durable governance culture

Yarnteen has exceptionally good corporate governance. The organisation is accorded legitimacy by external stakeholders and regulators—it has passed government-instigated reviews and financial audits, and continues to receive favourable assessments from the private sector. An annual report is published each year, and has been since its inception. Its administrative systems and planning processes are kept straightforward and are understood by staff and governing members, and management and staff are qualified in a range of skills and professional in their conduct.

The Chair of the Yarnteen Board convenes well run, minuted meetings, and board members say they are properly provided with clear information and considered advice by the Executive Director and Chair. There appears to be consistent attendance at meetings by board members. Their collective view is that there is a proper focus on the big issues during meetings, and that individual members come along prepared to do their job. A factor in the effectiveness of the board's decision making is that the members are confident in the accuracy of the financial information and strategic business advice they are provided. Board members ensure they understand the complex financial matters brought before them by consistently asking questions of management, and discussing potential business risks and options.

A primary factor in building these governance skills for business has been the provision by the Executive Director of ongoing, in-house training for board members on issues including their financial roles and responsibilities, business planning, risk management, consensus decision making, and board practice. In collaboration with the Executive Director, the board has developed a 'Board Values Statement' that seeks to promote the members' shared commitment to transparent, honest decision making, fairness, and internal and external accountability. As a consequence of these internal professional development initiatives, the board is familiar with strategic financial planning and their business transitions appear to be well managed (see Smith 1996, 2006).

The separation of powers between the board and Executive Director is generally understood and implemented, contrary to many Indigenous organisations. But importantly, the Yarnteen approach to this 'good governance' prescription remains a flexible one. There is a close working relationship of mutual support between the board and senior management. Individual board members also collaborate with staff on more operational tasks, and staff members periodically contribute to strategic planning and goal setting for the organisation. In other words, the governance arrangement could more accurately be described as 'separate, but working together'.

This 'governance partnership' is somewhat contrary to the standard principle that proposes a much stricter division between the roles and responsibilities of boards and management. Yet Yarnteen's approach seems to enable it to make better combined use of its knowledge, skills and experience across the layers of the organisation. This has promoted resilience and a strong shared commitment within the organisation.

Board members and senior management also espouse a joint approach to balancing the need for both business innovation and stability—a philosophy that has been described by the Executive Director as 'restless self-renewal'. In these diverse ways, the organisation has developed a valuable reserve of corporate governance capital to sustain its economic goals, which can be called upon in times of planned internal transition or externally instigated change.

Perhaps more importantly, though, alongside this corporate practice, Yarnteen's leaders have actively created a broader and durable 'governance culture' within the organisation, its subsidiaries and offshoots.

An organisation's 'governance culture' can be defined as the system of formal and informal traditions, collective values, and culturally-shared mechanisms for behavioural accountability, incentives and censure that direct staff, management and leaders to conform to the organisation's policies, vision and goals (see Bresser and Millonig 2003; Cornell and Kalt 1995; Hunt and Smith 2007). The formal components of an organisation's governance culture may include its written policy documents, dispute and appeal procedures, vision statements and strategic plans. Its informal aspects are typically unwritten, but nonetheless prevail in people's behaviour and interaction within the organisation; they tell individuals how to do things and how to relate to each other.

In practice, a great deal of what happens in organisational governance falls into this informal area. Informal governance works at the level of individuals, through processes such as how conflicts and appeals are mediated, praise and reward given, behavioural sanctions applied, collective identity reaffirmed, and through the style or personality of decision-making and management.

The leaders of Yarnteen have embedded a pervasive 'governance culture' within the organisation which actively promotes a particular set of norms. These include fairness, mutual respect, the value of personal contribution, accountability and teamwork in the work environment, and a shared commitment to the organisation's long-term success and autonomy. Importantly, these values are promoted in a manner that reinforces collective support for the style of governance as being distinctly Aboriginal and therefore legitimate.

This collective support is further reinforced by the prevalence of Aboriginal humour, a decision making style that resonates with Aboriginal consensus and conflict mediation processes, and the perception that all members of the organisation—from board members to young staff—are 'one family'. These characteristics are regularly articulated by people as valued qualities of the organisation's 'cultural identity' (Armstrong 2007: 75). And board members emphasise their desire to maintain this style of governance:

> We make decisions like a washing machine. First we just push it all around, everything round and round and have a good talk about every part of it. Then we come to a decision. Once a decision is made, board members think it is important to stick to it … then we agree as one. Once a decision is passed, that's it, it's finished. Then we're under one agreement, we get on with it (Yarnteen Corporation Board member).

This governance culture does not simply sit at the top with the Yarnteen Board and Executive Director; it has been seeded by the leadership throughout the management and staff, and the family of organisations. At the heart of this governance culture lies a process of institution building that has been deliberately embedded in Yarnteen's *modus operandi*.

Building institutional capital

Institutions can be defined as the 'rules of the game', the socially and culturally legitimated behavioural expectations that can be rewarded if followed, or sanctioned if violated. Rules and their related processes are the organising tools of governance. They tell the leaders, staff and members of an organisation how it should work, what decisions are made on behalf of members, and who may make them. Effective institutions are those that are capable of regulating and channelling both individual and collective behaviour.

Institutional weakness has been highlighted as a critical factor in the poor governance of many Indigenous organisations and governments (Cornell 1995; Hunt and Smith 2007; Sterritt 2002). In the case of Yarnteen, its leaders have created and sustained a range of governance institutions. These provide a system of incentives, rewards, constraints and limits, which direct the board, senior management and individual staff members to behave and perform in ways that support and strengthen the organisation's economic and service delivery objectives and strategies. Following Hunt and Smith (2007) and Oliver (1997), the richness or depth of this system creates a form of 'institutional capital' for Yarnteen.

In the context of economic development, institutional capital can be defined as the specific conditions in an organisation's internal and external institutional context that allow the formation of sustained business success and competitive advantage in the commercial arena (see Bresser and Millonig 2003: 225–2; and Scott 1995: 35–9). Scott (1995) and Bresser and Millonig (2003) distinguish three interacting components or pillars of institutional capital: regulative, normative, and cognitive. Each of these is applicable and evident in Yarnteen and its offshoot organisations.

Regulative institutions focus on rules (more often formal than informal) that are monitored and sanctioned in the case of possible corruption, bias, violation or poor corporate performance. To this end, Yarnteen's leaders have designed and implemented customised written policies, conflict resolution and appeals processes, procedures for the periodic review of individual performance, and regular internal reviews of its economic portfolio and community development functions. Senior and executive management participate in regular updates to monitor the organisation's commercial and corporate performance in respect to these.

These internal regulations are overwhelmingly seen as beneficial within the corporation, and so act as a source of institutional capital. Externally imposed government regulative mechanisms (such as mandatory government audits, departmental reviews, and financial and program reporting procedures) are invariably seen as overly burdensome and a source of erratic, but coercive pressure. The perception within Yarnteen is that the extent of regulatory scrutiny by government undermines its resilience and focus, rather than enabling its governance. The board and senior management of the organisation do give considerable attention to fulfilling their external compliance and financial responsibilities, but as the Executive Director notes, 'best practice organisations look to achieving this themselves and do not rely on external organisations to regulate or enforce this through external controls' (Armstrong 2003: 7).

Yarnteen's normative institutions comprise the norms and values which define the types of behaviours that are considered desirable, appropriate, and correct. The fact that these are uniformly seen as culturally legitimate by staff, management and board members means that they have deep acceptance and influence within the organisation. As a consequence, individual compliance with the organisation's codes of conduct, vision statement, the board's value statement and corporate responsibilities, and individual performance milestones, is considered to be both a behavioural and cultural obligation. The adoption and practice of a code of ethical values by the board is taken seriously as an example of the standards to be maintained by people throughout the organisation (see Armstrong 2003).

These normative institutions assist Yarnteen's leadership to modify structures, routines and business strategies as necessary, and so help to ameliorate potentially adverse affects that might arise from long-term board membership and employment of particular staff. Another influential aspect of the normative environment within the organisation is the expectation that members of the staff, management and board will routinely activate their networks into the wider business and public sector, and with regional Aboriginal communities. This further assists in preventing insularity of ideas and thinking.

The third element of Yarnteen's institutional environment is its cognitive capital. This relates to the ways in which individuals perceive and interpret their work and community life; a reality that is always a social and cultural construction. The cognitive institutional component of an organisation can be defined as the sum understanding of its internalised values and norms; that is, all the aspects of institutions that are *taken for granted* at a subconscious level.

Compared to the normative dimension, the cognitive component emphasises subjective assumptions, expectations and pressures. In this realm, Yarnteen has developed considerable collective cognitive capital shaped around members' close identification with its history, governance, goals and operation as a distinctly 'Aboriginal organisation', with Aboriginal values and behaviours, and 'family' relationships between the organisations. Within the corporation, these relationships and shared understandings are seen to positively facilitate success rather than undermine it.

The institutional strengths of the Yarnteen—regulative, normative and cognitive—are thus multidimensional and comprise both internal and external dimensions. Particularly influential institutions appear to be those that have been generated and embedded internally by the organisation's own leaders and staff, not those developed and imposed from outside.

These institutional strategies have taken time and commitment to implement. For many organisations they are the first things to go by the wayside when resources and people are stretched. Yet Yarnteen's rich institutional environment has generated considerable governance and economic benefits. Because they are shared and routinely followed by staff, management and board members alike, they become the vehicle for collective goal setting and action. The staff of Yarnteen say they feel part of this strategic institutional and governance approach and, as a consequence, a culture of teamwork and loyalty to the organisation has taken root. Not surprisingly then, in comparison with many other organisations, Yarnteen has had a very low turnover of employees and board members. Overall, its institution-building efforts are a form of capital that acts to buffer and neutralise the potential disadvantages of long-term board membership, select family representative structures, and debilitating external demands and pressures.

Leadership for economic development

The leadership of Yarnteen has been the catalyst for building the organisation's governance culture and institutional capital. In 2006, I carried out interviews and informal discussions with board members, the executive, managers and staff on the issue of leadership (see Smith 2006). The qualities of Aboriginal leaders seen to be necessary include:

- 'humility';
- 'being part of the Aboriginal community';
- 'having a passion for helping their community not just themselves';
- being 'selfless';
- 'having a vision of what's possible';
- 'experience in politics';
- being 'able to mentor younger people';
- 'able to talk to all kinds of people, and listen well'; and
- 'able to get agreement and consensus'.

Yarnteen's leadership is of a very high quality and has been a critical factor in the success of its governance for economic development. Its leaders are both male and female. They have strong links into the local and regional Indigenous community, and extensive networks into the state and national leadership.

Several have national experience on representative organisations, councils and boards. They are extremely well qualified in their management, governance and financial expertise.

The Executive Director and Chair of Yarnteen have an extremely sophisticated understanding of governance best practice and strategies. The concept is frequently discussed in board meetings. Governance training has been provided in-house; senior managers have participated in external leadership workshops; several board members and senior managers have presented conference and workshop papers on the topic; and the Executive Director has undertaken the Australian Company Directors' Course. The combined effect is to ensure that the board is not easily swayed by any particular subset of family or factional interests, and takes considered economic risks. Single, strong voices cannot prevail against the board's collective assessment of issues, and there are robust guidelines for fair governance that members actively attempt to meet.

Leadership succession is currently an issue on the table for the organisation and it is starting to trial different strategies. The resilience of Yarnteen's governance culture and institutional capital is intimately associated with its current senior leadership. A future test for the organisation will be the extent to which its institutional capital assists it to weather the turnover of any key leaders.

Conclusion: the business of 'governing for business'

> How do we live at this 'place' where the two worlds meet and remain Indigenous? Indigenous people want to participate in the wider economic, social and cultural lives that are enjoyed by other Australians. But they will not be successful and cannot be expected to succeed as long as they are denied the opportunities and the tools to enable cultural integrity and community survival (Leah Armstrong 2007: 75).

Yarnteen is an example of an organisation with effective, legitimate governance for economic development. It operates in a complex urban community environment and national context, where the challenges facing Indigenous businesses are substantial, and their corporate governance and financial failure is common. The Yarnteen family of organisations has an extremely high reputation in the wider private and public sectors, where it is seen to be a model for other organisations, and a sound investment opportunity. Its economic and strategic success is durable, and raises several important implications for other Indigenous organisations attempting to develop robust governance for sustained enterprise and cultural development.

First, the cultural 'self' in Yarnteen's governance is a complex pastiche that is a product of the Aboriginal history of Newcastle and its early organisations. This history is one of regional mobility and resettlement, long residence in the town by a core group of extended families, continuing strong cultural identities, and the incubation of a network of service delivery organisations in the town and surrounding region. The corporation's governance strategies and tactics have been based around understanding and managing both the constraints and benefits of that community environment and cultural identity.

Second, Yarnteen's leaders adopted a deliberate and effective strategy to insulate the organisation from debilitating community conflicts and jealousies by keeping its representative structure tight and sticking to its core enterprise development goals at the same time as ensuring that the organisation positively contributes to wider community cultural and social goals. In this way, the organisation manages to maintain a delicate balance between 'family' and 'community'. Alongside these structural strategies, the strength of its internal culture and institutional capital has enabled the corporation to create a set of workable limits and constraints on individual self-interest and family factionalism. Other organisations might consider the benefits that seem to flow from establishing a legal and structural demarcation between business and social/cultural initiatives, and from developing their governance representation and membership to support that distinction.

Third, fundamental to the organisation's economic success has been its internal governance culture and institutional capital. Effective governance is a prerequisite for mobilising other forms of capital and provides better conditions under which that capital can be developed and sustained. An organisation's institutional environment is a major driver of competitive commercial advantage. The leaders of Yarnteen Corporation have actively managed both their internal and external institutional contexts, and progressively built up deep reserves of regulative, normative and cognitive capital that have enabled it to remain proactive in assessing, taking up and managing economic opportunities.

And fourth, organisational leadership is essential if well designed governance and economic success are to be developed and sustained. Effective leaders are the fundamental drivers of institution building within an organisation. Without their commitment and demonstrated practice in this fundamental area, an organisation will lack the institutional environment that promotes flexibility, resilience and collective performance.

There is little doubt that it is the combination of governance, leadership, organisational flexibility, and institutional strength that has sustained this extraordinarily successful urban enterprise. Furthermore, in achieving this success the organisation has not had to turn its back on its cultural identity, its community and family relationships. Yarnteen not only works in an Aboriginal way, but also meets external demands for effective corporate governance, business standards and financial accountability.

Acknowledgements

My research engagement with Yarnteen Corporation commenced in 1995 and focused on factors contributing to their success in operating the CDEP scheme. The research on which this chapter is based was conducted over several visits between 2006 and 2007.

During my visits, the board members, management and staff at Yarnteen provided me with enormous support and assistance in the collaborative research carried out under the umbrella of the ICGP. I would especially like to thank Leah Armstrong, Executive Director of Yarnteen, and Jim Wright, Chair of the Yarnteen Board, for the considerable time, intellectual contribution, research feedback, editorial comments, friendship and enthusiasm they gave to my research and this paper.

The members of the Yarnteen Board welcomed the opportunity to assess how they were travelling in respect to their roles and responsibilities. They happily made themselves available for lively discussions and have been frank in their feedback on my various reports. This has made the research process a pleasure.

Senior managers of Yarnteen contributed valuable time when they were under heavy workloads. I thank them for their professional approach to engaging in and supporting my work. I would also like to thank the many staff members of Yarnteen who spent hours assisting me to organise interviews, meetings and discussion sessions, and who tirelessly assisted me with access to data and written reports. In particular, I would like to thank Pat Capper for her unstinting support and assistance during my several stays, and Uncle Rex Morgan who took the time to show me around town and the surrounding region and give me his history of Yarnteen.

References

Ah Mat, R. 2003. 'The moral case for Indigenous capitalism', Unpublished paper presented to the *Native Title Conference: Native Title on the Ground*, 3–5 June, Alice Springs.

Armstrong, L. 2003. 'Financial management and business systems: the backbone of an effectively resourced capacity for governance', Unpublished paper presented to the *Building Effective Indigenous Governance Conference*, 5–7 November, Jabiru, NT, available at <http://www.nt.gov.au/cdsca/indigenous_conference/web/html/papers.html> [accessed 19 May 2008].

——2007. 'Finding Australia's soul: rebuilding our Indigenous communities', *The Circle*, 1: 74–6, Social Ventures Australia, available at <http://www.socialventures.com.au/files/pdf/TC%20mag%20Leah%20Armstrong.pdf> [accessed 19 May 2008].

Arthur, W. S. 1994. 'The same but different: Indigenous socioeconomic variation', Unpublished report to the Australian Institute of Aboriginal and Torres Strait Islander Studies, Canberra.

Ball, R. E. 1985. 'The economic situation of Aborigines in Newcastle, 1982', *Australian Aboriginal Studies,* 1: 2–21.

Bresser, R. and Millonig, K. 2003. 'Institutional capital: competitive advantage in light of the new institutionalism in organisational theory', *Schmalenbach Business Review,* 55: 220–41.

Champion, M. 2002. 'Urban CDEPs as Indigenous Employment Centres: policy and community implications', *CAEPR Discussion Paper No. 228,* CAEPR, ANU, Canberra, available at <http://www.anu.edu.au/caepr/discussion.php>.

Cornell, S. and Kalt, J. P. 1990. 'Pathways from poverty: development and institution-building on American Indian reservations', *American Indian Culture and Research Journal,* 14 (1): 89–125, also available at <http://www.hks.harvard.edu/hpaied/pubs/pub_016.htm> [accessed 19 May 2008].

—— and ——1995. 'Cultural evolution and constitutional public choice: institutional diversity and economic performance on American Indian reservations', *PRS 95-3,* Harvard Project on American Indian Economic Development, Malcolm Weiner Center for Social Policy, John F. Kennedy School of Government, Harvard University, Cambridge, MA.

Daly, A. and Smith, D. E. 2003. 'Reproducing exclusion or inclusion? Implications for the wellbeing of Indigenous Australian children', *CAEPR Discussion Paper No. 253,* CAEPR, ANU, Canberra, available at <http://www.anu.edu.au/caepr/discussion.php>.

Dodson, M. and Smith, D. E. 2003. 'Governance for sustainable development: strategic issues and principles for Indigenous Australian communities', *CAEPR Discussion Paper No. 250,* CAEPR, ANU, Canberra, available at <http://www.anu.edu.au/caepr/discussion.php>.

Edmunds, M. 1990. 'Doing business: socialisation, social relations, and social control in Aboriginal society. A review in relation to the issues underlying Aboriginal deaths in custody', Unpublished discussion paper prepared for the Royal Commission into Aboriginal Deaths in Custody on behalf of the Department of Prehistory and Anthropology, ANU, and AIATSIS, Canberra.

Finlayson, J. 1991. Don't Depend on Me: Autonomy and Dependence in an Aboriginal Community in North Queensland, PhD Thesis, Anthropology Department, ANU, Canberra.

Hall, M. R. and Jonas, W. J. 1985. *On the Fringes of Newcastle Society*, Newcastle Aboriginal Cooperative Ltd, Newcastle.

Hunt, J. and Smith, D. E. 2006. 'Building Indigenous community governance in Australia: preliminary research findings', *CAEPR Working Paper No. 31*, CAEPR, CASS, ANU, Canberra.

—— and ——2007. 'Indigenous Community Governance Project: year two research findings', *CAEPR Working Paper No. 36*, CAEPR, ANU, Canberra.

Jonas, W. J. 1991. Awabakal, Bahtabah, Biripi, Worimi: Four Successful Aboriginal Organisations, Unpublished report, Aboriginal Education Unit, University of Newcastle, Newcastle.

Kaufmann, D. 2005. 'Back to basics: ten myths about governance and corruption', *Finance and Development*, 42 (3), available at <http://www.imf.org/external/pubs/ft/ fandd/2005/09/index.htm>.

Kaufmann, D., Kraay, A. and Mastruzzi, M. 2005. 'Governance matters IV: governance indicators for 1996–2004', *World Bank Policy Research Working Paper 3237*, available at <http://worldbank.org/wbi/ governance/pubs/govmatters4.html>.

Macdonald, G. 2000. 'Economies and personhood: demand sharing among the Wiradjuri of New South Wales', in G. W. Wenzel, G. Hovelsrud-Borda and N. Kishigami (eds), *The Social Economy of Sharing: Resource Allocation and Modern Hunter-Gatherers*, Senri Ethnological Studies 53, National Museum of Ethnology, Osaka.

Oliver, C. 1996. 'The institutional embeddedness of economic activity', *Advances in Strategic Management*, 13: 163–86.

Oliver, C. 1997. 'Sustainable competitive advantage: combining institutional and resource-based views', *Strategic Management Journal*, 18: 697–713.

Office of the Registrar of Aboriginal Corporations (ORAC) 2004. *Report—Forum on Risk Issues for Programs Funding Indigenous Corporations*, ORAC, Australian Government, Canberra.

Office of the Registrar of Aboriginal and Torres Strait Islander Corporations (ORATSIC) 2007. 'Duties of directors and other officers', *Fact Sheet*, October, Office of the Registrar of Aboriginal and Torres Strait Islander Corporations, Australian Government, Canberra, available at <http://www.oratsic.gov.au/about_ORIC/legislation/CATSI_Act.aspx#6.

Peters-Little, F. 2000. 'The community game: Aboriginal self-definition at the local level', *AIATSIS Research Discussion Paper No. 10*, AIATSIS, Canberra.

Scott, R. 1994. 'Institutions and organizations: toward a theoretical synthesis', in R. Scott and J. Meyer (eds), *Institutional Environments and Organization: Structural Complexity and Individualism*, Sage Publications, Thousand Oaks, CA.

——1995. *Institutions and Organizations*, Sage Publications, Thousand Oaks, CA.

Smith, D. E. 1991. 'Toward an Aboriginal household expenditure survey: conceptual, methodological and cultural considerations', *CAEPR Discussion Paper No. 10*, CAEPR, ANU, Canberra.

——1996. 'CDEP as urban enterprise: the case of Yarnteen Aboriginal and Torres Strait Islanders Corporation, Newcastle', *CAEPR Discussion Paper No. 114*, CAEPR, ANU, Canberra.

——(ed.) 2000. *Indigenous Families and the Welfare System: Two Community Case Studies*, CAEPR Research Monograph No. 17, CAEPR, ANU, Canberra.

——2005. 'Indigenous households and community governance', in D. Austin-Broos and G. Macdonald (eds), *Culture, Economy and Governance in Aboriginal Australia*, Sydney University Press, Sydney.

——2006. 'Evaluating governance effectiveness: a facilitated process with the board of Yarnteen Corporation', *ICGP Case Study Report* No. 2, ICGP, CAEPR, ANU, Canberra.

Sterritt, N. 2002. 'Defining Indigenous governance', Paper presented to the *Indigenous Governance Conference*, 3–5 April, Canberra, available at <http://www.reconciliation.org.au/igawards/pages/about-governance/conference.php>.

Sutton, P. 1998. 'Families of polity: post-classical Aboriginal society and native title', in P. Sutton, *Native Title and the Descent of Rights*, National Native Title Tribunal, Perth.

Taylor, J. 2006. 'Population and diversity: policy implications of emerging Indigenous demographic trends', *CAEPR Discussion Paper No. 283*, CAEPR, ANU, Canberra.

Yarnteen Aboriginal and Torres Strait Islanders Corporation (YATSIC) 2005. *Annual Report*, YATSIC, Newcastle.

9. Indigenous leaders and leadership: agents of networked governance

Bill Ivory

Introduction

In 2007, the Prime Minister of Australia, The Hon. John Howard,[1] introduced a policy of unilateral intervention into Indigenous communities in the Northern Territory (NT), purportedly to address the overwhelming incidence of child abuse. In doing so, he argued that 'The basic elements of a civilised society don't exist'.[2] His main Ministerial proponent of the intervention, The Hon. Mal Brough, the Minister for Families, Community Services and Indigenous Affairs, justified the nature of the initiative by characterising Indigenous people in the NT as having a dysfunctional society where 'strong men prevail' (Howard and Brough 2007). In addition, the Federal Health Minister, Mr Tony Abbott, referred to 'big men' who are 'terrorising' other Aboriginal people (ABC 2007).

These views are reminiscent of those of commentators such as Helen Hughes (2005: 16), who recently argued that 'Small elites of "big men" monopolise the layers of separate governance created for Aborigines and Torres Strait Islanders'. According to Hughes (ibid.), 'Sorcery and payback thrive. The ultimate results are murders and suicides'.

In a similar vein, another commentator (Hirst 2007) wrote in one national newspaper that 'in many Aboriginal communities … [t]he people have shown they are incapable of governing themselves. There is no point in consulting them about the creation of authority; authority has to be created for them'.

When issues arise about the functionality of Indigenous communities, politicians and public commentators regularly question whether there is, in fact, any extant Indigenous governance and leadership. Some argue that if it once existed, it has since become valueless or has disintegrated altogether. Many regard Indigenous leadership as being so politically under-developed and socially ephemeral that it is ineffective in mobilising law and order.

It is perhaps not surprising then, that when The Hon. John Howard's VIP aircraft landed at Wadeye (Port Keats) in the NT in early April 2005, Australia's national leader, accompanied by senior bureaucrats, appeared keen to make his visit as brief as possible. Receiving a salute from an Aboriginal soldier in army uniform,

---

[1] Prime Minister Howard's Federal Coalition party lost government during the Australian election held on 24 November 2007.
[2] Interview with David Koch and Melissa Doyle, *Sunrise*, Seven Network, 22 June 2007, transcript available at <http://pandora.nla.gov.au/pan> [accessed 24 April 2008].

he shook hands with a local Aboriginal landowner and council representative and then hurriedly moved on. Under a nearby tree, unnoticed by the official party, were several bemused elderly Aboriginal gentlemen, one in a wheel chair, patiently watching the events unfold, and waiting to welcome their official guest. These men were in fact senior leaders[3] of the Port Keats region, experts in group survival, directors of ceremony, and adept at negotiated decision-making and consensus building.[4] Most had spent time 'droving bullocky' as expert stockmen, working for the cattle barons of the NT, and more recently had been engaged in establishing representative organisations within the community. Later, they were briefly acknowledged by the Prime Minister as his party swept on through the community. Meanwhile, Aboriginal community residents, well aware of the importance of these old men, respectfully gave them their due deference and attention.[5]

In the wider historical context of Indigenous affairs and the NT intervention, this scene raises important questions. Why is it that in Australia, Indigenous leaders are often disregarded or at best grudgingly recognised by non-Indigenous people and their leaders? Why is Indigenous leadership seemingly invisible to non-Indigenous eyes? Is Indigenous leadership so politically under-developed that it is ineffective in today's post-colonial Australian society? Are the leaders themselves content to sit in the background and let the intercultural vortex marginalise them?

This chapter draws on field research conducted at Port Keats to examine the conditions for the reproduction and enactment of Indigenous leadership with the aim of bringing both the concept and practical workings of leadership into sharper relief in the contemporary Australian intercultural setting. A model of networked Indigenous leadership is proposed that enables us to better understand how Indigenous leaders are produced and developed, and how local Indigenous societies, at least to this point, have been able to promote cultural resilience and collective survival. To do so, the chapter looks back at the leadership history of the community and the personal life histories of people who are regarded by their peers and kin as 'leaders'. It also positions Indigenous leadership and governance within the wider environment of mainstream Australian governance

---

[3] These men were senior leaders (among others) within their clan-groups and also within the wider ceremonial arena. Each clan, and there are 20 within the Thamarrurr region, has senior leadership. As the Prime Minister was entering a particular clan's land, referred to as the *Kardu Diminin*, these men were the appropriate authority figures for this occasion.

[4] Two of these senior leaders have since passed away.

[5] The Prime Minister was at Wadeye to acknowledge its prominence as the selected NT trial site for a major Council of Australian Governments (COAG) initiative. In April 2002, COAG had introduced the initiative in order to develop integrated and flexible programs and services for Indigenous people in eight sites across Australia, one in each State and Territory. Each trial was led by one Australian Government and one State Government agency.

and explores possible options for creative engagement between the two domains, and for the sustainability of Indigenous forms of leadership.

Colonial views of Australian Indigenous leadership

There are many publications that provide important insights into Australian Indigenous leadership, particularly in its regionally differentiated, gendered and religico-ritual contexts.[6] Often the terms 'leader' or 'leadership' are not to be found in the text of these publications, as writers have referred to headmen, chiefs, bosses, elders and so on. Whilst the literature on contemporary Indigenous leadership illustrates a wide spectrum of views, in early colonial Australia descriptions were perhaps even more varied, although possibly more tightly bound by the conceptual constraints of the social evolutionist thinking that prevailed in early colonial accounts of Indigenous Australian life.

Debate has ensued since Captain Cook's first landing about whether Australian Aboriginal people even had systematic forms of 'leadership' and governance, and if they did, what they looked like. Early colonial assumptions and opinions were formed under the ideological umbrella of the European Enlightenment, which Burch and Ellanna (1994: 1) have described as 'political philosophy, not science' with its 'arguments and assumptions … based more on fantasy than fact'. One early commentator, in 1793, was concerned that there did not appear to be 'any civil regulations, or ordinances … [existing] among this people' (Tench 1961: 51).

Sixty years later, reflecting a common opinion of the time, a journalist and historian writing in 1853–54 argued that Aboriginal people had 'authority or unity of no description' and that they had 'no chiefs' (Flanagan 1888: 15).

These early constructs of Indigenous leadership were often based on European military and institutional paradigms as well as past colonial encounters with natives elsewhere. There was a yearning amongst British settlers and observers for visible structures of government, clear hierarchies of power and authority, plus written laws. The assumptions and biases of social evolutionist perspectives that emerged from the colonial era were further developed within public policy and anthropological thought in the nineteenth and early twentieth century. A summary of these chronological views is given in Table 9.1.[7]

---

[6] Table 9.1 outlines some of the writings about Indigenous leadership. Other researchers (Anderson 1988; Bern 1979; Edwards 1987; Hiatt 1986, 1996; Keen 2006; Smith 1976) have previously reviewed the literature on Indigenous politics and leadership.

[7] Table 9.1 reflects various perspectives on Indigenous leadership but it is not intended to be definitive. Some analysts employ a range of leadership descriptions, such as 'old men', 'mature men', 'men of power, authority and influence' (see e.g. Stanner 1979), and so on. For my purposes here, however, a particular analyst might be mentioned in only one category.

Table 9.1 Paradigms of Indigenous leadership

TYPE	PROPONENT & PERIOD	BRIEF DESCRIPTION
Chief or chiefs	Tench (1961) [1793], Batman [1835] in Billot (1979), Grey (1841), Taplin (1874), Dawson (1881), Thomas, W. [1898] in Bride (1969)	Chiefs but no 'civil regulations'; chief selected by family heads; authority over a certain territory; government is patriarchal.
Head of group	Collins (1804), Thomas (1906), Wheeler (1910), Elkin (1938), Biskup (1973), Von Sturmer (1978)	Family heads; assembly of elders; 'past masters'; local group headmen; ceremonial headmen/ political power.
No Chiefs	Wilkes (1845), Eyre (1845), Flanagan (1888) [1853], Radcliffe-Brown (1913)	'Laws'; no authority/ no chiefs; no tribal chief, nor any form of tribal government.
Old men	Smyth (1878), Spencer and Gillen (1938) [1899], Strehlow (1947), Stanner (1979) [1953], Sackett (1978), Rowse (1998)	Men who 'took the lead'; headmen of council; leaders; ceremonial chiefs; mature men.
Eminent, prominent, influential, and great men	Howitt (1967) [1880], Curr (1886), Elkin (1938), Maddock (1972), Kolig (1981), Keen (1994)	'Men of note'; prominent men; bosses or 'bunggawa'/ 'looking after' others; networks; local and personal authority.
Men of authority	Bern (1979), Keen (1982)	Prestige and authority through religion.
No headmen	Sharp (1958), Meggitt (1962)	No leaders, headmen, or chiefs; kinship-related social rules.
Senior men	Hiatt (1965)	Clan-based senior men
Big men	Berndt and Berndt (1965), Von Sturmer (1978), Sutton (1978), Chase (1984)	'Bosses'; kinship system of leadership/ hierarchical ordering.
Elders	Gould (1969), Collman (1988)	Elders but no official leader; tribal elders interacting with bureaucracy.
Leaders	Rigsby (1997) [1982], Sutton and Rigsby (1982), Tonkinson (1991) [1978], Williams (1987), Smith (1997)	Ritual leaders; 'politicks', political structures and leadership; context-based; hierarchical clan-based leadership/ networks.
Managers	Burridge (1973)	Middle-aged men who 'managed'.
Authority & Higher order	Myers (1976)	Authority through progressive growth/ 'looking after' others.
Masterful men	Sansom (1980)	Men with business acumen.
Dominant & adventurous men	Gerritsen (1981)	Control of public sector/ appropriation & sharing of benefits amongst followers.
'Experts'	Trigger (1992)	Context-based on two domains; joint status; middle-men.

NB: When the date of observation/description differs from that of publication it is noted in square brackets.

This summary suggests that major shifts in perspectives on Indigenous leadership have occurred at key periods of Australian history. Nineteenth century reports on Indigenous leadership favoured a social evolutionist approach, whilst during the early twentieth century, research began to be informed by the functionalist and structuralist approaches of British anthropology. More recent field-based research has drawn more widely from political science, political economy, and French structuralism, in order to yield more detailed knowledge of the complexity of Indigenous leadership in its local variations.

This more recent literature (see Table 9.1) can be summarised as proposing that Indigenous leadership in Australia has the following characteristics:

- it is founded on group-based structures, tending in some cases to be hierarchical (kinship, marriage and social bonds define and bind such groups, often to the point of being characterised as an inflexible blue-print for action);

- it is constructed and practised among groups with regional variations;
- it is highly contextualised and gender-specific;
- men (and women) commence their leadership 'training' from an early age and such socialisation continues through life;
- age and knowledge play an important part in defining one's position in the leadership hierarchy;
- some men and groups become more influential than others through their own personal attributes, or by the accumulation of power through ceremonial means, women, followers, and access to other desired resources; and
- such influential men can broaden their leadership base and prowess by further developing social ties through reciprocal obligations, which can develop into complex networks of authority and power, and may be influenced by contemporary arrangements and resources. The literature occasionally refers to such individuals as 'big men' and notes that such 'bigmanship'[8] may only be temporary.

Unlike the issues of Indigenous land ownership, territoriality, kinship models and religious life, there does not seem to have been a progression from these useful insights, towards a more cohesive theoretical analysis that illuminates the historical and contemporary conditions, workings and transformations of Indigenous leadership in the inter-cultural context.

Much of the research evidence so far has been developed by anthropologists and others observing specific groups in various areas of Australia. A key related challenge is whether such evidence can be generally applied across the whole of Australia, and whether regionalism and other cultural factors make for influential similarities and differences in the conditions and enactment of leadership.

Leadership in the Port Keats region

Research I conducted in the remote Aboriginal-owned area referred to as Port Keats[9] or Wadeye has enabled me to identify key conditions and features of Indigenous leadership over several generations. These inform a model that conceptualises how leadership operates to establish governing order and how it is reproduced and transformed, and which illuminates how that leadership has responded to external changes and contact over generations.

The reality of life and research in Indigenous Australia is that there is a gendered framework for how secret knowledge is maintained and passed on. There are distinct male and female rites of passage through which leaders pass, and gendered contexts where leadership may be performed. As a man, this has meant

---

[8] The term 'bigmanship' is used by Hiatt (1986: 14).
[9] Port Keats is the region and Wadeye is the town. Aboriginal people often refer to their 'home' as Port Keats.

that my research has inevitably focused on male leadership. An important caveat, then, in my attempt to develop a more cohesive, analytically useful model of Indigenous leadership, is that my research has been primarily about and with male leaders. It could legitimately be said that what I am describing is only half of a symbiotic system of overall leadership in community life. I would argue, however, that this does not detract from the salience and validity of the model and analysis presented here, as my research has also been informed over many years by numerous discussions and interactions with female leaders and senior women in families amongst all the clan groups in the community and surrounding region. I have travelled extensively with senior women, undertaken 'return to country' and site mapping with them, and worked with a number of women in their official capacities as representatives in community organisations.[10] To that extent then, my analysis has also been considerably influenced and moulded by women's views and information, as well as by those of male leaders in Wadeye.

My perhaps audacious hypothesis is that despite clear gender differences in the context and style of male and female leadership, research with women by a woman would generally confirm that the same broad structural, institutional, sociological and political conditions for the production and reproduction of leadership apply to both men and women's leadership. Accordingly, where relevant and to the extent of my knowledge, I have presented comparative information on female leadership at Wadeye; but the clear and primary focus of my analysis here is on male leadership.

The structural and systemic bases for contemporary Indigenous leadership

The Port Keats region is situated 320km southwest of Darwin in the NT. It is relatively isolated and is inaccessible by road during the wet season. The population of predominantly Aboriginal people was estimated to be 800 in the early 1970s, rising to its current total of approximately 2300 Indigenous languages and dialects in the region include Murrinh-patha, Marri Ngarr, Magati-ge, Marritjevin, Marri Amu, Emmi, Menhthe, Ngan.gi-tjemerri, Ngan.gi-wumeri, and Ngan.gi-kurunggurr.[11] Murrinh-patha is generally understood as the 'universal' language amongst the Aboriginal community residents. Some residents, particularly the elderly, also speak languages to the southwest including Djamindjung, Ngaliwuru and Miriwung.

---

[10] Female leadership is prominent in the Port Keats region but was not the primary focus of this particular research. Nevertheless, Indigenous female leaders provided valuable information, advice and assistance.

[11] This list of languages and dialects (and the spelling) corresponds to that of Dixon (2002).

Fig. 9.1 Port Keats/Wadeye regional map showing localities and pastoral stations (shaded areas) mentioned in the text

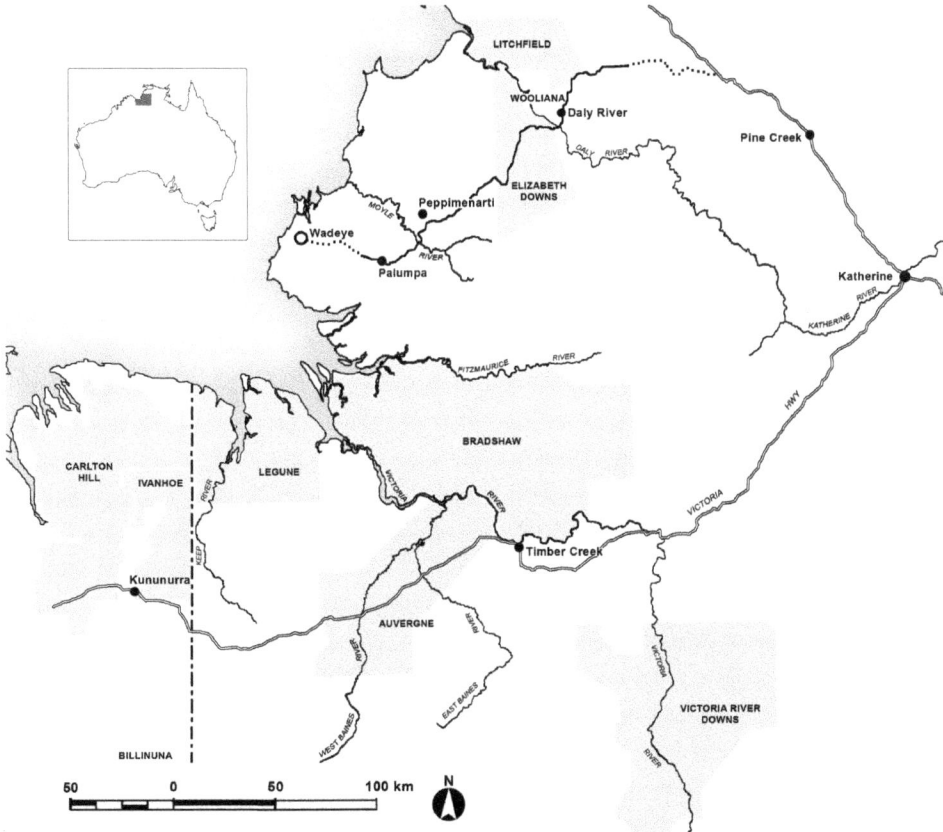

People from the region have a long history of contact with other Aboriginal groups particularly north toward the Daly River and south toward Timber Creek. These contacts have ebbed and flowed depending on events, but they were probably at their height when labour from Port Keats was accessed for pastoral work.

A tripartite ceremonial structure, made up of the *Dhanba/Wurlthirrii/Malkarrin*, *Wangga*, and the *Lirrga* ceremonial groups (and representing the various language groups), exists in the Port Keats region today.[12] This structure is foundational in determining relationships and interaction between individuals and groups.

---

[12] The spelling of these ceremonial and song genres varies. The spelling used in this case is that used by Marett (2005), an ethnomusicologist who has done considerable work in the region.

There are numerous patrilineal clan groups with specifically-owned estates in the region.[13] Each clan has a hierarchical structure of authority for the conduct of certain affairs that is recognised by its membership. The primary decision-makers for each clan are the men referred to as *kardu pule* or 'bosses'. By various means, some individuals also gain higher levels of authority across clan boundaries. Whilst such authority exists, it is also important to acknowledge the underlying egalitarian nature of the society and individualistic rights, for these form the foundation within which leaders function.

Fig. 9.2 Murrinh-patha age categories

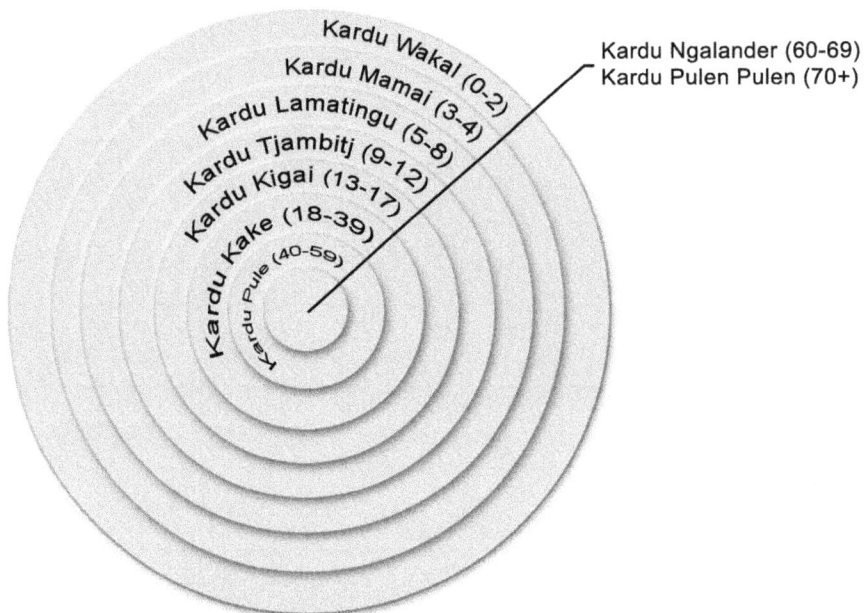

Kardu Wakal (0-2)
Kardu Mamai (3-4)
Kardu Lamatingu (5-8)
Kardu Tjambitj (9-12)
Kardu Kigai (13-17)
Kardu Kake (18-39)
Kardu Pule (40-59)
Kardu Ngalander (60-69)
Kardu Pulen Pulen (70+)

Murrinh-patha Age Categories

As they age, young boys progress from the outer circle toward the centre. Older men in the centre have superior knowledge and experience.

From a fairly early age, young men at Port Keats begin to proceed through certain rites of passage (see Ivory 2005b: 4–5). Such passage is marked by categorisation

---

[13] The use of the term 'clan', and its appropriateness, is debated in the anthropological discourse. Nevertheless, the Port Keats people regularly use the term to describe the basic land-owning group in their region and I have followed suit.

into particular age groups (see Fig. 9.2). Indoctrination and learning is conducted in formal and informal circumstances. Male and female leaders from the clan teach the young about their clan estate, its associated mythology, and how to survive using that knowledge. Formal learning is usually associated with three ceremonies where initiates learn about sacred aspects of Aboriginal religion, norms of the society, and build a special relationship with their peers and the senior leaders.

Today, social development is continuing in the Indigenous domain at Port Keats. The question then, is whether Indigenous leaders are able to participate in the non-Indigenous domain as well, and if so, how? And how has the leadership situation evolved over time to enable forms of inter-cultural leadership engagement?

Leadership in the intercultural domain

Leaders in Port Keats have, over the years, developed different structures for collective leadership in the intercultural domain.

A local council, Kardu Numida Inc, was established at the township of Wadeye in 1979 (Thamarrurr Regional Council 1995: 4). The council was to act as a stable form of local government authority and supply local government-type services. It was established under the *Associations Incorporations Act 1963* (NT), legislation that was originally intended for 'football clubs and bingo groups' (D. Read, Assistant Director of Northern Territory Department of Community Development, pers. comm., 1978). However, although the NT and Australian Governments recognised this entity, it was 'often not seen to be the valid decision making structure in the eyes of local Aboriginal people' (Desmarchelier 2000: 2).

The electoral process of the Kardu Numida Council required annual elections, with 15 people to be nominated from family groups belonging to each of the three larger ceremonial groups referred to above. Over time it became apparent that leaders from outside of the Kardu Diminin clan (*Dhanba* group) were feeling increasingly uncomfortable about making decisions related primarily to land on which the community was located, but which was traditionally owned by another clan. As a consequence, by 1994 the leaders outside of the Kardu Diminin had virtually withdrawn their participation from the Kardu Numida structure. Financial problems associated with inappropriate funding levels for a community that had doubled in population signalled the end for the council in this form.

The development of *Thamarrurr*

Commencing in 1996, at the end of the Kardu Numida era, a deliberate move was made by the Kardu Diminin clan leaders, in conjunction with other clan leaders, to correct what was seen as a past governance imbalance. The governance structure they now developed was a culturally-based concept of conflict resolution and power balance, referred to in the Murrinh-patha language as *Thamarrurr*. This model effectively recognises the relationships between individuals, groups and clans.

Formal recognition of the clan as a primary node of authority and the notion of the *Thamarrurr* model, in some of its dimensions, was transposed into a NT local government scheme under the *Local Government Act* for the region in 2003. The people of the Port Keats region perceived this as a major repositioning of the traditional authority structure with contemporary Australian governance. The leaders envisaged that with this model they would be able to engage more effectively with wider Australia and move forward. It was seen as the foundation for dealing with social, political and economic issues that had emerged for them as the dominant wider Australian culture further influenced and changed the Indigenous cultures of the region.

The concept of *Thamarrurr*

Prior to colonisation, the people of the Port Keats region lived on country that was rich in food and resources, and also rich in religious meaning. The land supported a relatively high density of population of approximately 3,000 people, compared to other parts of Australia (Ivory 2007). During visits commencing in 1934, the anthropologist William Stanner observed that the society was structured into segments, with the primary division being the clan. Each clan had a fairly strictly defined territory delineated by physical markers and sites associated with mythological beings that were known by both men and women (Stanner 1964: 32).

Clan estates were relatively small and close together. Each estate was zealously watched over by members of the clan and there was regular warfare related to disputes that differentiated and defined relationships and ownership of territories and resources. Social life, according to Stanner (1964: 31) was a volitional and purposive system deferring to tradition. Relationships between individuals and groups were governed by a system referred to as *Thamarrurr*. In the Murrinh-patha language, Thamarrurr Region Councillors articulated this concept as follows:

> It is our way of working together, cooperating with each other, and it is also the basis of our governance system.

> In the early days we looked after our families, our clans and our people through *Thamarrurr*. We arranged ceremonies, marriages, sorted out tribal disputes and many other things (in Taylor 2004).

According to Stanner (1964: 37), certain aspects of the local culture were 'working toward' a 'unified system or unified whole' in the 1950s, which eventuated in the 1960s. An example of this transition is the ceremonial structure, which over time became more and more isolated from countrymen in places such as Kununurra, Timber Creek, and the various cattle stations where they had worked. This had occurred primarily because of the breakdown of job opportunities outside Port Keats and a subsequent lessening of social interactions with these other Aboriginal groups.[14]

Today, the clan unit is still the key structure of importance. Clan members and outsiders are very knowledgeable about their clan estates and fulfil their responsibilities to such country to varying but significant degrees. On occasions in the past, a group might have been pushed off country by the might of the spear or a more amicable arrangement reached, but this is unlikely today as land rights enshrined in Australian law have brought a new definition and permanence to land ownership.[15]

The rights of the individual within a socially situated group context are still paramount today, as is the right to take matters to another level if one is considered to be aggrieved. Where there were once 'hordes', 'gangs' and 'fire-places' of anthropologically classified groups (Falkenberg and Falkenberg 1981: 69–75), now there are council houses in suburban enclaves, but still within demarcated cultural spaces. Alliances are constantly worked on and nurtured, particularly through marriage and kinship, and cultural trade referred to as *nandji kulu* continues and respective affiliations are cultivated.

Despite the influence of outside contact, many of the structures and aspects of culture today remain similar to when the missionaries first arrived in 1935. Ceremonies and rituals are maintained within the constraints of contemporary conditions and people hold strong family and clan affiliations and relationships. The reconfiguration of song genres in the 1950s onwards, as described by Furlan (2005), demonstrates a desire to reproduce Indigenous values within a paradigm of modernity. Individuals are socialised within a cultural context but amidst the environment of a burgeoning town. Leaders are identified and trained, and then eased on to a 'stage' that increasingly operates in the intercultural with various political, social and economic responsibilities.

The concept of *Thamarrurr* means all of the above and more. Local clan leader Tobias Nganbe[16] (pers. comm., 2005) describes it as 'a way of life' and a means of cooperation and governance. Further he advises that it is foundational to the mental construct and world-view of local people.

---

[14] Relationships are still maintained with such northern and southern groups but not to the same degree. People in the past would walk back and forth from Port Keats to Bradshaw Station, for example, but this has not happened for many years. Nevertheless, there are still air and road visitations when funds are available.

[15] The *Aboriginal Land Rights (Northern Territory) Act 1976 (Cth)* enabled some Aboriginal people in the NT to gain inalienable freehold title to their traditional land.

[16] Tobias Ngambe is co-principal of Our Lady of the Sacred Heart Catholic School, Wadeye, NT.

Adaptations of leadership: challenges from without

There has been a series of landmark events that have challenged the leadership model of Port Keats. My research (Ivory 2005b, 2006, 2007) indicates that these events include the:

- early intrusions by explorers, miners and others;
- advent of pastoralism and occupation to the south of Port Keats from 1870;
- introduction of associated diseases that decimated the Aboriginal population;
- arrival of missionaries in 1935;
- World Wars One and Two;
- opportunity to participate and work in mainstream economic society;
- advent of welfare payments, including unemployment payments or 'sit-down money', when suitable work ceased;
- establishment of a community council in 1979;
- establishment of the Aboriginal and Torres Strait Islander Commission (ATSIC) and a regional ATSIC council for the wider area in 1990;[17]
- establishment of a NT local government council in the Port Keats region in 2003 and then further local government reform from 2006; and
- pressure to participate in an Australia-wide Council of Australian Governments' (COAG) trial from 2003.[18]

Finally, the challenge that emerged in 2007, that continues today, is one of 'intervention' by the Australian Government, where many Indigenous leaders are being told that they are ineffective, irresponsible, and unable to deal with issues such as child abuse.

History reveals that Indigenous people in the Port Keats region have had to deal with significant social change in the past. My historical and ethnographic field research indicates that each time a challenge is thrown up for Indigenous leaders of the region they respond—repeatedly seeking positive engagement and making adaptations in the process. Below I present three examples from the above list to highlight the nature and impacts of this 'responsive engagement' by leaders.

---

[17] ATSIC was a key element of the Commonwealth Indigenous affairs administration and representation for 14 years. Representation was divided into regions and the Port Keats area was part of a wider representative region that included many other communities. There was effectively one representative from Port Keats. The Coalition Government abolished ATSIC in 2004.

[18] COAG is the peak intergovernmental forum in Australia, comprising the Prime Minister, State Premiers, Territory Chief Ministers and the President of the Australian Local Government Association (ALGA). In 2002, COAG, in a reaffirmation of its commitment to advance reconciliation and address social and economic disadvantage of Indigenous Australians, agreed to a trial of a whole-of-government cooperative approach in up to 10 communities and regions. The NT Government put forward Wadeye as its trial site.

Example 1: Pastoralism and occupation

Early European occupation on country south of Port Keats occurred from the 1870s. Settlers established Victoria River Downs, Bradshaw, Legune, Auvergne and other pastoral properties (see Fig. 9.1). There was an immediate response from Aborigines in the region, including Port Keats, to initiate relationships with the newcomers. Aboriginal men and women, with their families, moved to these cattle and sheep stations, often taking work for rations as stockmen, station hands, domestics and the like. Others camped on the outskirts of the properties, later moving closer to the respective station as relationships flourished.

Aboriginal people were keen to proffer their services in exchange for European goods such as tobacco, tea, sugar and flour. Whilst 'the network of relations' between Aboriginal groups in the wider region was disturbed (Stanner 1964: 109), it was also rapidly adjusted as leaders negotiated their positions. The decision to engage and adapt was made by the clan leaders. In doing so, they retained their own status as leaders whilst exposing their clan group to the influences of non-Aboriginal society, both positive and negative. The leaders and their followers also commenced engagement in a new phase of non-Indigenous economic life. Through Indigenous religious experience and ceremonial exchange, new political relationships between leaders from Port Keats and those further south were re-defined and reinforced.

Example 2: The arrival of the mission

The Commonwealth Government encouraged church endeavour during the early 1900s in the Top End, mainly due to their own inability at the time to deliver services. On hearing of the arrival of Father Docherty and fellow missionaries in 1935, the clan leaders, almost unanimously it seems, welcomed their arrival. The missionaries brought goods, a new economic and political system, as well as an alternate religion.

Aboriginal leaders led them to water supplies and suitable land for settlement and later agreed for the main community to be built at Wadeye on suitable high ground. They brought their children into the Church and entrusted them to the missionaries for education within the dormitory system. They supported and worked with the missionaries in market gardens, forestry, pastoral and other ventures.

The impact of this phase of engagement on the leaders and patterns of leadership was substantial. Some leaders were regarded as being 'in' with the missionaries and gained access to new resources and opportunities. The power base of those leaders who worked with the missionaries was enhanced, while others who were not so in favour moved further afield to cater for the needs of their group. Nevertheless, the dynamic nature of the leadership construct continued. Even though some leaders were engaging with the missionaries and others were not, the clan-based leadership construct remained strong, as did reliance on both the existing and newly established Indigenous networks of relationships.[19]

Example 3: Local government reform and Commonwealth intervention

In more recent times, and despite such efforts by the leadership to engage, both the NT and Commonwealth Governments began to move toward revised policies of intervention in 2006 and 2007.

From mid 2006, the Commonwealth Government began to intervene in community affairs at Wadeye. They were keen, through the Indigenous Affairs Minister, The Hon. Mal Brough, to effect practical changes in terms of law and order, housing, and individual behaviour. Following a NT Government report on child abuse, publicly released in June 2007 (Anderson and Wild 2007), the Commonwealth announced fundamental changes to its mode of policy intervention. This announcement primarily targeted law and order, education, and health.

Contemporaneously, in October 2006, frustrated at the level of perceived 'dysfunction' (Ah Kit 2002: 2) in Indigenous communities, the NT Government announced through their Minister for Local Government, The Hon. Elliot McAdam, a new policy of mandatory regionalised, amalgamated local government (see McAdam 2006). This, he argued, would provide better basic services and be economically sustainable.

The NT Government's initiative of local government reform meant that the Thamarrurr Regional Council, constructed by the Port Keats leadership only four years earlier, would no longer be the formal local government authority in the region. The Thamarrurr region will form a ward of a larger shire council on 1 July 2008 and have four representatives on the new council.[20] The leaders, having to readjust their quest for positive engagement once again, have reportedly now focused their attention on restructuring the Thamarrurr model to be the economic development body for the region, whilst also tacitly accepting the new local government regime.

Despite an ever-changing environment, these three examples suggest there has always been a substantial degree of willingness on the part of leaders and groups at Port Keats to actively engage with external agencies and survive. Indigenous accommodation and reconstitution has repeatedly occurred in response to massive interventions that, in some instances, included challenges on physical and

---

[19] Often those leaders who did not actively engage had an ongoing dispute with another family member (who had formed a relationship with the missionaries) and this impeded their own engagement.
[20] The draft business plan for the Victoria Daly Shire Council (December 2007) proposes that there be four representatives for Port Keats on a council of 12. See: <http://www.localgovernment.nt.gov.au/__data/assets/pdf_file/0009/32013/Victoria_Daly_Shire_Business_Plan_-_Main_Report_1st_Draft.pdf> [accessed 1 May 2008].

psychological fronts. It was only the resilience of the people and leadership adaptations that enabled them to re-engage with a succession of outsiders and continue their lives (see Ivory 2005a: 1–15). The evidence strongly challenges the supposition that Indigenous leadership was, and is, ill defined and unresponsive. However, challenges to Indigenous leadership at Port Keats have not all come from outside their local political domain, they have also come from within their own society.

Adaptations of leadership: challenges from within

During the late 1980s, groups of young men and women from Port Keats began to create their own social constructs and 'way of being' in the form of groups (sometimes referred to by the media and others as gangs). They increasingly manoeuvred themselves into a powerful bloc on the socio-political scene at Wadeye. The groups refer to themselves with often brazen names such as Evil Warriors, Judas Priest, Fear Factory, Big T and so on (see Ivory 2003). Many of the names are derived from western heavy metal band culture (ibid.: 65–6).

In general, the 'youth' in these groups have poor education, are unemployed, and aged between about 8–30 years. They might be described as the angry young men of Port Keats and have emerged post-mission.[21] Fifty years ago, Stanner (1964: 109) had written about the 'noticeable' change in young adult males as 'traditional circumcisions' ceased. The older men spoke about the 'indiscipline of the new generation' and their 'disrespect toward authority' (ibid.).

It is evident that the contemporary youth groups of Port Keats have characteristics of their own when compared to mainstream constructs of gangs throughout the world. In addition to 'normal' youth gang attributes, they have strong affiliations to Indigenous kin, country, and family, and a strong desire to be recognised positively from within their own Indigenous society. They have constructed their own subculture and developed a collective response—albeit a deviant one on some occasions—in order to resolve contradictions that are present in relation to their own culture (Ivory 2003). Whilst the middle-aged, in conjunction with the elders, have constructed and defined a positive role for their cohort, this third group has constructed its own networks and nodes of leadership based on a seemingly more negative worldview. Interestingly, however, many of these networks and constructs mirror the segmentation observed by Stanner 70 years ago and may not be quite as negative as they at first appear.

During the period of my research, particularly from 2002 until early 2006, relationships deteriorated between the youth of Port Keats and the older and middle-aged groups, as well as with the non-Indigenous sector. Conflict between

---

[21] The groups consist of both males and females; however, young men are predominantly associated with conflicts.

the youth groups was a common scene in Wadeye. It reached a point in March 2006, following a major outbreak of violence amongst the groups, when the leaders took affirmative and conciliatory action. The older and middle-aged clan leaders, aware of the affiliations, strength and positive connectedness of their societies' networked systems, but also aware of the divisiveness that could be generated, met as a group. Their previous strategy had been to attempt to ignore and not acknowledge the youth leadership and their dysfunctional behaviour. This time they decided to talk, recognise, and re-engage.

In conjunction with the youth groups, they developed plans enabling the youth to move back onto their respective land, be supported by the Council and the leaders, participate in positive work activities, and be recognised as a legitimate bloc. A key objective of the plan was to use kin relationships to reincorporate and re-centre the Indigenous youth back into family networks and life. This took the pressure off the community at the time, and although many of the younger groups later moved back to Wadeye, they now see living out on country as an option, particularly at times of stress. This solution, over simplified here, and precarious at times with a regular need for reconciliation, has enabled the wider community to move on. It is a further example of Indigenous leadership assessing the situation and readjusting their stance in order to retain the overall cultural fundamentals as well as their authority.

The life history of individual leadership development

An understanding of individual experiences of leadership development in the region is required to provide a greater level of understanding of how leadership operates. Individual case studies of three pre-eminent leaders, each from a different age group, are presented below.[22] The first is about a man in his seventies, the second of a man in his forties, and the final case study is of a youth group leader in his late twenties.

Case study A

Mr J was born in the Wadeye Church Hospital in 1942. The Japanese had bombed the town of Darwin only a few months earlier. He was initiated in the bush when he was about '8 or 9'. Mr J recalls spending much of his early life on his father's clan estate. It was a time of much tribal conflict. War parties intent on capturing women would come down from Daly River and Pine Creek. He said they were '*Ngan.gi-tjemerri, Brinkin, Wagaman, Mulluk-Mulluk* tribes and others'. He says:

> Sometimes the bastards would surprise us and we would have to run and hide until they left. But then my father and his brothers would join

---

[22] These case studies are based on interviews conducted with the individuals concerned. The names of the men have been abbreviated.

up with men from other clans and go and steal their women. It was wild days then!

Mr J informed me that a place of refuge when any intruders came on to country was a small sand island near the mouth of the Fitzmaurice River. Adults and children would walk across to the island at low tide, and because the going was treacherous they were not followed.

At the time of Mr J's youth, Stanner was excavating an archaeological site on Mr J's country. Stanner had befriended Mr J's father and they all camped at the site together. At this time, Mr J's father was still making spear and axe-heads out of stone. The women would collect seeds and berries and grind them in the rock hollows at the shelter.

Soon after, Mr J was sent to the dormitory at Port Keats to be educated by the missionaries. He was allocated an identification number, as were all the others in the dormitories. He recalls how he detested this life, because the missionaries were often very strict with their punishments. At the age of about 13 he ran away in the company of his uncle. They walked from Port Keats to Daly River (a distance of about 180km) and worked for a while at Elizabeth Downs Station and Wooliana Station (see Fig. 9.1). He has vivid memories of the station manager at Elizabeth Downs 'going off his head' and firing a rifle at all and sundry because someone had borrowed the truck without asking.

During this time, he recalls another uncle deciding to walk a long distance because he had run out of tobacco. The uncle then got very sick. Mr J made a bed of branches in a tree for his uncle to have some respite from the mosquitoes but during the night the old man fell out. Mr J. spent some hours trying to lift him back in and commented, 'by gee he was heavy'. Some time later, Mr J went back to Port Keats to pick up his promised wife. But she had been given to someone else. He 'got wild' and left for a life in the pastoral industry.

During the next 15 years Mr J worked at Litchfield Station, Carlton Station, Billinuna Station, Ivanhoe Station, Legune Station (see Fig. 9.1), Mirrawong, and other cattle properties in the NT and Western Australia (WA). He is known as having been an excellent stockman and rodeo rider (as were others from Port Keats), riding in various events in WA and the NT. During this period of his life, Mr J also attended 'five different types of ceremonies in Kununurra, Halls Creek and Billinuna' that were performed by Aboriginal people from WA. In the 1970s, Mr J came back to the Port Keats area and joined a stock camp at Palumpa Station. Mr J was later elected to the Northern Land Council and served for many years, at one stage visiting the United States for business.

In recent years, Mr J has lived on his country, which is about 20km from Wadeye. He speaks Murrinh-patha as his primary language, is the most senior leader of his clan group, and is also well-regarded as a ceremony leader. In 2003, when the first elections for the Thamarrurr Regional Council were held, each clan group, by constitution, had the right to elect two councillors each. I visited each of the 20 clans on their own country with local Aboriginal people and Council officials to explain why the council was being established, the process, and the need for each group to conduct an election. Mr J, as the leader of his clan, spoke with passion. He spoke about his life—'a bloody hard life I tell you'—and the need 'for the young fellas to stand up and work for their people'. He said that his life was almost at an end but he was happy with the new Thamarrurr Council entity because 'blackfellas could now have the same rights as whitefellas'.

After about an hour of oration, during which Mr J talked about the need for young people to 'stand up', he declared that he had decided not to sit on the council himself. On behalf of the clan, he said, two women would be the representatives. But he would be 'looking over their shoulder to make sure they do the right thing. They got to report back by geez!' The women have subsequently been regular attendees at council meetings. Mr J rarely attends, but when he does he always has something to say, which is accepted by those present with respect. On occasions, Mr J also attends some informal community meetings at places such as Peppiminarti, 'caucusing' on issues and he still has a very strong presence in the region. He is one of a number of elderly men who have heightened status across most clans and age groups.

Mr J has resided on his clan estate for many years now, driving into the Wadeye township each day to conduct social and business affairs. Despite ill health, he has no regrets, a contented attitude to life, is very proud of his career in the cattle industry, and interestingly, does not speak with any real bitterness about missionaries, stockmen or anyone else for that matter. His leadership style might be described as broad ranging, with leadership and social networks established far beyond Port Keats and extending into WA. Mr J maintains and nurtures such relationships with other leaders, often visiting for ceremonies, funerals and other activities.

Case study B

Mr N was born at the Wadeye mission hospital in 1957. His father's clan estate was the original landing site of the early missionaries in 1934. Mr N lived in the mission dormitory for 'about 6 or 7 years'. Like Mr J, he still recalls his dormitory identification number. On the weekends he was allowed home to stay with his family. Mr N remembers these days as being 'good fun—especially being with my friends in that age group'. This age group was made up of young men from all of the various tribes 'mixed up'.

Mr N describes a 'turning point' in his life. This was in 1970 when he visited Brisbane and other places. He says:

We saw how other people live. It was the first time we had seen a big city. We were very well looked after and respected by strangers. I started to realise that there are people out there that don't care where you come from.

He attended a private high school in Victoria during the period 1971–73 and went on to complete Year 12. He remembers it as 'good times', particularly when mixing with boys from Nauru and Central Australia. He says, 'I got to know a lot of people', but also that he saw racism—not so much directed at him but to other Indigenous students. These students were referred to with such names as 'the blackies'. After observing this, Mr N said that it actually made him more resolute—'So now I can take anything'.

Mr N underwent *djenbitj* (initiation) in Darwin Hospital. In 1978, he commenced his ceremonial introduction into the senior ceremonies. The initial ceremony took place at a site where a major gas pipeline is currently being built. Other men being initiated were from his dormitory group and they went through at the same time. He says, 'The old men really gave us a lesson. They made us sit down and talk things over'.

Mr N says that his father said to him as a young boy 'One day you will take my place as a leader'. But his father also said that 'I want you to go down south to study. It is better that way'. Mr N says, 'But I missed a lot of stuff [culture]'. In 1983 his father died. Mr N says that his father 'In Council meetings ... was strong but he would also let other people have their say'.

Mr N returned to Wadeye following his education in Victoria and began to pursue a career as a teacher at the Catholic school at Wadeye. Whilst rising through the ranks of the NT education system, he has also become a prominent and influential member of the local council.

Reflecting on where he is today as a senior educational official in the Wadeye community and an influential spokesperson on intercultural affairs, Mr N says: 'If we hadn't been made to speak English at school—I would never have gone on to matriculation'. He argues: 'This is important—you have to be able to speak English whether you like it or not'. Mr N maintains cordial relations with most clan leaders in the Port Keats region and is highly regarded. He often acts as a negotiator and peacekeeper. He is of the *Kardu Keke* age bracket (see Fig. 9.2) and has been delegated various responsibilities by senior clan leaders. Such status enables him to effectively operate and negotiate with non-Indigenous interests as well.

Case study C

Mr K is in his late twenties. He is a large man with an imposing presence. For many years he has been regarded as the leader of one of the youth groups or 'gangs'. He prefers to refer to the group as 'family'. Mr K attended boarding school in Darwin to Year 10. He has been charged by the police on many occasions, usually for assault, and has spent much of the last 10 years of his life in prison.

Mr K has a large following of male and female supporters, most of whom are younger than him. He is called on, and usually responds, to lead battles against other groups or to intervene in matters of contention. He is rarely involved in routine events in the community and for many years was not even seen enough to be recognisable by non-Indigenous residents (although most have heard his name).

Mr K has a reasonable knowledge of matters related to his estate but does not participate very often in ritual affairs. He regards this as the fault of elders in the community. The elders have often been reluctant, he says, to pass on information of sacred importance to some individuals in case it is used wrongfully. Mr K's relationship with the other two levels of leadership in Wadeye—the elderly and middle-aged—is terse, although is improving noticeably as he grows older. In more recent times, Mr K's relationship with the police has also improved and this has generally translated into a better state of community affairs.

Mr K is regarded as a strong leader by his young followers and many fellow clan members, and they revere his strength of character. However, unlike Mr J and Mr N, he is yet to gain credibility in the wider community arena of leadership. This could change if his style becomes more peaceful and embracing of others. The other leaders previously mentioned, Mr J and Mr N, have developed networks of leadership, particularly through their work experience, whilst Mr K's opportunities to construct a leadership base have been mainly restricted to prison or illegal activities.

These three case studies reflect the temporal related life-experience of leaders from the region.[23] They indicate not only that leadership development begins at an early age and builds over time, but that it also occurs in a particular historical period, which provides a range of associated opportunities that one might experience. Individuals who have worked or studied in environments outside of the immediate region may develop more constructive community roles later in life. The case studies highlight the continuing importance of ceremonial knowledge plus education (not necessarily in the same person), and also the importance of networks in the region. The studies also strongly point to negative styles of engagement, as some individuals progress through life-stages within prison walls.

---

[23] Numerous other case studies have been conducted. They are very detailed and reflect a 'journey' of leadership development.

A model of leadership and engagement

The general literature on Indigenous Australian leadership emphasises a range of western paradigms, none of which adequately explains the situation at Port Keats. Anthropological perspectives developed in more recent times, whilst examining other regional groups, provide more insight, but in their totality have not yet reached a cohesive analysis that might be both locally relevant and generally applicable.

My research at Port Keats has attempted to develop an ethnographically informed conceptualisation of leadership. The model presented here is of a socially and politically articulated form of leadership founded on inherited and acquired responsibilities of 'looking after' and working for others, which is reproduced by being born on certain country, by having relationships through kin and marriage, and by individual development within complex personal and group networks. In other words, leaders not only have to be born to lead, they also have to build up and maintain their respect.

More specifically, leadership is distributed and reproduced amongst senior men who own particular areas of land through patrilineal affiliation and descent. Their authority is absolute for very specific matters related to such estates and the other men, women and children within the clan, but is negotiable for other matters. Such men participate in regional ceremonial activities that celebrate a higher order of life and being. They extend and nurture their leadership domain by engaging with other leaders and groups in a flexible field of authority that often depends on demonstrating personal qualities such as the ability to understand and care for others. It is through the mobilisation of such networks and resources that such leaders get things done. This is referred to as 'nodal leadership' (see Hunt and Smith 2007: vii). Rarely does a leader become 'wealthy' in a material sense in this environment, although the thickness of their nodal networks suggests they are rich in the sense of human relationships and social capital. This lack of material wealth suggests that their 'bigness' remains vulnerable to the judgment of their peers.

Furthermore, the model acknowledges that leadership is inherently founded on Indigenous social constructs and culturally based institutions and systems. The important theoretical conclusion that can be derived from the daily condition of Indigenous life described here is that leadership must be conceptualised and understood as a form of networked governance based on a nodal framework of leaders across communities and regions. This model of Indigenous leadership has the following characteristics:

1.   The networks reflect 'enduring webs' of leadership relationships that are able to both accommodate and persevere in the midst of 'shifting alliances

and cleavages' between and amongst leaders and groups (Hunt and Smith 2007: 8).

2. Nodal leaders have the capacity to draw on shared histories and mobilise alliances and resources across networks in order to get things done.

3. Such leadership does not translate to the accumulation of material goods or even permanent rights, but represents a web of authority and knowledge that is utilised for the common goals of the group.

4. The system has the occasional prominent or eminent leader, but within a socially-sanctioned network where legitimacy has to continue to be 'earned', eminence relies on recognition within the overall system, the ability to work within the network, the ability to bring to fruition the local potential of that system (i.e. 'get things done'), and the 'thickness' of each individual's networks (nurtured and supported by generosity, reciprocity and other such cultural norms).

5. Leadership can be delegated to certain individuals in order to reproduce and maintain relationships within the colonial intercultural realm.

6. Leaders regularly attempt to engage with other cultural groups, but often fail because of mutual misunderstandings and competition for scarce resources (including followers). This results in misalignment and, occasionally, the fission and fusion of groups and organisations.

The last point is important in the context that Indigenous leaders currently find themselves; for the research at Port Keats indicates a desire by the people, despite years of confusion and misalignment, to continue to strategically engage in order to survive as a social, political and economic entity.

This model of nodal, networked leadership works and is sustainable because:

*   it is reasonably 'fluid', negotiable and adaptive to local circumstances in some situations, but constant and know-able (non-negotiable) in others; and
*   it reflects the essential duality of Indigenous society's egalitarian and hierarchical nature, incorporates the desire for individual decision-making rights, but is enabling in that it embodies and supports a capacity, in some of the leaders, to move across contexts and mobilise collective action.

The 'gap' in intercultural understanding

This model suggests that there is a considerable gap in understanding between Indigenous and non-Indigenous sectors about leadership and governance, and that this gap generates political contestation over power and authority in post-colonial Australian society. Some argue that today, delineating culturally distinct governance structures and supporting distinctly Indigenous forms of leadership is no longer relevant or possible and that an intercultural approach is required (Holcombe 2004; Martin 2003; Merlan 1998). While Aboriginal groups at Port Keats have seen over their contact history that their attempts to engage in an 'intercultural' domain are extremely problematic, they have initiated several innovative attempts to transform and insert their culturally-based model of leadership into their interactions with the Australian state. However, with limited legal or policy recognition of their own governance systems and leadership networks, Indigenous leaders at Wadeye remain firmly embedded within an Indigenous 'domain'.

Sinclair (2007: 128) argues that leadership identity is created within 'a negotiated process that takes place within a politically charged organisational and social space'. Further, she argues that people face pressures in mainstream society to produce the 'right' leadership identity (ibid. 131). Feel for the Indigenous leader then, who has to operate and engage in both 'traditional' and mainstream domains. There are high expectations to deliver outcomes within the kind of group-orientated Indigenous framework as described in this chapter; and the state and its implicit policy goal to create the 'right' types of Indigenous leadership has created a negative environment over a long period. It is not surprising therefore that despite recent positive events[24] the current restlessness of youth at Port Keats underlies another perspective from some locals. That is, that whilst their leaders lead at home, beyond the reserve boundary they are, as one old Murrinh-patha man said in the 1970s, 'makardu', a nobody, with limited power and authority (see Fr J. Leary cited in McCormack 2006).

Conclusion

My research indicates that Indigenous leadership today in northwest Northern Australia can be described as a model of networked authority, which is inter-relational and nodal in nature, and which provides a system of governing order for a given group or society and for individuals. It affords morals and meaning in a demanding, challenging and changing environment. Such nodal, networked leadership comprises a coherent internal entity and has been an important survival mechanism for many Indigenous groups. At its most effective, this Indigenous leadership model enables various loci of events and intercultural articulations to occur and be incorporated, and subsequently perpetuate the system. When the external power of the state overrides and prevails, the governance and transformative benefits of Indigenous leadership are greatly diminished.

Unfortunately, this system of authority is often imperceptible to those 'outside' it, and this 'invisibility' often has adverse consequences. Given this situation, the reality is that Indigenous leadership in many areas of remote Australia is

---

[24] In 2006, the senior men began an initiative to discuss key issues with the younger members of the community who were causing problems. A jointly planned move to re-establish some living areas on clan estates and land management activities was made to the satisfaction of most concerned. This relationship, and assistance, peaks and wanes depending on dysfunctional activities of the youth and conflict between groups.

under extreme threat. Nevertheless, the research has also outlined how, when under threat or challenge, Indigenous leadership can demonstrate its considerable resilience. Leadership is generally proposed as being a fundamental component of legitimate and effective, 'good' governance. If Indigenous people, irrespective of where they live in the world, are to be justly and fairly recognised in wider society, then this recognition needs to be founded in leadership and authority structures that are relevant to Indigenous people themselves, and which provide a recognised link to dominant institutions. It is important for non-Indigenous Australia to understand and work with the dynamics of Indigenous leadership, particularly as young leaders emerge. Just as important is the need for Indigenous people to appreciate the leadership constructs of the dominant society and the distinct nature of their own leadership.

Acknowledgements

Diane Smith has provided advice and assistance with the preparation of this paper. Her on-going support throughout this process has been gratefully received. Kate Senior, my principal PhD supervisor, has also provided valuable advice and support. I also thank Will Sanders, John Taylor, Janet Hunt, Stephanie Garling and fellow researchers at CAEPR for their advice and assistance and the two anonymous reviewers for their helpful comments. Dominic McCormack, Tobias Nganbe and Leon Melpi have always provided expert and insightful advice in the field. Kevin Wanganeen, Terry Bullimore, Dale Seaniger, Rick Bliss, Mandy Leggatt, Mark Crocombe and John Marchant at Wadeye as well as Kevin, Nicole and Andrew at the North Australian Research Unit have been very supportive and helpful, and I thank them. My research is supported by Charles Darwin University, the Menzies School of Health Research and CAEPR, ANU. Most importantly, I have been advised and guided over the years by Aboriginal men and women from the Port Keats region and I am extremely grateful for their patience, knowledge and support.

References

Ah Kit, J. The Hon. 2002. Ministerial Statement, delivered as Minister assisting the Chief Minister on Indigenous Affairs, 7 March, Northern Territory Government, Darwin.

Anderson, C. 1988. 'All bosses are not created equal', *Anthropological Forum*, 4: 507–23.

Anderson, P. and Wild, R. 2007. *Ampe Akelyernemane Meke Mekarle—Little Children Are Sacred, Report of the Northern Territory Board of Inquiry into the Protection of Aboriginal Children from Sexual Abuse*, Report to the Northern Territory Government, Darwin, available at <http://www.nt.gov.au/dcm/inquirysaac/>

Australian Broadcasting Corporation (ABC) 2007. 'We don't need the army: Indigenous leaders', *ABC News Online*, 25 June, available at <http://www.abc.net.au/news/stories/2007/06/25/1961525.htm> [accessed 26 June 2007].

Billot, C. P. 1979. *John Batman: John Batman and the Founding of Melbourne*, Hyland House, Melbourne.

Biskup, P. 1973. *Not Slaves Not Citizens: The Aboriginal Problem in Western Australia, 1898–1954*, University of Queensland Press, St Lucia.

Bern, J. 1979. 'Ideology and domination: toward a reconstruction of Australian Aboriginal social formation', *Oceania*, 50 (2): 118–32.

Berndt, R. M. and Berndt, C. H. 1965. *Aboriginal Man in Australia: Essays in Honour of Emeritus Professor A. P. Elkin*, Angus & Robertson, Sydney.

Bride, T. F. 1969. *Letters from Victorian Pioneers: Being a Series of Papers on the Early Occupation of the Colony, the Aborigines, etc.*, Heinemann, Melbourne.

Burch, E. S. and Ellanna, L. J. (eds) 1994. *Key Issues in Hunter-Gatherer Research*, Berg, Oxford.

Burridge, K. 1973. *Encountering Aborigines, a Case Study: Anthropology and the Australian Aboriginal*, Pergamon Press, New York.

Chase, A. 1984. 'Belonging to country: territory, identity and environment in Cape York Peninsula, Northern Australia', in L. R. Hiatt (ed.), *Aboriginal Landowners: Contemporary Issues in the Determination of Traditional Aboriginal Land Ownership*, Oceania Monograph No. 27, University of Sydney, Sydney.

Collins, D. 1804. *An Account of the English Colony in New South Wales*, Cadell & Davies, London.

Collman, J. 1988. *Fringe-Dwellers and Welfare: The Aboriginal Response to Bureaucracy*, University of Queensland Press, St Lucia.

Curr, E. M. 1886. *The Australian Race: Its Origin, Languages, Customs, Place of Landing in Australia and the Routes By Which It Spread Itself Over that Continent*, J. Ferres, Government Printer, Melbourne.

Dawson, J. 1881. *Australian Aborigines: The Languages and Customs of Several Tribes of Aborigines in the Western District of Victoria, Australia*, G. Robertson, Melbourne.

Desmarchelier, X. 2000. Background Presentation: A Historical and Cultural Overview to the Re-emergence of Thamarrurr a Traditional Form of Governance for the People of Wadeye Region, Unpublished report prepared by the people of Wadeye on behalf of Thamarrurr Incorporated, Thamarrurr, Wadeye.

Dixon, R. M. W. 2002. *Australian Languages: Their Nature and Development,* Cambridge University Press, Cambridge.

Edwards, W. H. (ed.) 1987. *Traditional Aboriginal Society: A Reader,* Macmillan, South Melbourne.

Elkin, A. P. 1938. *The Australian Aborigines: How to Understand Them,* Angus & Robertson, Sydney.

Eyre, E. 1845. *Journals of Expeditions of Discovery into Central Australia, and Overland from Adelaide to King George's Sound, Sent by the Colonists of South Australia, With the Sanction and Support of the Government: Including an Account of the Manners and Customs of the Aborigines and the State of Their Relations with Europeans,* T. & W. Boone, London.

Falkenberg, A. and Falkenberg, J. 1981. *The Affinal Relationship System: A New Approach to Kinship and Marriage Among the Australian Aborigines at Port Keats,* Universitetsforlaget, Oslo.

Flanagan, R. J. 1888. *The Aborigines of Australia,* E. F. Flanagan and G. Robertson and Co., Sydney.

Furlan, A. 2005. Songs of Continuity and Change: The Reproduction of Aboriginal Culture through Traditional and Popular Music, PhD Thesis, University of Sydney, Sydney.

Gerritsen, R. 1981. 'Thoughts on Camelot: from Herodians and Zealots to the contemporary politics of remote Aboriginal settlement in the Northern Territory', Paper presented to *The Australasian Political Studies Association 23rd Annual Conference,* ANU, Canberra.

Grey, G. 1841. *Journals of Two Expeditions of Discovery in North-West and Western Australia, During the Years 1837, 38, and 39 ... With Observations on the Moral and Physical Condition of the Aboriginal Inhabitants, &c. &c.,* T. & W. Boone, London.

Gould, R. A. 1969. *Yiwara: Foragers of the Australian Desert,* Collins, London.

Hiatt, L. R. 1965. *Kinship and Conflict: A Study of an Aboriginal Community in Northern Arnhem Land,* Australian National University, Canberra.

——1986. *Aboriginal Political Life,* Australian Institute of Aboriginal Studies, Canberra.

Hiatt, L. R. 1996. *Arguments about Aborigines: Australia and the Evolution of Social Anthropology,* Cambridge University Press, Cambridge.

Hirst, J. 2007. 'The myth of a new paternalism', *The Australian*, 26 June, available at <http://www.theaustralian.news.com.au/story/0,20867,21966257-7583,00.html>.

Holcombe, S. 2004. 'Socio-political perspectives on localism and regionalism in the Pintupi Luritja region of central Australia: implications for service delivery and governance', *CAEPR Working Paper No. 25*, CAEPR, ANU, Canberra.

Howard, J. The Hon. and Brough, M. The Hon. 2007. 'Joint Press Conference with The Hon. Mal Brough, for Families, Community Services and Indigenous Affairs, Canberra', Interview Transcript, 21 June, available at <http://pandora.nla.gov.au/pan/10052/20070823-1732/www.pm.gov.au/media/Interview/2007/Interview24380.html> [accessed 24 April 2008].

Howitt, A. W. 1967. 'The Kurnai: their customs in peace and war', in L. Fison and A. W. Howitt, *Kamilaroi and Kurnai: Group-Marriage and Relationship, and Marriage by Elopement, Drawn Chiefly from the Usage of the Australia Aborigines; also, The Kurnai Tribe: Their Customs in Peace and War*, Anthropological Publications, Oosterhout.

Hughes, H. 2005. 'Policies entrench poverty', *The Australian*, 23 September, available at <http://www.cis.org.au/executive_highlights/EH2005/eh30205.html>.

Hunt, J. and Smith, D. E. 2007. 'Indigenous Community Governance Project: year two research findings', *CAEPR Working Paper No. 36*, CAEPR, CASS, ANU, Canberra.

Ivory, B. 2003. Nemarluk to Heavy Metal: Cultural Change and the Development of Contemporary Youth Sub-culture at Port Keats, Northern Territory, BA (Hons) Thesis, Charles Darwin University, Darwin.

——2005a. 'Indigenous governance and leadership: a case study from the Thamarrurr (Port Keats) region in the Northern Territory', *ICGP Occasional Paper No. 8*, CAEPR, ANU, Canberra.

——2005b. 'Leadership: issues and principles from the Thamarrurr (Port Keats) region of the Northern Territory', *ICGP Occasional Paper No. 12*, CAEPR, ANU, Canberra.

——2006. 'The problem of leadership: research from the Port Keats region of the Northern Territory', Paper presented in *Anthropology Seminar Series*, 7 April, Charles Darwin University, Darwin.

——2007. 'Indigenous leadership: critical events in the northwest of the Northern Territory 1870–1935', Paper presented in the *Anthropology Seminar Series*, 20 April, Charles Darwin University, Darwin.

Keen, I. 1982. 'How some Murngin men marry ten wives: the marital implications of matrilineal cross-cousin structures', *Man*, 17 (4): 620–42.

——1994. *Knowledge and Secrecy in an Aboriginal Religion*, Clarendon Press, Oxford.

——2006. 'Constraints on the development of enduring inequalities in Late Holocene Australia', *Current Anthropology*, 47 (1): 7–38.

Kolig, E. 1981. *The Silent Revolution: The Effects of Modernization on Australian Aboriginal Religion*, Institute for the Study of Human Issues, Philadelphia.

McCormack, D. 2006. 'The substance of Australia's first men', Paper presented to the National Mental Health and Homelessness Advisory Committee of St Vincent de Paul Society, 20 July, Darwin, available at <http://www.bowden-mccormack.com.au/uploads/articles-papers/substance-first-men.pdf>.

Maddock, K. 1972. *The Australian Aborigines: A Portrait of Their Society*, Allen Lane, London.

Martin, D. 2003. 'Rethinking the design of Indigenous organisations: the need for strategic engagement', *CAEPR Discussion Paper No. 248*, CAEPR, ANU, Canberra.

Marett, A. 2005. *Songs, Dreaming, and Ghosts: The Wangga of North Australia*, Wesleyan University Press, Middletown.

McAdam, E. The Hon. 2006. 'Local government reform in the Northern Territory', Statement from the Minister for Local Government, 11 October 2006, available at <http://www.localgovernment.nt.gov.au/__data/assets/pdf_file/0018/5931/McAdam_Statement_061011.pdf> [accessed 5 May 2008].

Meggitt, M. 1962. *Desert People: A Study of the Walbiri Aborigines of Central Australia*, Angus & Robertson, Sydney.

Merlan, F. 1998. *Caging the Rainbow: Places, Politics and Aborigines in a North Australian Town*, University of Hawai'i Press, Honolulu.

Myers, F. R. 1976. To Have and To Hold: A Study of Persistence and Change in Pintupi Social Life, PhD Thesis, University of Michigan, Ann Arbor.

Radcliffe-Brown, A. 1913. 'Three tribes of Western Australia', *Journal of the Royal Anthropological Institute*, 43: 143–94.

Rigsby, B. 1997. 'Structural parallelism and convergence in the Princess Charlotte Bay languages', in P. McConvell and N. Evans (eds), *Archaeology and Linguistics: Aboriginal Australia in Global Perspective*, Oxford University Press, Melbourne.

Rowse, T. 1998. *White Flour, White Power: From Rations to Citizenship in Central Australia*, Cambridge University Press, Melbourne.

Sackett, L. 1978. 'Punishment as ritual: "man-making" among Western Desert Aborigines', *Oceania*, 49: 110–27.

Sansom, B. 1980. *The Camp at Wallaby Cross: Aboriginal Fringe Dwellers in Darwin*, AIAS New Series No. 18, Australian Institute of Aboriginal Studies, Canberra.

Sharp, L. 1958. 'People without politics', in V. Ray (ed.), *Systems of Political Control and Bureaucracy in Human Societies*, University of Washington Press, Seattle.

Sinclair, A. 2007. *Leadership for the Disillusioned: Moving Beyond Myths and Heroes to Leading That Liberates*, Allen & Unwin, Crows Nest.

Smith (von Sturmer), D. E. 1976. Past-Masters Now: A Study of the Relationship between Anthropology and Australian Aboriginal Societies, BA (Hons) thesis, Department of Anthropology, University of Queensland, St Lucia.

Smith, D. E. 1984. '"That register business": the role of the Land Councils in determining traditional Aboriginal owners', in L. R. Hiatt (ed.), *Aboriginal Landowners: Contemporary Issues in the Determination of Traditional Aboriginal Land Ownership*, Oceania Monograph No. 27, University of Sydney, Sydney.

——1997. 'From humbug to good faith? The politics of negotiating the right to negotiate', in J. Finlayson and D. E. Smith (eds), *Fighting Over Country: Anthropological Perspectives*, CAEPR Research Monograph No. 12, CAEPR, ANU, Canberra.

Smyth, R. B. 1878. *The Aborigines of Victoria: With Notes Relating to the Habits of the Natives of Other Parts of Australia and Tasmania*, Government Printer, Melbourne.

Spencer, B. and Gillen, F. J. 1938. *The Native Tribes of Central Australia*, Macmillan, London.

Stanner, W. E. H. 1964. *On Aboriginal Religion*, Oceania Monograph No. 11, University of Sydney Press, Sydney.

——1979. *White Man Got No Dreaming: Essays 1938–1973*, ANU Press, Canberra.

Strehlow, T. G. H. 1947. *Aranda Traditions*, Melbourne University Press, Melbourne.

Sutton, P. 1978. Aboriginal Society: Territoriality and Language at Cape Kerweer, Cape York Peninsula, PhD Thesis, University of Queensland, St Lucia.

—— and Rigsby, B. 1982. 'People with 'politicks': management of land and personnel on Australia's Cape York Peninsula', in N. M. Williams and

E. S. Hunn (eds), *Resource Managers: North American and Australian Hunter-Gatherers*, Westview Press for the American Association for the Advancement of Science, Boulder.

Taplin, G. 1874. *The Narrinyeri: An Account of the Tribes of South Australian Aborigines Inhabiting the Country Around the Lakes Alexandrina, Albert, and Coorong, and the Lower Part of the River Murray ...* , Shawyer, Adelaide.

Taylor, J. 2004. *Social Indicators for Aboriginal Governance: Insights from the Thamarrurr Region, Northern Territory*, CAEPR Research Monograph No. 24, ANU E Press, ANU, Canberra.

Tench, W. 1961. *Sydney's First Four Years: Being a Reprint of A Narrative of the Expedition to Botany Bay and a Complete Account of the Settlement at Port Jackson*, Angus & Robertson, Sydney.

Thamarrurr Regional Council 1995. Thamarrurr Council of Elders, Thamarrurr Regional Council, Wadeye.

Thomas, N. 1906. *Kinship Organisations and Group Marriage in Australia*, Cambridge University Press, Cambridge.

Tonkinson, R. 1991. *The Mardu Aborigines: Living the Dream in Australia's Desert*, Holt, Rinehart and Winston, Fort Worth.

Trigger, D. S. 1992. *Whitefella Comin': Aboriginal Responses to Colonialism in Northern Australia*, Cambridge University Press, Cambridge.

von Sturmer, J. R. 1978. The Wik Region: Economy, Territoriality and Totemism in Western Cape York Peninsula, North Queensland, PhD Thesis, University of Queensland, St Lucia.

Wheeler, G. C. 1910. *The Tribe, and Intertribal Relations in Australia*, J. Murray, London.

Wilkes, C. 1845. *Narrative of the United States Exploring Expedition, During the Years 1838, 1839, 1840, 1841, 1842*, Lea & Blanchard, Philadelphia.

Williams, N. M. 1987. *Two Laws: Managing Disputes in a Contemporary Aboriginal Community*, Australian Institute of Aboriginal Studies, Canberra.

Part 4: Contesting cultural geographies of governance

10. Noongar Nation

Manuhuia Barcham

Introduction

In the wake of the positive determination made in the case of the Perth metropolitan area in the Single Noongar (native title) Claim in late 2006, the idea of a Noongar Nation is gaining currency around Australia. The judgment made clear that Noongar constitute a single group—a Noongar Nation. Exploring how this came about is the aim of this chapter. The chapter begins with a discussion of the historical context of the southwest of Western Australia (WA), with its long history of European contact and the subsequent effects this contact had on Noongar language and culture. After looking at how Noongar historically constituted a discrete socio-cultural grouping, the chapter explores how Noongar socio-cultural forms adapted in the face of ongoing European contact and government interference. It then looks at the way in which the native title land claims have helped provide an organisational form that has enabled Noongar to speak as a single voice—as a Noongar Nation. Looking at the experiences of the Noongar Land Council and its successor, the South West Aboriginal Land and Sea Council (SWALSC), the chapter explores how, despite problems with administrative and governance issues, Noongar have been able to use the native title process to create an organisation that is not only representative of Noongar society, but that is able to articulate Noongar society's aims and desires. Following the successful ruling on the Perth metropolitan area in 2006, the chapter ends by looking at some of the issues that the Noongar Nation will need to face in the coming years.

Historical context

The southwest of WA has been inhabited for tens of thousands of years. At the arrival of European settlers, the Indigenous inhabitants of the southwest spoke variants of a language now known as Noongar (variously spelt Nyungar or Nyoongah). While the debate continues as to whether or not these were distinct but closely related languages or dialects of one single language, the original occupants of these lands were seen by both themselves and others as being qualitatively different—both culturally and linguistically—from their immediate neighbours to the north and east (see Berndt 1979: 81–3).[1]

---

[1] One of the key traditional indicators of difference was the circumcision band to the west that separated Noongar (who practised neither circumcision nor incision) from their neighbours (who practised circumcision and/or incision).

In the immediate post-contact era the key social unit was the band, which was an aggregate of people, the size of which depended upon the particular ecology of their own local territory (Howard 1981: 2). This band structure was based on totemic forms of social organisation, which were attached to particular sites of significance within their estate. Bands were comprised of members of several of these totemic groups and their spouses and children (ibid. 2–3). The relatively benign environment of the southwest meant that Noongar social groupings were relatively large by Indigenous Australian standards, as compared to those of the neighbouring Western Desert, for example. And so, in places like the Swan River, bands that shared a number of common socio-cultural features came together to form larger, loose forms of social alliances (ibid. 4).

Permanent European settlement of the southwest occurred in 1829 with the establishment of the Swan River colony. Increasing numbers of European settlers led to radical changes for the region's Indigenous inhabitants. The creation of towns and farms impinged on Noongar traditional practices and subsistence lifestyles, as well as traditional forms of social organisation. With foraging forms of subsistence becoming increasingly difficult to sustain in the face of encroaching Western civilisation, Noongar became increasingly dependent on the introduced economy. The Indigenous inhabitants of the southwest were also hit hard by the effects of new diseases (Berndt 1979: 87).

Combined, these forces meant that by the beginning of the twentieth century many formal aspects of Noongar youth education had largely broken down. As a result of this, many traditional ceremonial practices and traditional rites began to be practiced less and less, and the Noongar language began to be replaced by English as the main mode of social communication. In this period, traditional forms of social organisation along totemic and band lines also started to be replaced by kinship systems based along European-style family lines, although place of origin and kinship ties remained an important determinant of Noongar social and cultural life (Howard 1981: 9). This social adaptation was compounded further by the removal of Noongar children to residential schools in the early to mid-twentieth century. However, despite all this, Noongar managed to maintain a coherent corporate identity, in contrast to both white Australian society and much of Aboriginal Australia.

'All one family'

In much of the twentieth century, Noongar social forms thus tended to focus on discrete social groupings known as families.[2] Christina Birdsall (1988: 137) has argued that it was this form of kinship organisation that 'enabled the Nyungar people to maintain themselves as a discrete socio-political group within the wider Australian society'. Birdsall (ibid.) went on to argue that while

---

[2] Technically these families are examples of matrifocal, bi-lateral, cognatic descent groups.

through the pressures of the assimilation policies of previous decades and the search for work ... they are now a people of the towns and cities whose first language is English ... [Noongar nonetheless] remain a distinctive socio-cultural category, maintaining a particular form of kinship organisation.

These families, and Noongar individuals, generally identify themselves in terms of their descent from a particular ancestor, these individuals generally being those born as a result of a union between a white man and a Noongar woman. Each of these groups has a surname by which they identify themselves in relation to other Noongar families. Thus, the generic question 'what your mob is?' is greeted, in general, by respondents with the name of the family to which they feel their strongest allegiance. Recent estimates are that there are about 400 Noongar families (SWALSC anthropologists, pers. comm.).

Birdsall (1988) argued that these families generally number some 200 to 300 individuals, who can be widely dispersed across the southwest. Anecdotal evidence, however, would seem to point to the fact that some of the families, such as the Kicketts, are much larger than this. These families are then further subdivided into smaller sections, usually numbering 40 to 150 people. The smaller parts of the family are usually descended from a set of 'sibling-cousins', usually older women, who act to hold the family together 'through close and continuing cooperation over the years' (1988: 141). It is within these smaller sections of 'the family' that most Noongar social interaction occurs. These families are the key signifier of Noongar identity, both vis-à-vis the non-Noongar world and in relation to other Noongar families.

Noongar families are generally spread over a discrete set or 'run' of towns, which is recognised by other Noongar families as belonging to that family. And, within these families, Noongar individuals generally claim one town as their primary town. These links to country, and to other members of the family, are maintained by ongoing movement around these family runs. However, in the wake of the history of enforced transportation and institutionalisation of Noongar over the last century, many Noongar families often ended up residing great distances from their traditional country. What has happened in these situations is that people have generally tended to return 'home' when the situation permitted. In doing so, this process has created a 'line of towns' through which individuals and groups passed on their way home to their country. This process often took an extended period of time due to financial and other constraints, and as children were born and raised not all would carry on with their parents and would instead settle in one of these towns (Birdsall 1988). As a result of this process, Noongar movement tends to operate not only around family runs but also along these lines as well. One of the side effects of this forced relocation of individuals and families and their eventual return over time to their own 'country' has thus been the creation of a broader web of kinship across the southwest, as individuals from disparate regions of Noongar country married and had children together. This broader kinship web could play an important role in the creation of a Noongar nation—linking together as it does families across the entire southwest. In order to look more deeply into the emergence of a Noongar nation we need first to look at the process of native title in the southwest—as it is through this process that Noongar have been able to come together as a single corporate group.

Native Title Representative Bodies in Western Australia

In the wake of the recognition of native title in the Mabo case in 1992, and the subsequent passage of the *Native Title Act 1993* (Cth), representative bodies began to be established across Australia. The lack of suitable bodies in WA in the early 1990s to take on the functions of a Native Title Representative Body (NTRB) meant that the Aboriginal Legal Service of Western Australia Inc (ALSWA) was approached and asked whether or not they would be able to take on native title functions for the region. ALSWA already possessed some capacity in the area due to the existence of its Land and Heritage Unit. And so, in 1993 Greg Benn, former head of the Land and Heritage Unit, became the new head of the NTRB function within ALSWA. While ALSWA thus acquired the mandate to act as the NTRB in WA, this did not preclude the continued existence of other councils such as the Kimberley Land Council or the creation of new land councils. And by 1998, a number of land councils had been formed at a regional level in WA, including the Noongar Land Council.

Noongar Land Council

The Noongar Land Council was established in 1995. The impetus for its creation was a meeting in Narrogin convened by John Hayden, then Chair for the Kaata-Wangkanyini Aboriginal and Torres Strait Islander Commission (ATSIC) Regional Council. One of the key motivating factors in the calling of this meeting was that the work of the ALSWA was seen by Noongar as being too far removed from their aims and desires, especially in terms of land rights issues in traditional Noongar country. In addition, Noongar leaders felt that while other Aboriginal groups across Australia were engaging with State and Federal Governments, Noongar were being left behind. Noongar leaders felt that the establishment of a land council, that is, a single Noongar body, would provide a focal point through which Noongar desires around land rights—such as the prosecution of the 78 claims by Noongar over various sections of the southwest along with other issues—could best be articulated. Over 200 Noongar individuals came together and decided by a vote at the meeting that a land council would be established for the southwest and it would actively seek to obtain NTRB status.

The two ATSIC regional councils in the southwest supported this initiative through grants of about $100 000 in order to help form the Noongar Land Council.

At another meeting in Narrogin in late 1995, initial nominations were made for wards in the new land council. Nominations for these wards occurred with no consideration for linkage to country. Instead of standing in the wards to which they had traditional links, people were instead standing in wards that they thought they had the best chance of winning. As a regional representative structure, the Noongar Land Council thus had no explicit organisational linkage to traditional Noongar linkages to land. However, in their voting, Noongar family ties did play an important part in the success or failure of candidates. Explicit family support in the manner of votes was a key aspect in the success of Noongar individuals wanting to be voted on to the Noongar Land Council council.

The full council of the Noongar Land Council was composed of four Noongar people from each electoral ward, who were voted in by Noongar Land Council members. The 12 electoral wards were: Albany, Brookton, Bunbury, Gnowangerup, Manjimup, Merredin, Moora, Narrogin, Northam, Perth North, Perth South and Pinjarra. The Noongar Land Council executive committee was then elected from the 48 Noongar Land Council full council members, who would decide amongst themselves who would sit on the executive. At its establishment in 1995, Glen Colbung was elected as the first chair while Merv Kelly was appointed as the first Chief Executive Officer (CEO).

The Noongar Land Council was initially based at Narrogin, but various issues including difficulties sourcing staff eventually saw the Noongar Land Council move to Perth. The initial organisation was very small with a staff of two. However, right from the very beginning the new land council was beset by governance problems, many of which were a direct result of a lack of capacity within the organisation. This lack of administrative and management skills within the organisation saw ATSIC step in within a few months of the land council opening after claims emerged of financial mismanagement within the council.

Threatening to shut the Noongar Land Council down because of the mismanagement of funds, ATSIC appointed Dewesbury (a Perth law firm) to act as grant controllers and administrators of the council. In response to this, a special general meeting was held in Narrogin for Noongar concerned about the fate of the land council. At the meeting, people discussed whether or not the land council should just be wound up, but John Hayden argued that there was a need for it to stay in place as otherwise Noongar would have to start from scratch if they wanted their own NTRB for the southwest. Working with Dewesbury and the regional ATSIC Councils, the Noongar Land Council members decided to suspend the Noongar Land Council executive, and a four member management committee was put in place to manage the land council in order to bring it back to shape.

This management committee was composed of four Noongar— Geri Hayden, Mark Ugle, Brett Collard and Glen Kelly—who were mandated to work with Helen Griffith from ATSIC in order to oversee the running of the Noongar Land Council until new structures were put in place. Part of the problem in the running of the Noongar Land Council had been its constitution, which placed an inordinate amount of control in the hands of committee members. One of the key tasks of the committee was therefore to draw up a new constitution. Other tasks included putting in place robust financial management systems and dealing with the Office of the Registrar of Aboriginal Corporations in relation to the financial irregularities that had led to the initial intervention by ATSIC.

Another of the key tasks for the new management committee was the appointment of a new CEO. The job was advertised a number of times, but only two Indigenous Australians applied. In the end, John Hoare, an Indigenous man from Mount Isa in Queensland, was appointed to the position on a six-month initial contract. His primary task in his new role was to work with the management committee to rework the council and the constitution, in order to improve the internal governance systems. During this period, while an executive committee existed (comprising members from the Noongar Land Council council), final sign-off for any decision was required from the management committee.

At the end of his initial contract, John Hoare was signed on for another six-month term. In this second period, the management committee continued to have final say on any management decisions within the council. However, at the end of his second term Hoare called a meeting of the council executive in Albany, with no involvement of the management committee. At this meeting the council executive decided that Hoare's contract would become permanent and he became the full time CEO of the Noongar Land Council. After this event the management committee was no longer consulted on decision making processes and the executive council took on full decision making power.[3]

Problems continued under the new structure, however, with people claiming that the executive still had too much power and influence in the day-to-day running of the organisation, and that there was no real movement in terms of who sat on the executive. Some began to argue that there was no clear division of power under the Noongar Land Council's constitution between the governance and management functions of the organisation. In elections, there were accusations of vote stacking and candidates switching wards merely to maximise their vote. For some Noongar, this acted to reinforce the view held by some

---

[3] Subsequently, the management committee disbanded. An interesting point to note is that at the next election a number of members of the management committee became members of the executive council.

outsiders that Noongar as a group of people were more concerned with fighting each other than acting as a team. Meanwhile, the problems within the executive arm were being mirrored within the elected arm. Many of the same issues, such as favouritism and vote-stacking, began to arise in terms of the groups set up within the Noongar Land Council to manage the land claims process. Noongar were becoming increasingly concerned that not all Noongar interests were being represented in this process. This feeling, that the structures of the Noongar Land Council were not representative of all Noongar interests, was to set off a cascade of change within the organisation.

Native title claims in the southwest under the Noongar Land Council

Despite the existence of the 78 claims by Noongar over various sections of the southwest, limited capacity within the Noongar Land Council meant that they would only ever be able to fund a limited number of these claims. Because of this, the land council was forced to tell the various claimants that, as they would not be able to support all claims, they would need to choose certain claims to support over others. The distinction between which claims were to be supported was to be decided in terms of which would be seen as being most likely to achieve native title. This caused an outcry amongst many Noongar, who felt that their particular claims would thus be overlooked. A possible answer to this lack of capacity, so Noongar Land Council argued, was for these claims to be all folded into a single claim for the southwest as a whole.

Indeed, there had long been a desire amongst many in the Noongar leadership for the creation of a Single Noongar Claim In the course of my research, a number of Noongar individuals told me that the reason that there was a general consensus among Noongar in this period towards this, was the belief by many that Noongar constituted a single group—a Noongar Nation.[4] This desire, when coupled with the Noongar Land Council's inability to fully support all 78 existing claims, meant that early in 1998 the Noongar Land Council began a process to consolidate the various claims. In order to confirm this though, the Noongar Land Council undertook a period of consultation, going out into the communities to ensure that Noongar actually wanted to consolidate the claims. And, while there were some individuals and families who for various reasons opposed the consolidation process, the general consensus was that it should go ahead. However, despite this, it was decided by the Noongar Land Council executive that the move from 78 claims to a single claim would, for pragmatic reasons, be too risky, with the possibility that it could fail registration. Therefore, it was decided to undergo

---

[4] In talking with various Noongar individuals it appeared that the term 'Noongar Nation' began to be used by the Noongar leadership more often in the 1990s. Its roots may be older, however, and might be traced back to the impact of North American forms of activism— especially the idea of Native Nations—on Indigenous activism in Australia in the 1960s and 1970s.

an intermediate step whereby the 78 claims would be reduced to six, and from there the six remaining claims would then be consolidated into a single claim. And so, with this long-term goal in mind, in 1998 the 78 original claims were withdrawn and replaced by six larger claims covering the same total area (Noongar Land Council 1999: 3) (Fig. 10.1).

Fig. 10.1 Six Noongar claims

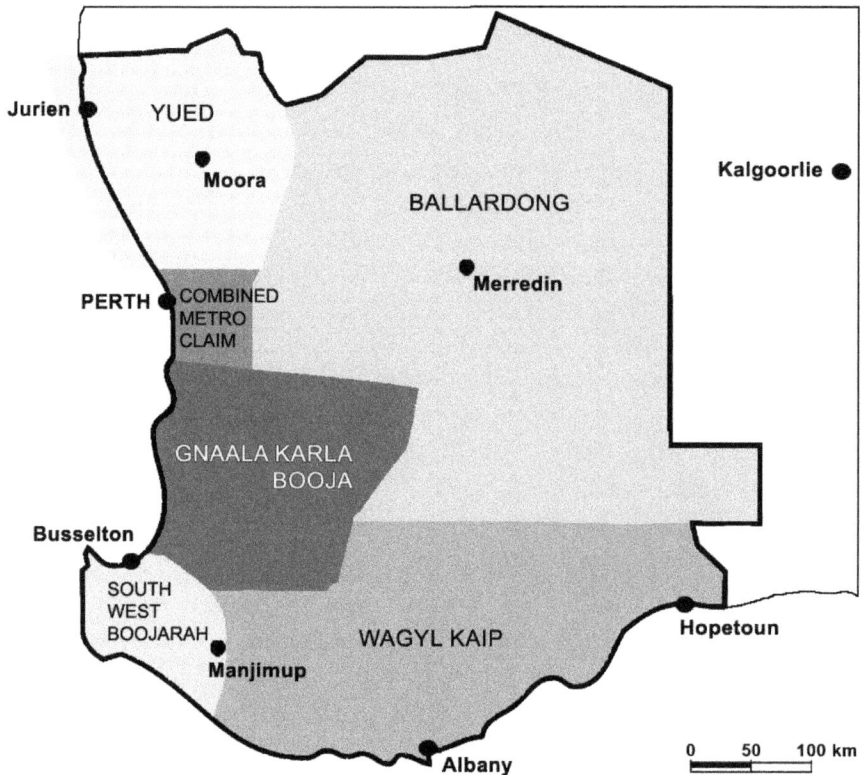

Source: SWALSC

In withdrawing their claims, the named applicants of the original claims were transferred over to become the named applicants on the six new claims. In addition, these individuals also became the initial members of the working parties for each of the claims. This process raised a number of issues about the governance and legitimacy of these new working parties. A number of Noongar families who had interests in various of the six new claims felt that their interests were not being either protected or served by the working parties as they were then constituted. With membership of the working parties restricted to those who had been named applicants of the initial 78 claims, or those individuals granted membership of the working parties by the aforementioned named applicants, a number of Noongar individuals and families felt that the native title process was being hijacked by certain other Noongar families and individuals who had managed to 'get in first'.

Problems with the working party system

After the initial working parties had been formed, a number of Noongar began to express interest in joining them. And, as working party meetings[5] began to be held, Noongar individuals would attend and be voted on to the working party. As would be expected, this process meant that working parties began to grow exponentially in size. This had a number of important ramifications, the most important being the negative effect it had on the achievement of quorums at any meeting, given that attendance by members was often sporadic. In addition, people felt as though power blocs, centred on certain families, were emerging within the working parties. People were concerned that meetings were being stacked by individuals and families to ensure advantageous results for either their families or for themselves. These issues led to the growth of a general feeling of dissatisfaction with the working party system, as it then existed, by the wider Noongar community. Many Noongar felt that the working parties were not representative of all Noongar interests within the community, and they were concerned that many families were not being consulted or informed about the ongoing processes of the claims.

Combined, these problems in the working parties and in the executive arm of the organisation, led to a rising feeling of discontent within the broader Noongar electorate in the southwest, which was to come to a head over issues to do with the registration of the Noongar Land Council as the NTRB for the southwest.

The Noongar Land Council and the Aboriginal Legal Service of Western Australia

As new representative bodies came into being in WA, some, but not all of them, were granted NTRB status. But the ALSWA continued to overlap them all and act as the major NTRB in the state. This overlapping system worked well initially, as the nascent councils were generally small and possessed low levels of capacity to deal with their new role as NTRBs. As a result, the ALSWA acted in a tutelary role to help the new councils create appropriate procedures and structures. A simple division of labour also sprung up between these land councils during this period, with the new councils dealing primarily with future acts while the ALSWA dealt with the actual native title litigation. However, the ongoing scarcity of resources in the native title field in the 1990s meant that a rivalry

---

[5] This of course had other impacts, such as increased need for funding. The funding for this process came from the monies provided to SWALSC by the Federal Government as the NTRB for the southwest.

began to develop between the various land councils, and particularly between the regional land councils and the ALSWA.

Things came to a head with the release of the Parker Report in 1995 (ATSIC 1995) and the native title amendments of 1998 under the Howard Government. One of the key recommendations of this report was that there should be only one representative body per region and that these bodies should be land councils. The Parker Report also recommended that the role of the ALSWA should be to act as a central agency through which land councils could contract native title services. The amendments to the *Native Title Act 1993* (Cth) also meant, among other things, that all NTRBs would have to reapply to retain their status. In the southwest region, both the Noongar Land Council and the ALSWA applied for NTRB status. Both were declined. Both, nonetheless, continued to function despite not receiving official recognition as a NTRB. However, a lack of funds for the ALSWA in the native title area meant that by 2000 the Noongar Land Council was the only remaining *de facto* NTRB in the southwest.[6] Its status was *de facto* because while the Noongar Land Council failed its re-registration, it was granted provisional NTRB status by the Federal Government.

Problems of infighting within the executive and governance and administration issues within the organisation, due largely to problems with the constitution, meant that the Government threatened to withdraw the Noongar Land Council's provisional NTRB status unless they amended their constitution. As a result of these processes, a new CEO was appointed in October 2000. Tasked with overhauling the governance structure of the organisation was the new CEO, Daryl Pearce, an Arrente man with extensive experience in the land rights field in the Northern Territory. One of the key points behind his appointment was that, as a non-Noongar Aboriginal man, he could bring cultural awareness to the position without himself being tied into Noongar family politics. One of the key tasks assigned to him was thus to restructure the organisation so as to make it more representative of as wide a range of Noongar interests as possible. However, changing the constitution of the council was, as the next few years were to show, going to be a mammoth task.

The emergence of the South West Aboriginal Land and Sea Council

As explained above, from 2000 the Noongar Land Council was the sole NTRB for the southwest. However, the Wik decision and the 1998 amendments to the *Native Title Act 1993* (Cth) meant, amongst other things, that the Noongar Land Council had to continue to reapply to maintain its status as a NTRB. As a result

---

[6] Unfortunately, ALSWA's lack of funding for native title work, as a result of its application being turned down, meant that the Parker Report's recommendation that the ALSWA act as a resource for the land councils never came to fruition. It also meant that ALSWA had to either make redundant, or re-deploy to new positions within its organisation, those people with native title experience.

of these legislative changes, the Noongar Land Council executive began moves in 1999 to change the council's constitution in order to pave the way for its reapplication for NTRB status; this appeared to be the major stumbling block to its recognition as the official NTRB for the southwest.

Over the next three years, the executive attempted to change the constitution seven times. Each attempt, however, was met by defeat.[7] Yet, as these attempts continued, albeit unsuccessfully, the Noongar Land Council nonetheless continued to attempt re-registration with the constitution as it stood. And, just as before, each attempt met with refusal. It should be noted again though, that even though the Noongar Land Council continued to fail the registration test, it nonetheless kept being granted provisional NTRB status and hence funding from the Federal Government, as the representative body for the southwest. This is an important point to make, as the only real income flow of sizable proportions available for the Noongar Land Council at this time was the money allocated to it as an NTRB.

The reason that the Noongar Land Council kept failing its re-registration was a perceived lack of good governance. This was in turn seen as flowing largely from a number of issues to do with a loosely defined constitution (Noongar Land Council 2000: 3). Poor management and ongoing Noongar factionalism also contributed to this deleterious state of affairs. However, as discussed above, these problems of governance were only the latest in a long line of governance and mismanagement issues for the Noongar Land Council.

Concerned that their provisional status would not continue to be granted indefinitely, the executive decided that the only way out of its predicament would be through the creation of a new peak body to act as a NTRB for Noongar. The SWALSC was thus created by the Noongar Land Council executive in an attempt to overcome the deadlock amongst Noongar that threatened to derail its re-registration yet again. In 2002, both the Noongar Land Council and SWALSC were submitted to the Minister for registration as the NTRB for the southwest. The only substantive difference between the two submissions, names aside, was the submission of a new constitution with the SWALSC bid. Once again, the Noongar Land Council failed the test but, with their new constitution, SWALSC passed, and so became the recognised NTRB for the southwest.[8]

SWALSC, the organisation, is made up of an executive and an elected arm. The executive arm operates under the CEO who controls the day-to-day running of

---

[7] Under the rules of the then Noongar Land Council there was a need for 75 per cent agreement amongst the full council for changes to the constitution to occur.

[8] The Noongar Land Council was never officially wound up and continues to exist to this day in a shadowy form of half-life. Certain families claim it is the 'legitimate' NTRB for the southwest, but it has no real legitimacy with either the majority of Noongar or government.

the operation, while the elected arm operates through a council system. In the SWALSC system Noongar country was initially split into 14 wards (see Fig. 10.2).

Fig. 10.2 SWALSC wards (Source: SWALSC)

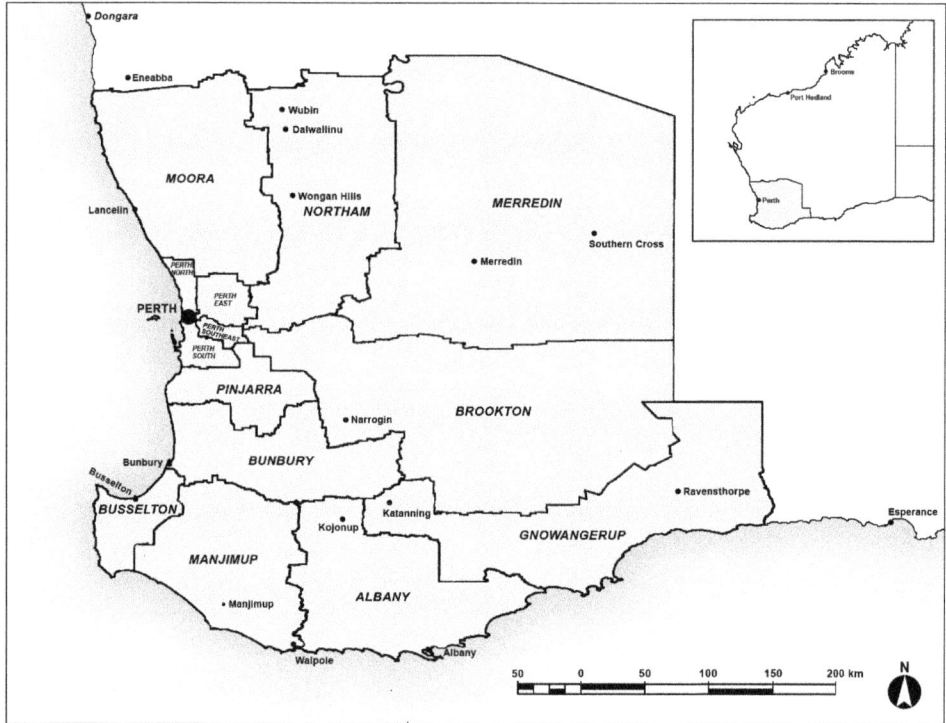

Each ward elected four members to full council, with the full SWALSC council thus comprising 56 individuals. These four members were in turn elected to fill certain positions within their ward, these being: an executive committee member, a ward representative, a women's representative and an older person. While all four sat on full council, they also sat on their respective sub-committees. The key task facing the newly recognised land council, as they came together for the first time in 2002, was the continued prosecution of their native title claims.

The Single Noongar Claim

In February 2003, SWALSC held a number of claimant meetings across the entire southwest where they asked whether or not Noongar wanted to carry on with the process begun by the Noongar Land Council and proceed with the creation of a single claim. Given the status of native title in Australia in that period—especially in the wake of the negative Ward and Yorta Yorta decisions[9] —and the degree of native title extinguishment asserted in the southwest, a

---

[9] See, *State of Western Australia v Ward* (2000) 170 ALR 159, (2000) FCA 191; and *Members of the Yorta Yorta Aboriginal Community v Victoria* (2001) 180 ALR 655.

single native title claim was seen by many Noongar as providing a much stronger position to argue from and as having the greatest potential for securing a negotiated outcome. In addition, the other reason for moving from six claims to a single claim, as discussed above, was partly to do with capacity—or more precisely a lack of it. Despite being reduced to six claims, SWALSC still did not possess the capacity to fund all of them simultaneously. As discussed above, the intention had always been to reduce the 78 claims to one single claim but, for pragmatic reasons, it was decided that this process would be best achieved through an intermediate step—in this case a transition from 78 to six claims, and then from there down to a single claim (Lynette Lund, pers. comm., 25 November 2004).

However, while it was decided that SWALSC would move towards a single claim, they decided as an organisation that they would continue to retain the existing structure of six working parties. But, concerned with the negative feedback they had been receiving about the working party system, SWALSC presented an alternative working party structure to Noongar at the claimant meetings they held across the southwest. In this new system, the old working party arrangements would be completely overhauled and each family who had interests in the region would choose two family members to represent them on their regional working party. These representatives could be named applicants on the original claim or on the new single claim but this need not necessarily be the case. The only criterion was that they needed to be appointed by their families, although the exact selection process used was to be determined by each family. Both resolutions, that SWALSC move towards the creation of a Single Noongar Claim and that the working party system be restructured, were carried at all of the claimant meetings.

In order to go forward with this restructuring of the working party system, the original applicants needed to agree. Not all applicants agreed to this though, as despite assurances by SWALSC and other Noongar that removal as an applicant did not remove applicants from the group or from their standing in traditional lore and custom, they nonetheless felt that there was more risk involved in them going with this new structure. While this small group did not prevent the transfer and creation of a new working group structure, it did present problems that at a later date were to come back to haunt SWALSC and the creation of the Single Noongar Claim.

Family meetings and the Single Noongar Claim

From February 2003, SWALSC began restructuring the working party system and developing the single claim. SWALSC researchers began to compile lists of genealogies and family names associated with various regions across the southwest, linked back to lists of 99 identified 'apical' ancestors.[10] Once these lists were compiled, a meeting would be called in the respective regions and the lists of 400 identified Noongar family names would be put up in the room; Noongar present at the meeting would add or subtract names until agreement was reached that only families who had interests in the region and could speak for country were left on the list. From late May until December 2003, the researchers then called a meeting with each of the Noongar families to confirm genealogies and connections to country. In some meetings, family runs were also mapped out, but research capacity issues prevented this being achieved for all families.

In addition, it was at these meetings that each family nominated two members who would become its representatives on the new regional working parties. As mentioned above, the method by which each family selected their representatives was left up to them to decide. Some families chose to have a show of hands, others voted, while still others decided to have private discussions without the researchers present and then tell SWALSC of their decision.[11] During these meetings and the ensuing decision making process, weight was given to the opinion of the elders of each family.[12] These meetings also gave SWALSC an opportunity to explain how the single claim process would run, including the relationship between the working parties and the named applicants and how decisions would be made and then acted on.

While this process was underway, SWALSC began to restructure the boundaries of the six working groups. Whereas previously the boundaries of these groups had matched those of the original six claims, SWALSC began to restructure them so as to fit more neatly alongside the WA shire boundaries. The reason behind this move was a desire to facilitate the eventual 'fit' of the six working groups with the 14 electoral wards of SWALSC, which were developed from within the geographic confines of the state's shire boundaries. Ultimately, however, the working group boundaries emerged from the consolidation of the various native title claims in the southwest. What this meant was that there was no relation between the working group regions and SWALSC's electoral wards. By redefining the working groups' boundaries along the electoral ward's boundaries the hope was to create a 'neater' administrative structure for SWALSC.

After much work, the Single Noongar Claim was lodged in the Federal Court in September 2003. In this structure, the working parties were seen by many Noongar as being the true decision making bodies for Noongar. There was

---

[10] Some overlap, between not only families but also apical ancestors, naturally occurred across regions.

[11] Research officers were ordered to ensure that each family adopted a decision making structure, whatever that may be, and then to record how this structure operated; that is how the family came to their decision.

[12] In the smaller families, the decision making was structured around the oldest male, while larger families structured proceedings around the oldest surviving sibling set (including cousins).

widespread support for this, as the regional working groups comprised over 240 endorsed family representatives, with each Noongar family represented in the areas in which they held land interests. The working groups are the sites where Noongar social structures connect with the modern organisational form of the NTRB—to present a united voice in the prosecution of native title claims and other issues. Noongar have argued that the new working party structure is much more representative of Noongar society and has brought new faces to the table and stopped old power plays.

Promise and problems with the Single Noongar Claim

However, all was not to stay so positive. As noted above, some legal issues with the six claims remained, as a small minority of original claimants refused to allow their names to be taken off the applications (and thereby lose their individual right to negotiate). Taking this into consideration, on Tuesday 15 June 2004 Justice French dismissed the Noongar attempt to combine the remaining claims into a Single Noongar Claim.

Disappointing as this was to many Noongar, SWALSC pushed on with the process of combining the six claims into a single claim, despite the Federal Court continuing with proceedings for the underlying claims. Things looked even more grim for the Single Noongar Claim as initial support for it in the WA Office of Native Title began to wane. The Office of the State Solicitor and the Federal Government were pressing for one of the six underlying claims, the Combined Metro claim, to go to trial. And, despite SWALSC's opposition to the hearing of this claim area (they would rather have proceeded with the single claim), the Metro case went to court in October 2005. The decision on this claim came down on 19 September 2006 (Bennell v Western Australia [2006] FCA 1243).

In making his determination, the presiding judge, Justice Wilcox, was primarily interested in establishing two issues: that in the Metro area there was a single community with shared law and customs through which they were connected to land and waters for native title purposes at the time sovereignty was asserted in 1829; and that this same community continued to exist and continued to acknowledge those same laws and customs in the present day. In making his decision, Justice Wilcox found that the evidence did indeed show that at 1829 the laws and customs governing land and water throughout the whole claim area were those of a single Noongar community. In contrast to the claims made by the state, that Noongar could not be seen as constituting a single society as they were not aware of each other and there was no overarching central authority in the region, the judge noted that the normative system derived its force through observance and not through a central authority. That is, he found that the existence of a right was not necessarily dependent on a formalised system of enforcement and sanction. In his ruling, the judge also concluded that this same community continued to exist and continued to acknowledge those same laws and customs in the present day.

Despite being appealed by the State and Federal Governments, this ruling effectively confirms what many Noongar have argued for a number of years. That is, they constitute a single Noongar people, a Noongar nation, which continues to exercise traditional laws and customs in the southwest.

Where to from here?

The ruling on the Metro claim area was pivotal for Noongar land claims in that it was seen by many—both Noongar and non-Noongar—as being probably the most difficult to prove ongoing connection to in native title terms. However, now that they have had this positive ruling, the remaining claims—which many feel are much stronger cases—should be easier to prosecute. The Metro case has shown that not only do Noongar exist as a discrete community across the southwest, but that even in a place with as long a direct contact history as metropolitan Perth they have maintained their traditional laws and customs.

While this ruling is important for Noongar, it is also important for other Aboriginal groups living in settled Australia. For too long, and especially in the wake of the Yorta Yorta decision, native title rulings in settled Australia have appeared to depend on socio-cultural forms abstracted from remote areas of Australia such as the Western Desert and the Kimberley. However, to do this is to enact yet another form of violence on peoples who have already endured two hundred years of oppression. With its very different ecology, southern Australia was home to very different Aboriginal social forms to those found in the north. Evidence such as that presented in the Metro claim shows that Aboriginal groups in the southwest came together in much larger socio-cultural groupings than those found in much of the north. The successful Metro claim is an important case, therefore, in that it provides a valuable corrective to this flawed form of inferential reasoning.

That said, in many cases the hard work has only just started. After the appeal the other remaining cases will need to be heard, although as noted above, the success of the Metro case makes the prosecution of the other cases simpler in many respects. But a flow-on point from this is that as rulings are made on these cases, then funding for SWALSC as the NTRB for the southwest will begin to disappear. Will SWALSC be able to source money from other areas to remain as the peak body for the Noongar Nation? This chapter has shown that SWALSC and the Noongar Land Council have played a pivotal role in making concrete the notion of a Noongar Nation. Questions need to be asked about how the aims and desires of this nation can be articulated without a single peak Noongar body to provide coherence to the multitude of voices that make it up; and about the relationship of the Prescribed Bodies Corporate, which will need to be established in the wake of the successful native title determinations, to SWALSC or other Noongar bodies.

As I have noted elsewhere (Barcham 2006), in the post-ATSIC environment there has been a push to create regional governance organisations. The existence of the Noongar Nation as a large 'natural' grouping provides an ideal opportunity for the creation of a Noongar Regional Authority. Two problems, however, need to be considered before this could come into effect. The first is the issue of funding. Under current government policy there is no opportunity for regional authorities to obtain recurrent budget funding, and as the Noongar native title cases are settled, funding for SWALSC will cease. Opportunities for funding do exist, such as through service delivery arrangements for government organisations or through Shared Responsibility Agreements. However, none of these options is ideal as they do not necessarily provide long term funding opportunities. The other question that needs to be asked concerns the issue of historic peoples. The southwest is home to many non-Noongar Aboriginal people. Under current policy, any regional governance authority would be expected to work for all Indigenous people in its jurisdiction—not just traditional land owners. If SWALSC or some other Noongar body was to become the regional authority for the southwest, then there would be a need to explore how historic peoples could be fitted within the structures of the organisation.

Conclusion

Despite the formidable amount of work that remains to be done, Noongar have every reason to be happy with the major victory they have achieved with the positive determination made in the Metro claim. In his judgment, Justice Wilcox has reaffirmed what Noongar already knew—they are a single people, a Noongar Nation.[13] This notion of a Noongar Nation has played out in the revamped organisational structure of SWALSC. The restructured working party system offers a much more representative structure for Noongar interests in the southwest and, so far, has a relatively high degree of support by Noongar. As this chapter has shown, despite a long history of European contact and government interference, Noongar have been able to maintain their identity as a Noongar community—a Noongar Nation. Using the native title process, Noongar society has been able to successfully create an organisation that is not only representative, but which is able to articulate its aims and desires. While

---

[13] On 23 April 2008 the full bench of the Federal Court upheld a West Australian and Australian Government appeal against the 2006 ruling by Justice Murray Wilcox on the grounds that Justice Wilcox had made two errors in law in his ruling. The decision was set aside and referred to a new hearing. However, the judges did not agree to rule that there was no native title over Perth. WA Deputy Premier, Mr Eric Ripper, subsequently stated that the WA Government recognised the Noongar people's traditional connection to the southwest of WA and hoped the matter would be settled by negotiations. The Federal Attorney-General also indicated that he would consider the detail of the decision, including opportunities it might present for negotiation.

problems remain, and many issues will need to be confronted in the upcoming years, the future indeed looks bright for the Noongar Nation.

References

Aboriginal and Torres Strait Islander Commission (ATSIC) 1995. *Review of Native Title Representative Bodies*, ATSIC, Canberra.

Barcham, M. 2006. 'Regional governance structures in Indigenous Australia: Western Australian examples', *CIGAD Working Paper Series No. 1*, Centre for Indigenous Governance and Development, Massey University, Palmerston North.

Berndt, R. 1979. 'Aborigines of the south-west', in R. Berndt and C. Berndt (eds), *Aborigines of the West: Their Past and Present*, University of Western Australia Press, Nedlands, WA.

Birdsall, C. 1988. 'All one family', in I. Keen (ed.), *Being Black: Aboriginal Culture in 'Settled' Australia*, Aboriginal Studies Press, Canberra.

Howard, M. 1981. *Aboriginal Politics in Southwestern Australia*, University of Western Australia Press, Nedlands, WA.

Noongar Land Council 1999. *Annual Report 1998/1999*, Noongar Land Council, Perth.

——2000. *Annual Report 1999/2000*, Noongar Land Council, Perth.

11. Regionalism that respects localism: the Anmatjere Community Government Council and beyond

Will Sanders

Introduction

The Anmatjere Community Government Council (ACGC) in central Australia was established in 1993 as part of a push by the Northern Territory (NT) Government towards larger regional, multi-settlement groupings within its emerging local government system. Fifteen years on, as part of another such push, ACGC is about to be amalgamated into a much larger Central Desert Shire. The shire, which will begin operations during 2008, will merge ACGC with five other local governing bodies and cover a population some four times ACGC's current constituency.

This chapter reflects on the history of ACGC within the NT local government system and on ideas of regionalism and localism. It argues that ACGC has been a reasonably successful experiment in regional, multi-settlement local government, and that this is partly because it has respected and built on single-settlement localism. The chapter will discuss how the early constitutional design of ACGC respected such localism and how that respect has developed and endured since, albeit at times under stress. I will also argue that this respect for single-settlement localism points the way forward for local government in the NT under the new larger shires arrangement. Regionalism must build on localism, rather than devalue or disparage it.

The emergence of ACGC

The Anmatjere region sits astride the Stuart Highway about 200km north of Alice Springs. The name derives from the region's Aboriginal language, which is still widely spoken among the predominantly Aboriginal population of 1,000 or more people.[1] European settlement in the area dates back to the 1870s, when a repeater station on the Overland Telegraph Line was established at Ti Tree well. Pastoralism followed in the early years of the twentieth century, with most land then being leased to settlers for pastoral purposes. In later years, some small horticultural blocks were also developed by settlers, along with a roadhouse or two. The only town in the region is Ti Tree, gazetted in 1980, straddling the

---

[1] The 2006 Census enumerated 966 usual residents in the Anmatjere area, 88 per cent of whom identified as Indigenous and 56 per cent of whom listed Anmatyerr as the language spoken at home. Another 12 per cent each spoke Warlpiri and Arrernte at home.

Stuart Highway on a five mile square (ca. 64km^2) parcel of land, which was formerly the old telegraph reserve.

In the late 1970s, the Ti Tree Station pastoral lease surrounding the town was acquired for Aboriginal people by the Commonwealth's Aboriginal Land Fund Commission. In the early 1980s, a successful land claim converted this lease to Aboriginal freehold, as the Ahakeye Land Trust. While this might suggest that the region fared quite well in the early years of the Commonwealth's land rights system for Aboriginal people in the NT, this was not the predominant perception among local Aboriginal people. In the late 1980s and early 1990s, a movement developed among Aboriginal people in Anmatjere for a breakaway regional land council, separate from the larger Central Land Council based in Alice Springs. The Commonwealth Minister for Aboriginal Affairs was not convinced that the requirements for such a breakaway land council had been met, and did not support the move (Morton 1994). However, the NT Government, through its local government Minister, saw the opportunity to support a regional local government in the area, and thus the ACGC emerged.

At self-government in 1978, the NT had just four local governments in its major urban centres. During the 1980s, the NT Government encouraged the development of local governments in smaller urban centres and outlying areas, under the Community Government provisions of its Local Government Act (Coburn 1982; Phegan 1989). At first, as one commentator of the time noted, the approach was 'laissez fare' and the pattern that began to emerge was of small, single-settlement local government incorporations (Wolfe 1989). However, in time, the NT Government became more directive and promoted the idea of larger, regional, multi-settlement incorporations. The first of these to emerge was Yugul Mangi Community Government Council in southeast Arnhem Land in 1988, which brought together eight non-contiguous parcels of land and their associated discrete Aboriginal communities.[2] The second, in 1993, was ACGC, which was proudly proclaimed by the local government Minister in the Legislative Assembly of the Northern Territory (LANT) as the twentieth community government council (LANT 1993a: 8583). The Minister also noted in the Assembly a month later that the ACGC's first meeting had been held and that Eric Panangka had been elected as chair (LANT 1993b: 8854). As well as being prominent in the movement for a breakaway land council, Panangka had been a Country Liberal Party (CLP) candidate for the Legislative Assembly seat of Stuart in the 1991 elections. So, there were clearly quite close and amiable connections between the CLP Government of the time and the emerging ACGC.

In its 1993 incarnation, ACGC brought together nine wards containing discrete Aboriginal communities. Three of these wards were the Ahakeye Land Trust,

---

[2] Yugul Mangi CGC was dismissed in 2001 and reformed in 2003 to cover one larger land area. Like ACGC, it is now about to disappear into a much larger shire.

divided into western, central and eastern portions, each of which had one significant discrete Aboriginal settlement on it. Around this large central block of incorporated land were six other wards on much smaller land parcels. These were Aboriginal living area excisions from surrounding pastoral leases, measured in hectares rather than square miles (see Fig. 11.1). As well as having very different land bases, these nine wards also had very different population bases, with some settlements having over 200 residents and some less than 50. However, in a classic federal move, each of the wards was given an equal representation of two potential members on the council, irrespective of its population size. Another interesting constitutional provision was that a quorum for council meetings required a member to be present from every ward that currently had members. Like the ward representation rule, this very high quorum rule indicated a guarded regional federalism that had considerable respect for the autonomy of its constituent parts.

Fig. 11.1 Area and wards of the Anmatjere Community Government Council

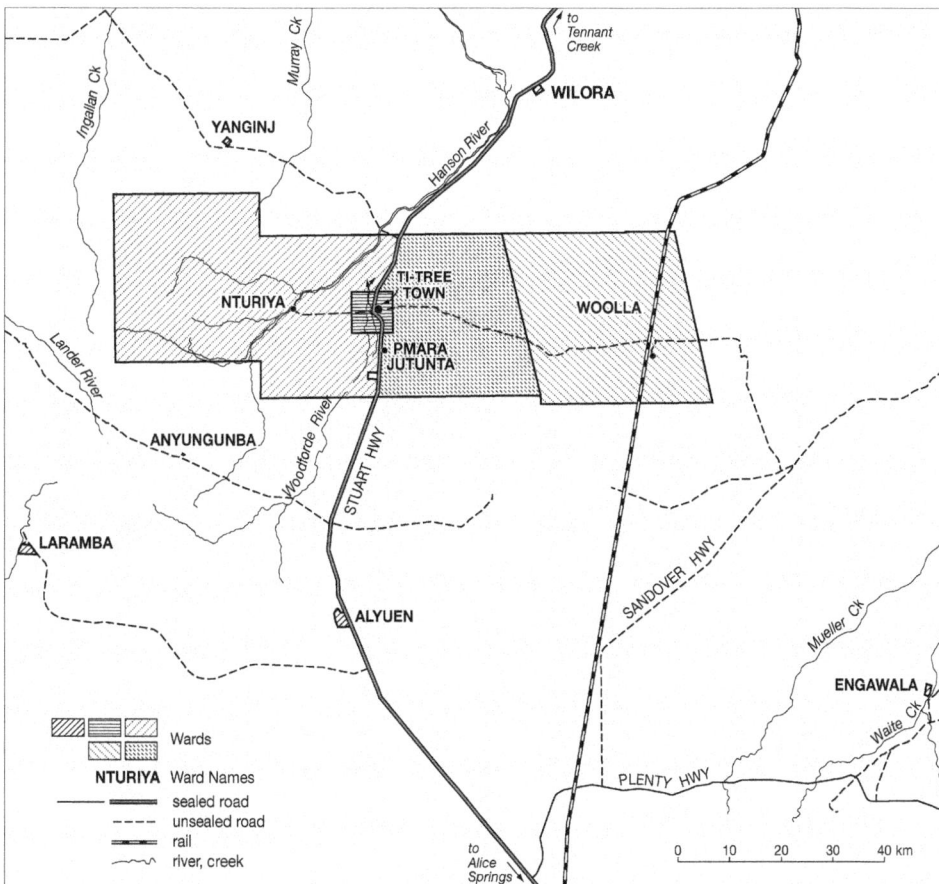

This original ACGC in 1993 was an all-Aboriginal affair. Settler interests in the region, such as pastoralists, roadhouse residents, horticulturalists and Ti Tree town residents, were all left outside the scheme, on about 90 per cent of the region's land area, covered by nine or 10 pastoral leases and other non-Aboriginal land tenures. However, the NT Government's intention from the outset was at least to bring the residents and land area of Ti Tree town into the scheme. The move to do this in 1995 met with considerable resistance from the existing organisational guardian of the town, the Ti Tree Progress Association. In previous years, under the dominance of settler interests, this organisation had developed town facilities like a park and an airstrip. Now, these assets were to become the responsibility of ACGC, and Ti Tree town residents were being asked to throw in their lot as one additional ward, with two members, within a predominantly Aboriginal local government. The one concession to Ti Tree's rather different status as a small open roadside town, rather than a discrete Aboriginal settlement, was the residence requirements for voting or standing for office. In this ward, the requirements were to be just three months before the closure of the rolls, rather than one year in the previous three years as in the other wards. This reflected the fact that many people from elsewhere moved through Ti Tree in quite short periods of time as public sector employees at the school, the health clinic, the police station or in ACGC.

At the time the Ti Tree town ward was included in ACGC in 1995, there was some controversy over who was on the electoral roll for the ward. The Labor member for Stuart, and Opposition Leader in the NT Legislative Assembly, suggested that some Aboriginal town residents who had supported the inclusion might have been improperly removed from the roll, which only had 27 eligible voters on it. Controversy was also aroused by the fact that the Council Clerk of the ACGC was nominating to be an elected member for the Ti Tree town ward, which the Opposition Leader saw as a significant conflict of interest (LANT 1995a: 4680, 1995b: 4796).[3]

Clearly, the early years of ACGC were quite contested and difficult. One source of this contestation was the attempt to mix Indigenous and settler town interests. Another, however, was the multi-settlement nature of the Indigenous regionalism. This required council members to travel into town once a month for meetings from settlements which were, in two cases, up to 150km away, and in five cases, 50km away (see Fig. 11.1). Council members pushed for vehicles to enable them to get to meetings and to attend to constituency matters in between times. The inaugural Council Clerk responded to this pressure by leasing a number of vehicles for the use of members under standard public sector arrangements. This

---

[3] The ACGC Clerk was successful in this bid, but in time the NT Government amended its Local Government Act to say that council employees could only stand for elected office with the permission of the minister. Subsequently, the policy followed was generally only to give such permission to non-managerial employees, and not to council clerks or other significant managerial employees.

worked well until the three year term of these leases was looming, and the vehicles had done far more kilometres and were in far worse condition than the terms of the leases allowed. Due to lease penalties that would need to be paid, in late 1996 and early 1997, ACGC was facing a financial overrun of some $150,000. The Council Clerk chose, at that time, to vacate his position, leaving the problem of bringing in the vehicles and dealing with the financial overrun to his deputy and successor.

Elsewhere, I have written about how this first Council Clerk is, in fact, well remembered and how it is difficult to judge his vehicle leasing arrangements entirely adversely (Sanders 2006a). At one level, leasing vehicles was innovative and entrepreneurial management, at another, somewhat naïve and un-strategic, at least in the longer term. At base, the episode illustrated a problem of small scale organisation that I have labeled 'isolated managerialism', and which the NT Government's push towards larger, regional local governments was, at least partly, intended to overcome (Sanders 2005, 2006a). At this point, therefore, I will briefly turn back to the NT Government and its promotion of larger, regional, multi-settlement local governments before returning to pick up the story of ACGC in later years.

Actively promoting voluntary regionalism: the Northern Territory Government 1999–2005

In early 1999, The Hon. Loraine Braham, the local government Minister in the long-serving CLP NT Government, announced to the Legislative Assembly a 'reform and development' agenda for local government. She argued that while the development of community government over the previous 20 years had been 'useful in bringing small remote communities into the wider local government industry', it was 'now time to make changes … which build upon the knowledge and experience' of those years. She noted that of the Territory's then 68 local governments, many had 'populations of around 300 people' and that in these situations 'the amount required for even a basic level of administration impacts seriously on the amount of money available for services'. She also noted that some of these local governments 'face continuing difficulties in attracting sufficient numbers of qualified, competent and ethical staff' and that 'many fail to do so'. Many 'current councils', she argued are 'simply too small' to allow 'for the achievement of any economies of scale' (LANT 1999: 2769–70).

Braham detailed the way in which numbers of local government councils were being reduced in places like Victoria and Tasmania, and said that it was 'the Government's view that there should eventually be less councils in the Territory' as well. She insisted that 'no minimum population' was being 'set' but argued that 'councils with a population of less than about 2,000 people encounter greater difficulties in maintaining adequate levels of administration and service delivery over the longer-term'. However, she also noted that:

a movement towards larger, more sustainable councils does not mean that the Government is seeking to deny small, remote communities the opportunity to make decisions at the local level … It is essential, therefore, that in developing constitutions for larger councils, the capacity is maintained, to an appropriate degree, for smaller communities to make decisions specific to them (LANT 1999: 2771).

In many ways, therefore, while the NT Government was clearly pushing strongly for larger, regional, multi-settlement local governments in 1999, it was also still acknowledging respect for single-settlement localism.

The most obvious product of this 1999 policy push was the Tiwi Islands Local Government, which emerged in 2001, combining three former community government councils (Campbell 2001). In central Australia, however, there was little evident change, and ACGC remained the one clear instance of a regional, multi-settlement local government.

After the election of a Labor Government in the NT in August 2001, the local government portfolio was taken on by the Territory's first Aboriginal Minister, The Hon. John Ah Kit. In March 2002, in a Ministerial statement to the Legislative Assembly, The Hon. Ah Kit indicated that he would be re-casting the local government reform and development agenda 'to look at regional governance issues relating to specific service delivery functions, rather than looking narrowly at the amalgamation of Community Government Councils' (LANT 2002b: 1112). Fourteen months later, The Hon. Ah Kit announced a *Building Stronger Regions—Stronger Futures* package, which did indeed cast regional development somewhat more broadly, as economic development, local government and other service delivery (Ah Kit 2003). However, in the local government area, the new reform agenda also essentially came down to voluntary regional up-scaling and amalgamation, albeit under the new label of 'regional authority'. In August 2003, Ah Kit told the Legislative Assembly of the Northern Territory that:

the creation of regional authorities will only occur where it is the wish of the communities involved to adopt this model for service delivery. The concept of regional authorities that we propose is straightforward. They will be established under the *Local Government Act*. The constitutions of regional authorities will give them power to govern, and make by-laws for the area they cover.

We are not inventing a new tier of government, but we are creating the capacity for councils to voluntarily come together for improved service delivery (LANT 2003: 4861)

The Hon. John Ah Kit identified that two new regional groupings had already emerged in 2003, the Thamarrurr Regional Council at Wadeye, 350km southwest of Darwin, and the Nyirranggulang Mardrulk Ngadberre Regional Council to the east of Katherine. One other grouping was also being discussed as a possibility in the West MacDonnell Ranges area of central Australia (LANT 2003: 4862; see also NT Government 2003: 12). However, as it turned out, this last never came to fruition.

Voluntary regional up-scaling of remote area local governments seemed to be a fairly slow and variable process. Some in the tropical 'top end' of the NT were slowly embracing the idea, but the arid 'centre' seemed more problematic and resistant.

ACGC around the millennium: centre/periphery tensions

During these years around the millennium, ACGC was not under particular pressure from the NT Government to be reformed. Along with Yuendumu, ACGC was the only remote area local government in central Australia that could claim a population of over 1,000. So, the reform effort was in many ways directed much more to the 20 or so other such local governing bodies in central Australia that serviced populations of well under 1,000 (see Sanders 2006b). ACGC's challenge, either side of the millennium, once it had recovered from its financial overrun of 1996–97, seemed to be managing emerging centre/periphery tensions.

Once Ti Tree town had been added as a ward in 1995, it became very clear that the town was becoming the centre of ACGC operations. Housing began to be built there for managerial staff and a new, quite substantial office complex and council chambers began to be planned and developed there, which was finally opened in 2002. ACGC also developed a new Aged Care Day Centre in Ti Tree during these years, as well as having its major works yard there (see Fig. 11.2).

With all this development of ACGC infrastructure occurring in Ti Tree town, there were clearly times when some of the council members and their constituents from the outlying discrete Aboriginal settlement wards wondered whether they were getting an appropriate share of the ACGC's attention and resources. The two most outlying and quite populous settlements, Laramba to the southwest and Engawala to the southeast, had little to gain from infrastructure and services being developed in Ti Tree town, as they were the best part of 150km and two hours drive away (see Fig. 11.1). Each maintained their own community association and office, and ran a Community Development Employment Project (CDEP) for local people separate from ACGC.[4] Also, their power and water systems were stand alone and not always run by ACGC. So, there were several times when Laramba, in particular, felt it was gaining little from ACGC and threatened to break away with a grouping of settlements to its west. At one

---

[4] CDEP is often referred to as the Indigenous work-for-the-dole scheme. However, CDEP pre-existed the general Australian Government 'Work for the Dole' scheme, introduced in 1996, by almost 20 years, and there are some pertinent differences between the two. Perhaps the most important is that CDEP participants are employees of the organisation running CDEP, whereas Work for Dole participants are Centrelink payment recipients, who are directed to undertake an activity with a placement organisation.

point, Laramba's secession ambitions were even discussed in the NT Legislative Assembly (LANT 2002a: 934).

Fig. 11.2 Ti Tree town and Creek Camp

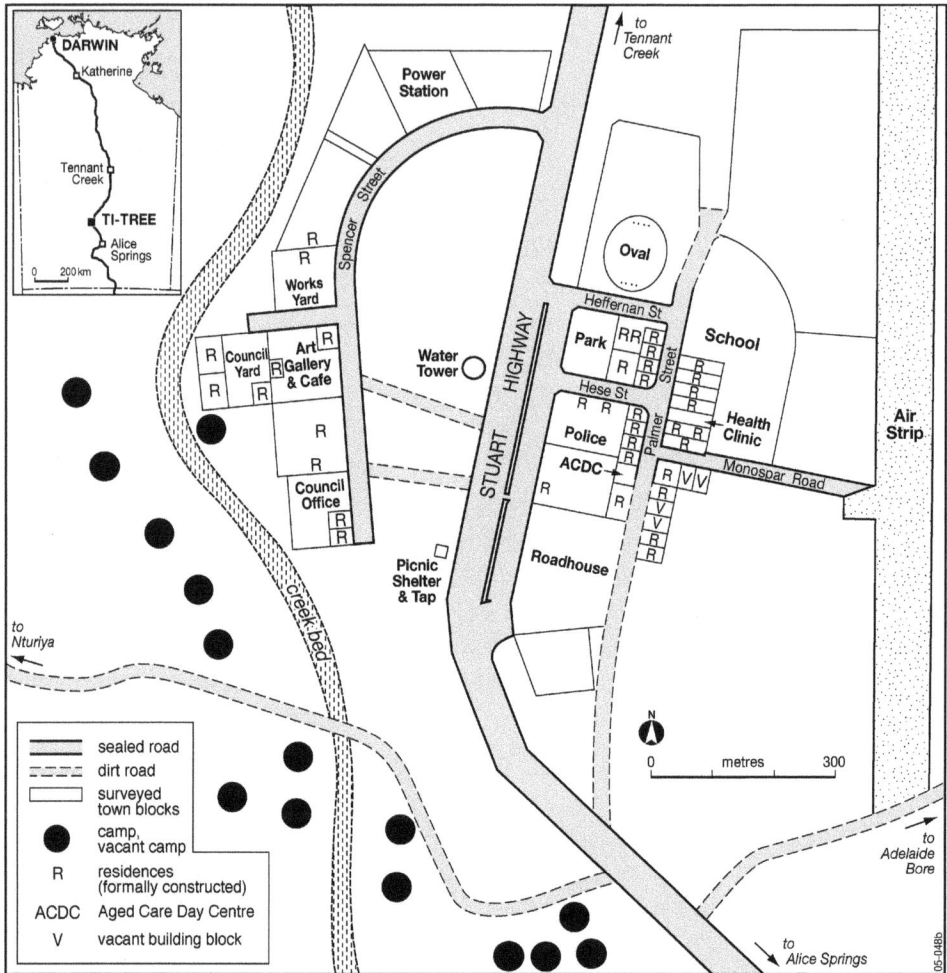

Some of the settlements closer to Ti Tree also had cause to wonder about the efficacy of the ACGC arrangement during these years. Three settlements 50km from Ti Tree on dirt roads, Yanginj, Woolla and Anyungunba, had just basic water, electricity and housing services managed by ACGC, and were having trouble retaining residents. As numbers of residents fell, so did service levels. Two other settlements 50km from Ti Tree, but adjacent to the highway, Alyuen and Wilora, seemed to be doing better at retaining their residents, but in some sense this was not primarily due to ACGC services. Alyuen had access to a nearby roadhouse for stores, and Wilora had access to a small pastoral station store, a

CDEP run independently of ACGC, and a small school. Again, ACGC really only oversaw the water, electricity and housing in these communities.

The two closest settlements to Ti Tree, Pmara Jutunta and Nturiya, were experiencing different issues again. Already among the more populous settlements in the regional grouping, their populations seemed if anything to be growing, but at the same time, their service levels seemed to be falling. Being only 10km and 17km respectively from Ti Tree, there had been a judgment made by the ACGC administration in previous years that the residents of these two settlements could use the ACGC office in Ti Tree and no ACGC office presence was maintained in Pmara Jutunta or Nturiya. While this may have seemed acceptable for a while, when the community store run by the Aboriginal pastoral company closed at Nturiya early in 2002, that settlement was effectively left without any local place for even basic administrative business. Nturiya was now simply a housing estate from which people were obliged to commute to Ti Tree for virtually all services. Pmara Jutunta, by contrast, still had a community store, although it was becoming run down.[5]

While the decline of store services in Nturiya and Pmara Jutunta was not the direct responsibility of ACGC, when combined with the lack of ACGC offices in the settlements it did not augur well. Service levels generally in these two more populous settlements seemed to be contracting back to just housing, water and electricity, as in some of the less populous settlements 50km out of town. This contraction of service levels in the discrete Aboriginal settlements surrounding Ti Tree was clearly going to have ramifications for ACGC as the local governing body, particularly when contrasted with ACGC's growing level of infrastructure in Ti Tree town. There were thus, it seemed, some centre-periphery tensions developing in ACGC around the turn of the millennium, which needed to be managed.

Building relationships: working with Anmatjere Community Government Council 2004–06

When Sarah Holcombe and I approached ACGC to be part of the Indigenous Community Governance Project (ICGP) in the early months of 2004, our arrival coincided with that of a new Chief Executive Officer (CEO). The appointee was an officer of the NT local government department who, towards the end of his career, wanted to take the opportunity to show that a regional, multi-settlement local government like ACGC could work. He was open to our involvement and, as a new arrival, was not at all defensive about the existing situation at ACGC. We attended our first council meeting in June 2004, and council too seemed open to our involvement, though somewhat tentative.

---

[5] The Pmara Jutunta community store ended up closing in mid 2006.

Two months later we heard from the CEO that council had been dismissed. The reason was that members from some of the nine wards that then had members were not turning up to monthly meetings and the rules clearly stated that if council did not meet its quorum rule for two consecutive meetings it was dismissed and new elections called. The numbers on the electoral roll for each ward for this election in August 2004 are set out in Table 11.1. Clearly, the tenth ward, Anyungunba, which had not had members in the previous council, was not going to have members in the new council either, as the one person on the roll there could not self nominate. Woolla and Yanginj were also very low in numbers on the roll and it was known that these few enrolled people were not currently residing in the settlements.[6]

When the new council was elected in October 2004, it did, however, have a full complement of 18 members from nine wards, Anyungunba aside. None of the elections was contested, so it appeared that community discussion had delivered just the right number of nominees for vacancies. About half the members were returnees from the previous council, including the previous chairman and the one non-Indigenous member for the Ti Tree ward. At the first meeting of the new council, the previous chairman nominated again for that position, but so did a new member who had developed a working relationship with the new CEO as a liaison officer during the period after the dismissal of the previous council. This new council member won the position of chairman in a fairly close vote.

Table 11.1 ACGC Election 2004, enrolments by ward

Ward	Number Enrolled
Alyuen	20
Anyungunba	1
Engawala	57
Laramba	158
Nturiya	92
Pmara Jutunta	119
Ti Tree	109
Wilora	59
Woolla	14
Yanginj	8
Total	637

Our relationship with the new council developed comfortably, though we moved away from using 'governance' as the key descriptive term for our project. The 'governance' terminology seemed to be associated with the idea of elected member 'training' of one sort or another, and we did not want to be cast in the role of a 'training' provider. We began to talk about 'working with Council' on 'issues

---

[6] Lack of current residence in these wards did not disqualify these enrollees from standing for office, as the formal criterion was one year's residence in the previous three.

of importance or concern' to them, because we were interested in 'how' ACGC worked and, without pre-judging the matter, how it might work better.

The issue that emerged in late 2004 was the number of Aboriginal people camping informally along the western side of Ti Tree town, without reticulated water or electricity (see Fig. 11.2). The local member of the NT Legislative Assembly for Stuart, and senior Minister in the Martin Labor Government, Peter Toyne, had just written to ACGC expressing disquiet at the low level of servicing for significant numbers of campers in this area and asking whether ACGC might be able to do some more.[7] ACGC agreed to run a boxed water service in the camps over the summer of 2004, funded by the NT Government, and we offered our services to do a study of who was living in the camps and for what reasons, and to report back to council. The camping seemed to be an 'issue of importance and concern' at least for Peter Toyne, and therefore also for the council.

Sarah Holcombe's chapter in this volume discusses in greater detail how this work proceeded, and we have also reported on it elsewhere (Holcombe and Sanders 2007; Sanders and Holcombe 2007). Suffice to say here, that the work proved a very useful way for us to get to know council members and their constituents, and for us to come to grips with life-ways and service patterns in the region. Declining service levels at Nturiya and places like Yanginj were clearly boosting numbers in 'Creek Camp', but so was trouble further afield, outside the Anmatjere region, in places like Willowra to the northwest. Among the 15 camps, which accommodated towards 100 people at times, there were about 25 very well established core, permanent residents. Some of these were public sector employees in Ti Tree, who were not offered housing with their employment. Employment-linked housing was restricted to senior employees mainly recruited from elsewhere. Two ACGC houses were available in Ti Tree for local Aboriginal employees, but this was far from enough, and one ACGC worker who had occupied one of these houses for a period had ended up living back in Creek Camp, sick of 'other people' using his 'lounge room as a bedroom'. There were also old and disabled people among the core residents of Creek Camp, who liked it as a quiet, spread out place to live, with dogs, close to town services and family, but away from the whitefellas of the compact eastern residential area and with a bit of service support from the Aged Care Day Centre. Most of the 25 or so core residents of Creek Camp saw themselves as continuing to live there for some considerable time, and were more interested in exploring development options there than the idea of moving into houses on the east side of Ti Tree (see Fig. 11.2).

---

[7] Toyne had previously raised the issue of inadequate services for people camping in this area in the Legislative Assembly of the NT, soon after the closure of the community store at Nturiya (LANT 21 May 2002c: 1426).

This last finding led us to explore the attitudes of other Ti Tree residents and NT Government officials to the idea of developing Creek Camp with reticulated services and possibly some buildings. Many were open to the idea, however, key interests within the NT Department of Planning and Infrastructure were not so keen and, in support of that stance, cited NT Government policy against the further recognition of Aboriginal community living areas in urban areas. The obstacles to reticulated services and other development at Creek Camp at this higher level of government seemed insurmountable, and ACGC itself also had some reservations, both on council and among its key managerial staff. So, after three reports to council over 18 months, we saw no option but to step back from this difficult issue for a while. Our probing had put a more positive and quantified image of Creek Camp in the public domain, but there was still no obvious way forward to ameliorate the existing situation.

In the middle of 2005, as we were first reporting to ACGC on the Creek Camp work, the one settler member of council resigned due to family commitments. Being replaced by an Aboriginal resident, council then became all-Aboriginal again, in a way that it had not been since 1995; and it has remained that way since. Late in 2005, council was once again dismissed for not meeting its quorum rule for two consecutive meetings. A new issue that was thus emerging was whether the quorum rule should be made less demanding. The 2005 council was reluctant to change the rule, with some of the long-serving members arguing that it was good to have people from all wards in the meeting when making decisions generally, but also that members from particular wards needed to be there for making decisions specific to their ward. Indeed, during 2005 we observed a tendency to defer to and support people from particular wards in decisions relating specifically to their wards.

For example, during 2005 the issue was often raised of reinvesting in electricity infrastructure at Yanginj and Woolla. Without residents permanently present, the generators in both places had gone missing over recent years. Some money was available for re-investment, but the CEO's argument was that, in order to safeguard assets, ACGC could only reinvest if there was some assurance of people residing in the two settlements. However, none of the four members of council from these two wards who were raising this issue could clearly commit to resuming residence themselves, or on behalf of members of their families. Other council members were generally supportive of their re-investment push, but essentially deferred on the matter to the ward members and the CEO. The issue gradually lost currency in council meetings as it became clear that the ward members could not commit to residence and the CEO was maintaining the need for such commitment in order to re-invest.

The new council that was elected in early 2006 only had 13 members from eight wards, nine of whom were returnees, including the chairman, and all of whom were, once again, elected unopposed. Woolla had no members in the new council, and Yanginj and two other wards had dropped down to just one member each, which potentially made meeting the quorum rule even harder, as these three single ward members had to be present at all meetings. We thought, at the time, that council was losing interest, as they were finding the CEO somewhat 'hard', even though procedurally he was scrupulous in keeping members well informed and involving them in decision making.[8] Council members were also coming to understand that the CEO was a stickler for the rules, and we realised that probably in the past, the council had often not met its quorum rule, but that clerks and CEOs had simply not invoked the rules.[9] Faced with this strict adherence to the rules and the prospect of being dismissed yet again, council began to shift, pragmatically, on the idea of changing the quorum rule. At the first meeting of the new council in February 2006, no quorum was achieved. At its second meeting in March, when a quorum was achieved, council passed a resolution that the quorum rule be changed to a simple majority of elected members. However, ACGC could only request such a change; the power to effect it lay with the NT local government Minister, and because of consultation requirements this would take some time.

From March 2006 onwards, the CEO seemed to soften somewhat. He gently let it be known that now that council had passed its resolution to have the quorum rule changed he would not dismiss it for not meeting the higher quorum rule—and in July 2006 this declared intention was indeed tested. After almost two years in the job, the CEO also seemed to be softening because he was benefiting from some build up of other managerial staff around him. A new social services director and staff were strengthening the level of ACGC activity in aged and disabled services, sport, recreation and youth services, and also child care services, not only in Ti Tree but in the outlying communities as well. The corporate services section had built a Rural Transaction Centre within the council office in Ti Tree and was increasing ACGC's level of both Centrelink and personal financial services. There was thus a sense that ACGC was growing and expanding its servicing roles a little, beyond electricity, water and housing, and back out from Ti Tree town into the outlying communities. This seemed to allow the CEO to relax a little with council and to take some credit for ACGC's modest recent expansion of services.

Another aspect of this expansion of service roles was that during late 2005 and early 2006, ACGC was being encouraged by the Commonwealth Department of

---

[8] Folds (2001: 41) reports Indigenous views of managers being 'hard' in another NT Indigenous community governance context as follows: 'Managers who withhold "institutional" resources from Pintupi, as individuals, in order to fulfil their official purposes, are considered to be "hard" bosses, careless of relationships through their unreasonable greed'. Being a 'hard' and a 'good' manager in Indigenous community governance are related in quite complex ways (Sanders 2006a).

[9] Under changes to the NT *Local Government Act*, council clerks were redesignated as CEOs in 2003.

Employment and Workplace Relations (DEWR) to become involved in running CDEP. This had two aspects. One was taking on the running of the existing CDEPs at Laramba and Engawala, and the second was developing CDEP for the first time in the settlements closer to Ti Tree. This second aspect was a substantial new opportunity for ACGC to offer quite large numbers of part-time jobs to local Aboriginal people in Pmara Jutunta, Nturiya, Ti Tree and Alyuen. This clearly had great potential for making ACGC more relevant and present in the lives of the residents of these settlements. However, the other aspect of ACGC taking on CDEP was somewhat more fraught, as it could easily be seen in Laramba and Engawala as ACGC muscling in on their long-standing, local, autonomous office and CDEP arrangements.

When DEWR awarded the CDEP contract for Laramba and Engawala to ACGC, the CEO knew that they would have to do some work allaying fears and building support in these communities. The local CDEP manager in each place, who doubled as a general office manager, would now for the first time become an ACGC employee, rather than being autonomously employed by a local committee. This new ACGC employee would clearly need to work with the local committees in these places if the new arrangement was to endure. Consequently, ACGC contracted the consultancy firm Burdon-Torzillo to do some 'CDEP governance' work in these two settlements, and we were encouraged to work with them. At the same time, an officer of the NT local government department was charged with the responsibility of consulting constituents about the proposed quorum rule change and helping the Minister ascertain that people were satisfied with it. We became adjuncts to both these processes, travelling frequently to Laramba and Engawala and less often to some of the other outlying settlements.

Our role in the quorum change consultations was educational. We developed some graphics to explain the proposed new quorum rule in comparison to the existing rule, one version of which was designed for notice boards and is reproduced in Fig. 11.3. These graphics seemed to work well as an educational tool and meant that the NT local government department officer had a sounder basis on which to assess that people understood and were supportive of the new rule. Like the Council, constituents seemed pragmatic about the rule change once they understood why council was being repeatedly dismissed. The Minister approved and promulgated the new quorum rule, which came into effect from November 2006.

Fig. 11.3 Graphic of ACGC quorum rules

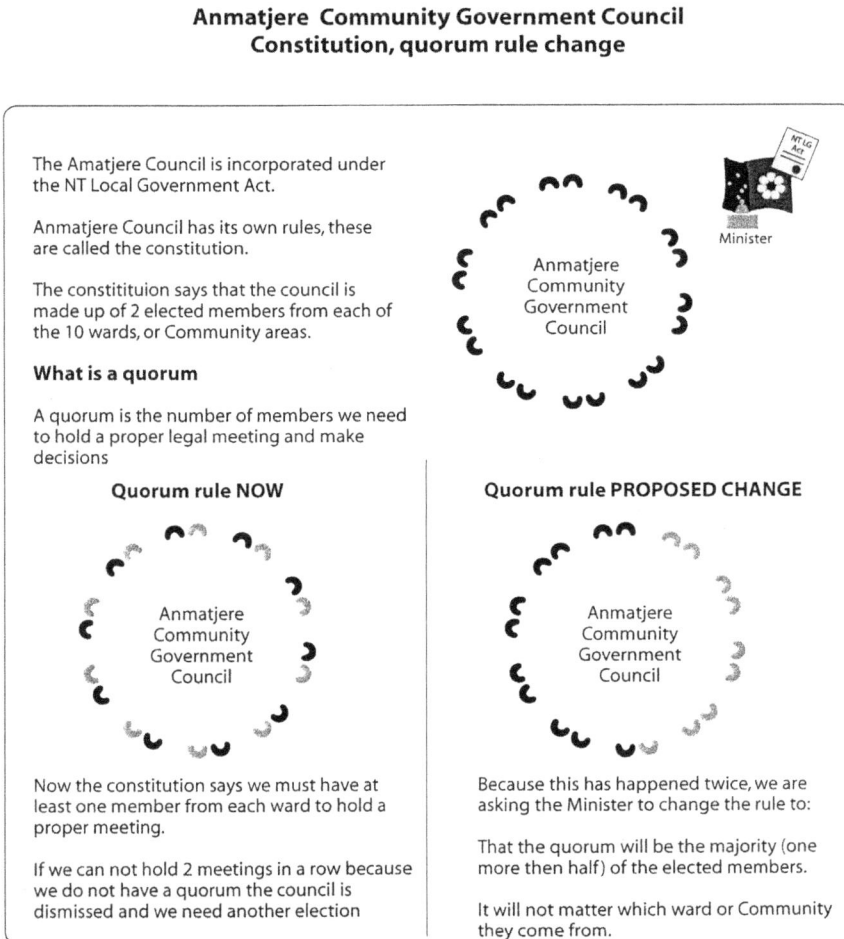

**Anmatjere Community Government Council
Constitution, quorum rule change**

The Amatjere Council is incorporated under the NT Local Government Act.

Anmatjere Council has its own rules, these are called the constitution.

The constituion says that the council is made up of 2 elected members from each of the 10 wards, or Community areas.

What is a quorum

A quorum is the number of members we need to hold a proper legal meeting and make decisions

Anmatjere Community Government Council

Minister

Quorum rule NOW

Anmatjere Community Government Council

Now the constitution says we must have at least one member from each ward to hold a proper meeting.

If we can not hold 2 meetings in a row because we do not have a quorum the council is dismissed and we need another election

Quorum rule PROPOSED CHANGE

Anmatjere Community Government Council

Because this has happened twice, we are asking the Minister to change the rule to:

That the quorum will be the majority (one more then half) of the elected members.

It will not matter which ward or Community they come from.

Source: Diagram developed by Burdon-Torzillo

Our role in the Laramba and Engawala 'CDEP governance' work was largely to assist Burdon-Torzillo in holding discussions with the 'committee' in these two settlements about the new administrative arrangements. In one of these settlements this meant meeting with a relatively small group of local people and in the other it meant large community meetings. In both settlements there were some fears about the changes to CDEP and local office staffing arrangements, but there was also a willingness to work with ACGC on refining the new arrangements. The main concern was to keep some degree of local settlement autonomy in the utilisation of the local CDEP workforce and equipment, and in the running of the local office and other local services. In light of this, Burdon-Torzillo developed the idea of local-regional agreements between ACGC and the two settlement committees, which would be signed by each (see Fig. 11.4). These agreements were developed during the second half of 2006 and signed in December. The significance of this work, however, was as much in the process as the product. The ACGC administration was showing considerable respect for single-settlement localism in dealing specifically with Laramba and Engawala in this way. Indeed, by the end of the process, the CEO was hailing Laramba and Engawala as ACGC's best organised settlements and wondering whether local committees and offices on other settlements could be usefully re-instituted as part of the introduction of CDEP.

Fig. 11.4 Depiction of regional/local relationships in Anmatjere (Source: Burdon-Torzillo)

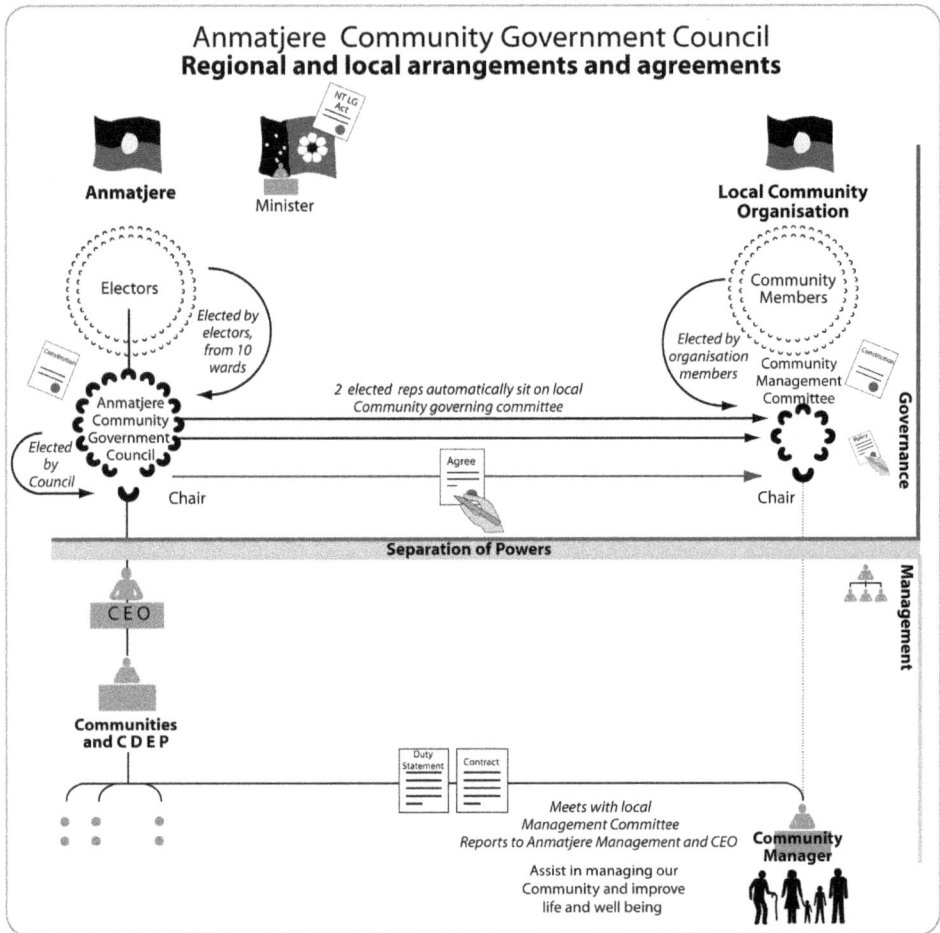

In the later months of 2006, an old settlement office in Pmara Jutunta was indeed refurbished and re-opened as part of the introduction of CDEP. A non-CDEP, settler staff member of ACGC was out-posted to this office for administrative and logistical support, commuting out daily from Ti Tree. A Pmara Jutunta settlement committee was also encouraged and established among CDEP participants, though with a broader remit than just helping organise CDEP in the settlement. Our next 'research' task, looking forward to 2007, was identified as supporting and working with this committee and the out-posted ACGC officer, helping them to address Pmara Jutunta settlement issues and to liaise with council regionally.[10] There was also the suggestion that a similar arrangement might be developed at Nturiya, though that settlement no longer had an old office that could be easily refurbished, nor as yet, a coherent group of CDEP workers who could be drawn on to develop a settlement committee.

At the end of 2006, therefore, ACGC seemed to have rediscovered the need to support strong single-settlement localism within its larger multi-settlement regionalism. This seemed to us a very positive development that in some ways revisited the guarded regional federalism of ACGC's early constitutional design. Laramba and Engawala, rather than being seen as troublesome regional outliers, were now being recognised anew for their autonomous settlement strength. The introduction of CDEP to other ACGC settlements was being seen as an opportunity to reinvigorate their single-settlement strength as well, within the larger regional framework.

Times of change: working with ACGC in 2007

The year 2007 was looming as one of quite considerable change for ACGC. Towards the end of 2006, the CEO had let it be known that he was intending to move on at the expiry of his three-year contract in April 2007, and was therefore instituting a process for recruiting his successor.

Also in October 2006, after many months of rumours, the NT's new, and second Aboriginal local government Minister, The Hon. Elliot McAdam, had announced that there was about to be another round of local government reform. The new framework was to develop municipalities and 'regional shires' that would cover the entire Territory from July 2008, rather than just the piecemeal incorporation of about eight per cent of its land area as under the existing arrangements. While the number of municipalities and shires was not specified, the Minister had stated that:

---

[10] Having moved away from the language of 'governance' to describe our own task and tried the phrase 'issues of importance or concern', we realised in time that council members were simply using the words 'research' and 'researchers' to describe our role. Hence once, when introducing us to a third party, the ACGC Chairman commented: 'We like our researchers, they came with a blank page'. The idea that council could experience 'research' and 'researchers' as similar, irrespective of their substantive interest, and that 'good researchers' are those whose substantive interests are flexible enough to recede from view, raises interesting implications for engagement between academics and Indigenous organisations.

it is evident from research undertaken on the sustainability of local governments in other jurisdictions that a shire of less than 5000 people would struggle to be sustainable in the long term (McAdam 2006: 4).

Clearly, the intention was to move to larger groupings than at present, including for ACGC.

Then in January 2007, Minister McAdam announced that there would be just four municipalities and nine shires, and he published a map of their suggested boundaries (McAdam 2007; see Fig. 11.5). ACGC was to be combined with five other local governing bodies in a Central Desert Shire which would cover a band of land from the Queensland to the Western Australian borders north of Alice Springs. Central Desert Shire's constituency would be about 5,000 people.

A proposal of roughly this sort had been foreshadowed by the CEO at ACGC meetings during the later months of 2006, and when it was announced there was no great sense of surprise, or indeed of hostility, among members. Rather, there seemed to be a sense that restructuring local government is just something that higher levels of government do from time to time. There was also a sense that members would now wait, watch and gradually reposition themselves as the framework was further developed. We suggested that this development increased the importance of having local single-settlement committees operating, as when ACGC disappeared these might become a way in which people living in particular settlements could have some input to and influence on the shire. This diagnosis seemed readily accepted and reinforced the idea that our research task for 2007 would be to encourage and support the work of single-settlement committees.

Another unexpected source of change in March 2007 was the resignation of the ACGC Chairman of the previous two and half years. While the CEO, ourselves and others had all found him a capable and constructive colleague, there were some signs that the pressure of the job was taking a personal toll. Having been picked up by the police for a driving offence, it came to light that the Chairman was still on parole for a more major past offence and should not, by the rules, have been on council for the past two and a half years anyway. The Chairman resigned from council and his younger deputy was thrown into the role of Acting Chairman at precisely the time when the recruitment of the new CEO was reaching its conclusion.

Fig. 11.5 Proposed shires and municipalities in the Northern Territory from July 2008

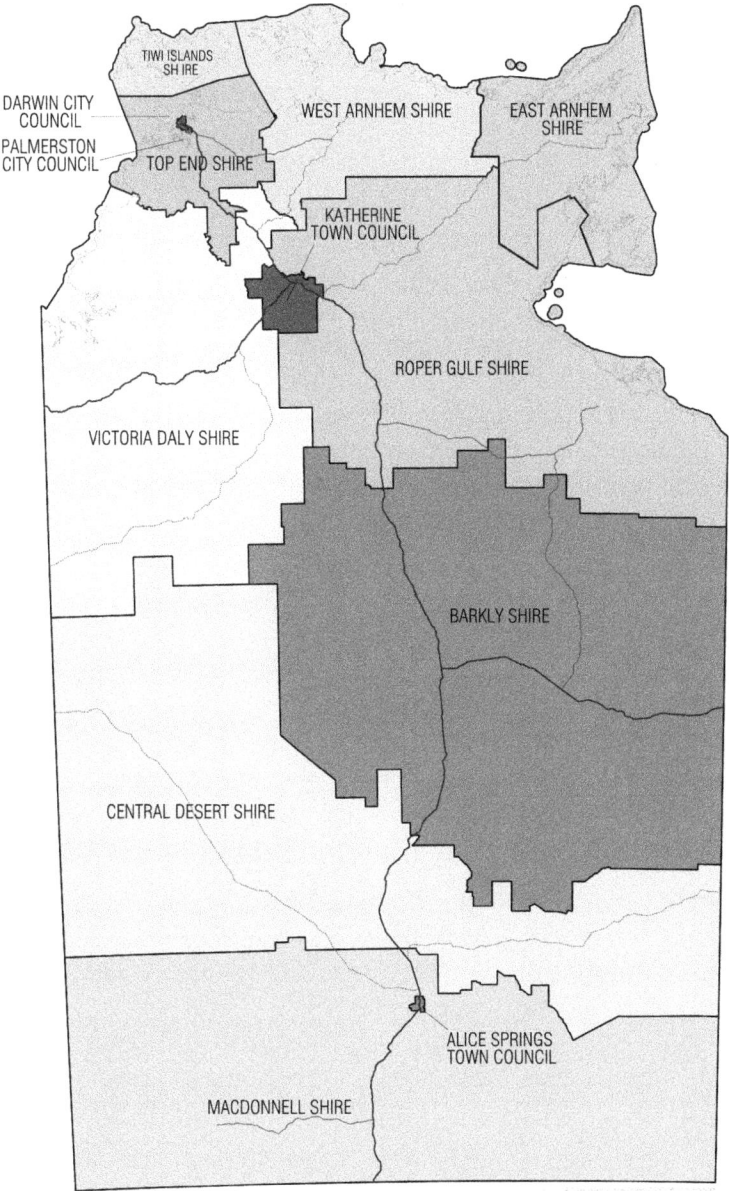

All this was, in fact, handled very smoothly during March 2007, and by the April council meeting both a new CEO and a new Council Chairman were in place. The new Chairman was the previous deputy and the new CEO a woman who had served in a senior managerial post within ACGC for a period of eight months in 2006. There was, thus, a very strong element of continuity in the leadership change at ACGC in April 2007. However, the new CEO clearly also had ideas for change based on her past experience and the new, younger Chairman was also going to put his own stamp on the job.

The final source of change for ACGC in 2007 was the Howard Commonwealth Government's 'national emergency' intervention into NT Aboriginal communities, which was announced on June 21. This comprised 11 areas of proposed change, ranging from alcohol restrictions and compulsory income management in prescribed areas to health checks, increased numbers of police, Commonwealth leases and the end of the permit system in settlements on Aboriginal land, plus the appointment by the Commonwealth of Government Business Managers (Brough 2007). A month later, the intended abolition of the CDEP scheme in the NT over the next year was also announced as a twelfth intervention measure (Brough and Hockey 2007; see also Chapter 2, this volume).

This last intervention measure, in particular, clearly had major implications for ACGC and its growing network of local offices and committees in its discrete Aboriginal settlements. Initially, ACGC was given a CDEP closure date of late October 2007 and informed that participants should be sent on leave before then to serve out their annual leave entitlements. However, in early October ACGC was given a revised CDEP closure date of February 2008. This possibly reflected lobbying from ACGC for the maintenance of CDEP, but also that closures of CDEPs south and west of Alice Springs had been somewhat contested and difficult, and were taking longer than anticipated.

With the defeat of the Howard Coalition Government in November 2007 and the election of the Rudd Labor Government on a platform of continuing the intervention, but reviewing it after 12 months, and of reforming rather than abolishing CDEP, this foreshadowed closure of CDEP in February 2008 has not proceeded. So, the role of CDEP in helping ACGC maintain and develop local settlement offices and committees looks likely to continue until ACGC itself disappears in mid 2008.

On the other intervention measures, ACGC was informed during October 2007 that the Commonwealth now had a lease over at least some of its outlying discrete Aboriginal communities and that it should 'continue to operate' its 'housing service according to existing policies and requirements' until contacted by the relevant Commonwealth department. It was also informed that an Australian Government Business Manager would be starting work in the region from October

29.[11] From the perspective of the ACGC CEO, however, little had resulted from the intervention by that time, except for uncertainty about the future of CDEP and demands for a large number of meetings with visiting Commonwealth officers. No new resources had flowed to ACGC as a result of the intervention.

The larger prospect of change for ACGC at the end of 2007 was still dominated by its foreshadowed amalgamation into Central Desert Shire in the middle of 2008. The ACGC Chairman, CEO and one other councillor had attended shire transition committee meetings during 2007, and a number of decisions had been made. The Anmatjere region will be one of four wards within the Central Desert Shire, with four representatives out of 12, calculated on a rough population basis. The shire is to be headquartered *outside* of its own boundaries in Alice Springs, though there will still be substantial offices focused on service delivery in each of the four wards. Hence, the large ACGC office complex and Council Chambers in Ti Tree will be a shire branch office, rather than a headquarters, even though Ti Tree is geographically quite central within the Central Desert Shire and there was some debate in the transition committee about possibly having a headquarters *within* the shire. These are major changes for Ti Tree and the Anmatjere region, which after 15 years of having its own distinctive regional, multi-settlement local government is about to lose it.

Achievements and limitations: from Anmatjere Community Government Council to Central Desert Shire

I began this chapter by noting how ACGC emerged out of an attempt by the NT Government to encourage regional up-scaling in its local government system and now, 15 years later, how it is set to disappear into the much larger Central Desert Shire as part of another such local government up-scaling exercise. In this final section I will reflect more generally on both ACGC's achievements and its limitations during its 15 year life. I will also speculate a little on how Central Desert Shire might further develop local governance in this region, pointing to differences with ACGC as well as similarities.

ACGC's major achievement of the last 15 years has been holding together and providing basic services to a disparate group of discrete Aboriginal settlements in the Anmatjere region. Though there has at times been tension within the group, none of the settlements has in fact broken away from ACGC. Three of the smaller settlements appear to have withered over this period, but the six other settlements have endured in a useful, and respectful, small regional federation. The level of servicing that ACGC has been able to provide to these enduring settlements has sometimes been rather basic, covering just water, electricity and housing. But, over time, ACGC has also built up its presence in

---

[11] This information was contained in letters to ACGC tabled at the monthly meeting on 24 October 2007.

social services, such as aged care, child care and youth, sport and recreation, as well as in Centrelink support and personal financial services. Since 2006, ACGC has also been able to increase its contribution in the region as a provider of base-level, part-time employment for Aboriginal people through the CDEP scheme. These are modest, but by no means insubstantial achievements for a regional local government in a remote area of the NT.

In the period that Sarah Holcombe and I have observed, ACGC also appears to have overcome some of the worst problems of 'isolated managerialism', whereby very small organisations that rely on just one or two managerial staff, periodically collapse through the departure of a key person. In 2007, we observed an orderly transition from one CEO to the next at ACGC. More generally over the four years, we have also observed a high degree of administrative continuity at ACGC through a managerial team which, at any one time, numbers more like seven or eight people, rather than just one or two. The period that we have observed may not be entirely typical, as in the seven years from 1997 to early 2004, ACGC had six Council Clerks or CEOs, most of whom stayed less than a year. This rate of turnover of senior managers is somewhat worrying, but there does seem to have been basic continuity of administration in ACGC and, as the period 2004–07 has demonstrated, managerial stability can indeed be achieved in an organisation the size of ACGC.

Against these two basic achievements, there can I think be counter-posed an essential failing or limitation of ACGC, which is that it never really achieved a coming together of Aboriginal and settler interests in the Anmatjere region. Such a coming together of interests was certainly the intention of the NT Government when it pushed Ti Tree town and its Progress Association into ACGC in 1995. However, the settler interests of Ti Tree town went into ACGC somewhat unwillingly and have perhaps never really been entirely comfortable within it. I have noted above that in the early days of the research there was one settler member of ACGC for the Ti Tree town ward, but that in mid 2005 this member withdrew due to family commitments and that since then council has been all Aboriginal. Holcombe and I are also aware that in the late 1990s there was another active settler member on council, but by the time of our engagement in 2004 that person had not only left council, but also left town. Hence, there is a sense in which settler interests, as elected members, seemed to withdraw from ACGC after a while, possibly because they found its predominance of Aboriginal members and concerns quite difficult to engage with.[12]

---

[12] This is a speculative comment that suggests a hypothesis to be investigated as much as an argument for which I am giving evidence. Neither Holcombe nor I have had contact with the settler member of ACGC from the 1990s and have only heard of his supposed frustrations with council second hand. The settler member whom we observed in 2004–05 has always emphasised family commitments as the reason for withdrawal.

This limitation of ACGC might seem counter-intuitive in light of our Creek Camp work. For in many ways the central story of that work was that a historical pattern of residential segregation between settler and Aboriginal people in the Anmatjere region was being maintained. Ti Tree town was still essentially the residential area for settlers and Aboriginal people were still generally encouraged to reside in outlying settlements. The fact that ACGC, as the local government body, had predominantly Aboriginal members somehow had not greatly changed this historical pattern of residential segregation. Settler interests still dominated in Ti Tree town, partly through the policies and influence of certain departments of the NT Government. However, ACGC members were also quite hesitant and unsure about whether and how this pattern of residential segregation might change.

Nevertheless, it was the case that settler interests tended to leave the role of elected representatives on ACGC to Aboriginal interests, and that ACGC did not, as a result, realise its full potential as a local governing body that brought together Indigenous and settler interests. One reviewer of an earlier draft of this paper noted that Holcombe and I were undertaking this research as part of an *Indigenous* community governance project and wondered whether we thought local government was in fact an appropriate vehicle through which Aboriginal people could work.[13] My approach has long been that Aboriginal people can and should be able to take opportunities to participate in general political institutions, like local government, as well as Aboriginal-specific organisations, like land councils (Sanders 1996). In a geographic region like Anmatjere, in which over 80 per cent of the resident population is Aboriginal, there is clearly a very good electoral base from which Aboriginal people can participate in general political institutions, and this in no way restricts their ability to also participate in Indigenous-specific institutions.

Under the Central Desert Shire, the issue of mixing Indigenous and settler interests will no doubt arise anew, both in the Anmatjere ward and in the other three wards to the west and east. As it incorporates all land areas, Central Desert Shire could potentially draw in more settler interests than ACGC ever could or did. However, with a constituency that is also over 80 per cent Aboriginal, it is possible that settler interests will also stand back from the Central Desert Shire and that it too will fail to be a meeting place for Indigenous and settler interests in quite the way hoped for by the NT Government. In a sense, what the history of ACGC demonstrates, and what Central Desert Shire may yet in time also demonstrate, is that it is very hard in remote areas of the NT to genuinely combine Indigenous and settler interests in one local government organisation.

---

[13] This issue also came up at the very first council meeting we attended, when the CEO noted that ACGC was not an Indigenous-specific organisation. We acknowledged this, but argued that Indigenous community governance should also be seen as covering situations like ACGC's.

The Central Desert Shire may also face a greater challenge than ACGC even in just bringing together Indigenous interests. Whereas ACGC was named after a single Aboriginal language group, Central Desert Shire also covers the Warlpiri to the west and the Alyawarr and Eastern Arrernte language groups to the east. As well as straddling these four language groups, Central Desert Shire will cover discrete Aboriginal settlements that are over 1000km apart, rather than just 100 or 200km apart as in ACGC. Travelling to centrally located council meetings will be a matter of days, rather than hours, and feeling common interests over such substantial geographic and social distances may also be a considerable challenge. So, Central Desert Shire may need to work even more assiduously than ACGC in bringing together the Indigenous interests of its larger geographic area, and in developing a multi-settlement regionalism that respects and builds on single-settlement localism.

The fundamental argument of this chapter, however, is that ACGC has shown that regional, multi-settlement local government in the remote areas of the NT can survive, can provide representation for diverse Indigenous interests and can offer its residents some useful services, if it respects and builds on the strengths of single-settlement localism. ACGC, as a regional, multi-settlement local government, has worked best when it has valued its constituent settlements for their autonomous, local strength and has worked with them cooperatively. Whether Central Desert Shire will be able to do likewise, across a far larger regional grouping, will only emerge over time and will be of considerable interest to observe.

Postscript

In February 2008, the new Henderson Labor Government in the NT pulled back a little from some of this fore-shadowed local government reform. It announced that the proposed Top End Shire, in the Darwin hinterland, would not proceed and that existing local governments in that area would remain. However, further afield, in remoter areas with fewer settler interests and more predominantly Aboriginal populations, reform of local government was to proceed as planned (Henderson 2008). This change of heart led the Aboriginal local government Minister, The Hon. Elliot McAdam, who had initiated the reform proposal back in late 2006 and early 2007, to resign from the cabinet and ministry. A new non-Indigenous Minister will now oversee the completion of the process.

In Anmatjere and the larger Central Desert Shire area, the local government reform process still looks likely to proceed. Indeed, in February 2008, the new ACGC CEO of 10 months standing left to take up a position in the newly emerging MacDonnell Shire to the south. The new shires were thus beginning to have an effect, simply by drawing experienced managers out of the existing local governments. Administrative continuity was, however, once again maintained at ACGC in February 2008, as the existing social services manager took on the job of CEO for the final four months of its existence.

With all its achievements and limitations, ACGC now seems destined to disappear from the landscape of NT local government in mid 2008. Hopefully, ACGC will be remembered as a modestly successful experiment in multi-settlement regionalism, which respected and built on single-settlement localism.

Acknowledgements

As well as being part of the ICGP supported by the Australian Research Council and Reconciliation Australia under Linkage Project No. 0348744, this work has also been supported by the Australian Government Cooperative Research Centres (CRCs) Programme through the Desert Knowledge CRC, at first through its Governance Theme and later through its Core Project on Sustainable Desert Settlements. The views expressed herein do not necessarily represent the views of the Desert Knowledge CRC or its participants.

References

Ah Kit, J. The Hon. 2003. 'Building stronger regions—stronger futures', Address as NT Minister for Community Development to the Local Government Association of the Northern Territory, 14 May, Alice Springs.

Brough, M. The Hon. 2007. 'National emergency response to protect Aboriginal children in the NT', Media Release by Minister for Families, Community Services and Indigenous Affairs, Australian Government, 21 June, available at <http://www.facsia.gov.au/internet/minister3.nsf/content/emergency_21june07.htm>.

—— and Hockey, J. The Hon. 2007. 'Jobs and training for Indigenous people in the NT', Joint Media Release by Minister for Families, Community Services and Indigenous Affairs and Minister for Employment and Workplace Relations, Australian Government, 23 July, available at <http://www.facsia.gov.au/internet/minister3.nsf/content/cdep_23jul07.htm>.-

Campbell, D. 2001. 'Double exposure: the story of the formation of the Tiwi Islands Local Government', Research paper prepared for the Department of Community Development, Sport and Cultural Affairs, Local Government and Regional Development Division, NT Government, Darwin.

Coburn, W. 1982. 'Aboriginal community councils and the delivery of services', in P. Loveday (ed.), *Service Delivery to Remote Communities*, NARU Monograph, North Australia Research Unit, ANU, Darwin.

Folds, R. 2001. *Crossed Purposes: the Pintupi and Australia's Indigenous Policy*, University of New South Wales Press, Sydney.

Henderson, P. The Hon. 2008. 'Local government changes', Media Release by Chief Minister, Northern Territory Government, 12 February, available at <http://newsroom.nt.gov.au/index.cfm?fuseaction=viewRelease&id= 3598&d=>.

Holcombe, S. and Sanders, W. 2007. 'Accommodating difference? The socio-politics of an Aboriginal fringe camp in a small north Australian town', *The International Journal of Interdisciplinary Social Sciences*, 2: 339–48.

Legislative Assembly of the Northern Territory (LANT). 1993a. *Parliamentary Record No. 16*, Sixth Assembly, First Session, 26 May 1993, Darwin.

———1993b. *Parliamentary Record No. 17*, Sixth Assembly, First Session, 29 June 1993, Darwin.

———1995a. *Parliamentary Record No. 14*, Seventh Assembly, First Session, 22 August 1995, Darwin.

———1995b. *Parliamentary Record No. 14*, Seventh Assembly, First Session, 23 August 1995, Darwin.

———1999. *Parliamentary Record No. 14*, Eighth Assembly, First Session, 17 February 1999, Darwin.

———2002a. *Parliamentary Record No. 3*, Ninth Assembly, First Session, 28 February 2002, Darwin.

———2002b. *Parliamentary Record No. 3*, Ninth Assembly, First Session, 7 March 2002, Darwin.

———2002c. *Parliamentary Record No. 4*, Ninth Assembly, First Session, 21 May 2002, Darwin.

———2003. Ministerial Statement, Building Stronger Regions—Stronger Futures, *Parliamentary Record No. 6*, Ninth Assembly, First Session, 20 August 2003, Darwin.

McAdam, E. The Hon. 2006. 'Minister's Speech' as Minister for Local Government, *Local Government Association of the Northern Territory (LGANT) Conference*, 11 October, Alice Springs, available at <http://www.localgovernment.nt.gov.au/new/minister/ministers_speech>.

McAdam, E. The Hon. 2007. 'New local government structure announced', Media Release by Minister for Local Government, Northern Territory Government, 30 January, available at <http://newsroom.nt.gov.au/ index.cfm?fuseaction=viewRelease&id=1319&d=5>.

Morton, J. 1994. The Proposed Anmatjere Land Council: Its Historical Antecedents and an Estimation of Levels of Support, Unpublished report to ATSIC, Canberra.

Northern Territory Government 2003. *Building Stronger Regions—Stronger Futures: Northern Territory*, Department of Community Development, Sport and Cultural Affairs, Darwin.

Phegan, G. 1989. 'Community government models for small towns in the Northern Territory', in P. Loveday and A. Webb (eds), *Small Towns in Northern Australia*, NARU Monograph, North Australia Research Unit, ANU, Darwin.

Sanders, W. 1996. 'Local governments and Indigenous Australians: developments and dilemmas in contrasting circumstances', *Australian Journal of Political Science*, 31 (2): 153–74.

——2005. 'Dispersal, autonomy and scale in Indigenous community governance: some reflections on recent Northern Territory experience', *Australian Journal of Public Administration*, 64 (4): 53–62.

——2006a. 'Being a good senior manager in Indigenous community governance: working with public purpose and private benefit', *CAEPR Discussion Paper No. 280*, CAEPR, ANU, Canberra.

——2006b. 'Local governments and Indigenous interests in Australia's Northern Territory', *CAEPR Discussion Paper No. 285*, CAEPR, ANU, Canberra.

—— and Holcombe, S. 2007. 'The Ti Tree Creek Camp study: a contribution to good governance', *Ngiya: Talk the Law*, 1: 71–91.

Wolfe, J. 1989. *'That Community Government Mob': Local Government in Small Northern Territory Communities*, North Australia Research Unit, ANU, Darwin.

Part 5: Rebuilding governance

12. Incorporating cattle: governance and an Aboriginal pastoral enterprise

Christina Lange

Drought and dying cattle have always been part of life on pastoral stations in Australia. Banjo Paterson's poem from 1896 captures the desperation of droving cattle to greener pastures in times of drought:

> We cannot use the whip for shame
> On beasts that crawl along;
> We have to drop the weak and lame,
> And try to save the strong;
> The wrath of God is on the track,
> The drought fiend holds his sway,
> With blows and cries and stockwhip crack
> We take the stock away.
> As they fall we leave them lying,
> With the crows to watch them dying,
> Grim sextons of the Overland that fasten on their prey ...
> (Paterson 1896).

On a more contemporary note, the manager of a family run cattle station near Meekatharra in the Murchison Gascoyne region of Western Australia (WA), articulates the inevitability of losing some cattle during periods of extended drought: 'It can be tough during drought years having to deal with the pressure of dying cattle and dragging animals out of dams'.[1]

In early February 2005, the WA Department of Agriculture and Food (DAFWA) received a complaint about animal neglect on an Aboriginal owned pastoral lease in the northeastern goldfields region of WA. A chain of bureaucratic responses flowed from this complaint. These responses included intervention by the Royal Society for the Prevention of Cruelty to Animals (RSPCA) Western Australia Inc; a proposal by the State Government to forfeit the lease; an investigation by the Office of the Registrar of Aboriginal Corporations (ORAC);[2] issuance of a care, control and management order over the station by the Pastoral Lands Board (PLB); and intervention by the Indigenous Land Corporation (ILC) and DAFWA.

---

[1] Getaccess, n.d., 'Cattle station manager—Ben Forsyth', Government of Western Australia, available at <http://www.getaccess.com.au/careers/myjob/data/BenForsyth.asp?> [accessed 13 July 2007].
[2] As of 1 May 2008, this Australian Government office is now called the Office of the Registrar of Indigenous Corporations.

This chapter explores the role of Aboriginal governance at the intersection between economic activity, corporate responsibility and community aspiration. A lack of attention to governance issues contributed to the problems experienced by the lessees. The preparedness of the community to refine its understanding of its corporate responsibilities, fuelled by an unwavering determination to retain its pastoral enterprise, was instrumental in the resolution of the issue. This chapter also touches on tensions within the community and the pastoral industry relating to Aboriginal pastoralism.

In WA, the 'pastoral industry' refers to the 'grazing industry which occurs on sheep and cattle stations in more remote areas of the state'.[3] The PLB has the statutory authority under the *Lands Administration Act 1997* (LAA) to administer pastoral leases. Under s.96 of the LAA, the relevant minister, currently the Minister for Planning and Infrastructure, has the power to direct the PLB with respect to the exercise of its powers. The PLB is required by the LAA (s.137) to establish an 'administrative mechanism' with the Commissioner for Soil and Land Conservation to exchange relevant information about pastoral lease holdings.[4] In discharging this responsibility, the Commissioner, through DAFWA, provides an annual report to the PLB on the current condition of land under pastoral lease, and also provides ad hoc reports at the request of the PLB. In 2006, DAFWA prepared 116 reports to the PLB (DAFWA 2006: iii). This high level of exchange of information between the agencies is indicative of a significant sharing of responsibility for pastoral rangelands.

PLB figures show that as at July 2007 there were '527 pastoral leases covering 474 pastoral stations'.[5] Pastoral leases held by Aboriginal entities account for approximately 12 per cent of pastoral leases in WA. The majority (39) of these leases are in the Kimberley region. However, there are a further 26 Aboriginal owned leases in the regions south of the Kimberley.

Windidda Station, the Aboriginal owned pastoral lease that is the subject of this chapter, is situated in the Shire of Wiluna approximately 200km east of the town of Wiluna (Fig. 12.1). The town lies close to the western border of the shire boundary and is the only town in the shire. It is approximately 1000km northeast of Perth, and 550km north of the regional centre of Kalgoorlie. The town is the starting point of both the Canning Stock Route, which runs northeast to Halls Creek, and the Gunbarrel Highway, which runs east to Warburton.

---

[3] Department of Planning and Infrastructure (DPI) website, 'Western Australia's Pastoral Industry', Government of Western Australia, available at <http://www.dpi.wa.gov.au/pastoral/1597.asp> [accessed 3 July 2007].

[4] The position of the Commissioner of Soil and Land Conservation is established by the *Soil and Land Conservation Act 1945* (WA). The Commissioner administers the Act for the Minister of Agriculture.

[5] DPI website, 'Western Australia's Pastoral Industry', Government of Western Australia, last updated 9 January 2006, available at <http://www.dpi.wa.gov.au/pastoral/1597.asp> [accessed 3 July 2007]. The differences in the figures indicate that some pastoral stations consist of more than one lease.

Fig. 12.1 Location of the local government Shire of Wiluna and the township of Wiluna, WA

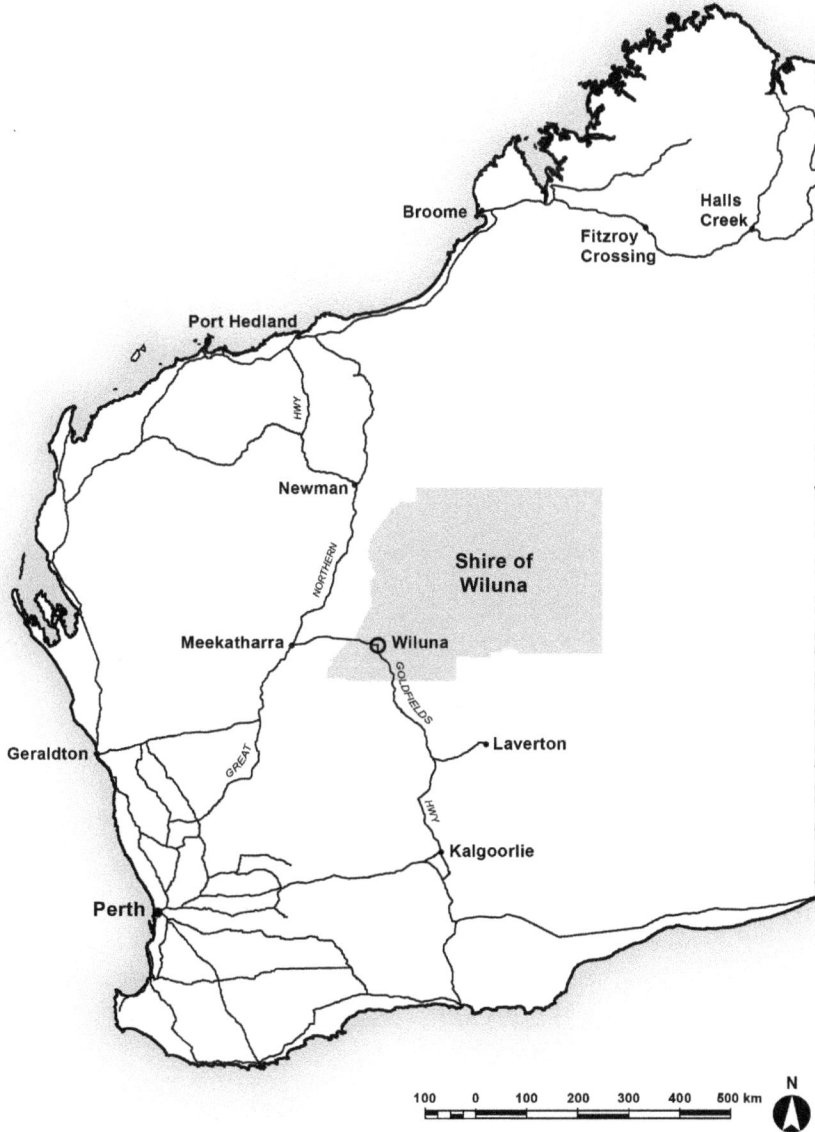

I have been involved with this community since 2005 through my PhD research undertaken in Wiluna, and I also had contact with members of Aboriginal families from Wiluna while working on a native title claim to the south of Wiluna from 2001–04. From late 2005 and throughout the period discussed in this paper, I provided mentoring to the Windidda community and continue to do so. During 2007, I was engaged as a consultant trainer to deliver governance training to Windidda community members.

The Shire of Wiluna covers an area of 184,000km^2 and is predominantly mining and pastoral land. Mining and pastoralism are part of the 'culture' of the Shire. There has been a merging of the pastoral and mining industries through the acquisition of pastoral stations by mining companies in the region. The lack of conformity in the way different agencies categorise pastoral lands creates difficulties in the compilation of data for a more concise area, such as within a shire boundary.[6] However, research reveals that there are 27 pastoral leases within the Wiluna Shire.[7] Ten leases are owned by mining companies, some of which have been destocked. The WA Department of Environment and Conservation (DEC) has acquired two of the leases, which have been fully destocked and are run as nature reserves.[8] The remaining 15 leases are held by family groups or pastoral companies. The Windidda lease is included in this category.

Windidda Station was once part of a larger pastoral station owned by three brothers. In 1992, the large leaseholding was broken up into three smaller leases.[9] The Windidda lease of 384,000 hectares was purchased at that time by Ngangganawili Community Incorporated (henceforth Ngangganawili), an organisation set up by Aboriginal people in Wiluna. The lease was purchased without any government assistance; funds for the purchase were obtained 'from people saving up for it through a chuck in account'.[10] It is the only Aboriginal owned pastoral lease in the shire.

Around 1994, Ngangganawili was wound up and its assets distributed to the three dominant kin based groups in Wiluna. The pastoral lease was one of the assets distributed. The extended family group that acquired the lease had a long association with the area previously covered by the original three leases, and a senior member was born and later worked on the leases. In common with the

---

[6] For instance, the PLB refers to three regions—the Kimberley, Pilbara, and 'the Gascoyne, Murchison, Goldfields and Nullabor'—and DAFWA refers to two broad categories—the 'northern rangelands' and the 'southern rangelands'. There is some conformity between the 'Kimberley' and the 'northern rangelands', but for areas south of the Kimberley it is difficult to correlate data.

[7] This means that there is a margin for error as my data have been compiled from a range of sources, including from informants with a long association with the industry in the shire.

[8] DEC has entered into joint management negotiations with the native title applicants' representative relating to the leases.

[9] One brother retained one of the leases and still runs it.

[10] Windidda Aboriginal Corporation committee member, pers. comm., 2006.

other family groups to whom Ngangganawili's assets were distributed, it was necessary for this group to become incorporated in order to hold the assets and to receive Australian Government funding for infrastructure. The group incorporated as Windidda Aboriginal Corporation (WAC) under the Commonwealth *Aboriginal Councils and Associations Act 1976* (ACAA) in 1994.[11]

The transfer of the pastoral lease from Ngangganawili to the newly formed Aboriginal organisation was not properly completed at that time or subsequently. Ngangganawili remained on the books as the leaseholder until the lease reverted to the Commissioner for Fair Trading under the provisions of the *Associations Incorporation Act 1997* (WA).

WAC members were apparently aware that the lease had not been put into the corporation's name but understood that 'DIA were doing something about it'.[12] This view appears to be justified by a Department of Indigenous Affairs (DIA) report which states that the DIA 'Land Branch is arranging [for the] Pastoral Lands Board and Commissioner for Trading [sic] to transfer [the] pastoral lease' (DIA 2004).

Since 1994, WAC has run the station, paid the rates and taxes, and seen itself—and has been acknowledged by others including government agencies—as the owner of the lease. Between 15 and 40 community members live and work on the pastoral lease. In common with most Aboriginal owned leases, the station workers were participants in the Community Development Employment Projects (CDEP) program.

The failure by WAC to ensure that the lease was properly transferred in the intervening years was a sign that something was amiss in the governance process of the corporation. The lack of attention to the transfer also points to some other realities: that land tenure and the transfer of land are arcane to most of us, that these matters are usually left in the hands of people with experience in conveyancing; that in remote areas it is difficult to gain access to professional services; and that there was an underlying assumption that government agencies would conclude the transfer as part of their bureaucratic processes.

Regardless of the perceptions held by the corporation or its understanding of bureaucratic processes, securing the lease in its own name was an important matter that should have been pursued more diligently. It was in the corporation's interests to have done so.

When a complaint was made to DAFWA in early February 2005 that there was insufficient water for the cattle on the lease, the region was in a period of drought. DAFWA (2005: 19–21) stated in its 2005 annual report to the PLB that:

---

[11] On 1 July 2007, the ACAA was replaced by a new package of laws called the *Corporations (Aboriginal and Torres Strait Islanders) Act 2006* (Cth) (CATSIA).

[12] WAC committee member, pers. comm., March 2005.

'To the east of Meekatharra, around Wiluna the run of good seasons ending ... resulted in a number of properties moving stock out of the district in response to the very dry conditions'.

A Bureau of Meteorology (BOM) rainfall deciles[13] map for the period 1 January to 30 June 2005 shows that rainfall in the area of the pastoral lease was 'very much below average', and that rainfall just to the east of the station was the 'lowest on record'.[14]

The complaint to DAFWA triggered a cascade of events over the following months:

February 2005

- DAFWA referred the complaint to the RSPCA;
- the RSPCA seized the cattle at the pastoral station;
- PLB placed the pastoral lease under a temporary care, control and management order; and
- cattle were mustered from the station by the RSPCA, transported to Geraldton and sold.

February–May 2005

- extensive media coverage focused on 'dead cattle' and 'Aboriginal leaseholders'; and
- questions in Parliament suggested that the Minister should rescind the lease.

May 2005

- WAC was advised by ORAC that its affairs would be investigated under s.60 of the ACAA.

November 2005

- charges were laid against the corporation and three members by the RSPCA.

This was not the first time concerns about the station had been raised. There had been a previous occasion, in December 2002, when DAFWA had cause to assess rangeland conditions on the lease and report to the PLB. Following that report, the PLB requested that the corporation prepare and submit a management plan, but this request had not been complied with.

On any assessment, the organisation was in trouble. It was in danger of forfeiting its pastoral lease and thereby losing an asset that was the foundation of its

---

[13] Deciles provide a measure of the spread of rainfall experiences in the past. Rainfall in a current year can be compared against decile information to see where it stands in relation to historical records. The BOM generally categorises rainfall as 'below average', 'average' and 'above average'. 'Below' and 'above' average' rainfall are sometimes further categorised according to the degree of deviation from the average.
[14] BOM website, 'Western Australian Rainfall Deciles 1 January to 30 June 2005', available at <http://www.bom.gov.au> [accessed 19 July 2007].

community and work life; it was facing prosecution by the RSPCA; and it was being investigated by the corporate regulator. It was also the subject of a negative media campaign that by any objective criterion was distorting the facts.

The remainder of this chapter takes a closer look at these events and at the remedial strategies that enabled the organisation to favourably resolve the situation over an 18 month period.

RSPCA

DAFWA had referred the complaint that there was insufficient water for cattle on the station to the regional RSPCA office on 8 February 2005. Over the next week, RSPCA officers visited the station and inspected the watering points. In the period they were on the station, the daily temperature was averaging around 41°C. The officers noted that a number of the watering points appeared to have been de-commissioned and others were not fully operational. In the officers' opinion, the watering points on the station were not producing enough water to sustain the cattle. At many of the watering points only minor repairs were necessary to make them productive. The RSPCA subsequently made arrangements for water to be carted to the station.

On 16 February 2005, the RSPCA seized the cattle on the station under s.42(1)(a) of the *Animal Welfare Act 2002* (WA). On 18 February, the Minister transferred temporary care and control of the station to the PLB.

Following these actions, there was a period of negotiation between WAC, the RSPCA, and the PLB to reach agreement on how to resolve the issue. The community was assisted in these negotiations by a legal representative arranged by the Goldfields Land and Sea Council. Agreement was reached on 3 March 2005 that the cattle would be mustered and sold and the proceeds, less costs, would be returned to the corporation.

The muster was completed by 18 March, six weeks after the complaint. The RSPCA mustered 'just over 1800 head of cattle from the station' (Grieve 2005c). The cattle were understood to be in good condition when they arrived at the sale yards, a fact supported by the good sale price received.

The WAC and three of its members were each charged under s.19(3)(d) of the *Animal Welfare Act 2002*. The charge was that the corporation and each member, '[b]eing a person in charge of animals, namely approximately 1500 head of cattle, was cruel to the animals as they were not provided with proper and sufficient water' (Magistrates Court 2005). The Aboriginal Legal Service provided legal representation when the case was heard in the Magistrates Court in May 2006. A plea bargain saw the charges against the three members of the corporation dropped in exchange for a guilty plea by the corporation. The corporation was fined $10,000 and ordered to pay costs.[15]

An independent assessment of the condition of station infrastructure and the peril of the cattle raises the possibility that the RSPCA's initial response to the allegation of insufficient water on the lease, may have been disproportionate (Centre for Management of Arid Environments 2006). In fact, the RSPCA's statement of material facts read out in the court hearing stated only that 'some dead animals were sighted' when its officers went the station in February. The statement did not identify whether the 'dead animals' were cattle or feral animals. Similarly, all the initial media reports, including RSPCA media comment, sensationalised the incident by claiming that large numbers of dead cattle had been found on an Aboriginal-run station. The following extracts from some of the media reports at the time show it took a while for accurate reports to be given coverage:

> [RSPCA] Spokeswoman ... says the pastoral lease, about 200 kilometres east of Wiluna, is held by an Aboriginal corporation, and it's the second time in 12 months the RPSCA has had to intervene (ABC Rural 2005).[16]

> You might recall, last week, RSPCA inspectors found around five hundred cattle dead on Windidda Station and a further 2500 in need of assistance (Grieve 2005b).

> The pastoral lease for a remote West Australian station where 500 cattle were found dead and another 2,500 were struggling to survive must immediately be cancelled, a parliamentarian and a farmers' group said today (AAP 2005).

Later in the same press article, the president of the Pastoralists and Graziers Association stated his view that:

> Obviously the lease has got to be taken off them immediately, the cattle removed and the fines that everyone else has to stand by have to be enforced for them as well ... There can't be one rule for Aboriginal stations and one rule for the white stations (AAP 2005).

These media reports show that the Aboriginality of the station management was a significant factor in the outcry about the incident.

By early March, the dead cattle were now only in 'the tens': 'Initial estimates of animal fatalities on the property, provided by State Government staff, appear

---

[15] Plea bargaining is not unusual in this type of legal proceedings. In this case, concessions were made by the defence and prosecution to expedite the process, protect individuals and arrive at an outcome that all could live with.

[16] This statement by the RSPCA is incorrect. The last intervention was in 2002.

to have been high and ongoing assessment suggests the actual figure would be in the tens rather than the hundreds' (RSPCA 2005).

By mid April reports were more circumspect: '[B]ack in February, the RSPCA found a number of dead cattle on the station' (Grieve 2005a).

The fact that a large number of healthy cattle were mustered from the 385,000 hectare property in the last month of summer, following a period of high temperatures and 'very much below average rainfall', is jarringly at odds with the media reports and public statements made by the RSPCA and other instrumentalities about the extent of animal neglect.

The Pastoral Lands Board

A care and control order issued in February 2005 transferred responsibility for the running of the station to the PLB. The order was to stay in place until the PLB was satisfied that satisfactory care, control and management of the land had been demonstrated by the community.

Following the imposition of the order, the relevant Minister advised the corporation that she intended to go further and rescind the lease. The corporation, through the Goldfields and Sea Council, appealed this decision. The appeal was supported by the independent assessment of the station, which showed that the watering points were generally in sound condition and able to support the station's requirements. The appeal also set out concerns expressed by members of the community that the pumps and bores had been vandalised by outsiders prior to the initial complaint. The RSPCA's statement to the court could be construed as supporting this possibility. It describes how only minor repairs were required to get a number of the watering points back into working order. It stated that wires had been disconnected from some solar pumps, which made them inoperable, and animals were found in a couple of wells, which contaminated the water. The RSPCA attributed these problems to a lack of regular maintenance. The community did not disagree entirely with this view, acknowledging that it had experienced difficulty at times attending to the maintenance of all the watering points on the station. However, community members also believed that there had been acts of sabotage that had interfered with the operation of the wells. For example, the community members pointed out that the animals down the wells cited by the RSPCA were kangaroos that had been shot and then placed there.

Attention to governance issues, particularly in regard to decision making, planning and maintenance of the pastoral station, was identified by the PLB and accepted by the Minister as fundamental to the question of the corporation regaining control of the lease. The Minister demonstrated some confidence in the community by advising that she would 'consider deferring forfeiture action to give the Windidda community the chance to show it can implement an acceptable management plan for the station' (ABC News 2005).

The WAC was required to satisfy a number of conditions, initially to forestall the forfeiture and, in the event that this was successful, further actions would be required to meet the conditions for the transfer of a pastoral lease. In this regard, the PLB had responsibility for assessing the competence of the community to run the lease and for providing advice to the Minister prior to a decision being made about the transfer of the lease.

Just as the community were coming to terms with these events, another hurdle arose. In June 2005, ORAC advised the WAC that it had authorised an examination of its affairs under its statutory powers.

Office of the Registrar of Aboriginal Corporations

ORAC has a range of regulatory powers under the ACAA, including power under s.60 to examine the documents of a corporation and to report on any financial irregularities.[17] The genesis of this particular s.60 examination is unclear. It was possibly undertaken as part of ORAC's 'program of rolling examinations', under which 61 corporations were investigated in the 2004–05 financial year (Department of Immigration, Multicultural and Indigenous Affairs (DIMIA) 2005: 335). ORAC also acts on complaints about corporations from other bodies, and it is probable that the s.60 examination was triggered by the PLB raising concerns about the governance of the corporation in relation to the pastoral lease.

ORAC's standard terms of reference for a s.60 investigation require the examiner to:

(a) Assess the level of the Corporation's compliance with its Constitution and the Act.

(b) Assess the viability/solvency of the Corporation.

(c) Check whether any conflicts of interest exist within the Governing Committee.

(d) Report any lack of control, direction and overall management of the affairs of the Corporation by the Governing Committee.

(e) Report on the ability of the Governing Committee and staff to deliver an effective standard of services to its members and the community.[18]

---

[17] Section 60 of the ACAA states that: 'The Registrar may, at any time, cause a person authorised by the Registrar for the purposes of this section to examine the documents of an Incorporated Aboriginal Association and to report to the Registrar on the results of that examination, drawing attention to any irregularity in the operations or financial affairs of the Association disclosed by that examination'.

[18] This document, entitled 'Terms of Reference of the proposed examination of [name removed by ORAC] Aboriginal Corporation', ORAC 2005, was provided to me by ORAC as an example of the terms of reference for a s.60 examination. Under the CATSIA 2006 (see Chapter 10, parts 10.2–10.4), the Registrar has more extensive regulatory and enforcement powers.

The s.60 investigation was carried out in September and October 2005, and the Examiner presented his final report to ORAC in December 2005.

It is relevant to note at this point that the community had been running the lease and the corporation over the past 12 years with little or no assistance or intervention from WA or Australian Government agencies. The members of the governing committee had assumed—not unreasonably under these circumstances—that since they had not attracted any interest from the regulatory body or the funding bodies, they were adequately fulfilling their responsibilities. The previous attention they had attracted from the PLB appeared to have settled of its own accord.

Staying under the regulatory body's radar is relatively formulaic for a small organisation once it has been set up; namely, hold a general meeting and elect a governing committee on an annual basis, and if possible apply for exemptions for the lodgement of annual reporting requirements. ORAC has a realistic understanding that many organisations receive little or no funding and therefore 'have no capacity to apply for an exemption' (DIMIA 2005: 326). In fact, non-compliance has been the norm under the AACA. In the 2004–05 financial year, ORAC reported that over 60 per cent of corporations were 'not fully or partially compliant' and less than 30 per cent were 'fully compliant' (DIMIA 2005: 326). WAC's records indicate that in most years it would fall into the category of 'partially compliant'. It held general meetings and elected a governing committee on a regular basis throughout its incorporation, and either fulfilled or had been exempted from most of its reporting requirements.

In March 2006, the Registrar advised the organisation that 'the examination identified many instances where the Corporation has not complied with the Act and the Rules of the Corporation's Constitution', and that a notice under s.60A of the ACAA would be issued.[19] The notice required the corporation to remedy a number of matters within a 28 day period. The matters that needed to be addressed focused mainly on the need for the governing committee to exercise greater control of financial and administrative record keeping. The s.60A notice stated that 'due to inexperience, members of the Governing Committee may not understand the importance of some of the requirements of the ACAA and [the] Constitution, and the reasons behind each rule'.

Receipt of the notice challenged the community's assumption that a lack of interest from the regulatory body equated to the satisfactory fulfilment of

---

[19] Section 60A of the ACAA states that: 'If the Registrar suspects on reasonable grounds that: (a) an Incorporated Aboriginal Association has failed to comply with a provision of this Act, the regulations or the Rules; or (b) there has been an irregularity in the financial affairs of an Incorporated Aboriginal Association; the Registrar may, by notice served on the public officer, require the Governing Committee to take the action specified in the notice within the period specified in the notice, for the purpose of complying with the Act, the regulations or the Rules or remedying the irregularity, as the case may be'.

corporate responsibilities. The serving of the notice also demonstrated that incorporation under the AACA was more complex and far reaching than the community had previously contemplated.

The PLB had assumed responsibility for the lease under the management order and in September 2005 put a manager on the station for a six month period. The PLB had advised the community that it must develop a comprehensive management plan for the future operation of the station and to be able to demonstrate its capacity to put in place best practice management standards on a day–to-day and long term basis.

Following the issuance of ORAC's s.60A notice, the PLB advised that a further condition for transfer was that the corporation had fully complied with ORAC's requirements under the s.60A notice.

Support for the community

In a relatively short period of time, the community had been confronted with a series of challenging incidents: its organisation and three of its members faced prosecution under the *Animal Welfare Act 2002* (WA); it was required to fulfil a bewildering array of conditions imposed by ORAC to prevent the corporation being deregistered; and the PLB had outlined a series of steps that it would need to take to regain control of the lease. In addition, the ground rules had shifted. It was becoming increasingly clear that the running of the corporation and the running of the pastoral lease, which had previously been ticking along without attracting any sustained attention, had been scrutinised in a new and more searching way, and had been found wanting. This time, the problems would not slowly dissipate over time but would require sustained action to overcome them.

The community saw that many of its difficulties could be attributed to a combination of farm management and governance problems, in particular, decision making and the implementation of decisions. This encompassed the need to plan for and develop budgets for maintenance and improvements on the station, to ensure work was carried out at the right time and was properly supervised, and all aspects of record keeping.

The dilemma facing the community was that these adverse events posed a real threat to its ongoing stability, and it had little or no resources on which to draw to fulfil the array of conditions that had been imposed and thus successfully extricate itself from its situation.

Over this period of crisis, assistance for the community came from a number of sources. The Goldfields Land and Sea Council[20] provided advocacy support for the community in its dealing with the RSPCA, the PLB and the Minister. This support included regular reporting to the PLB on the progress the community was making and interceding on its behalf when necessary to forestall unwanted actions.

I worked with the governing committee of the WAC throughout 2006 as it progressively dealt with the issues identified in the s.60A notice from ORAC. In November 2006, ORAC confirmed that the committee had satisfactorily addressed all the actions set out in the notice. Concurrently, the ILC funded a facilitated group planning session for the community so that it could outline and document its plans for the lease. Following the workshop, the community's aspirations were paired with the PLB's requirements for the transfer of the lease, and a package of planning, reporting and training was developed. At this point, FarmBis, a partnership between the WA and Australian Governments that supports training in land and business management,[21] provided training support for the community. FarmBis and the ILC jointly funded a comprehensive training package covering on-farm skills and governance training for community members and the governing committee. These training packages were designed specifically to match the training needs of the community and were delivered over a 12 month period.

FarmBis approached its relationship with the community as a partnership that shared the goal of reaching a point where the corporation could run the station as a strong and financially successful pastoral business. A principal objective for the training package was to get the corporation ready to take part in an Indigenous Management Support Services project run by DAFWA and jointly funded by ILC. This project, which has been operating successfully in the Kimberley and Pilbara, provides an Agriculture Department adviser to work closely with the community to improve pastoral station management practices and to increase the quality and quantity of the cattle herd. The reciprocity in this partnership was that FarmBis brought the training and the opportunity to be involved in the management service support project to the table, and in return the community demonstrated its commitment by attending and contributing to the extensive training programs, and putting the new information into practice. Qualifying to be 'project ready', that is, part of the Indigenous Management Support Services project, was a powerful incentive for community members to actively participate over the many months of training.

---

[20] Although Ngaanyatjarra Council was the representative body for the Wiluna area at the time, there was an agreement between Ngaanyatjarra Council and the Goldfields Land and Sea Council that the latter would provide support to the community on this matter.
[21] In WA, FarmBis is administered by DAFWA.

The governance training component involved sixteen days of face-to-face training, delivered in Wiluna and on the pastoral station, between June and November 2007. In this training program, the ambit of 'governance' encompassed more than a narrow focus on compliance. Governance was presented comprising a bundle of tools that the community could use to move its aspirations beyond the planning phase into reality. With this perspective in mind, the community used the training sessions to explore its proposals for future development on the lease and drew on the tools of governance to forge a way forward.

Incorporation and the community

In common with many Aboriginal organisations that incorporated in the last two decades, the need to incorporate was externally driven rather than arising from the community's desire to be part of the mainstream, corporate world. Arguably, the motivation for incorporation affects the way the community understands the relationship between its aspirations and its corporation, and between its corporation and the requirements of the ACAA. The s.60A notice raised some issues about the governing committee's understanding about the interaction between community activities and corporate identity. The community had used incorporation in 1994 to achieve practical outcomes, which were: (a) to hold the pastoral lease when Ngangganawili, the larger community organisation, was dissolved; and (b) to attract funding for community infrastructure and essential services associated with maintaining the pastoral station. However, the identity of the incorporated body was merged with the identity of the community, rather than being seen as an entity separate from the community. Working with the community as it grappled with a range of governance issues, it became clear that it was important to appreciate the interplay between 'community', 'members' and 'the corporation', and to engage the participants in identifying the components of each of these concepts and to disengage each from the other.

An example of the interrelatedness between corporate responsibilities and community activity arose during discussion with the committee about the level of financial record keeping required under the ACAA. The governing committee was surprised and concerned to learn that it was required to provide details of all the corporation's financial transactions to ORAC, including what it termed 'community money'. The need for accountability of government funds to government was not disputed, but the committee made a distinction between 'government money' and 'community money'. The committee's view was that ORAC should only be interested in 'government money', that is, the funding allocated to the community by the regional resource agency.[22] 'Community

---

[22] The regional resource agency applied to relevant government departments for funding for the 13 communities it serviced. The resource agency also acquitted these funds. From its funding pool it

money' was money collected and used for the running of 'community' aspects of life on the pastoral station. An example of 'community money' is 'chuck in', which refers to money deducted from each community member's CDEP payments to fund a range of activities, such as attendance at funerals, the purchase of food supplies in bulk, rent and repairs. The committee felt it was inappropriate and unnecessary for 'community money', which was carefully accounted for, to be subjected to public scrutiny through the ORAC reporting process. However, the complication was that since the funds were held in bank accounts in the corporation's name, they were therefore seen as corporation funds and corporations are required to report to ORAC on all activities undertaken in its name.

On the one hand, the notions of 'the community' and 'the organisation' had been conflated by depositing all the funds in the corporation's name, yet on the other hand, there was a desire to maintain the autonomy of 'the community' and to shield it from the public arena of corporate reporting. The reality of day-to-day community life, compared to the requirements of bureaucratic reporting, illustrates that the distinction between community and corporation is an artificial one from a community perspective, and one that is not always easily achieved. For example, there is the practical difficulty of finding an alternative 'body', other than the corporation or an individual, to establish an account to hold the funds of this nature and to distribute them when appropriate.

On 26 November 2007, the Minister wrote to the most senior member of Windidda advising that she had decided to withdraw the management order and 'to approve the transfer of the lease to Windidda Aboriginal Corporation'. The Minister added that: 'Your commitment to the pastoral lease and to the involvement of your family and community to ensure that the lease is run as a successful pastoral enterprise is to be commended'. The State coordinator of FarmBis attended the corporation's Annual General Meeting in November 2007 and advised the meeting that Windidda had acquired 'project ready' status and, pending funding approval from the State Government, would be included in the Indigenous Management Support Services project from July 2008.

Conclusion

Close attention to governance in its broadest sense was integral to reaching this stage. Over an 18 month period the community was confronted with a barrage of bureaucratic and legislative challenges including the RSPCA, the justice system, the pastoral industry, the PLB, ORAC, and the public through the media. Its primary focus throughout was to regain the pastoral lease by resolving outstanding corporate compliance issues, acquiring skills in governance and

allocated resources to each community to meet their individual requirements for infrastructure and municipal services.

farm management, and by employing this expertise in good station management practices. This encompassed planning for the future, making decisions that matched those plans, managing income and assets in a structured way, talking to the local community as well as to industry, keeping records that show what has been done and why, what worked and what did not.

Although it was important for the community to draw a distinction between 'the community' and 'the corporation' to achieve and maintain corporate compliance, governance for pastoral success and governance for community success are intermeshed. The pastoral station is regarded by the community as an important and valuable asset. The station usually turns off between 300–500 head of cattle each year, and provides both meaningful work for members of the community and an alternative living environment for workers and their young families away from the negative aspects of town life, including alcohol. There are more than 25 children of primary school age in the community, which creates a tension between the members' aspirations to live and work on the station and their obligation to be in town so the children can attend school. The community is investigating how to arrange on-station schooling so that workers, their families and other community members are able to stay for extended periods on the pastoral station.

The establishment of additional infrastructure on the station to support community life will directly enhance the likelihood of a stable workforce living on the station, able to support its growth. This infrastructure, identified by the community as recreational facilities, a communal garden and education alternatives for the children, will require an expansion in the income the station generates. The current level of activity on the lease barely covers the costs of rates, maintenance and improvements necessary to maintain the lease, let alone to fund the community's plans. Additional income can potentially be achieved through the Indigenous Management Support Services project which has the potential to provide the long term financial, physical and technical assistance the community will need to drawn on to continue in a positive direction.

One indicator of good governance is having a network in place to call on for help when there is trouble. The community was given initial assistance to put this in place and it has garnered further support along the way. It will need to draw on its own resources and its external network to maintain and build on what it has achieved to date.

Acknowledgements

I would like to acknowledge the assistance I have received from the members of Windidda Aboriginal Corporation and in particular the governing committee. Thanks for their generous support during a period when there were many demands being made on their time and energy.

References

Australian Associated Press (AAP) 2005. 'Pastoral lease must be cancelled after 500 cattle died', 18 February, available at <http://www.rummage.com.au/AAPView.aspx?id=68680> [accessed 3 July 2007].

ABC News 2005. 'Board to decided [sic] on Windida [sic] Station lease', ABC online, 18 March, available at <http://www.abc.net.au/news/stories/2005/03/18/1326422.htm> [accessed 16 July 2007].

ABC Rural 2005. 'Big cattle deaths at WA station', Rural News Week, *Country Breakfast—Story Archive*, 19 February, available at <http://www.abc.net.au/rural/breakfast/stories/s1305859.htm> [accessed 16 August 2005].

Centre for the Management of Arid Environments 2006. Report on Inspection of the Pastoral Property, Unpublished report, 16 May, Curtin University of Technology, Kalgoorlie.

Department of Agriculture and Food Western Australia (DAFWA) 2006. *Annual Report to the Pastoral Lands Board 2005/2006*, DAFWA, Government of Western Australia, Perth.

——2005. *Annual Report to the Pastoral Lands Board of Western Australia 2004/2005 Financial Year*, DAFWA, Government of Western Australia, Perth.

Department of Immigration and Multicultural and Indigenous Affairs (DIMIA) 2005. 'Part 2, Report on performance—Outcome 5', in *DIMIA Annual Report 2004-2005*, Commonwealth of Australia, Canberra.

Department of Indigenous Affairs (DIA) 2004. *Services to Indigenous People in the Shire of Wiluna: Mapping and Gap Analysis Report*, Government of Western Australia, Perth, available at <http://www.dia.wa.gov.au/Our-Business/Reports--Publications>.

Grieve, J. 2005a. 'Government forfeits Windidda lease', *WA Country Hour Summary*, ABC Rural online, 20 April, available at <http://www.abc.net.au/rural/wa/stories/s1349734.htm> [accessed 16 August 2005].

——2005b. 'PLB addresses animal welfare on Windidda Station', *WA Country Hour Summary*, ABC Rural online, 24 February, available at <http://www.abc.net.au/rural/wa/stories/s1310366.htm> [accessed 16 August 2005].

——2005c. 'RSPCA welcomes Windidda decision, but doesn't rule out legal action', *WA Country Hour Summary*, ABC Rural online, 21 April, available at <http://www.abc.net.au/rural/wa/stories/s1350816.htm> [accessed 16 August 2005].

Magistrates Court of Western Australia 2005. Prosecution Notice issued by the RSPCA Headquarters, Malaga, WA, Attachment 1, 17 June 2005.

Paterson, A. B. 'Banjo' 1896. 'With the cattle', *The Australasian Pastoralists' Review*, 15 September.

Royal Society for the Prevention of Cruelty to Animals (RSPCA). 2005. 'Windidda Station Drought', Media Release, 8 March, available at <http://www.rspcawa.asn.au/news_mediareleases.php> [accessed 14 March 2005].

13. Mapping expectations around a 'governance review' exercise of a West Kimberley organisation

Kathryn Thorburn

Introduction

The term 'governance' relating to the management of Australian Indigenous organisations and communities became increasingly common in the late 1990s. By the early 2000s, a suite of training packages were being developed to address particular deficiencies identified as part of a new focus on capacity building in Indigenous organisations.[1] The focus of such training, however, along with the considerable range of meanings associated with the term 'governance' itself, was wide ranging and variable in its effectiveness.[2]

Since around 2000, there have also been policy shifts encouraging the amalgamation of smaller organisations into larger 'umbrella' structures. This process has seen smaller, historically distinct entities losing their previous role as independent recipients of government funding, and retaining a representative function only. This has certainly been the case in the Fitzroy Valley, the geographical region serviced by the township of Fitzroy Crossing in the West Kimberley. In this region, the number of independent CDEP grantees decreased from 13 in 2000, to four in 2005, all of which are umbrella organisations.[3] While benefiting from the economy of scale that comes with having a larger membership, such organisations are inevitably afflicted with conflicts over authority across subsidiary groups; the position of Chairperson in these kinds of entities can be especially fraught for that reason. It is this kind of organisation I am describing here.

---

[1] A number of submissions to the House of Representatives 2004 Inquiry into capacity building in Indigenous communities argued for 'building governance training and monitoring into the design and delivery of every major funding program' (House of Representatives Standing Committee on Aboriginal Affairs 2004: 113).

[2] See, for example Willis (2004: 17), who reviewed the governance training on offer in the Northern Territory (NT) in 2004, and drew the distinction between that which focuses on compliance and conformity to rules, versus that which focuses on decision making and power over future development. She noted a general lack of definition across training packages, which undermined the 'capacity building' exercise across the NT, and contributed to her assessment of it being 'segregated and uncoordinated' (ibid. 18). A 2004 forum on Indigenous corporate governance also calls repeatedly for better evaluation of the effectiveness of training programs on offer (Office of the Registrar of Aboriginal Corporations and Reconciliation Australia 2004).

[3] See also Taylor (2006: 57), who noted that the number of CDEP organisations in the West Kimberley, that is, including the towns of Broome and Derby, had decreased over the last five years, from 17 to eight.

In this chapter, I propose to explore an internal governance review episode that took place in late 2005 at Kurungal Inc. This organisation was itself the result of an earlier amalgamation, and was experiencing considerable tensions. My aim is to demonstrate that there are a range of meanings or interpretations associated with the term 'governance', and that this lack of clarity has implications for organisational change and development, and indeed for Indigenous community empowerment. There are positive and negative elements to this uncertainty. On the negative side, it can result in unrealistic expectations being generated around governance-related exercises such as the one described here. More positively, however, the ambiguity around 'governance capacity building' can act as an open and flexible space, where organisations and communities can address any number of concerns they may have. Because developing 'good governance' has been identified as a priority for many government funders, there are often resources available for these kinds of exercises.

I will begin by providing a brief history of Kurungal Inc, which will explore some of the tensions and limitations that are built into the entity. I then examine the various understandings that contributors to the governance review exercise—including staff, the 'community' and the 'consultant'—brought to it. I also note here my own perceptions of the organisation, which were derived from fieldwork completed in the second half of 2005. In doing so, I demonstrate what it means in practice that there is a lack of consensus around exactly what 'governance' is. In this context, such an openness of meaning proved useful because it allowed local interpretation and prioritisation around concerns as broad as councillor roles, legal responsibilities of incorporated bodies, and forms of respectful communication across the two cultures.

Kurungal Inc: a brief history

Kurungal Inc is an organisation situated around a group of communities, which are located about 120km to the southeast of Fitzroy Crossing in the central west Kimberley, northwest Western Australia (WA). The organisation is based in a reasonably remote part of Australia and provides specific government funded services to surrounding Indigenous communities. These incorporate the communities of Wangkatjungka, Kupartiya, Ngumpan, Gilly Sharpe, and a seasonally inhabited outstation, Ngarantjadu (see Fig. 13.1).[4]

Kurungal Inc is an umbrella organisation, that is, it has five subsidiary organisations associated with each of these five communities as its members (see Fig. 13.2). The term 'kurungal' itself refers to the country adjacent to Christmas Creek, and incorporates Christmas Creek Station. It was also how the group of

---

[4] The organisational membership at this subsidiary level, however, is not strictly based on geographical residency. These groupings relate more to historical and kin connections, with the geographical location being a kind of marker.

people who lived and worked on Christmas Creek Station, prior to the Pastoral Award decision of 1968, became known—the 'kurungal mob'.[5]

Fig. 13.1 West Kimberley region showing Kurungal Inc's communities

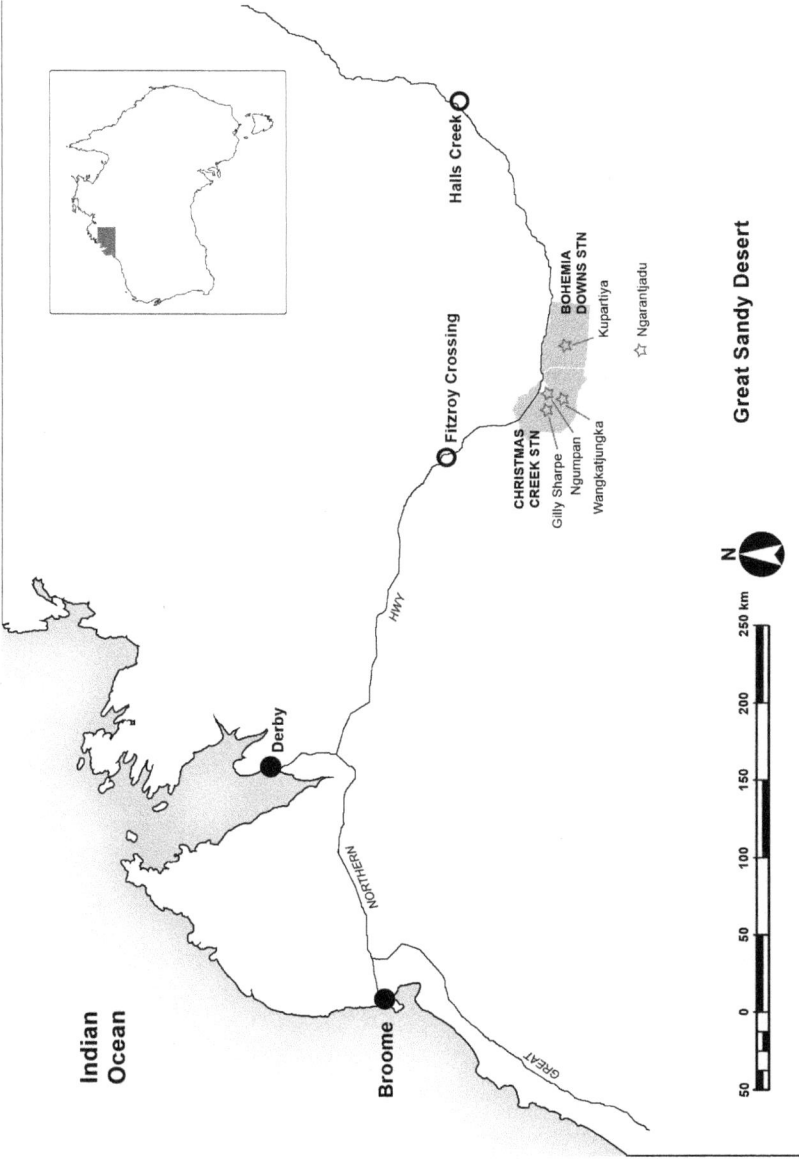

---

[5] Indeed, the community now named Wangkatjungka was originally named 'Kurungal'; see for example, Davey (1979). See Bunburry (2002) for discussion of the impacts of the Pastoral Award decision throughout the Kimberley and the NT, which meant that Aboriginal station workers had to be paid the same as non-Indigenous workers. In the case of Christmas Creek station, this meant that the station management moved off over 200 people (Commissioner of Native Welfare 1969). The majority moved back over time, to land adjacent to the station boundary.

The five subsidiaries all predate Kurungal Inc, and one of them, Wangkatjungka Community Inc, was one of the earliest organisations to be established in the area. It was set up in 1975 by the Wangkatjungka people who were camping in Fitzroy Crossing at the time, having recently been forced off Christmas Creek Station following the Pastoral Award decision.[6] Wangkatjungka is also by far the largest subsidiary organisation in terms of membership, having around 200 members. The majority of these reside in the community of Wangkatjungka, which is situated on an Aboriginal Lands Trust lease on the boundary fence of Christmas Creek Station. The other four subsidiaries are all substantially smaller. Kupartiya and Ngumpan both have a similar number of members, between 30 and 50, while Gilly Sharpe and Ngarantjadu are much smaller outstations with between 10 and 30 members.

Fig. 13.2 Structure of Kurungal Inc

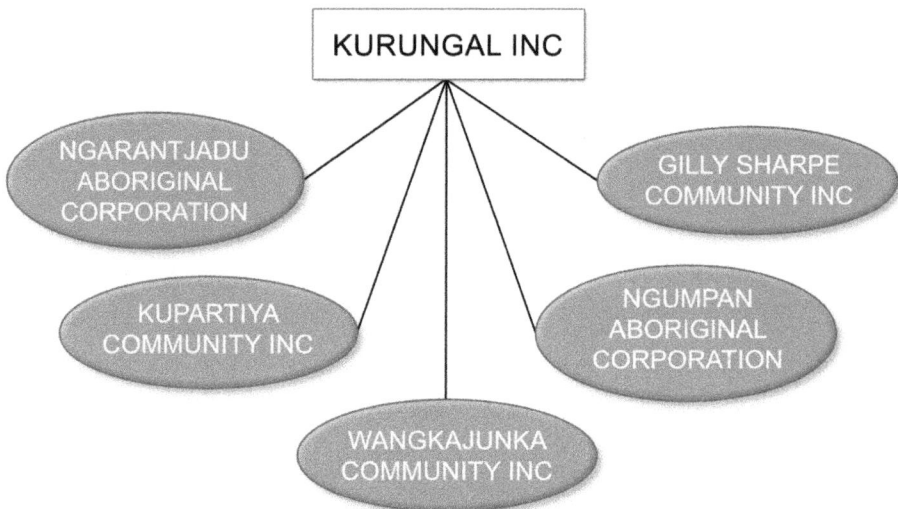

Many of the residents of Wangkatjungka in particular are members of the Wangkatjungka language group, who began moving out of the Great Sandy Desert along the Canning Stock Route around the time of World War Two (Bolger 1987).[7] Some were still moving into the area from the Great Sandy Desert as late as the 1950s and 1960s. Consequently, they are not in the strict sense 'traditional owners', although some of their descendants have been given, or have acquired, responsibilities relating to the surrounding country. Intermarriage has further blurred the distinctions between language groups. There is a handful of resident

---

[6] While the decision itself was taken in 1968, pastoralists in the Kimberley did not have to start enacting it until the following year, and some stations retained significant populations until well into the mid 1970s.

[7] For Wangkatjungka language, see Thieberger (1993), McGregor (1988) and Tindale (1974: 43).

people who have a stronger claim to traditional owner status—that is, those of Walmajerri/Gooniyandi[8] heritage (see McGregor 1988; Thieberger 1993). For the vast majority of Kurungal Inc members, English is their second or third language, after Wangkatjungka, Walmajerri and often others.

Kurungal Inc was established in 2001 under the *Associations Incorporation Act 1987* (WA), at the instigation of Derby-based officers of the Aboriginal and Torres Strait Islander Commission (ATSIC), through which Wangkatjungka Inc had previously received funding. They had a number of motivations for initiating this shift. Foremost, there had allegedly been ongoing problems with non-Indigenous staff residing in Wangkatjungka and being subject to violent acts or assault; the community office had also been vandalised on more than one occasion. The 'problem' as ATSIC saw it was a lack of leadership in Wangkatjungka at the time, which meant that there was little sanction of aberrant behaviour. Strong leadership, however, was evident on the surrounding much smaller communities, including Kupartiya on Bohemia Downs station, which local ATSIC staff at the time considered a much 'quieter' place. There had also been a number of breaches by Wangkatjungka Inc of its funding agreements, although whether these were trivial or not was not made clear to me.[9]

Prior to the creation of Kurungal Inc, the communities of Kupartiya on Bohemia Downs Station and Wangkatjungka had no administrative connection, although they did have strong cultural and historic ties. Prior to 2001, Wangkatjungka Inc had itself been an umbrella, managing the Community Development Employment Projects (CDEP)[10] of Ngumpan and Ngarantjadu, as well as the larger Wangkatjungka community.

The creation of Kurungal Inc saw an important shift occur in the dynamics amongst these geographic and political communities. In particular, the administrative centre (the office) and its associated resources, moved from Wangkatjungka to newly built premises at Kupartiya, some 60km distant on Bohemia Downs Station. The initiation of a new umbrella—Kurungal Inc—represented a significant shift in the balance of power and access to resources between the communities of Wangkatjungka and the much smaller Kupartiya.

The vast majority of Kurungal Inc's business, since its inception in 2001, has related to either managing government monies and providing related services, or attempting to draw in new sources of government funding. At the time of

---

[8] Davey (1979) noted that many of the original people from around Christmas Creek had moved east to GoGo Station and Bayulu community.
[9] Organisations such as these can be breached by their government funders for a variety of misdemeanors ranging from the serious to the arguably insignificant.
[10] CDEP monies were the main source of government funding for Kurungal Inc, representing almost 75 per cent in 2005. There was also funding available for a housing officer to manage the maintenance of housing across the communities.

my fieldwork, there was one full-time non-Indigenous staff member, a 'CDEP coordinator'; his partner worked part-time for the organisation between her stints away in New South Wales. They were assisted in the office at Kupartiya by one or two local residents on CDEP 'top-up',[11] performing tasks such as answering phones and cleaning. Part of the role of the coordinator, and a requirement of the funding agreements, was to hold regular meetings of the Kurungal Council, which is the governing body of Kurungal Inc. While the communities of Kupartiya and Ngumpan had shared ownership of a cattle station, Bohemia Downs, and Wangkatjungka had a community store, the organisation of Kurungal Inc did not have any business interests beyond managing funds allocated by government agencies. Its major concern was running a CDEP program for around 80 participants across the five membership groups. However, it also received funding to maintain housing stock, deliver municipal services, and to provide a meals-on-wheels service and other aged care help in Wangkatjungka.

In the context of this discussion around a review of governance, there are a few important things to note:

- the organisation had in-built, imposed tensions and imbalances;
- its only concern was managing government money, so it had limited scope in addressing community priorities beyond those deemed worthy by government;
- the coordinator, apart from the shopkeeper and his wife in Wangkatjungka, was for the most part the only whitefella working directly for these communities;[12]
- the 'office' was 60km away from the 'main' community; this resulted in a limited sense of ownership by that community, and inter-community problems of trust and jealousy; and
- there was an uneven claim across groups to traditional owner status. The majority of members were of 'historical' status,[13] although in this context the distinction was not always totally clear or uncontested.

It is my contention that these historically evolved tensions, which are inherent to this organisation and many others, are crucial to the way in which their governance functions. Gaining an understanding of these historical dynamics can be very difficult, especially when there are shameful 'failures' of previous ventures or entities, which people may not wish to discuss. In the case of

---

[11] The work requirements under CDEP were 16 hours per week—generally four hours per day. However, participants could earn more money, known as 'top-up', if they chose to work longer hours.
[12] Sanders (2006: 14–17) has developed the concept of 'isolated managerialism', which was clearly at play at Kurungal Inc.
[13] By 'historical status' I mean that the majority were not people, or descendants of people, who would be clearly considered traditional owners.

Kurungal Inc, a pre-existing subsidiary organisation had been investigated and its assets liquidated by the Office of the Register of Aboriginal Corporations (ORAC) in 2003. This entity was reconstituted under the WA legislation. Such a negative experience may have contributed to the reluctance of certain authority figures to become closely involved in the formal governance structure of Kurungal Inc.

Organisation identifies need for governance review

As part of my doctoral fieldwork on governance, I was granted permission to observe meetings and broader interactions within the organisational environment, including those with outsiders. I was seeking insight into people's relationships to country and to each other, and into people's histories, and how all of these manifest in an organisational context. While I was there, a number of senior community members and the non-Indigenous CDEP coordinator agreed that a review of governance was necessary. It was one of the few occasions when they agreed so wholeheartedly, but probably this was because each had completely different understandings and hopes about what such an exercise might involve. These different understandings incidentally did not arise in a vacuum. Some people had attended 'governance training' in other contexts, such as around station management. Some had been involved in developing cross-cultural training courses for non-Indigenous people, and believed that a governance related exercise might allow them to apply some of this experience to the coordinator. In any case, there was consensus that something had to be done to improve the internal workings of the organisation.[14]

That 'the community'[15] and the staff member had different understandings need not have been problematic, particularly as the review was to be undertaken by a very experienced practitioner who quickly picked up this gap in expectations. The community had ongoing strained relations with the coordinator, although this was not a phenomenon that related only to this particular individual, or this organisation. Indeed such a position—being the only official non-Indigenous employee in a remote community—has always been very difficult, but was perhaps increasingly so in this particular policy climate. The relationship between the community and previous coordinators had also been problematic. Because of Kurungal Inc's history of a high staff turnover rate (generally a new coordinator every year or so since it started), the organisation

---

[14] Some six months beforehand, the community had called a big meeting to attempt to clarify the extent of the co-ordinator's authority. However, by the time of the training described here, tensions were again very high.

[15] I shall refer to the 'community' here simply to distinguish the broad constituency from 'the Kurungal Council', and these from the co-ordinator. While 'the community' was rarely a totally coherent entity, in relation to (or opposition to) the co-ordinator, it was often reasonably united. See Holcombe (2005: 228) for a similar observation. The concept of 'community' has been problematised by many, see for example Rowse (1992: 50–8).

did not sit particularly favourably with the local Indigenous Coordination Centre (ICC), through which it received its main sources of Commonwealth funding. It had informally been made clear that it was 'on notice'. To assist Kurungal Inc sort through some of these ongoing issues and to support what the ICC had identified as elements of strong leadership there, they were allocated $15,000 to build governance capacity. The consultant was chosen largely on the basis of a pre-existing relationship that he had with one senior man, having worked together in another 'capacity building' exercise relating to station management.

The review process was to see the consultant spend time with both the staff and 'the community', including community leaders, and to listen to their concerns about the organisation. He was interested as well to understand the formal structure of the organisation and how it had evolved. In doing so, he was seeking to identify whether the tensions were structural ones, interpersonal/intercultural ones, or process-related.

Background to the review: the coordinator's concerns

The coordinator hoped that a review of governance would bring to light the need to improve both councillors' and constituents' understanding of the parameters of his job. This, he hoped, would encourage both groups to temper their expectations accordingly. He also hoped that it would clarify for people '[w]hat Kurungal is, what it is for [and] is trying to achieve'. He hoped such improved understanding would mean the councillors would take more of an active interest in the activities of the organisation. He had had limited success in organising regular council meetings, and was understandably frustrated. He also hoped to use the review process to inform councillors and members more generally about the legally binding nature of the service agreements that they had signed. In other words, he wanted them to understand that government had given the organisation certain monies, and in return the organisation had to demonstrate that agreed objectives were being met. He believed it was important for him to 'go by the book', to ensure that the agreements that were signed with government were strictly adhered to. It is important to note that for him to have taken a less hardline approach, in terms of organisational compliance with various agreements with government, would have jeopardised the organisation's funding and hence its entire existence. He was acutely aware of this. He also strongly believed that 'the community' was in need of 'cross-cultural' training to deepen their comprehension of non-Indigenous cultural systems and values, a rather unusual perspective.[16] He believed that the communities' lack of understanding of the complex structures of

---

[16] Martin (2003: 13), however, has made a similar suggestion: 'To be truly effective then, "capacity building" needs to be seen as a particular form of cross-cultural education in which indigenous peoples' enhanced capacity to achieve self-determination through their own institutions provides an important bridgehead to strategic engagement with the institutions (formal and informal) of the wider society'.

'government', or concepts such as 'business', was undermining his role and limiting the communities' potential to positively engage with government programs.

The community's concerns

At the same time, community members and councillors reported finding the coordinator rude and offensive, and described him as too hard, too bossy, and as exercising too much agency *outside* of the bounds of the office. People believed that a governance review might 'pull him up' and make him better understand the limitations of his role. While the coordinator could not understand why people had limited interest in Kurungal Inc since it was *their organisation*, the 'community' considered that it was really more of a *kartiya* [17] thing, something that was *his* responsibility to tend to. From the community perspective, its function was fundamentally as a conduit to resources, and the job of the coordinator was to keep the money story looking good for government so that this would continue.

Members of the community had raised a number of issues about how this particular coordinator carried out his job. Some of these were more sensitive than others, and included a perception that he talked down to women and 'shamed people'.[18] He was also criticised for not properly listening, which related to his inability to pick up on more subtle forms of communication, such as body language in meetings, which indicated that people were not engaged with his statements or were offended by his directive manner. 'Not listening' also related to the problem that his latitude in carrying out community requests or demands was in fact very limited, but he found it difficult to dismiss such requests outright, especially when made in a public meeting.

There was also the perception that he spent too much time out of the office and in the communities, assisting in a 'hands on' way with CDEP work, instead of making sure all of the government 'paperwork' requirements were being dealt with. Obviously, this individual's style departed somewhat from his predecessor's, who had remained more office-bound by comparison. There was also a perception that he did not attend to internal paperwork properly, including that which some people had become accustomed to around meetings: minutes and their follow-up, setting out clear agendas beforehand, following up matters

---

[17] '*Kartiya*' (pronounced gardeeya) is the term that is used across the Kimberley and into the NT both for non-Indigenous people and as the adjective for matters pertaining to that world.

[18] See, for example, Myers (1986) on the subject of 'shame'; a very powerful and not neatly translatable concept. To avoid it, Myers (1986: 121) notes that a show of humility on the part of the speaker (the potential 'shamer') is required that indicates 'that he does not think he is better than the others. Similarly, direct contradiction is avoided lest it cause "shame" … by exposing a person's egotism'. Such an indirect and non-hierarchical approach to communication is somewhat diametrically opposed to whitefella preconceptions around being a 'boss', in this example, having to manage 80 CDEP workers and encourage their productivity.

from previous meetings and so forth. Arguably, some members of the community had higher expectations of acceptable governance practice than the coordinator.

Another common criticism of the coordinator was that he was too much of a gatekeeper. He insisted that any contractors, government agencies or service providers who were seeking to do business or talk to any people living in any of the five communities inform him first. He saw this as an important aspect of his role, making sure outsiders had gone through the proper channels—via Kurungal Inc—to engage with these places. The people, however, had a different idea, and resented what they perceived to be his meddling in their business. He was perceived by some as an empire builder, as trying 'to take over everything'.

Finally, his desire to 'play by the book' was perceived by people as being overly inflexible and unimaginative, and demonstrative of his loyalty to 'government side' rather than 'community side'. As one senior woman posed it: 'we got all this *milli milli*, this paper, but then other things can happen, can't they?'[19] What this question encapsulates, it seems to me, is the increasing gap between a community's expectation that such *kartiyas* are there to 'help' them, and the government's expectation that such positions are there to unforgivingly, and with very little latitude or concern for cultural difference, implement policy. Straddling such very different expectations makes a position such as that of the coordinator described here an extremely difficult and uncomfortable one.[20]

My observations

During my time with Kurungal Inc, there were a number of 'community' meetings, generally called by the community, rather than the coordinator, to address issues of concern to them. These meetings were generally attended by dozens of people, including many 'councillors'. The difficulty for the coordinator, who was invited to attend most of these, was perhaps that he made a distinction between these very open ended meetings and a 'council meeting'. And yet from my discussions with people, Kurungal Council meetings had always taken this kind of format. The 'council', as conceived by the coordinator, was too abstracted from the much more inclusive and meaningful sociality expressed in larger meetings. As such, his more strictly delimited notion of the council held little interest for people, and arguably limited legitimacy. Nor did it have precedent. And yet the inefficiency of such big, inclusive meetings, at least when measured in terms of addressing a particular list of agenda items, meant that large

---

[19] *Milli milli* means, roughly, paperwork. In this context, the woman was referring to the various service agreements, Shared Responsibility Agreements (SRAs) and so forth.

[20] One of the reviewers of this chapter commented that most of the communities' concerns recorded here focused on the coordinator, rather than the organisation more broadly. Indeed, it was the case that for whatever reasons, the coordinator was held accountable for all kinds of problems that arguably were beyond his influence. This in itself could be considered as contributing to the overall difficulties around communication between the coordinator and the community.

community meetings were a frustrating kind of vehicle for the coordinator to engage with.

Kurungal Inc's limited legitimacy in part related to the nature of the organisation itself—its genesis and its physical locality—which meant that the majority of members had a very minimal sense of ownership of it, or comprehension of its business. The other interesting thing about the organisation was that those who *had been* elected as councillors did not necessarily have much cultural authority, or much experience in dealing with *kartiyas*. This combination of discomfort and limited authority also translated into a limited engagement with the process of attending meetings for many councillors. In any case, the four community leaders who *did* have both authority and experience with *kartiyas*, formed a group that was named the 'elders group', as a kind of informal advice-giving group. It was from this group that the coordinator in practice sought sanction for his actions.

While the members of this group had no official position in the organisation, their input was crucial in allowing it to continue functioning with a degree of legitimacy, at least as far as the constituency was concerned. Arguably, such legitimacy would not have been garnered from having council meetings of the kind imagined by the coordinator, or indeed demanded in the organisation's rules. Nevertheless, the coordinator remained extremely frustrated at official meetings not occurring, in part because he was required to provide evidence that they were to the ICC. Minutes of meetings and related documents would demonstrate that he had the necessary community sanction for particular decisions.

The 'elders group' gave legitimacy to decisions, and in a sense represented the absolute minimum group required to give approval, not unlike the way a quorum works in a formal governance context. Of course, while decisions they made tended to have *sufficient* authority, they did not have *absolute* authority and were still open to question by others outside of the group. Nevertheless, the influence of this group greatly upset the coordinator's sense of justice and democratic process. But he also wished to understand and respect edicts of the 'cultural side', which he recognised the 'elders group' as signifying. On the one hand, this group, whose role was to provide necessary sanction to the coordinator's actions, further undermined the formal council, and made it even less likely to become a functional, practising entity of any influence. However, it was also true that on the basis of traditional ownership of surrounding country and the strength of one's claims on that front, there were substantial variations in the authority and power of the subsidiaries and their members. The 'elders group' had very strong claims to country, and this was largely the basis of their legitimacy—although they also had considerable experience with *kartiyas*. A council that ignored these claims, or pretended to generate some kind of authority outside of them, was destined to be symbolic at best, dysfunctional at worst.

The 'elders group' operated as a quorum *in practice* if not in law, and as such, the decisions being implemented by the coordinator managed to avoid intra-community conflict, partly because of a degree of distrust amongst the four, which demanded ongoing transparency. That is, the 'elders group' accounted for the main competing interests. Such an achievement is not insignificant in organisations of this nature. However, this practice—that is, prioritising communication with the 'group that calls the shots'—contributed to the aforementioned criticism within the wider community that the coordinator was not listening to people. It is difficult to argue, however, that he had any choice but to engage with this informal, and yet legitimate, decision making process.

It should be noted that none of the 'elders group', at least prior to the 2005 AGM when two of the four allowed themselves to be elected, had positions on the Kurungal Council. As one elder had stated earlier in the year: 'I don't want no *kartiya* looking over my shoulders'. There was a definite sense in which their engagement with the formal council, in particular via the Chairman's position, was a new attempt to exercise greater control over the coordinator. The irony is that people of influence started to engage with the formal mechanisms of Kurungal Inc not because of the coordinator's efforts, but in spite of them.

The consultant's view

After some discussion between the consultant, the coordinator and a senior community member, it was decided that a review of governance could involve a process by which the breadth of their concerns could be explored. The consultant suggested that some of the negative reaction coming from the community might in fact relate to the particular policy climate, with its very limited flexibility for expenditure, and particular policies such as the much stricter implementation of the CDEP 'no work, no pay' rule, which had come in during this particular coordinator's tenure. He guessed that there might be a general sense of insecurity amongst the membership, and fear about what the future holds and what the government might decide to do next. He also proposed that there was little appreciation of the limits to government largesse, including the fact that Indigenous policy shifts were often driven by mainstream Australian politics and voter perceptions. He thought it would be worthwhile to include in the discussion some of these matters, and explore people's fears about the future.

The consultant spent six days in total in the various communities associated with Kurungal. He spent one and a half days with the coordinator and his partner, working through their identified concerns, one of which was the conduct of a day long 'cross-cultural workshop' for their benefit. He then spent three days with various families and groups from within the organisation's membership, going bush, spending time on a stock camp and generally canvassing the issues people had with Kurungal.[21] He also spent time with the coordinator in the office, attempting to find all of the documentation relating to Kurungal Inc and its subsidiaries: constitutions, membership lists, rules, titles to land, and so forth. Some of this material could not be found.

Broadly speaking, the consultant concluded that there were major issues of cross-cultural misunderstanding at play, and that these were contributing to other stresses built into the organisation, and to those bearing down from the policy environment.

The review workshop

On the final day, the consultant held a workshop that explored three areas:

1. Working between the two worlds;
2. Understanding the Kurungal governance arrangements; and
3. Identifying solutions.

In the morning, after a handful of cars and the school bus had done the 120km round trip to pick up as many people as possible from the member communities, there was a further surprise. Two consultants and a senior officer from the ICC were waiting at the Kupartiya office to raise with the Kurungal Inc membership the issue of designing new regional governance structures, which could feed into the former ATSIC region of Malarabah. These community consultation sessions were taking place throughout the geographical reach of the Derby ICC. They had apparently provided the coordinator with less than a week's notice of their intended visit. Various governance models were overviewed, and those present were asked to attend another meeting in Fitzroy Crossing for further discussion. The visitors were very impressed at the two dozen or so people who had turned up to attend their discussion, and no one had the heart to tell them that people had gathered together for another purpose that had been much longer in the planning.

That discussion was completed by around 11am, and after morning tea, the workshop began. The first aspect, on the difficulties of working in 'two worlds'[22] —was facilitated by two members of the community who attempted to capture the difficulties on 'both sides' of communicating well with those in another

---

[21] The views of the coordinator and of 'the community' above were expressed to me via interviews, both before and after the training took place. I was not privy to the discussions between the consultant and either party, although I did provide some logistic and administrative support to the consultant during his time at Kurungal.

[22] This is the consultant's terminology, not my own.

cultural milieu.[23] The discussion, however, remained very general, with law, culture and country characterising the Indigenous cultural side, and money hoarding behaviour, possessions, governments and skyscrapers characterising non-Indigenous culture.

The second phase of the workshop, about understanding Kurungal Inc governance arrangements, started with the consultant demonstrating the various agreements to which the organisation was party by laying them out on the floor—all 13 of them, which included three Shared Responsibility Agreements (SRAs)[24] and various service agreements. He then went through the various Acts available to become incorporated under, and looked at each subsidiary organisation, asking whether all requisite paperwork was there: rules/constitutions, signed list of members and so forth.[25] He described the difference between an organisation that was a company, one that was incorporated, and how they differ structurally, in terms of reporting responsibilities and also in their capacity to carry out various functions such as holding Aboriginal Lands Trust leases. He also described the various parts of an incorporated body—the board/executive, the members and the staff—and explained how they must relate to each other, and yet remain distinct, for the whole to operate. This part of the workshop was to explain to participants the actual legal structure of Kurungal Inc.

The final aspect of the workshop, 'identifying solutions', essentially focused on how to sort out some of the missing paperwork for the subsidiary organisations, including membership lists. The consultant also raised the possibility of restructuring Kurungal Inc to reflect 'actual leadership and community political behaviour', but there was insufficient time or energy to really generate discussion on the matter, and the workshop came to a close. Everyone headed back to their communities and the consultant left the following day.

Whilst the review had been useful in certain respects, and the missing membership lists were discovered, which was important, the fractured relationship between the coordinator and the community had not been addressed. In truth, a one day workshop had only sufficed to begin exploring aspects of

---

[23] Both of these individuals had been involved in presenting cross-cultural training in other contexts, generally to a largely non-Indigenous audience.

[24] SRAs were introduced in 2004 as part of the 'New Arrangements in Indigenous Affairs': 'SRAs will set out clearly what the family, community and government is responsible for contributing to a particular activity, what outcomes are to be achieved, and the agreed milestones to measure success. Under the new approach, groups will need to offer commitments and undertake changes that benefit the community in return for government funding' (Office of Indigenous Policy Coordination 2004: 18). See Arabena (2005) for a critical look at SRAs and at the 'new arrangements' more generally.

[25] Not all of these subsidiary incorporated bodies had been incorporated under the same legislation. In general, the older ones came under the Commonwealth's *Aboriginal Councils and Associations Act 1976*, which requires up-to-date membership lists, and the latter ones, including Kurungal Inc, had come under WA's *Associations Incorporation Act 1987*. The latter allows for incorporated bodies to be members; the Commonwealth Act did not.

'Kurungal Inc' as a *kartiya* and bureaucratic cultural artefact. It had failed to address the meanings, or lack of meanings, attributed to the entity by its membership, and it had not directly touched on the ongoing emotional tension that had come to characterise the organisation. There was much talk amongst community members about getting the consultant to return in 2006 and help resolve the ongoing tensions. This had been one of the original terms of reference of the exercise—that is, to 'Assess the feasibility and viability of a governance development project at Kurungal'. The consultant's report certainly suggested that 'community members consider reforming the current governance arrangements for Kurungal and its affiliated organisations', although it contained no explanation as to why such reform might be necessary. However, by April 2006 the Kurungal Council had terminated the coordinator's contract. As so often occurs though, it took some two months for Kurungal to fill the position, by which time there was a significant backlog of reporting and other requirements, representing further slippage for the organisation to catch up on.

The consultant's report

The consultant's report to Kurungal Inc on the review exercise is interesting in a number of respects. Firstly, the breadth of issues that were raised by people as part of a 'governance review' points to the lack of clarity about exactly what governance is. He records that there were a number of people who raised concerns about the connection between Kurungal Inc and subsidiary organisations, although the exact nature of these concerns is not elaborated in the report. Elsewhere he reports on comments that:

> there was something structural [sic] wrong and that the communities were only living places with little to do and little opportunity to develop something new. Concern was expressed that the CEO [i.e. the coordinator] did not discuss possible solutions rather he already had them and 'just told people'.[26]

This comment alone points to confusion about the role of the organisation and its limits.

The concerns about the relationship between Kurungal Inc and its subsidiary organisations were probably related to the historical disenfranchisement of Wangkatjungka as the administrative hub community for the area in 2001. It would also have related to a lack of clarity around the relationship between Kurungal Inc (the organisation) and Kupartiya/Bohemia Downs stations (where the office was situated). Clearly, there are benefits for a community that 'hosts' the administrative centre and these were apparent to the other communities and community leaders. Many of these relate to the more informal, day-to-day services

---

[26] Unpublished consultant's report of the governance review to ORAC.

provided by such organisations (Thorburn 2007: 21). I would suggest that the expressions of concern about the 'governance structure' related more to these (and other) issues around the internal power dynamics of the different communities. Arguably, they also reflected the inevitable problems of transparency that arise when the administrative hub is situated on a community which is 60km away from where the majority reside, and on country where this majority might have diminished rights.

The crux of the issue, it seems to me, is that a community based organisation such as Kurungal Inc can become the focus of a very broad sense of discontent amongst constituents, largely because there is no other avenue available for such sentiments to be expressed. Great care needs to be taken, however, in mistaking the expression of discontent about a whole range of issues with the need to reform the internal governance structure of an organisation. As others have recently argued, the entire system of service delivery to Indigenous communities has become increasingly torturous, and is itself badly in need of reform (see Dodson 2007; Morgan, Disney and Associates Pty Ltd 2006).

In this case, the consultant's report recommended a broader review of the organisation, which included input from various government agencies. It went on to suggest that subject to the outcomes of such a review process, the community ought to consider 'reforming the current governance arrangements'. Arguably, the highly generalised nature of the terms of reference for the review discussed here left the consultant little option but to make highly generalised recommendations, which really did not clarify at all the nature of the problems at hand, or how to rectify them. The adoption of the generalised language of 'governance', in circumstances that are highly locally specific and complex, can contribute to the likelihood of outcomes, which are arguably simplistic at best and difficult to translate into practical or applied solutions.

Finding practical solutions (meeting half way)

In providing such a very site and time specific example of how problems can play out around one organisational entity, this chapter has sought to demonstrate the acute necessity to avoid generality in talk and analysis about Indigenous organisational practice, and for attention to specifics. It also shows that even when all of these specifics are laid out, their resolution might be far from straightforward. That is, identifying 'problem areas' is not difficult. It is likely, however, that certain of these 'problem areas' are themselves solutions to some other imbalance. The 'elders group' is an example. The Kurungal Council had little legitimacy because of the way it had developed historically, and because its main business—implementing government programs—held little interest for people. The formal councillors therefore also lacked authority, and in any case, their decision making scope was similarly limited and of minimal interest. This 'problem' related to the organisation's history (that it was externally imposed to address other identified 'problems'[27] and was an unpopular attempt to centralise) and to the nature of its affairs (it was fundamentally a service provider, mostly of CDEP, although in a narrowing policy climate).

Nevertheless, despite the limited engagement of the Kurungal Inc constituency, action occurred and decisions were made. The 'elders group' was able to give the necessary direction to the coordinator to implement processes and allocate resources across the five subsidiary groups with a degree of legitimacy. While it was not enough to satisfy all community members, there was no suggestion amongst constituents that a solution to the group's contingent legitimacy was simply to hold regular council meetings.

Somewhat in contrast to this approach, the coordinator was keen to 'go by the book', or at least that was certainly his position in public forums. However, arguably if he had actually attempted this in practice, his position within the organisation would have been terminated much sooner. Attempting to 'go by the book' is probably unwise for either party to a cross-cultural interaction, because generally only one party is privy to the content of 'the book', that is, a set of culturally-specific rules. Rather, careful and steady mutual exploration of workable solutions to the difficult dilemmas that arise might be a better approach. Of course, while compromise does seem desirable and pragmatic, taking this path can open up another Pandora's Box: which organisational rules can be bent, which ones broken, and which must be adhered to? This particular coordinator was accused of being inconsistent, treating some families and communities favourably, and being paternalistic in the way he selectively bent rules, rewarding certain behaviours and punishing others. According to Sanders (2006), such perceptions are entirely to be expected. The trick is in managing them: 'Defending actual material distributions in the language of public purposes is what strategically balancing different accountabilities and perceptions is largely about' (Sanders 2006: 12). Maintaining legitimacy and consensus around correct processes is something that must be constantly worked at.[28] Such ongoing negotiation, however, requires time and resources which are not provided under the service agreements of organisations like Kurungal Inc.

Finally, that this organisation received funding to carry out a governance review relates specifically and primarily to the fact that the ICC had identified a deficit.

---

[27] This point, that externally imposed 'governance solutions' may have limited traction, was noted recently in Hunt and Smith (2007: xvi), but was also made back in 1990: 'Organisations that have emerged from within the Aboriginal community and which reflect Aboriginal aspirations and priorities are functioning better than other structures that are imposed by the government' (House of Representatives Standing Committee on Aboriginal Affairs 1990: 162). My understanding is that while there were a number of community meetings held between the member communities of the now Kurungal Inc and ATSIC prior to its creation, there was limited scope for arrangements to be developed outside of those which eventuated.

[28] Sullivan (2006: 27–8) argues that a focus on building appropriate processes, as opposed to structures, is crucial. See also, Sanders (2004: 20–21).

The 'community', however, was arguably seeking help across a number of areas, but had no other avenue available through which to make such a request from an outside, expert party, than via a one-off exercise in governance capacity building such as that which occurred.

Conclusion

This case study demonstrates that the language of governance can open a space and draw in resources that allow time and consideration of a range of issues. Arguably, the resolution of these, which include the dynamics of operating within an intercultural environment, as well as ongoing policy shifts, is likely to not be an endpoint but rather an ongoing process.

And yet there remain questions around whether the promise that a focus on 'governance' holds out can actually be realised. In this example, each party hoped that through a 'governance review' they might better communicate their expectations of each other in a process that was considered somehow neutral ground. In this sense, the potential space opened up by the prospect of this review might have been extremely valuable. But the time and resources allocated to the exercise were insufficient, and there was inadequate short term follow-up, which might have built on the momentum begun by the review. As Lange's chapter illustrates (Lange this volume, Chapter 12), ongoing support for organisations—such as that provided by FarmBis to Windidda Aboriginal Corporation—rather than sporadic events such as the exercise described here, is of much greater value. In addition, it is likely that some aspects of organisational governance practice might be less open to compromise or 'capacity building' than others, especially given the climate of diminishing trust between these organisations and governments. That is, the costs in accepting the 'help' offered by governments, particularly in terms of loss of autonomy and pressure for particular outcomes, is for many starting to outweigh the benefits. The crucial role such organisations have played in the past as cultural and political mediators may be in the process of changing so fundamentally that before long, those that survive may no longer be characterisable as 'Indigenous' in any meaningful way.

Acknowledgements

I would like to acknowledge the generosity of the membership and council of Kurungal Inc, and I thank in particular the councillors, members of the elders group, the coordinator, and the consultant who facilitated the review. The conclusions drawn in this chapter are solely my own and do not necessarily reflect the opinions of any of the research participants.

References

Arabena, K. 2005. 'Not fit for modern Australian society: Aboriginal and Torres Strait Islander people and the new arrangements for the administration of Indigenous affairs', *Research Discussion Paper No. 16*, AIATSIS, Canberra.

Bolger, A. 1987. 'Wangkajunga women: stories from the desert', *Aboriginal History*, 11 (2): 102–16.

Bunburry, B. 2002. *It's Not the Money It's the Land: Aboriginal Stockmen and the Equal Wage Case*, Fremantle Arts Centre Press, Fremantle.

Commissioner of Native Welfare 1969. *Annual Report*, Perth, WA.

Davey, S. 1979. Kroonull Community Development: An Overview, Unpublished report to the West Australian Department of Community Welfare, 7 March, Perth.

Dodson, P. 2007. 'Reconciliation—200 years on, is dialogue enough?' Centre for Dialogue Annual Lecture, La Trobe University, Melbourne.

Holcombe, S. 2005. 'Luritja management of the state,' *Oceania*, 75 (3): 222–33.

House of Representatives Standing Committee on Aboriginal Affairs 1990. *Our Future, Our Selves*, AGPS, Canberra.

House of Representatives Standing Committee on Aboriginal and Torres Strait Islander Affairs 2004. *Many Ways Forward: Report of the Inquiry Into Capacity Building and Service Delivery in Indigenous Communities*, AGPS, Canberra.

Hunt, J. and Smith, D. E. 2007. 'Indigenous Community Governance Project: year two research findings,' *CAEPR Working Paper No. 36*, CAEPR, CASS, ANU, Canberra.

Martin, D. 2003. 'Rethinking the design of Indigenous organisations: the need for strategic engagement,' *CAEPR Discussion Paper No. 248*, CAEPR, ANU, Canberra.

McGregor, W. 1988. *Handbook of Kimberley Languages*, Pacific Linguistics Series C No. 105, Dept. of Linguistics, RSPS, ANU, Canberra.

Morgan, Disney and Associates Pty Ltd. 2006. *A Red Tape Evaluation in Selected Indigenous Communities: Final Report for the Office of Indigenous Policy Coordination*, OIPC, Australian Government, Canberra.

Myers, F. R. 1986. *Pintupi Country Pintupi Self: Sentiment, Place and Politics Among Western Desert Aborigines*, Australian Institute of Aboriginal Studies, Canberra.

Office of Indigenous Policy Coordination (OIPC). 2004. *New Arrangements in Indigenous Affairs*, information booklet, August, OIPC, Canberra.

Office of the Registrar of Aboriginal Corporations (ORAC) and Reconciliation Australia2004. *Report from the Corporate Governance Forum*, Commonwealth of Australia, Woden, ACT, available at <http://www.orac.gov.au/about_orac/publications.aspx#8>.

Rowse, T. 1992. *Remote Possibilities: The Aboriginal Domain and the Administrative Imagination*, North Australia Research Unit, ANU, Darwin.

Sanders, W. 2004. 'Thinking about Indigenous community governance,' *CAEPR Discussion Paper No. 262*, CAEPR, ANU, Canberra.

——2006. 'Being a good senior manager in Indigenous community governance: working with public purpose and private benefit,' *CAEPR Discussion Paper No. 280,* CAEPR, ANU, Canberra.

Sullivan, P. 2006. 'Indigenous governance: the Harvard Project on Native American Economic Development and appropriate principles of governance for Aboriginal Australia,' *AIATSIS Research Discussion Paper No. 17*, AIATSIS, Canberra.

Taylor, J. 2006. 'Indigenous people in the West Kimberley labour market,' *CAEPR Working Paper No. 35*, CAEPR, ANU, Canberra.

Thieberger, N. 1993. *Handbook of Western Australian Aboriginal Languages South of the Kimberley Region*, Pacific Linguistics Series C No. 124, Dept. of Linguistics, RSPS, ANU, Canberra, available at <http://coombs.anu.edu.au/WWWVLPages/AborigPages/LANG/WA/contents.htm> [accessed 1 July 2007].

Thorburn, K. 2007. 'Managing dilemmas in Indigenous community-based organisations: viewing a spectrum of ways through the prism of accountability', *Ngiya: Talk the Law*, 1: 2–23.

Tindale, N. B. 1974. *Aboriginal Tribes of Australia*, University of California Press, Berkeley.

Willis, C. 2004. Review of Governance Training for Indigenous Organisations and Communities in the Northern Territory: Final Report to the Department of Community Development, Sport and Cultural Affairs, NT Government, Darwin.

Key ICGP Publications

Gray, B. and Sanders, W. 2006. 'Views from the top of the "quiet revolution": Secretarial perspectives on the new arrangements in Indigenous affairs', *CAEPR Discussion Paper No. 282*, CAEPR, ANU, Canberra.

Hunt, J. 2005. 'Capacity development in the international development context: Implications for Indigenous Australia', *CAEPR Discussion Paper No. 278*, CAEPR, ANU, Canberra.

Hunt, J. and Smith, D. E. 2006. 'Building Indigenous community governance in Australia: Preliminary research findings', *CAEPR Working Paper No. 31*, CAEPR, ANU, Canberra.

Hunt, J. and Smith, D. E. 2007. 'Indigenous Community Governance Project: Year two research findings', *CAEPR Working Paper No. 36*, CAEPR, CASS, ANU, Canberra.

Sanders, W. 2006a. 'Being a good senior manager in Indigenous community governance: Working with public purpose and private benefit', *CAEPR Discussion Paper No. 280*, CAEPR, ANU, Canberra.

Sanders, W. 2006b. 'Local governments and Indigenous interests in Australia's Northern Territory', *CAEPR Discussion Paper No. 285*, CAEPR, ANU, Canberra.

Smith, D. E. 2004. 'From Gove to governance: Reshaping Indigenous governance in the Northern Territory', *CAEPR Discussion Paper No. 265*, CAEPR, ANU, Canberra.

Smith, D. E. 2005. 'Researching Australian Indigenous governance: A methodological and conceptual framework', *CAEPR Working Paper No. 29*, CAEPR, ANU, Canberra.

See also, the papers contributed to *Ngiya: Talk the Law—Volume I, Governance in Indigenous Communities*, June 2007, Jumbunna Indigenous House of Learning, University of Technology, Sydney, available at <http://www.jumbunna.uts.edu.au>.

All the Indigenous Community Governance Project's publications—including Annual Reports, Research Reports, ICGP Case Study Reports, Occasional Papers, Discussion & Working Papers, the *Community Governance* newsletter, *Community Governance Research Update*, the online *Indigenous Governance Matters* issue brief series, and an Annotated Bibliography—can be accessed from the project's web pages on the CAEPR website at <http://www.anu.edu.au/caepr/ICGP_publications.php>.

Full details of all publications and other communications arising from the ICGP are given in the project's Annual Reports.

CAEPR Research Monograph Series

1. *Aborigines in the Economy: A Select Annotated Bibliography of Policy Relevant Research 1985–90*, L. M. Allen, J. C. Altman, and E. Owen (with assistance from W. S. Arthur), 1991.

2. *Aboriginal Employment Equity by the Year 2000*, J. C. Altman (ed.), published for the Academy of Social Sciences in Australia, 1991.

3. *A National Survey of Indigenous Australians: Options and Implications*, J. C. Altman (ed.), 1992.

4. *Indigenous Australians in the Economy: Abstracts of Research, 1991–92*, L. M. Roach and K. A. Probst, 1993.

5. *The Relative Economic Status of Indigenous Australians, 1986–91*, J. Taylor, 1993.

6. *Regional Change in the Economic Status of Indigenous Australians, 1986–91*, J. Taylor, 1993.

7. *Mabo and Native Title: Origins and Institutional Implications*, W. Sanders (ed.), 1994.

8. *The Housing Need of Indigenous Australians, 1991*, R. Jones, 1994.

9. *Indigenous Australians in the Economy: Abstracts of Research, 1993–94*, L. M. Roach and H. J. Bek, 1995.

10. *The Native Title Era: Emerging Issues for Research, Policy, and Practice*, J. Finlayson and D. E. Smith (eds), 1995.

11. *The 1994 National Aboriginal and Torres Strait Islander Survey: Findings and Future Prospects*, J. C. Altman and J. Taylor (eds), 1996.

12. *Fighting Over Country: Anthropological Perspectives*, D. E. Smith and J. Finlayson (eds), 1997.

13. *Connections in Native Title: Genealogies, Kinship, and Groups*, J. D. Finlayson, B. Rigsby, and H. J. Bek (eds), 1999.

14. *Land Rights at Risk? Evaluations of the Reeves Report*, J. C. Altman, F. Morphy, and T. Rowse (eds), 1999.

15. *Unemployment Payments, the Activity Test, and Indigenous Australians: Understanding Breach Rates*, W. Sanders, 1999.

16. *Why Only One in Three? The Complex Reasons for Low Indigenous School Retention*, R. G. Schwab, 1999.

17. *Indigenous Families and the Welfare System: Two Community Case Studies*, D. E. Smith (ed.), 2000.

18. *Ngukurr at the Millennium: A Baseline Profile for Social Impact Planning in South-East Arnhem Land*, J. Taylor, J. Bern, and K. A. Senior, 2000.

19. *Aboriginal Nutrition and the Nyirranggulung Health Strategy in Jawoyn Country*, J. Taylor and N. Westbury, 2000.

20. *The Indigenous Welfare Economy and the CDEP Scheme*, F. Morphy and W. Sanders (eds), 2001.

21. *Health Expenditure, Income and Health Status among Indigenous and Other Australians*, M. C. Gray, B. H. Hunter, and J. Taylor, 2002.

22. *Making Sense of the Census:Observations of the 2001 Enumeration in Remote Aboriginal Australia*, D. F. Martin, F. Morphy, W. G. Sanders and J. Taylor, 2002.

23. *Aboriginal Population Profiles for Development Planning in the Northern East Kimberley*, J. Taylor, 2003.

24. *Social Indicators for Aboriginal Governance: Insights from the Thamarrurr Region, Northern Territory*, J. Taylor, 2004.

25. *Indigenous People and the Pilbara Mining Boom: A Baseline for Regional Participation*, J. Taylor and B. Scambary, 2005.

26. *Assessing the Evidence on Indigenous Socioeconomic Outcomes: A Focus on the 2002 NATSISS*, B. H. Hunter (ed.), 2006.

27. *The Social Effects of Native Title: Recognition, Translation, Coexistence*, B. R. Smith and F. Morphy (eds), 2007.

28. *Agency, contingency and census process: Observations of the 2006 Indigenous Enumeration Strategy in remote Aboriginal Australia*, F. Morphy (ed.), 2008.

For information on CAEPR Discussion Papers, Working Papers and Research Monographs (Nos 1-19) please contact:

> Publication Sales, Centre for Aboriginal Economic Policy Research,
> College of Arts and Social Sciences,
> The Australian National University, Canberra, ACT, 0200

> Telephone: 02–6125 8211
> Facsimile: 02–6125 2789

Information on CAEPR abstracts and summaries of all CAEPR print publications and those published electronically can be found at the following WWW address: http://www.anu.edu.au/caepr/